Reflexive Governance for Global Public Goods

Politics, Science, and the Environment
Peter M. Haas and Sheila Jasanoff, series editors

For a complete list of books published in this series, please see the back of the book.

Reflexive Governance for Global Public Goods

edited by Eric Brousseau, Tom Dedeurwaerdere, and Bernd Siebenhüner

The MIT Press
Cambridge, Massachusetts
London, England

MIT Press books may be purchased at special quantity discounts for business or sales promotional use. For information, please email special_sales@mitpress.mit.edu or write to Special Sales Department, The MIT Press, 55 Hayward Street, Cambridge, MA 02142.

This book was set in Sabon by Toppan Best-set Premedia Limited. Printed and bound in the United States of America.

Library of Congress Cataloging-in-Publication Data

Reflexive governance for global public goods / edited by Eric Brousseau, Tom Dedeurwaerdere, and Bernd Siebenhüner.
   p.   cm.—(Politics, science, and the environment)
Includes bibliographical references and index.
ISBN 978-0-262-01724-4 (hardcover : alk. paper)—ISBN 978-0-262-51698-3 (pbk. : alk. paper) 1. Public interest—International cooperation. 2. Common good–International cooperation. 3. Public interest—Environmental aspects. 4. Common good—Environmental aspects. 5. Public interest—Economic aspects. 6. Common good—Economic aspects. 7. Environmental protection—International cooperation. 8. Sustainable development—International cooperation. I. Brousseau, Eric. II. Dedeurwaerdere, Tom. III. Siebenhüner, Bernd.
JC330.15.R45   2012
303.44—dc23

2011038145

10 9 8 7 6 5 4 3 2 1

Contents

Series Foreword

As our understanding of environmental threats deepens and broadens, it is increasingly clear that many environmental issues cannot be simply understood, analyzed, or acted upon. The multifaceted relationships between human beings, social and political institutions, and the physical environment in which they are situated extend across disciplinary as well as geopolitical confines, and cannot be analyzed or resolved in isolation.

The purpose of this series is to address the increasingly complex questions of how societies come to understand, confront, and cope with both the sources and the manifestations of present and potential environmental threats. Works in the series may focus on matters political, scientific, technical, social, or economic. What they share is attention to the intertwined roles of politics, science, and technology in the recognition, framing, analysis, and management of environmentally related contemporary issues, and a manifest relevance to the increasingly difficult problems of identifying and forging environmentally sound public policy.

Peter M. Haas
Sheila Jasanoff

Acknowledgments

The contributions to this book are the result of an international research project on reflexive governance, financed through the European Commission's Sixth Framework Programme from 2005 to 2010 (see http://refgov.cpdr.ucl.ac.be). By approaching global public-good problems through the lens of governance, this research project aimed to place individual preferences, democratic deliberation, and the role of knowledge center stage in discussions about the provision of goods in the general interest. More specifically, the work presented in the book was generated by an interdisciplinary network of researchers who wanted to analyze the nexus between global public goods, the building of collective preferences, the production of knowledge, and effective governance regimes. Three international workshops were organized to take stock of the state of the art on this matter. The first was organized in Berlin in March 2006, the second was held at the Université catholique de Louvain in Belgium in June 2006, and the third at the Vrije Universiteit Amsterdam in the Netherlands in May 2007 as part of a conference of the International Human Dimensions Programme.

The overall framework and the key concepts that are at the basis of this book were developed in a process of gradual convergence on cross-cutting themes among the researchers in this network. This process of convergence was made possible by the three state-of-the-art workshops and regular interactions within the core group of researchers. The process of writing the various chapters of the book was also highly interactive and quite demanding for the authors who accepted the challenge of a joint publication on this topic. We would like to thank the authors for their efforts to comply with the discipline of this collective effort. Chapter 3 was based on a published article. It was added to the volume because of its importance for introducing the global challenges involved in public goods provision. A longer version of this chapter was originally published as Todd Sandler and Daniel G. Arce, "New Face of Development Assistance: Public Goods and Changing Ethics," *Journal of International Development* 19, no. 4 (May 2007): 527–544. It is being republished with the kind permission of John Wiley & Sons, Ltd.

It is of course difficult to thank all the people who contributed to this project, but who are not authors of chapters in the book. In particular, we would like to thank the researchers at the Centre for the Philosophy of Law, and in particular the director, Jacques Lenoble, for their invaluable support and for hosting this project in such a stimulating research environment. We would also like to thank Anne Liesse for her support in the coordination of the network, Valérie Hilson for the careful editing of the manuscript, Alison Kelly for her English language revision skills that greatly improved the manuscript, and Frank Biermann for his support in hosting the 2007 workshop. Financial support from the EU Sixth Framework Programme (RTD FP6 CIT3–513420 REFGOV) and the Belgian Science Policy Interuniversity Attraction Poles (IUAP VI-06) is also gratefully acknowledged.

Contributors

Daniel G. Arce Professor of Economics, University of Texas at Dallas

Eric Brousseau Professor of Economics and Director of EconomiX, University of Paris West, France

Kamyla B. Cunha Research Fellow, Energy Planning Program of the Faculty of Mechanical Engineering, State University of Campinas, Brazil

Tom Dedeurwaerdere Professor, Faculty of Philosophy, Université catholique de Louvain at Louvain-la-Neuve, Belgium

Peter Feindt Senior Lecturer in Environmental Planning, School of City and Regional Planning, Cardiff University, United Kingdom

Bruno S. Frey Professor of Economics, University of Zurich, Switzerland

Oliver Fritsch Research Fellow, National Environmental Research Institute, Aarhus, Denmark; and Department of Politics, University of Exeter, United Kingdom.

Olivier Godard Researcher, National Centre for Scientific Research, France; Associate Professor, Ecole polytechnique;and Lecturer, Sciences-Po, Paris, France

Torsten Grothmann Research Fellow, Potsdam Institute for Climate Impact Research (PIK), Potsdam, Germany, and Carl von Ossietzky University of Oldenburg, Germany.

Neil Gunningham Professor, Regulatory Institutions Network and the Fenner School of Environment and Society at the Australian National University, Australia

Inge Kaul Adjunct Professor, Hertie School of Governance, Berlin, Germany.

Anna Lawrence Research Fellow, Environmental Change Institute, Oxford University, United Kingdom

Star Molteno Research Fellow, Environmental Change Institute, Oxford University, United Kingdom

Jens Newig Professor for Governance and Sustainability, Leuphana University, Lüneburg, Germany

Fernando Rei President of São Paulo State Sanitation, Technology and Environment Protection Agency (CETESB), São Paulo, Brazil

Todd Sandler   Vibhooti Shukla Chair in Economics and Political Economy, University of Texas at Dallas

Mare Sarr   Research Fellow at the School of Economics, University of Cape Town, South Africa

Bernd Siebenhüner   Professor of Ecological Economics, Carl von Ossietzky University of Oldenburg, Germany

Sigrid Stagl   Department of Socioeconomics, WU—Vienna University of Economics and Business, Vienna, Austria

Timothy M. Swanson   Chair of Environmental Economics, the Graduate Institute, Geneva, Switzerland

Arnaldo Walter   Assistant Professor, University of Campinas, Brazil

Introduction

Eric Brousseau, Tom Dedeurwaerdere, and Bernd Siebenhüner

Global Public Goods and the Governance Issues They Raise

A broad range of fundamental goods and services can be categorized as global public goods (GPGs). The problem of the change in the world's climate through greenhouse gas emissions is global in nature since it has the potential to affect all the world's inhabitants directly or indirectly. Put positively, everyone will benefit from a stable climate. The same holds true for the conservation of biodiversity on the Earth (global biodiversity). Potentially, everyone benefits from the guarantee it provides for the long-term adaptability of the earth's ecosystems to evolving conditions. Other examples of GPGs include public health, peace, and economic security (Kaul, Grunberg, and Stern 1999; Kaul et al. 2003).

The multilayered and multifaceted nature of many global public goods clearly challenges the effectiveness of current methods for tackling problems and conflicts in public good provision on several counts. First, there are often no established individual preferences for complex goods that provide benefits on multiple scales. Second, aggregating individual preferences and building collective preferences for the provision of these goods have to be done at different levels, which raises complex coordination problems. Third, uncertainty leads to important gaps in our knowledge of how the issues should be defined and solutions adopted.

As a result, the problem of the provision of global public goods has become increasingly intertwined with the question of governance. In the absence of given preferences or consensual knowledge, the characteristics of the goods to be provided and their public nature have to be collectively defined. In this process, the communities that benefit from the goods have to find legitimate ways to define themselves as communities, and to elaborate common norms and beliefs. Cases in point are complex goods such as global economic security, global biodiversity, and the global climate, for which there is no consensual set of norms and beliefs.

Since the publication of Kaul's ground-breaking work on GPG governance more than a decade ago (Kaul, Grunberg, and Stern 1999) many political initiatives have been taken and governance experiments run, and much research has been carried out at the frontier between environmental sciences and the social sciences. This transdisciplinary book addresses the new challenges in the provision of GPG and takes stock of the knowledge that has been accumulated over the years, while remaining dispersed. The aim is to contribute to the emerging understanding of the appropriate governance regimes that need to be considered for different types of goods.

The Challenges of Global Governance

The provision of GPGs is essentially a question of global governance. Building upon the debate in the academic literature (Young 1997), the term *global governance* designates any process of rule making and implementation at local, national, regional, and global levels that addresses issues of global concerns. This process is characterized by several challenges. First, there is no state to be the key actor in organizing the provision of these goods and services. A complex web of non-state actors and governments undertakes this task (Levi-Faur and Jordana 2005). Multilevel and international coordination and cooperation are needed to ensure efficiency. Second, as stated above, there is a lack of knowledge about needs and solutions. This is partly because it is often difficult to assess the impact of the provision of GPGs on individual situations. These problems are exacerbated by the interrelated and partly conflicting nature of the demand for the provision of public goods such as economic development and biodiversity.

Governance mechanisms are needed to overcome these problems. In this book, we want to go beyond the usual discussion of the insufficiencies of the dominant approaches to international governance. These insufficiencies include a lack of consistency in conventional rule setting by nation-states, the weaknesses of multilateral agreements, and the lack of powerful global institutions. All these approaches are based on the traditional command-and-control (or regulatory) model. The same holds true for the solutions based on market or pseudo-market mechanisms that are favored by several international organizations and lobby groups. These solutions assume that the goals (preferences) and solutions are well known and established. This book sets out to explore the principles of governance that will not only ensure consistency between the preferences of citizens and the efficient provision of GPGs, but also bridge the existing knowledge gap as a necessary prerequisite for building preferences and imagining workable solutions.

The GPG concepts as used today are not aligned to the understandings and the incentives of the actors. In essence, this book seeks to analyze the mechanisms by which certain issues can be recognized by global citizens (and decision makers) as being of common concern across the world. This implies that individuals have to recognize their interdependencies and their dependence on the global community to address certain issues. They then have to assess the value of the related "goods" and to rank them in the hierarchy of their individual preferences. In addition, the costs have to be assessed on an individual basis. Then mechanisms of aggregation are needed to compare the costs and benefits both at a collective and at an individual level. In any event, these costs and benefits are strongly dependent upon the institutional solutions chosen to provide the good.

These various operations do not only consist of revealing and aggregating individual preferences and assessment. In a world of bounded rationality, all of them are dependent upon the production of knowledge and its diffusion to citizens and decisions makers. Without this, individual preferences for collective goods cannot be generated, nor can individual and collective cost/benefit assessments be made. Such knowledge covers the nature of the goods, the technical solutions needed to provide them, and an analysis of the distribution of the costs and the interdependencies among them. We therefore seek an improved understanding of how efficient and effective alternative institutional solutions are in generating knowledge and ensuring its diffusion, so that well-informed citizens can make collective decisions.

This volume aims to overcome the misalignment between GPG policies on the one hand and the actor's incentives and understandings on the other. To this purpose, the various contributions to this volume, within the various disciplines that study GPG, propose theoretical models to bridge this gap. On the basis of these models they develop new empirical research with the view to gain insights into ongoing experiments in the field of GPG provision, by analyzing the complex impact of incentives, the involvement of stakeholders in collective decision making, and the specific coordination needs for the generation of knowledge. Collectively, the authors show that the effective governance of global public goods needs to be democratic, reflexive, and knowledge based. This demonstration is organized into five parts.

Conceptualizing Global Governance and Global Public Goods

Part I, "The Challenges in Governing Global Public Goods," focuses on the new ways of conceptualizing and analyzing global public goods. The chapters in this part examine the analytical challenge of conceptualizing public goods in a context of bounded rationality and heterogeneous collective preferences. They seek to study how the new challenges of multilayered public goods—from regional to global—can best be addressed and what effects the contrasted nature of the different goods have.

Chapter 1 by Eric Brousseau and Tom Dedeurwaerdere provides a rationale for the specific approach to GPGs in this book. This chapter initially recalls the conventional approach to GPGs in terms of non-rival and non-exclusive use. It then introduces the various reasons why this conventional approach is insufficient to deal with the complex global problems that face humanity today. First, as mentioned above, the publicness of any particular GPG is the result of social and political processes, which contribute to defining the nature of the GPG as it is perceived by various communities. Second, the definition of this collective interest is influenced by players who have both selfish and altruistic motivations, and who participate in both quid pro quo transactions and social interactions based on the logic of gift and social recognition. Neither a social-planning perspective (involving a "neutral" social engineer), nor a market perspective (where all interactions are organized on a quid pro quo basis) can do justice to this complex combination of motivations and interactions. Therefore, governance mechanisms based on a combination of the two approaches will play a main role in GPG governance. Third, bounded rationality, and the emergence of new issues due to societal evolution, call for the generation of new knowledge. New knowledge is needed to identify the issues and their possible solutions, and stakeholders have to be made aware of the issues to be able to express their preferences.

In chapter 2, Inge Kaul builds further on the fact that the publicness of a good is not a natural fact, but rather the product of a social and political process. Kaul points out that what particularly characterizes many governance problems today is that they go beyond the national/state level (because many externalities extend across national boundaries), and therefore there is no match between the organization of the collective decision (at the state level) and the scope of the problem being dealt with. Her contribution therefore calls for a change from the traditional public good theory to the governance approach, because the problems encountered are less about matching funding capabilities with the means of provision than about establishing the nature of the relevant communities for different types of collective goods. Consequently, the main challenge is to build ad hoc governance mechanisms to establish both collective preferences and efficient ways of providing collective goods. Kaul's contribution emphasizes the necessity of matching the degree of concern of each individual with the design of mechanisms for collective choice that give citizens a voice in the collective decision-making process.

The idea that the scope of transnational public goods varies from regional to truly global, as well as varying in their nature, is at the heart of the contribution by Todd Sandler and Daniel Arce that forms chapter 3. Sandler and Arce assert that one of the issues to be dealt with when managing transnational public goods is the strong inequalities between nations. This raises a dilemma. On the one hand, rising transborder externalities (due to the globalization of the economy and the pace of technological development) increase the convergence of interests, and hence the necessity to manage transnational issues cooperatively. On the other hand, mounting inequalities among and within nations tend to amplify the divergence of interests. So chapter 3 shows the necessity of identifying new governance mechanisms to provide transnational public goods.

Framing Individual and Collective Actions: Challenges in Designing Incentive Schemes

Part II of the book, "Designing Complex Incentive Schemes," addresses the institutional design problems that arise when dealing with complex and heterogeneous collective preferences. Reflexive regulation should rely first on the manipulation of traditional incentives to guarantee win-win situations. Compensations should be managed when sustainable practices translate into higher costs or loss of revenue for some. Second, reflexive regulation needs to focus on the transformation of beliefs, so that agents internalize collective issues in their own system of preferences. This is the reason why "crowding out" becomes a central issue. The contributions to this section analyze questions such as: How can equal concern for all individuals be squared with their varying abilities at influencing decision making during the collective decision process? Given the heterogeneous nature of collective preferences and the varying impact of incentives on communities at different levels, what is the best way to design incentive schemes? What are the effects of new incentive tools?

Chapter 4 by Bruno Frey reviews the efforts made by psychologists and social scientists to understand individual motivations in their social context and to analyze the potential counterproductive effects of incentives. Several contributions to this book converge on the claim that contemporary environmental policies should both attempt to influence beliefs and rely on those beliefs. This balance is precisely the issue addressed by Frey. As he points out, when individuals have a strong intrinsic motivation to contribute to public goods, crowding out is expected to dominate any incentive policy. Environmental issues and sustainable development issues are probably two domains to which a large proportion of the world's population is already willing to contribute. Incentives as tools to influence beliefs should therefore be employed with caution, probably along the lines suggested by Neil Gunningham in chapter 5.

Generating more knowledge is a necessary condition for managing the provision of environmental and global public goods more efficiently and more effectively. Better knowledge cannot guarantee, however, that any recommendation will be implemented. Many of the new approaches to regulation attempt to address this implementation issue. Chapter 5 highlights the fact that many of the regulatory tools that have been invented to replace the traditional command-and-control approach, can be understood as neoliberal strategies that aim to implement regulations by recognizing self-interest and utilizing incentives to reach a social goal. They can also be understood as ways of transforming preferences. New types of regulations combine more or less subtle incentives to take initiatives that address collective issues. These approaches include shaming bad performance, diffusing methodologies that favor reflexive processes of management (based in particular on methodological standards and the systematization of reporting and performance analysis), and sharing information and cooperation between regulators and regulated. All these strategies promote the internalization of environmental and social goals by all socioeconomic players. The logic is clearly to switch from manipulating extrinsic motivation to building intrinsic motivation to adopt environmentally friendly behavior and promote sustainable development.

The resulting challenge is to convince every member of the society that each individual will benefit from economic activity that takes the long-term viability of the world into account. The manipulation of taxes, reputation effects, and liability principles are ways of making individual incentives compatible with the collective interest. The development of new methods of regulation can therefore be understood as a systemic approach to regulation in which the state is more a catalyst for social change than a social planner. Its role is to encourage social actors to assume more responsibility, to internalize their own contribution to the environmental and global challenges, and to modify their behavior accordingly.

The state is needed because stakeholders' involvement does not per se guarantee the accumulation of knowledge or the efficient implementation of innovation to improve available solutions or fix problems once assessments have been made. Indeed, stakeholders may suffer from having a too narrowly focused vision, from lack of competence, or from an inability to agree on the best solution (e.g, the prisoners' dilemma or the battle of the sexes). This is why third parties are central to the debate. Public decision makers—provided they are appropriately motivated—can arbitrate between protagonists in the debates and help them to reach consensus or optimal solutions (in particular by managing Hicks-Kaldor compensation, by guaranteeing agreements, and by favoring fair and efficient negotiations). The other important third party is the scientific community. Being less directly involved than stakeholders, and knowledgeable about the issue, scientists can help stakeholders to work out the actual nature of the issues and the potential of possible solutions.

This is well illustrated in the contribution by Mare Sarr and Tim Swanson in chapter 6 of this book. Their chapter provides a direct contribution to the analysis of one of the policy instruments often put forward to promote biodiversity, namely granting intellectual property rights to traditional communities. It also nicely points out how scientific reasoning and academic methodology can help to frame socioeconomic decision making appropriately by identifying the scope of a given issue. Sarr and Swanson seek to analyze the efficiency of the Access and Benefit-Sharing agreements between the North and the South promoted by the 1992 Earth Summit in Rio. Rather than reviewing actual contracts, which are hard to collect and compare, and whose outcomes are difficult to identify, they propose a theoretical industrial-organization model of research and development (R&D) and discuss vertical integration and contracting in the light of alternative intellectual property rights (IPR) regimes. This allows them to point out that, given the North's control over downstream marketing, the South is never in the most favorable bargaining position. The North is therefore always able to extract the majority of the rents, whatever the property rights regime. A stronger IPR regime in favor of the South is desirable. However, vertical integration remains the best way of minimizing transaction costs and maximizing joint profit. This chapter is powerful in providing essential insights into the limits of the development and/or reinforcement of property rights to protect traditional knowledge and biological resources as a way of sustaining development. It sheds light on the social and political debate and should allow stakeholders to organize more informed negotiations and more relevant innovation strategies.

A Web of Mechanisms to Ensure Compliance

Part III "Compliance: From Legal Tools to Moral Norms" draws on the burgeoning literature about new legal principles and modes of citizen involvement. It starts from the intricacies of preference formation vis-à-vis GPGs and discusses the shifting role of governmental policies and the relationship between legal instruments and other incentive mechanisms in the interaction between national and international policies. The contributions deal with the following questions: How should the scope of the relevant communities concerned with these different types of collective goods be determined? Can international treaties and new modes of citizen involvement be used to bypass conflicts of interest among nation-states and among communities within nation-states, and to increase compliance with collective rules?

Chapter 7 by Oliver Godard examines how the combination of international treaties and new modes of citizen involvement can be a strong driver for bypassing conflicts of interest among nation-states. At first sight, national interests and sovereignty can appear to be inhibitors to any global governance mechanism if national governments exercise a power of veto. However, Godard shows that legal principles limit the capability of national governments to ignore international agreements. Once adopted, international treaties and national laws have an impact in the sense that they modify behavior. Because credibility matters, governments cannot ignore the agreements they have signed. Legal tools can be activated by all kinds of interest groups, and economic and social actors take them into consideration when making decisions. This mechanistic impact of treaties and laws is reinforced by citizens, consumers, and public opinion. When they become conscious of cross-boundary interdependencies, groups of citizens in many nations push national governments and economic actors to comply with treaties. In turn political and economic decision makers may consider the adoption of, and compliance with, principles and norms oriented toward the interests of the whole of humanity as a way of strengthening their legitimacy. Citizens and consumers appreciate the importance of abiding by regulations consistent with essential legal principles and basic socioeconomic rights. So there is a dynamic of declining national/state sovereignty, which does not rely on the emergence of a global government or any international organization per se, but results from a combination of the development of legal and institutional frameworks, and of the activism of interest groups (e.g., citizens, consumer groups, scientific advocates).

The complex mechanisms of international law and the interaction between international policies and other levels of governance produce some specific challenges in developing nations. Chapter 8, by Kamyla Borges Cunha, Fernando Rei, and Arnaldo César Walter, illustrates the case of subnational climate-friendly governance initiatives. Climate-change policy in Brazil has to deal with two conflicting trends. On the one hand, large emerging countries such as Brazil, India, and China have taken hostile positions with respect to their involvement in the international regime for environmental protection. In general, they argue that their historic and current emissions are much lower than those of developed countries. Moreover, growth and the reduction of social inequalities are higher priorities for them than the management of environmental externalities. On the other hand, the initiatives of states at the subnational level and the influence of transnational advocacy groups have led to climate-friendly policies being adopted at the regional level. The analysis in chapter 8 shows how these proactive steps in infra-state spheres (sometimes driven by demands from abroad) have become a means of exerting moral pressure on national/federal governments, as well as offering an alternative way of dealing with environmental problems. Indeed, by integrating the concerns of transnational civil society, local citizens' demands for ecological measures, and science advocacy, subnational governments can increase their reputation in the global arena, where the incorporation of pro-climate strategies is increasingly important in attracting foreign investment and political support.

The analysis by Peter Feindt in chapter 9 complements this approach by pointing out that the evolution of legal principles highlighted by Olivier Godard might be the result of a process of the elaboration of moral norms. To a large extent the concept of "sustainable development" that should lie behind most public policies, draws from the progressive stance of taking into account global and intergenerational interdependencies. Sustainable development seeks to satisfy the needs of the present generation—to guarantee a good life for everybody—without compromising the ability of future generations to meet their needs and choose their own lifestyles. It corresponds to a principle of intra- and inter-generational justice. However, the implementation of this rather abstract principle requires the design and implementation of governance mechanisms that translate it into a concrete form. This is why reflexive governance is needed. Deliberative and participatory processes are important, not only to guarantee due consideration of a wide diversity of interests, but also to incorporate multiple experiences and visions.

Reflexive Processes of Governance

Part IV, entitled "Multi-Stakeholder Coordination: How to Manage Heterogeneity," takes stock of two decades of experimentation with tools for reflexive governance. Mechanisms that involve multiple stakeholders in participatory governance processes rely upon different knowledge backgrounds and mechanisms of legitimacy from conventional representative policy processes. Despite the often-voiced approval of such mechanisms, they need to be scrutinized with regard to their actual outcomes.

Chapter 10, by Oliver Fritsch and Jens Newig, focuses on participatory governance and highlights some of the trade-offs involved. They highlight the ambivalent nature of participatory processes in environmental decision making: they have different effects depending on the sociopolitical context, the characteristics of the decision process, and the characteristics of the actors. The core finding of Fritsch and Newig's meta-analysis of case studies is that there exists a trade-off. On the one hand, participatory processes tend to increase compliance with the final agreements. The most important factor in increasing compliance appears to be the degree to which the decisions reflect the interests and the goals of the actors participating in the process. On the other hand, the agreed goals tend to be watered down by participants who capture the process and use it to promote their own interests. So, the targets resulting from participatory processes tend to be less ambitious than those set by governmental agencies or other external bodies. However, some factors can be identified that tend to improve both compliance and the adequacy of the agreed measures: first, compliance increases if there is a clear set of external policy goals; and second, effectiveness is improved by the inclusion of a wider selection of social interests. Moreover, context and stakeholders' interests matter more than the process itself in shaping governance outcomes

The concern with stakeholder involvement is at the heart of current research on democratic experimentalism. In this context, it is interesting to see how research on mutual monitoring between teams within firms has inspired promising experiments on collective learning with respect to sustainability targets. One example, the experimentation with forest groups in Flanders, is analyzed by Tom Dedeurwaerdere in chapter 11. The main concern in decentralized natural resource management, which is also discussed in chapter 10, is to involve the broadest possible set of stakeholders in making effective contributions to the learning process. This helps to prevent capture by private interests, and to ensure that new opportunities for reaching better collective outcomes are explored. Mutual monitoring and reporting, and comparison among different self-organized collective management organizations, appear to be effective ways to gradually scale up the level of environmental protection. However, as the case study shows, such a decentralized self-organized learning process can be quite costly for small private owners of natural resources, which may hinder their willingness to get involved. Better participation can be achieved through targeted subsidies and appropriate steering by a coordinating entity. Hence, the importance of combining a variety of different governance mechanisms is pointed out again.

In chapter 12, Sigrid Stagl addresses the problem of coordination among various stakeholders with heterogeneous collective preferences. The systematic overview of experiments of participatory assessments shows an interesting trade-off between more instrumentally oriented forms of participatory assessment (geared toward selecting among operational solutions) and more exploratory forms (geared toward the building of new collective preferences and actor representations). The instrumental forms, such as deliberative monetary valuation, are best suited to the appraisal of projects whose impacts are quite well understood and relatively short term. The more exploratory forms, such as multi-criteria mapping, work better when addressing complex interrelated issues characterized by uncertainty.

The Necessity and Difficulty of Knowledge Generation

Part V, "Knowledge Generation on Global Issues," focuses on the specific coordination needs of the generation of knowledge. Central questions include: What role does knowledge play in various governance processes vis-à-vis GPGs? Who should take part in the knowledge generation processes? How are its costs to be kept manageable, and its results to be disseminated widely? What are the preconditions and qualifications required for successful reflexive governance?

As Eric Brousseau, Tom Dedeurwaerdere, and Bernd Siebenhüner point out in chapter 13, one of the challenges of dealing with global governance issues is that there is a double lack of knowledge. Collective goals are unknown because individuals and communities can only develop preferences when they become conscious of what is actually at stake, and of the way in which alternative choices would impact on their own individual situation, the situation of others, and future members of society. Moreover, the solutions are also unknown, both because the most efficient means of dealing with an issue is unclear, and because diffusion of the relevant knowledge is problematic. Brousseau, Dedeurwaerdere, and Siebenhüner highlight the importance of the orientation and organization of the process of decision making. Relevant knowledge of how to deal with the diversity of environmental/global issues is largely dependent on the scope of the interests actually considered in the decision-making process, and the organization of this process to avoid the duplication of effort and boost diffusion. Hence, participatory dialogue, devolved decision making, local implementation (rather than uniformity), inclusiveness, transparency, information diffusion, collective deliberation, and consensus-based practices all play an important role.

Decentralized participatory processes do not always lead to better knowledge of GPGs, even when the inclusiveness of the process has a positive impact on implementation. An alternative way of proceeding is to have recourse to central government, which can organize a learning process without the possibility of capture by private interests, and which is more oriented toward the systematic integration of all available knowledge. In chapter 14, Anna Lawrence and Star Molteno analyze the experience of the United Kingdom Biodiversity Action Plan (UKBAP), which has been gathering data on species and habitats in the United Kingdom since 1994 and has developed target-based action plans. Its main strength has been to produce clear targets for sustainability, which have allowed cumulative and systematic knowledge gathering. However, biodiversity conservation requires knowledge of the interaction of different species and habitats in ecosystems and mechanisms for distributional bargaining among the various interests. Integrating complexity and flexible goal formulation in the knowledge generation process has been one of the main difficulties of the UKBAP. At the same time, the plan has been able to learn from these challenges and introduce some original approaches to managing complexity. General assessment is now combined with local biodiversity assessment and planning exercises, and transparency and interaction with stakeholders have been increased.

This study of participatory processes in environmental assessment shows how actors and communities can be involved in an intense process of experimentation and permanent reform. This highlights once again a key point in our analysis of reflexive governance. Processes more oriented toward knowledge generation should produce more human welfare. The capacity of actors to experiment with new governance mechanisms to challenge existing frameworks is key to the process. It is thus essential to explore practical strategies to increase this capacity. Whereas the discussion of civic and democratic skills has a long tradition in educational research, specific skills and actors' competencies must play a role in any discussion of the governance of environmental issues. This is shown in chapter 15 by Torsten Grothmann and Bernd Siebenhüner, who analyze the role of individual actors' competencies in dealing with uncertainty in adaptation to climate change. As already discussed in chapter 7, scientific uncertainty over outcomes and the development of complex systems have led to new moral tenets such as the precautionary principle. However, practical ways of dealing with uncertainty in distributional bargaining are still underdeveloped. The analysis in chapter 15 suggests some original training and education activities that could help us to meet this challenge.

The Potential of the Reflexive Governance Approach

The argument presented in this book aims to provide a roadmap for the analysis of the various dimensions that contribute to the efficient and legitimate provision of GPGs. The chapters analyze various possible governance schemes in the light of, inter alia, their ability to take into account complex social preferences and to generate appropriate knowledge on GPG provision in an efficient way. By focusing on these common reflexive insufficiencies of the current approaches to GPG, the volume proposes a novel integration of economic, political science, and science and society approaches to GPG governance. Collectively the various chapters aim to shed new light on the contribution of governance processes to overcome the gap between the GPG concept and the actor's incentives and understandings, thereby adding a new perspective to the existing models of reflexive governance.

The concept of reflexive governance as used in this book builds on the seminal work in the 1990s by Jurgen Habermas (1992, 1996) on the theory of deliberative democracy, which focuses on the formal conditions that should govern deliberative governance processes in the public sphere. One of the implications of his work is the importance of agreeing collectively upon the formal procedures, such as transparency and equity, that can ensure the normative legitimacy of the processes of deliberation. However, this formal approach should be completed with a more fine-grained analysis of the conditions that have to be satisfied when applying these formal conditions to practical action contexts. It fails to address the impact of real-world social possibilities in selecting possible outcomes of the learning process (Dedeurwaerdere 2005; Lenoble 1996) and the subjective genesis of the actor's involvement in the reflexive processes (Lenoble and Maesschalck 2010; Maesschalck 2010). For these reasons, which have been developed elsewhere, the approach in this book also aims to overcome the problems with the formal approach to deliberation, by developing an innovative approach to reflexive governance that considers both the formal deliberative processes that lead to more legitimate decision making over GPG and the real world constraints on the processes of social learning and knowledge generation. Although the focus of this volume is not on the genesis of the actor's involvement in the reflexive processes, the analysis in this book also recognizes the need for a better understanding of the conditions for building the actor's capacities for effective involvement in reflexive governance processes.

One possible caveat of such a nonformal approach to reflexive governance is that most empirical research has taken place in the field of environmental governance and sustainable development. Indeed, the concept of reflexive governance initially emerged within the context of the discussion on the study of environmental risks (Beck 1992), and a lot of work on reflexive governance has been carried out in this domain. Nevertheless, the need for more reflexive and deliberative collective decision making processes is a common feature shared by many global public good issues. Therefore the analysis in this book, even if it builds upon the existing scholarship in the field of environmental governance, directly addresses the role of reflexive governance processes in related areas of GPG provision such as global health, food security, and technological risks. The overall aim is to conduct a consistent comparison of the features of reflexive governance throughout various fields of study.

Improving Institutional Fit

The analysis of GPG governance in this book shows how the combination of complex preferences, uncertain knowledge on issues and solutions, and the multilevel nature of the goods necessitates and generates different types of governance mechanisms that often interact and are hybridized in global governance. The key question that needs to be addressed in this context is how to improve the institutional fit between the new governance mechanisms and the features of GPG provision that are highlighted in this book.

Let us consider the variations within each of these dimensions in turn. First, some GPGs are characterized by well-established and stable individual preferences (e.g., about global health and food security), while others are characterized by changing or even nonexistent individual preferences (in particular toward such abstract goods as global genetic diversity). Second, some GPG issues are characterized by limited uncertainty; that is, only a small range of development scenarios can be envisaged, even though precise predictions cannot be made. By contrast, there are situations in which future scenarios are completely unknown, either because our understanding of the current situation is incomplete or because future developments are too complex to be predicted. Third, the degree of globality/locality refers to whether a given collective action problem should be treated as a set of (linearly) cumulative local problems or as a set of interlinked problems requiring a systemic approach. Each of these dimensions, taken in isolation, influences the choice of the mode of governance, and their combination crucially complicates the task of choosing the appropriate way to govern GPGs.

The many possible combinations of these dimensions have an impact on the complexity of the collective action problems being considered, and on the difficulty of their governance. However, it is necessary to analyze how governance solutions interact with the various dimensions of GPGs.

Reflexive governance has emerged as a promising field of research to tackle the challenge of understanding and providing guidance in this new governance landscape. It is based on the analysis of the processes leading to changes in the cognitive and normative framing of the issues involved in the provision of GPGs, both at the level of state and non-state actors. Reflexive governance is not a panacea however. One of the claims of the book is that reflexive processes are also prone to a set of cooperation failures. A common cooperation failure in this context occurs when participants free ride upon other participants, and attempt to improve their own position by providing misleading information on their preferences or by extracting rents from information asymmetries. In some cases, exogenous institutional regulation is required to correct such behavior and produce a form of cooperation influenced by a hierarchy. This is illustrated in the contributions on multi-stakeholder coordination in part IV. In other cases, an appropriate transformation of the game structure, for example by a system of graduated sanctions or monetary incentives, might be sufficient to deter free riding. This option is particularly relevant when extrinsic social preferences play an important role, and such situations are analyzed in the chapters on complex incentive schemes (part II) and compliance (part III). Deliberate institutional design is used to turn the non-cooperative equilibrium into a cooperative outcome.

Coordination failures may also occur. For example, generating knowledge, which benefits everyone, might be hampered by insufficient guarantees of inclusiveness. Cases in point are the collective action needed to generate knowledge on new technological solutions to deal with climate change, or to develop vaccines for global pandemics. In the absence of guarantees that the other parties will make a similar investment, actors may be tempted to hide crucial information or under-invest in new knowledge. Here, uncertainty about the intentions of the other players is a rationale for non-cooperation. Solutions to these dilemmas can be found in devices for providing information on the intentions of the participants, or in mechanisms for binding the participants to agreements. These and other solutions to the coordination problems have led to a rich literature on establishing cooperative practices through the diffusion of models of innovative practices. This is illustrated in the debates on experimentalist governance in chapters 5 and 11, and on the building of institutional frameworks for knowledge generation in part V.

In order to deal with the complex coordination and cooperation problems embedded in evolving GPGs, various architectures of governance are proposed that may enhance the institutional fitness needed to deal with the management of knowledge generation and the building of collective preferences. These architectures range from self-governance and regional multi-stakeholder coordination mechanisms to the building of new global hierarchies and political constituencies. By combining knowledge from different research approaches to GPGs, it should be possible to identify which governance architectures are most appropriate for different types of GPGs, given their specific comparative benefits. Since the world is often characterized by second-best outcomes, it is important to consider not only the problem of designing the most appropriate governance solutions, but also the constraints of the actual decision-making process, and the problems of compliance associated with the instruments adopted.

I

The Challenges in Governing Global Public Goods

Governance mechanisms are needed to overcome GPG provision problems. The first part of this book explores the principles of governance that will ensure consistency between the preferences of citizens and the efficient provision of GPG, and it will also bridge the knowledge gap (which is a necessary prerequisite for building preferences and devising workable solutions). To avoid any moral (or immoral) bias, the first chapter shows that even starting from a set of minimal assumptions—self-interested individuals with bounded rationality—raises problems of global concern that should be governed by a combination of political and economic institutions. Among these is the provision of public goods of concern to all, which requires mechanisms for making collective decisions and managing motivations so that contributions are guaranteed. To address certain issues, individuals also have to recognize their interdependencies and their dependence on the global community.

The second and the third chapters show the necessity of broadening the categories of traditional GPG analysis. The second chapter, by Kaul, argues that the traditional public-economy theory of public good provision is oversimplified as it is fundamentally state-centered (at the national level) and fiscally focused, and therefore fails to consider the broader politics of multi-stakeholder and transnational public-good provision. In particular, various non-state actors contribute to GPGs, which increases the problem of coordination. The next chapter, by Sandler and Arce, provides a classification and definition of the various types of public goods, their interactions, and the implications for determining public-good aid to developing countries. This overview shows that there are many synergies and positive externalities between the provision of various public goods (e.g., between the conservation of biodiversity and global food security). It also adds to the overall argument of this first part, by showing that many public goods should be provided at levels that are neither national nor global. Regional public goods, such as the local ecosystem services provided by natural resources, probably pose the greatest difficulty, because often there is no clear political entity at the level of the ecosystem, and there are no clear benefit spillovers to the national or international levels. Transregional public goods require institutional arrangements that network the whole area in which the impact is felt.

1

Global Public Goods: The Participatory Governance Challenges

Eric Brousseau and Tom Dedeurwaerdere

This book addresses the topic of the governance of global public goods (GPGs). As explained in the introduction, the specific problem in the governance of GPGs is not only their multilevel character, due to the absence of a supreme global political constituency that shapes collective preferences and makes collective decisions. It is also the lack of clear-cut knowledge on collective preferences and solutions. This intricate combination of a collective-choice issue and a cognitive lack makes it worth discussing an analytical framework aimed at disentangling the various dimensions of the questions to be analyzed and debated.

It should not be forgotten that the concept of a global public good is questioned by many people. At first, the idea that there are problems of concern for all humankind may be considered a heroic assumption, or the result of a set of moral beliefs and assumptions about the necessary solidarity among human beings in a global society that considers their mutual interests. It is worth noting that such concepts can lead to requests that would certainly not be acceptable to some groups. For instance, the developed North could request the South not to develop, so as to preserve biodiversity, slow the process of global warming, and avoid resource depletion. To avoid any criticism of moral (or immoral) bias, we show in this chapter that even if we accept a set of minimal assumptions—starting from self-interested individuals—problems of global concern are raised that should be governed by a combination of political and economic solutions. To put it another way, even if we ignore the potentially altruistic orientations of human beings, the coordination needs of individuals and the existence of biophysical interdependencies on a global scale enable us to identify several issues that have to be dealt with collectively. Among these is the provision of goods of concern for all, which requires mechanisms for collective decision making and the management of motivations so that contributions are guaranteed.

To demonstrate this, we assume a world of individuals who pursue their own ends, but who recognize that they belong to communities in which two types of social relationship are built. On the one hand, exchange is at the basis of many social interactions by which agents align their individual interests through bargaining, ending in quid pro quo transactions. On the other hand, the logic of gifts (without quid pro quo compensation) is at the basis of the social interactions by which agents align their interests by recognizing a common interest encompassing and surpassing individual preferences. The definition of this "collective interest" can be influenced by players who may push their own interests, but who nevertheless take the interests of other members of the community into account.

The argument presented here aims to provide a roadmap for the analysis of the various dimensions that contribute to the efficient and legitimate provision of GPGs. First we show how the two logics of social interaction generate different types of governance mechanisms that often interact and are hybridized in global governance. We then point out why, in the context of the provision of GPGs, bounded rationality and the global context combine to demand the generation of new knowledge. New knowledge is needed to identify the issues and their possible solutions, and stakeholders have to be made aware of the issues to be able to express meaningful preferences. We also highlight the fragmentation of today's global society into communities without clear hierarchies, and the inclusiveness necessary for processes resulting in compromises about the definition of goods of common and global concern. Finally, we discuss the potential of the principles of reflexive governance and their practical limits. The concluding section shows how the various dimensions of GPG governance analyzed in this chapter are further developed in the five parts of the book.

The Governance Issues Raised by the Many Features of Public Goods

To define the common background of the chapters in this volume, it is important to start with a brief reminder of the basic economics of public goods. We first recall the standard definition and then show how the conventional approach has to be reconceptualized and extended to take into account the multilevel and partially socially constructed nature of global public goods. This explains why we then develop a theoretical framework aimed at pointing out the challenges raised by the governance of GPGs.

Pure and Impure Public Goods

Public goods are goods of common concern, more appropriately called "collective goods" (Sandler 2004). They are characterized by the properties of nonrivalry in consumption of the good (their use by one individual does not diminish the possibility of their use by another) and nonexcludability (it is costly and sometimes impossible to exclude a user from access to, or use of, the good). Pure public goods are both non-rival and non-excludable. Other types of public goods have only one of these properties: common-pool resources (land, water, livestock, etc.) are partially rival and non-excludable, and club goods (e.g., encrypted TV programs or intellectual property rights) are non-rival but excludable.

Partial rivalry can arise when additional users detract in some way from the benefits available to others, through crowding/congestion costs. Partial rivalry in common-pool resources has been extensively dealt with in the literature on the new commons. For example, in the new globally distributed digital commons (such as the Internet), collective action problems related to partial rivalry (such as a conflict of priorities, overuse, and congestion) have been increasingly recognized (Hess and Ostrom 2007). Similar problems of rivalry have been the focus of analyses of the global environmental commons (such as biodiversity and carbon sequestration), because localization and geographical scope brings unequal benefits and costs to stakeholders (Dolsak and Ostrom 2003). Public goods with global and nonexclusive, but partially rival, benefits, thus raise coordination issues that go beyond the problems of free riding and undersupply (see Carraro 2003 for a discussion of global environmental agreements).

In terms of provision, club goods do not pose major collective-action problems, as they can be efficiently supplied by members of the club, financed through tolls or user fees. However, as has been shown for scholarly publications, club goods raise delivery issues (Boyle 2007). The artificial transformation of pure public goods into club goods through the use of (digital, in the case of publication) fences, can produce a major decrease in social welfare. There is therefore a trade-off between the loss of social welfare resulting from the reduced availability of a nonexclusive resource, and the benefits in terms of a reduction in free riding that increases the contributions to provision.

Heterogeneity in Consumption and Contribution

Other important issues around the provision of public goods are linked to the heterogeneity of benefits and contributions among the various stakeholders. Some goods benefit different actors in different ways. For example, a preserved natural area benefits not only the local inhabitants, but also visitors who come to enjoy the scenery. The area can be used for recreational purposes or it can be managed so that it contributes to the global conservation of biodiversity. In such a context, the nature of the governance solution may impact upon the weighting attached to alternative users' preferences. For instance, pseudo-market solutions may favor wealthy urbanites to the detriment of farmers; while "democratic" mechanisms may mean that local interests prevail over more global or distant stakeholders.

The heterogeneity of contributions leads us to consider the issue of aggregation technology, which refers to how individual contributions to the collective good determine the quality of the goods available for consumption (Hirschleifer 1983; Cornes and Sandler 1984). With summation goods, each unit contributed to the public good adds identically and cumulatively to the overall level of the good available for consumption. For example, any reduction in the emission of greenhouse gases corresponds to the aggregate (summed) cutbacks of the polluter countries. Other important types of aggregation technologies are weakest-link public goods, (where the smallest contribution fixes the quantity of the public good for the entire group, as in pest control), best-shot public goods (for which the overall level of the public good equals the largest single individual provision level; e.g., finding a cure for a disease), and weighted-sum public goods (where different contributions can have different impacts, as in the cleanup of polluted sites). The main message of this research is that aggregation technologies other than summation often provide hopeful signposts to feasible collective action to produce the collective good where no state (or alternative coordinator of a large population of individuals) has control, so as to ensure an efficient level of contribution by all (Sandler 2004). In the case of knowledge it is often better to focus efforts on gathering the contributions of the most efficient providers, even when the end product remains freely available to all, as has been shown for free software communities (Nguyen and Pénard 2007).

Public Goods as Societal Issues

Public good provision is a social issue that raises social challenges. Provision is considered a social issue because dealing with GPGs is not just a technical or natural problem. Fundamental social choices include the definition of the boundaries of communities and the nature of the social contract, in particular the recognition of social groups within those boundaries. Public goods raise social challenges because the way to deal with them depends upon the design of adequate governance structures, in at least two distinct ways. First, the provision of public goods in general, and of GPGs in particular, raises the question of coordination among different communities and authorities. This is the central issue dealt with by fiscal federalism (see Oates 1999). However, specific to GPGs, no global government exists to coordinate the various authorities and communities involved in their production. Moreover, the jurisdictions involved in the production of GPGs are of various kinds. There are governments (at all levels), and self-regulated communities of many kinds (from rural communities to international business associations). The specificity of incompletely hierarchized coordination among heterogeneous providers is a true challenge for the social sciences. Second, it is important to stress that many of the properties of rivalry and excludability, and the aggregation technology, are neither absolute nor natural. They partly depend upon processes of social construction. For instance, rivalry in consumption of a good is directly related to population density, and the notion of exclusion is socially constructed and can evolve with the development of new technologies.

A Framework for Analyzing Collective Governance

To understand the properties of alternative models of governance, we need to take into account how complex individuals interact in a society and the logic of alternative governance principles in that perspective. This is why we first highlight a double logic in individual interactions, before pointing out the existence of four basic models of social interaction. These clearly refer to different logics, but in practice they coexist and are blended in varying proportions in different societies.

Self-Interested and Boundedly Rational Individuals

To present our argument, we use an analytical framework derived from new institutional economics (initiated by Coase, North, and Williamson; see Brousseau and Glachant 2008 for an overview). We consider global society as a collection of individuals embedded in social structures, who are characterized by individual preferences (which can be collectively built). These individuals have bounded rationality (as defined by Simon 1978, 1986), and more precisely, procedural rationality. Individuals and collectivities are nevertheless repositories of knowledge. Individuals know how to solve problems (including learning procedures for solving new problems, which is the idea behind the notion of procedural rationality). They also have a social capability to interact with other individuals who can help them to solve problems. The unit of analysis is therefore a collection of individuals, who are both stakeholders and knowledge holders. They have their own interests, and they also have personal capabilities to solve problems, to learn and to interact with other knowledge holders.

Individuals have their own set of preferences and ranking among these preferences, depending on such factors as personal history, beliefs, and societal position. Because these preferences are ordinal and subjective, they cannot be weighted and aggregated to yield a collective preference function (May 1954; Savage 1954). An individual's system of preferences is incomplete and therefore unstable. Since their rationality is bounded, individuals can discover new options enabling them to revise their whole system of preferences (Simon 1957, 1983, -1986; Selten 1990).

Self-interested individuals are concerned, above all, with the realization of their own ends (according to their own system of preferences). They know that this realization depends upon successful coordination with the other individuals in society. Individuals do not, however, always spontaneously recognize themselves as being members of a local, national, or global society that encompasses all living individuals, or even all the individuals leaving in a common territory, or belonging to the same group. To be consistent with the idea that individuals have bounded rationality, idiosyncratic hierarchies of preferences, and specific beliefs, it must be recognized that the concept of society is subjective and has little chance of being implemented consistently in every individual's set of preferences. To put it another way, not everyone has the same vision of what society is, and not everyone shares the idea that humankind per se is a society. This raises the issue of the definition of problems of global concern (see below). While recognizing this, we assume nevertheless that people are social beings. They know that they belong to collectivities. Collectivities are characterized by the existence of common rules of behavior, drawn from the convergent beliefs of members with shared interests, which justify constraints in the name of collective action. These collectivities can be labeled "communities," to point out their subjective aspect and its consequences.

In such a context, governance is not just a question of designing techniques to aggregate preferences (so as to manage collective choices) and implementing incentives to harmonize individual behavior. It also involves producing and sharing information to allow individuals to establish and modify their preferences. Furthermore, governance is about innovating and enhancing the collective capability to influence behavior so that individuals can discover and share new beliefs, more effective ways of resolving issues, and better techniques for confronting problems of collective action.

Four Articulated Models of Social Interactions

Individuals recognize that the realization of their ends necessitates interactions with other members of their communities. At this stage of our reasoning let us consider interactions among individuals in a given community, rather than interactions among communities. Interactions among individuals within a community can be based upon two alternative principles (trade/compensation or sharing/compromise) that are implemented in different ways. According to the trade/compensation principle, an individual agrees to renounce something (the benefit of a good, a right, or even having to make an effort) if and only if he or she is compensated by the provision of a good or service that balances the loss of satisfaction entailed by the renouncement. The sharing/compromise principle states that individuals, while recognizing their individual ends, use the community as a tool for reaching these ends. Individuals contribute to realizing the ends of the other community members and (expect to) benefit in return from the community's contribution to their own ends. Of course free-riding is an issue, but it is not always the best individual strategy, and mechanisms can be implemented to control it. Here, there are no transactions but only gifts (with the social consequences highlighted by Mauss 1924). Both these principles can be implemented either centrally (by means of collective decision mechanisms encompassing all the members of the community at the same time) or through bilateral negotiations between individuals.

This leads to four models of collective interaction, which have long been recognized and analyzed in the social sciences, and which are characterized in table 1.1.

- The (neoclassical) social-planner model indicates a situation in which an entity is in charge of optimizing the performance of the social system. This entity should act as a neutral engineer. There is no collective interest per se, but individual interests can be summed. The social planner overcomes coordination difficulties due to information

Table 1.1
Four models of social interaction

	Transaction (trade/ compensation) Relationships among individuals are based on exclusive (individual) interests	Gift (sharing/ compromise) Relationships among individuals are based on inclusive (common) interests
Centralized (collective decisions) Relationships among individuals are organized, because this increases the efficiency of managing interdependences	(Neoclassical) social planner	Communism/family/ nonprofit organizations
Decentralized (bilateral negotiations) Relationships among individuals are spontaneous	Market	Social networks (gift/ counter-gift)

costs, indivisibilities, and other factors, and thereby allows the maximization of each individual's welfare. It applies a Pareto principle and can organize compensation among individuals *à la* Hicks-Kaldor to reach a Pareto-improving situation that may harm some members of the society.

- The market model describes a situation in which a central, neutral agent cannot emerge, or cannot perform the social-planning task to the benefit of all. All social interactions are organized on a quid-pro-quo basis. Market failures may exist, but alternative ways of organizing transactions also have drawbacks.

- The communism/family/nonprofit model represents the situation in which an elite governs the society for the benefit of all, either because it is enlightened or because it has been consensually chosen. Its aim is to provide goods to each member of the society as a function of individual needs, and to request contributions proportional to everyone's means. There is, therefore, no perfect match for individuals between what they give and what they get, and constraints are required to manage this de facto redistribution. The redistribution can be justified in various ways (such as ethical principles, political need to strengthen the collectivity or maintain its consistency, and economic need to invest in collective resources benefiting everybody).

- The social-networks model refers to settings in which individuals freely choose to contribute to a collective venture without expecting compensation proportional to their contribution. The word *community* is often applied to such an arrangement (for example, open-source software communities or local communities).

Of course, none of the pure principles illustrated by the boxes fully characterizes any real society; while some societies are essentially based on market interactions, others exemplify collective compromises. The principles apply to various degrees in any society or community. This has an impact on the motivations for individuals' actions. It also has an impact, of course, on the logic of governance, which is different in each of the four modes of social interaction.

Disentangling the Logic and the Mechanisms of Coordination

Our goal in this section is to clarify the drivers of individual social behavior. The dominant vision is to contrast two facets of human psychology: selfishness and altruism. The first is a core assumption in economics, and leads to a vision of society in which central coordination is useless (or completely neutral). The second is a core assumption in ethics (and politics). Our analysis shows that both types of interests can be dealt with in either centralized or decentralized institutional systems–allowing us to disentangle the logic of coordination (driven by individual or collective interest) from the mechanism of coordination (which refers to how collective decisions are made). This distinction is useful in understanding the properties of alternative governance mechanisms and institutional architectures.

The first column of table 1.1—labeled transaction (cost/compensation)— refers to a cost/benefit analysis (managed either at the individual or the collective level), in which collective action is based on the logic of exchange. The second column—labeled gift (sharing/compromise)— refers to a universe of ability to influence the behavior of others in which collective action is based on social constraints and conviction. In brief, the first column refers to economics, the second to politics. Since individuals do not perceive the world as either a purely economic or a purely political entity, they understand that the realization of their individual ends relies on both mechanisms.

This results in complex motivations. Individuals have both what are usually called individualistic preferences (which in our nomenclature are economic preferences linked to the logic of transactions) and collective preferences (in our terminology, political preferences linked to the logic of sharing and compromise). Obviously these preferences differ from one individual to another, and are balanced in different ways for different purposes within individuals. However, individuals clearly have complex motivations because they simultaneously take into account their immediate interest—let us say their individual wealth—and a broader collective interest. They know that the wealth of the community or society impacts on their individual situation. To put it another way, individuals have both exclusive interests (they decide in terms of their own situation) and inclusive interests (they consider the impact of their actions and decisions on other stakeholders in the society and have their own preferences for that society).

Governance in such a framework consists first and foremost of the choice of a social interaction model for a given domain of collective life. Sets of individuals have to agree on the respective domains of self-interest and collectivity in a given society and on the scope of collective coordination in each of these domains. Then of course, actual governance mechanisms have to be implemented and operated.

Public Goods in a World of Bounded Rationality

There are two categories of problems that individuals have to solve that, by definition, are collective. The first is the provision of an infrastructure to manage the interactions between people (from a common language to marketplaces, and including the institutional framework in the sense defined by Coase [1988] and North [1990]). The second is methods of managing external effects. External effects occur when, for some reason, the use of an asset by one individual impacts (positively or negatively) on the utility of a nonuser of that asset, and it is either technically impossible, or prohibitively expensive, to confine the use of that asset to a particular person or group. What Samuelson (1954) called a public good is simply an extreme case of an externality. A service is automatically provided to everybody, but this provision does not deprive anybody of the benefits of the service.

As even economists of the Austrian school, such as Hayek (1979), recognized, the pure logic of decentralized trade fails to provide these goods because of the free riding that generates the "tragedy of the commons." This does not mean that the provision of these goods should rely on an organization called the state. It does, however, mean that there should be a mechanism to force individuals to contribute, either through social constraints or conviction, which applies to all the members of the community who benefit from the good.

It has been well documented, by Ostrom (1990) in particular, that compulsion can emerge spontaneously at the local level. Local communities can control the behavior of their members due to the stability of groups, the repetition of interactions, the high cost of exclusion through ostracism, and the easy diffusion of information on the behavior of members that sustains reputation effects. Spontaneous "cooperation" therefore flourishes in small, stable groups. However, as well demonstrated and argued by Milgrom, North, and Weingast (1990), the larger the group, the more formal and institutionalized the coercion mechanisms must be. In any case, collective goods raise the issue of how the provision of a service that is available to everybody on the basis of mandatory contributions is to be organized.

While the acceptance of formal or more informal means of coercion allows public goods to be provided, the problem of how to select those that will actually be provided among the many potential public goods (assuming that scarcity prevents the provision of all of them) remains. There is also the question of how they should be supplied. In a world of perfectly rational agents (in Savage's [1954] sense) each individual has a complete and stable set of preferences. Individuals are therefore able to value each potential public good, and a benevolent and costless social planner can implement a revelation scheme so that individuals show their preferences in a way—their propensity to pay—that allows their individual preferences to be aggregated.

In a world where agents do not have perfect rationality, however, two problems occur. First, bounded rationality means that agents are unable to value their individual utility for each possible public good according to a common currency. Even if they were able to rank their preferences (which presupposes knowledge of the complete list of potential public goods), in the absence of common currency, a social planner would be unable to aggregate their preferences because the Condorcet-Arrow paradox of social choice would apply (Arrow 1950). Second, bounded rationality could result in agents ignoring the complete list of potential public goods. In that case, it would be impossible for any social planner to decide which projects should be undertaken on the basis of individual wishes. In such a world, the transaction/trade/compensation model cannot be used to decide the amount and type of public goods to be provided.

In addition, in a world of bounded rationality, the scope of the community concerned by the provision of a public good remains an open question. The very notion of public good carries with it the notion of community. There are two conditions for the existence of a public good in this respect. The members of a community should recognize themselves as such (whatever the purpose, nature, and boundaries of the community). In addition, they should recognize that a given good is a public (or collective) resource. The first condition leads each member to accept the legitimacy of constraints placed on him or her by the group. The second one legitimates the constraints that are actually implemented in the provision of a given good.

Thus, in a world of bounded rationality, the provision of a public good necessarily entails mechanisms of governance pertaining to the logic of collective cooperation, based on inclusive (common) interests (see the first column in table 1.1), since the aggregation of individual preferences is neither possible nor the only issue.

Public Goods in a Global Context

One of the topics this book seeks to address is the mechanisms by which human beings recognize the existence of global public goods and agree on priorities and on ways to provide them. There are two main topics to be dealt with. First, agents have to recognize the existence of goods of common concern at the global level, which means that they must recognize the existence of a global community (i.e., a community encompassing all human beings, both present and future). We have already mentioned this issue, and we will return to it below. Second, agents have to establish a collective hierarchy of preferences for any particular GPG and between this GPG and alternative public (i.e., local public) and private goods. In a world of scarcity there is always competition among the various goods that could potentially be provided. This second topic requires an understanding of two sets of intertwined questions. First, the relationships among (the alternative ways to provide) the various GPGs have to be understood, since if these goods are not independent of each other (i.e., there are complementarities and/or substitutabilities between them), this has to be considered when establishing the hierarchy of preferences. Second, the cost of providing a GPG, which is in competition with providing other goods, is not independent of the establishment of the hierarchy of preferences. Agents have to know the costs (in terms of renouncing the provision of alternative goods) of providing GPGs, in order to take production constraints and the possible interdependencies among GPGs into account.

Since we assume that our individuals do not have perfect knowledge, we see any agreement on the type of global public goods to be produced and the way to achieve this end as being not only a problem of the revelation and aggregation of preferences, but also one of discovering issues and ways to deal with them. Put another way, while we acknowledge that the alignment of individual interests and the building of compromises is an issue, we also claim that the development of knowledge to identify GPGs, to understand the complex web of causal relationships that link them, and to discover how they can be delivered is another requirement.

Our analysis therefore covers the need to consider mechanisms for building the collective interest in the context of global governance. Beyond multi-stakeholder governance, the issue is to define how compromises, and the definition and hierarchization of GPGs, can be achieved in a world without an entity that can ultimately arbitrate among citizens' interest and settle conflicts among their agents (governments, organizations, political groups, etc.). Governance of GPGs necessarily leads to the logic of the gift exchange contained in the bottom right box of table 1.1.

The Role of Knowledge Communities in Global Governance

Inspired by the new institutional economics (NIE) approach, we feel that it is unnecessary to analyze alternative institutional frameworks from scratch. We are not working in the framework of "Nirvana economics" (Demsetz 1969). While we recognize that the notion of communities is linked to individual beliefs, we also recognize that individuals participate in preexisting communities that are organized on the basis of either jurisdiction or shared interests. Thinking about governance issues should therefore start from the fact that individuals are already grouped into communities, although the global community is not yet fully organized. Hence, there are various types of sub-global communities in which individuals develop their strategies to have an impact on the provision of public goods in general and global ones in particular.

For the purpose of our analysis, we can distinguish between two types of such communities. First there are those organized on a sociopolitical basis by a geographically delimited jurisdiction. These communities, which are essentially linked by spatial proximity, are generally made up of individuals with highly heterogeneous preferences. They usually already have formal institutional frameworks to manage this heterogeneity, while providing their members with a set of services. They therefore often benefit from (constitutional) collective decision-making mechanisms aimed at governing the community and providing it with an infrastructure for interacting (i.e., a legal and political order). Other communities are organized on the basis of mutually shared interests and/ or proximities of preferences. They group individuals on the basis of the realization of a common end, which can be such factors as the advancement of knowledge, the promotion of beliefs, or the wealth of the members. While such communities might be very formally organized, they tend to rely more on informal coordination mechanisms since they have to manage less tension linked to divergences and differences among their members.

Since there is no established global community recognized as such by all its members, the designation of a good as a GPG does not result from any agreement among all human beings or from any process of aggregating their will or consent. Some goods are claimed as GPGs by communities that, on the one hand, consider the externalities among existing communities, but, on the other hand, have strategies to promote their own interests. Indeed, they can seek to benefit from the contribution of others to providing a good that primarily benefits their community. They can also promote the production of the public good they prefer. One consequence of the subjective nature of GPGs is that their qualification as global, and the ranking of preferences for them, will always remain open to challenge.

In this context, generating knowledge should allow human beings to benefit from more information about the interdependencies among individual interests through the provision of goods. The more knowledge, the more individual interests will be included in collective choices, and therefore the better the nature and hierarchy of GPGs will be recognized, and the more efficiently they will be produced. In turn, the identification of interdependencies should allow each individual to express more informed preferences, since everyone will have a better understanding of the links between their own and the collective interest. Thus the more knowledge, the more complete the set of individual preferences, which will impact positively on the formation and expression of collective preferences.

Reflexive Governance for Collective Learning about the Provision of GPGs

Since there are no established collective preferences or solutions for the provision of GPGs, the design, choice, and implementation of the most appropriate rules should result from a reflexive governance process in which multiple actors are involved. The importance of reflexive governance has repeatedly been demonstrated in debates on participatory governance in domestic, regional, and local contexts. Numerous approaches have shown the applicability of deliberative formats for solving collective issues, with the inclusion of various stakeholder and citizen groups. Examples include planning cells, citizen juries, and consensus conferences. These participatory procedures not only diffuse information, allow for consultation, and support sharing in anticipation of the future, they also support the coordination of different forms and fields of knowledge, the coproduction of solutions, and social learning. While the existing literature has shown that participatory approaches are particularly suitable for integrating various bodies and forms of knowledge, concerns have been raised about their limited legitimacy. The need for direct interaction restricts the number of individuals who can be involved. The representation of different stakeholder groups and their knowledge and interests is possible, but the representation of larger fractions of the population cannot be guaranteed by these procedures. What needs to be further explored, therefore, is whether and how far these and other reflexive governance approaches can play a role in addressing the complex collective choice and cognitive problems involved in the provision of GPGs.

There are two aspects of reflexive governance processes: social and cognitive reflexivity. The first is the dynamic adjustment of collective beliefs among a variety of social actors. For instance, some collective rules result in the involvement of new groups and citizens, and this process transforms and builds new collective preferences. In such a perspective, a mode of governance can be considered as reflexive if it aims at including the perspectives, values and norms of a variety of actors. The second aspect concerns the revision of the cognitive framing; for example, the representation of the issue and of the governance problem at hand. The issue is to delineate the problems and decisions to be considered. New knowledge can change such aspects as the vision of the world, the issues to address, and the hierarchy of problems to solve, as illustrated by the issue of global warming or the precautionary principle in life sciences.

In general, what seems needed for the legitimate and efficient governance of global public goods is the broadening of our categories of public debate, both through deliberation in international organizations, and through more local forms of participatory governance and the involvement of communities and citizens in collective learning on GPG issues. This does not mean that traditional representative democracy will not be needed in the final decision-making phase, or that markets and hierarchies are not needed in the implementation phase. The implementation of reflexive governance also depends on a variety of mechanisms including regulation, incentive mechanisms, and information-based mechanisms. In essence, from our perspective, the appropriate provision of global public goods will require a combination of public ordering, market exchange, public debate, and the diffusion of information and knowledge to everybody.

2

Rethinking Public Goods and Global Public Goods

Inge Kaul

Public policy-making realities have, during recent decades, changed in often fundamental ways. Openness of national borders has increased; the roles of markets and governments have been rebalanced; an ever more densely networked global civil society has emerged; technological advances have been accomplished; and policy-making instruments have become more diversified and refined.

Some of these changes have already been incorporated into the main-stream theory of public economics as, for example, presented in the text-books of this discipline. Yet one core element of this theory, the concept of public goods, has so far remained largely unchanged. It still reflects the era when its present contours were shaped, notably the 1950s to 1970s.

This should give rise to concern, considering the growing importance of global challenges on national and international policy agendas and the gravity and urgency of some of those, including first and foremost global climate change.

This chapter therefore pursues a twofold objective. The first section identifies the major discrepancies that have arisen between the theory and reality of public goods. The discussion shows that the conventional concept now covers but a part, perhaps even a shrinking part, of the total reality of public goods. It focuses on national public goods and on the state's role in providing these goods. Largely excluded from the analysis are issues pertaining to transnational—regional and global—public goods, international cooperation in support of these goods, as well as aspects of voluntary and private provision.

Against this background the second section of the chapter suggests possible conceptual modifications that would be important for a fuller understanding of global public goods (GPGs) and their provision.

The main conclusion emerging from the analysis in this chapter is that for the provision of a particular public good to be considered adequate, at a given point in time, it is important to match the circle of stakeholders (those affected by the good's benefits or costs) with the circle of decision makers. In other words, where *publicness in consumption* is matched by *publicness in decision making* the resultant provision of the good is likely also to generate *publicness in utility*, that is, a distribution of net benefits that concerned stakeholders perceive as adequate—relatively efficient, effective, fair, and, therefore, also legitimate.

However, for the feedback processes between these three dimensions of publicness to work swiftly, reality has to be constantly reassessed and policy making has to be a fair process, providing all with an effective voice in matters that concern them. Reflexive governance is critical to an adequate provision of public goods. This holds especially true in the case of GPGs because socioeconomic, cultural, and political differences are often wider globally than nationally, and hence, preferences for GPGs are likely also to vary more across than within nations—as the 2009 United Nations Climate Change Conference in Copenhagen has shown only too clearly.

Out of Step: The Current Concept and Reality of Public Goods

Studies examining policy challenges and processes through the lens of public goods are likely to soon notice that the conventional concept of public goods—for example, as presented in most public economics (PE) textbooks—is, in many respects, out of step with current realities. The discrepancies concern the definition of public goods, and the analysis of the provision process of these goods, as elaborated in the following sections (these sections draw on Kaul, Conceição, Le Goulven, and Mendoza [2003], Kaul and Conceição [2006] and Kaul [2007]).

Non-Excludability and Non-Rivalry as Poor Predictors of Publicness

According to the conventional definition of public goods presented in chapter 1 the main properties of these goods are: non-excludability and non-rivalry for consumption. If goods have both properties, they are considered to be pure public; and if they have only one of these attributes, they are called impure public.

However, even a cursory look at various public domains will reveal that not all goods with these properties are necessarily public; that is,

Table 2.1
Gaps between the conventional concept and the reality of public good provision—with suggestions on overcoming the gaps

Conventional concept (1)	Reality of public goods (2)	Suggested re-conceptualization (3)
Non-rivalry and non-excludability as predictors of publicness	Goods with these properties may or may not be in the public domain, and goods with opposite properties may in effect be public	Expanded two-tier definition, distinguishing between a good's potential to be public and actual publicness
Public goods are being enjoyed by all	Public goods are often of a contested nature	Formulation of an empirical, value-neutral definition
Publicness perceived primarily as the opposite to privateness	Globalness and regionalness have emerged as special dimensions of publicness	Added definition of transnational, regional, and global public goods
Public goods are state-provided	Public goods are multi-actor provided	Introduction of the tool of provision-path analysis
Primary focus on national public goods	Transnational— regional and global— public goods are of growing importance	Explicit definition of regional and global public goods
Primary focus on goods that are already public	Major focus on who decides on whether or not to make a particular good public or private	Bringing the full political process and the public back in
Public goods as a case of economic market failure	Political markets like intergovernmental negotiations also fail	Expanding the theory of market failure
Focus on fiscally balanced provision	Concern about overall allocative efficiency	Formulation of a concept of full provision, design of distribution-sensitive assessments of investing in enhanced public good provision, complemented by notions of adequate and legitimate provision

there for all or affecting all. Knowledge of commercial value, which is non-rival in consumption and often difficult to make excludable, might be "protected" against use by individuals other than the inventors through intellectual property rights (often for important purposes such as dynamic efficiency, but sometimes for less socially desirable reasons). Conversely, excludable goods such as unhealthy fumes and noise are often left public, although exclusion would be feasible as well as economically desirable.

Publicness and privateness are not innate properties of a good. As soft and hard technologies advance, they can increasingly be altered, shifting goods from the public into the private domain or vice versa. Publicness and privateness are in most instances a policy choice that may vary and evolve as circumstances and preferences change. Therefore, the two conventional defining criteria of public goods—non-rivalry and non-excludability—are increasingly poor predictors of publicness, given scientific and technological progress, as well as faster changes due to increased competitiveness.

Sometimes Enjoyed by All But Also Frequently Contested

Most textbooks refer to publicness in consumption as a good's being available for all to enjoy. The use of the term *enjoy* has given rise to a widespread perception of public goods being good in a value sense—that is, good as opposed to bad.

Yet the controversy that often surrounds public goods today suggests otherwise. Preferences for public goods vary, depending on such factors as geography, sociocultural context, or income level. What some perceive as "good" and desirable may be viewed by others as generating disutility for them individually, their community, or the world at large, and, hence, as "bad." No doubt, some public goods are in the general public's interest, spreading their net benefits rather widely and evenly. Yet many are contentious, not enjoyed by all.

Sometimes Supplied by the State Alone But Mostly Multi-Actor Provided

Although the main defining criterion of a public good is its publicness in consumption, many textbooks also refer to public goods as state-provided goods. In the past the state certainly played an important role in public goods provision. But today, public goods often emerge based on inputs from multiple actor groups, state and non-state. Just think of the involvement of private security forces and other private providers in military operations, hospital and prison services, or the growing trend toward self-regulation, for example, in the extractive industry.

Figure 2.1 depicts the provision path of national-level public goods today. It illustrates how different actor groups interact at different stages of the process. All their diverse inputs have to come together for the good to emerge.

The growing trends toward privatization and public–private partnering have taken many cases of public good provision out of the fold of governments. In some instances governments still play a critical role, helping non-state actors to overcome collective-action problems. But they rarely deliver public goods in their entirety. Through various incentive measures, they mostly facilitate public good provision by non-state actors.

Sometimes National in Scope but Also Transnational in Reach

Most PE textbooks still assume a single, closed economy. Consequently, their discussion on public goods relates primarily to national public goods. However, governments themselves have had an active hand in promoting greater openness of national borders; for example, through the removal of trade barriers and financial controls. They fostered cross-border institutional and policy compatibility through behind-the-border policy harmonization. And once borders were opened up, cross-border economic activity intensified, bringing with it not only intended and desired effects but also unintended consequences, like cross-border spill-overs or externalities in the form of spreading communicable diseases, financial contagion, new knowledge and information, and other effects that are now—often with high speed—spreading from country to country, roaming the global public domain.

As a result, many hitherto national public goods have become globalized—either because governments promoted behind-the-border policy harmonization or because national public domains became exposed to cross-border externalities and policy choices made in other countries or by global non-state actors. (See also figure 2.2.)

While some PE textbooks make brief mention of transnational public goods like global climate change, few have so far revised the assumption of a single, closed economy and presented a definition of transnational— regional and global—public goods.

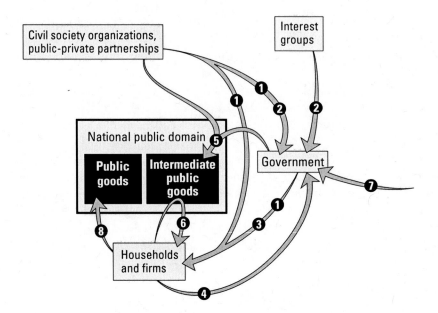

① Incentives
Encouraging actors to deliver direct and indirect inputs or to change behavior to account for social concerns

② Political pressure
Lobbying governments to fund or deliver goods and services

③ Coercion
Compelling individuals and firms to change their behavior to account for social concerns

④ Domestic preferences
Reflecting the choices on desired state action by national constituents

⑤ Opportunity
Offering households and firms the possibility of consuming goods and services that generate externalities that enhance the provisions of the public good

⑥ Consumption
Consuming goods and services made available to enhance the provision of the public good

⑦ External preferences
Reflecting the choices on desired state action by international constituents

⑧ Externality
Emerging as a result of individual action

Note:
The figure is based on the assumption that the good follows a "summation" aggregation technology.
Intermediate public goods (like norms and standards) serve as inputs to a final public good.

Figure 2.1
The production path of national public goods

Production path of global public goods

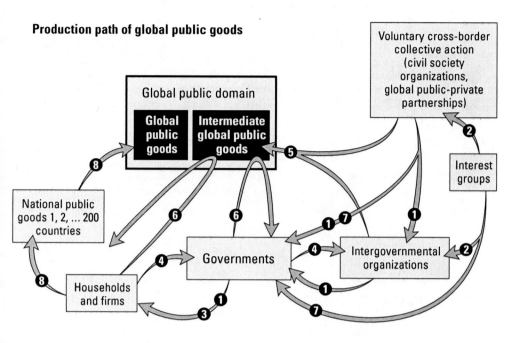

① **Incentives**
Encouraging actors to deliver direct and indirect inputs or to change behavior to account for social concerns

② **Political pressure**
Lobbying governments to fund or deliver goods and services

③ **Coercion**
Compelling individuals and firms to change their behavior to account for social concerns

④ **Domestic preferences**
Reflecting the choices on desired state action by national constituents

⑤ **Opportunity**
Offering households and firms the possibility of consuming goods and services that generate externalities that enhance the provisions of the public good

⑥ **Consumption**
Consuming goods and services made available to enhance the provision of the public good

⑦ **External preferences**
Reflecting the choices on desired state action by international constituents

⑧ **Externality**
Emerging as a result of individual action

Note:
The figure is based on the assumption that the good follows a "summation" aggregation technology. Intermediate public goods (like norms and standards) serve as inputs to a final public good.

Figure 2.2
Production path of global public goods

A Focus on Already-Public Goods

Mainstream PE theory primarily takes an interest in public goods once they are made or left public in consumption. The political processes that lead to the choice of placing a good either in the public or private domain receive only limited attention.

Yet, judging from current news reports it seems that the most heated public debates concern the question of where to place a good. For example, should social security schemes be shifted more into the private realm? Should railways or water systems be privatized? Or, should international trade rules be changed to allow a freer movement of goods and services across borders, and with it, more international competition? The general public participates in these debates in manifold ways. National elections are only one of those. Increasingly important are international negotiations, and the growing participation of non-state actors in the global public domain, including the participation of some 70,000 civil society organizations and a similar, perhaps even higher number of transnational business actors (cf. Anheier et al. 2004; UNCTAD 2007).

Yet policy makers or members of the general public, who today turn to standard PE theory, find only limited answers on how the politics of public goods provision work. Textbooks seem to address themselves primarily to the executive part of government; and they discuss how policy makers may gauge what people's preferences for certain already-public goods are. The questions they examine are: How much of each public good is to be provided nationally? In which way? And at what net benefit to which national constituencies?

Recognition of Economic Market Failure but Not Political Market Failure

In the world of PE textbooks, public goods are seen as presenting a risk of market failure, and consequently, a case for potentially desirable state intervention. Public choice theory in particular has pointed to the risk that in correcting market failure governments may also fail due, for example, to the pursuit of self-interest by organizations or individual bureaucrats (Buchanan and Musgrave 1999). Although these types of government failure are important, they are not the ones meant here with the term *political market failure*.

Rather, political market failure refers to governmental limitations that are evident particularly in the case of transnational, regional, and global public goods. They stem from the fact that in the international cooperation realm governments tend to behave like private actors nationally. They, too, pursue particularistic, namely national interests and attempt to free ride on the other nation-states' efforts.

Thus, it is not rare to see global civil society actors or representatives of transnational corporations pressing governments on the delivery of global public goods like climate stability, the spread of harmonized technical standards, or the universalization of human rights. This shows that public goods may make economic markets as well as political markets fail, especially in the case of international negotiations for cross-border cooperation. For this reason, all actor groups now seem to keep a watchful eye on each other.

Concern About Fiscal Balance Not Macro Allocative Efficiency

Due to the statist focus of conventional PE theory, the definition of what constitutes efficient provision of a public good is also state centered. It is the condition Paul Samuelson formulated in his 1954 article, "The Pure Theory of Public Expenditure." According to this article, pure public goods are efficiently provided when the marginal cost of providing the public good equals the sum of the marginal willingness to pay for it by all individuals affected by the good, a condition which in mathematical terms can be written as follows:

$$\sum_{i=1}^{n} MWTP = MC$$

However, several assumptions underlie this equation, including that people fully understand the short- and longer-term consequences of providing the good at a certain level; that policy makers can correctly read the public's preferences; and that no government failures of the public-choice types occur.

All of this cannot be taken for granted. Thus, one can find that public goods, which, according to the Samuelson condition, appear to be efficiently provided are de facto severely underprovided, because governments increasingly provide only some of the goods' building blocks, if any at all; and national-level interventions are often complemented by international-level inputs.

In sum, standard PE theory presents a conceptualization of public goods and public good provision reminiscent of earlier policy decades, notably the period between 1950 and the late 1970s, when, in both the

"East" and "West," the state had a strong, direct, economic role. That static, nationally oriented and state-centered perception has been overtaken by reality. Transnational public goods, notably GPGs are of growing importance; and public goods provision today is increasingly a multi-actor, multilevel process subject to rising expectations of participatory and transparent decision making as well as competitive provision.

Narrowing the Gap between the Theory and Reality of Public Goods

In light of the foregoing analysis, a fitting reconceptualization of public goods would have to meet the following conditions:

- Take account of transnational public goods and of today's multi-actor, multilevel provision of these goods.
- Incorporate the notion of change to recognize that globalization often comes accompanied by intensified competition and faster policy shifts.
- Recognize that preferences for public goods as well as policy paths may vary.
- Consider that democracy has advanced nationally, and increasingly also internationally, leading to more public debate and controversy about public policy, including the provision of public goods.

Put differently, a fitting reconceptualization of public goods would offer an expanded, dynamic, and value-neutral perspective; and importantly, it would put more of the politics back into public good provision. The modifications proposed in the following points try to meet these requirements. They suggest for further research and study, reconceptualizations that could help reduce the discrepancies noted in the previous sections.

Formulating an Expanded, Empirical Definition of Public Goods

The current discrepancies between the standard definition of public goods and what public goods actually are could be resolved through a redefinition that would aim to be empirical as well as value-neutral. The following two-tier definition would meet this criterion.

Definition 1 Goods have a special potential for being public if they have non-excludable benefits/costs, non-rival benefits/costs or both.

Definition 1.2 Goods are de facto public if they are nonexclusive and potentially affecting all.

Recognizing Transnationalness as a Special Dimension of Publicness

The creation of national borders in a way constitutes an act of privatization, the laying of a claim to a particular territory and to the exercise of policy making authority within this territory. Removing at-the-border barriers by, for example, reducing trade barriers or financial controls thus creates renewed openness or publicness, and in its wake, policy interdependence of countries.

This policy interdependence comes about in two ways. States may deliberately accept and promote it (e.g., by fostering policy harmonization); or they may simply experience it (e.g., by being affected by cross-border spillovers such as financial contagion effects or spreading diseases.)

Due to both deliberate and unintentional transnationalization, more and more hitherto national (including local) public goods become regionalized or globalized. Accordingly, one could define these goods in the following way:

Definition 2.1 Transnational public goods are goods with costs or benefits that extend across national borders.

Definition 2.2 If a good's public effects pertain only to a particular group of countries, it is a regional public good (if neighboring countries are affected) or club good (if countries with other common features like being landlocked or having a high income are concerned).

Definition 2.3 If the good's public effects are of a global reach or extend beyond generations, it is a global public good.

Introducing the Tool of Provision Path Analysis

As previously discussed, a full understanding of public goods requires not only assessing the span or range of their benefits and costs but also plotting their overall provision path, as figures 2.1 and 2.2 show. Such a provision path analysis could help identify the constituent building blocks of the good, as well as the actors currently involved in their provision. Against this background, one could then assess whether all inputs are actually being provided, and whether they are provided by actors who have a comparative advantage in delivering them.

Such a provision path analysis would also reveal that public goods often do not abide by just one of Hirshleifer's aggregation technologies introduced in chapter 1. Rather, different building blocks may have different underlying incentive structures and would thus also have to be assembled in different ways. To illustrate, while on the whole the provision path of "global climate stability" follows a summation process, some of its building blocks might follow a different path, a best-shot approach; for example, research aimed at developing required new energy or agricultural technologies.

A provision path analysis could also contribute to a better understanding of the institutional implications of public goods provision. If the state is no longer the sole or main manager of the provision process, then who is? How in a multi-actor world would the various components of a public good come together? Is the growing trend toward more single-issue organizational entities, so-called vertical programs like the Global Fund to Fight AIDS, Tuberculosis and Malaria or the Global Environment Facility, perhaps signaling a possible, early response to this management challenge?

Developing a Theory of Actor Failure in Public Goods Provision

The current market failure theory would perhaps have to be rethought in several ways. First, it would be important to develop a theory of political market failure, covering in particular intergovernmental negotiations on the provision of transnational public goods. These negotiations can be viewed as a political market, because participants meet in the negotiating venues as quasi-private, particularistic actors; and the purpose of their encounter often is to exchange policy reform outputs or policy reform promises and outputs against financial aid and compensation.

Also, these political markets may sometimes fail to achieve an efficient outcome for much the same reasons that may make economic markets fail, including information asymmetry, the existence of externalities and public goods—notably transnational public goods—and power structures reminiscent of situations of monopolistic or oligopolistic competition.

Another aspect to explore would be to what extent economic markets today actually fail. Or, in other words: How to explain what appears to be a growing trend toward voluntary and private provision of public goods, or at least, of inputs to these goods? Has the greater porosity between the private and the public sectors perhaps reduced the incidence of market failure in the case of public goods? Is it politically more acceptable today for private actors to add to public goods provision? Does it also perhaps pay for them to do so, because the general public is politically more active and holds corporations directly accountable—not just via state interventions?

Much of the voluntary and private provision of non-state actors to public goods is today being discussed under headings such as corporate social responsibility or the role of civil society. A comprehensive and systematic public goods analysis of why and how these actors become involved in public goods provision is still to be formulated.

Taking Account of the Full Political Process and Life-Cycle of the Good

The emergence of global public goods and the controversies surrounding goods like the multilateral trade regime have driven home the realization that public goods do not come ready made as public goods. Often they are being made public by policy design, including such choices as fostering economic or financial liberalization.

A proper public goods theory would thus have to consider how—by whom and according to which criteria—such choices are being made or not made. In this connection, it would also be interesting to examine why certain excludable goods are actually public and who derives which net cost/benefit from this fact; and why in other cases the public's access to goods like health-related knowledge is being blocked, or at least partially so.

Such a discussion on the politics that lead to a good being placed in either the public or private domain could generate an interesting typology of public goods, indicating:

- Infeasibility of exclusion—goods that at least for now are technically or economically non-excludable. The moonlight is a case in point.
- Intentional publicness—goods that have been placed or left in the national, regional, or global public domains by policy choice. The multilateral trade regime and the basic human rights norms provide examples for this category of public goods.
- Inadvertent publicness—goods about which requisite knowledge and understanding are lacking and which, for these reasons, are allowed to linger on in the public domain. This condition often applies to environmental hazards like pollutants.
- Policy neglect or hesitation—goods that are allowed to linger in the public domain, although it is known that they generate net costs. A case in point is global climate change and the slow progress to date in responding to it.

Developing a Concept of Adequate Public Goods Provision

The conceptual and methodological challenges in this respect are considerable and only just about to be explored systematically (see, for example, Touffut 2009). First, the Samuelson condition of optimal public goods provision remains important for analyses that focus on the economic role of states. But it also needs to be placed in a wider, public/private and national/global context (see, for example, Kaul and Conceição 2006). Today, we even lack the most basic data on the actual—public and private—spending on GPGs not to mention empirical global studies on how preferences (and, hence, willingness to pay) for particular GPGs vary and could potentially be aligned through international compensatory finance or other incentive measures.

Second, it would be important to encourage more studies that aim at assessing the net benefits of an enhanced provision of public goods to various communities—local, national, regional, and global. The concept of full provision developed by Conceição and Mendoza (2006) might be helpful in this respect and worth a more in-depth exploration. According to these authors, full provision is defined as "the [provision] level from which no further enhancements are feasible, given the good's innate or defined (physical) properties and the current state of knowledge and technology" (332).

In many instances, achieving full provision of a public good of national, regional, or global reach could generate significant net gains. Thus, a nation or the international community could approach allocative efficiency, if they were to invest in enhancing the provision of those public goods that promise the relatively best returns on the investment.

Conceição and Mendoza (2006) demonstrated how such assessments could be structured in the case of select global public goods. Since some of the expected global net benefits that they identified may take a long time to emerge or may be unevenly distributed, they also explored how international cooperation in support of these goods could, nevertheless, be unlocked. Their response is that distribution-sensitive assessments of expected net gains and international compensation measures could be a step in this direction, allowing international cooperation to make sense for all.

The Stern report (Stern 2006) provides an example of a global cost/benefit analysis of (in)action on the issue of climate change. Yet it looks at this issue from the (abstract and detached) perspective of a global social planner. Its results tell us why humanity as a whole should have an interest in taking prompt corrective action but not how preferences on such action differ across countries and communities. Yet these differences often constitute the stumbling block in international negotiations as the negotiations on a follow-up agreement to the Kyoto Protocol have demonstrated.

In sum, narrowing the current gap between the theory and practice of public goods provision requires concepts that capture, make allowances for, and explain and predict diversity, variability, and change in policy responses. It requires a focus not primarily on the state but on public goods as such—a proper theory of public goods, not just one of public goods provision as one aspect of public economics. In particular, it calls for a multidisciplinary approach, combining insights from economics as well as international relations theories and political science so as to take full account of the fact that the general public—civil society as well as business—plays a stronger, more active role today in setting policy priorities and delivering inputs to public goods. And what matters in the context of the present volume, all of this holds especially true in the case of GPGs.

The Role of Reflexive Governance in Fostering an Adequate and Legitimate Provision of Global Public Goods

Public goods provision today is more complex and less circumscribed than it was in earlier decades. To demonstrate this, the present chapter has identified a number of discrepancies between the current standard theory of public goods and the reality of public goods provision and suggested conceptual and methodological modifications for narrowing those. The main conclusion emerging from the discussion is that what constitutes an adequate provision of public goods can no longer be defined in fixed, technocratic, and purely economic terms. The concepts of efficient and optimal provision remain important. They provide important points of reference, even goalposts that we should strive to meet.

But we also need to recognize that people's and nation's notions of well-being and welfare, as well as their response to such factors as risk and uncertainty, vary, as do their preferences for different types of policy approaches (e.g., "more state" or "more market"). Adequate provision of public goods, notably GPGs, would therefore be more appropriately conceptualized as resulting from a process of participatory decision making or reflexive governance, and therefore as being in flux—that is,

Triangle of publicness

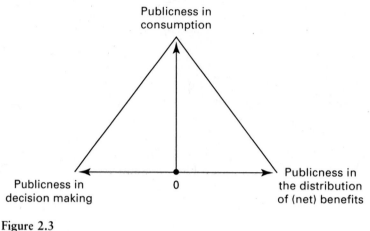

Figure 2.3
Triangle of publicness

changing as realities (e.g., technologies, economic conditions, and power relations) change.

Adequate provision would combine efficiency, effectiveness, and fairness concerns; and if such adequacy were to result from fair negotiation and decision making, it would also be likely to enjoy legitimacy, notably input legitimacy.[1]

Thus, adequate and legitimate provision of public goods can be depicted, as shown in figure 2.3, as a triangle of publicness the sides of which are *publicness in consumption*: the span of a good's stakeholders (the people affected by its costs or benefits); *publicness in decision making*: an effective voice for all stakeholders; and *publicness in utility*: an even distribution of net benefits across concerned population groups.

If the circles of stakeholders and decision makers are well matched, then policy making on, and delivery of a public good are likely to be competitive and produce efficient and fair outcomes, and hence, results that concerned constituencies and actors accept under the given circumstances as adequate and legitimate.

However, reflexive governance—the feedback loop between policy decisions, implementation, outcomes, change, innovation and policy redesign—will work well only if conceptualizations of public goods provision avoid over-generalizations of particular historic or geographic conditions. This calls for effective democracy at national and international levels, and importantly, also an examination of the implications of international democracy for national-level democracy. Because on whose policy preferences and priorities will governments act—on those of national constituencies; on those of external powers? Or, would they seek to act as an "intermediary state" (Kaul 2006), combining policy preferences of domestic and external constituencies?

As these questions indicate, we are only at the beginning of understanding GPGs and GPG provision. But GPGs like global climate change and biodiversity preservation are a reality, requiring urgent policy responses. It would be important for theory to catch up with reality, in particular to develop a proper theory of public goods that looks beyond the role of individual states and sees these goods as what they are today—goods in the public domain, depending on public and private, national and international input, for their adequate provision.

Notes

1. On the concept of fair negotiation, see in particular Albin (2001). The concept of legitimacy employed here follows Scharpf (1999) in distinguishing between input and output legitimacy. The former is given when concerned parties feel that they have an effective and fair say in matters that concern them. The latter requires public policy initiatives to lead to effective problem solving.

3

New Face of Development Assistance: Public Goods and Changing Ethics

Todd Sandler and Daniel G. Arce

Traditionally, foreign assistance provides private goods and social overhead capital to less-fortunate nations as a means to relieve abject poverty. Social overhead capital—for example, bridges, communication systems, schools, courts, and law enforcement—often consists of national public goods (NPGs), whose benefits are non-rival and non-excludable to those in the recipient country. As a precondition for markets and sustainable growth, some social overhead capital is necessary. An important motivation for traditional forms of foreign assistance is altruism as donors transfer income and goods to help those in need to achieve a higher standard of well-being.[1] Within multilaterals (e.g., World Bank), this altruistic motive was attenuated somewhat in the 1980s by conditionality, particularly when aid was conditioned on purchases such as technical assistance from the donor (Collier 1997). Bilateral aid was also modified to promote non-altruistic concerns such as security and trade-related gains to the donor nation.

In recent years, there has been an increased interest in the provision of aid in the form of NPGs and transnational public goods (TPGs). TPGs' benefits transcend the borders of the recipient country[2] and may assist other countries including the donor itself. This focus on TPGs was sparked in part by Kindleberger's (1986) article that noted the growing importance of these goods in international transactions among nations. Sandler (1997) brought the concept of public good aid to the attention of the World Bank and the United Nations Development Program (UNDP) when he wrote: "A new form of foreign aid—'*free rider aid*'—may come from the provision of TPGs and may increasingly replace traditionally tied and untied foreign aid of the post–World War II period" (183). This increased interest in public good aid is reflected not only by the increased portion of overseas foreign assistance that supports public goods, but also by the millennium development goals (MDGs) that include many targets involving NPGs and TPGs.

Public good aid incorporates an additional ethic for giving, founded more on donor self-interest. For instance, assistance for less-developed countries (LDCs) to foster substitutions from ozone-depleting chloro-fluorocarbons to non-ozone-depleting hydrofluorocarbons helps the donor country achieve a thicker stratospheric ozone layer that protects its own citizens along with others. Peacekeeping efforts to end civil wars in LDCs can limit the conflict's spread to neighboring countries, where rich donor countries obtain essential resources. Such examples underscore that publicness can align donor–recipient interests. This new focus on self-interest-based public good aid may augment giving and limit the aid fatigue of the 1990s, when the share of donors' gross national product (GNP) devoted to foreign assistance dropped from 0.33 percent in 1990 to 0.24 percent in 1999 (World Bank 2001, 87–89).

Unfortunately, recent studies suggest that enhanced giving to public good aid has crowded out traditional forms of foreign assistance (Anand 2004; te Velde, Morrissey, and Hewitt 2002). This raises a real concern because reduced poverty in the form of increased private goods and NPGs is a prerequisite for LDCs to absorb TPGs. A healthier, more-educated, and less-hungry population can better utilize TPGs so that private goods have a facilitating role. In addition, a recent study by the World Bank (2001) characterized NPGs as a complementary activity for TPGs in developing countries. Globalization has raised the importance of TPGs as nations are more susceptible to externalities (i.e., uncompensated interdependencies) that cross borders. For select TPGs, their overall level—for example, the eradication of a disease or financial stability—is disproportionately determined by the lowest provision level. As such, the well-being of developed countries is greatly tied to the ability of LDCs to obtain an acceptable provision level.

Public good aid raises many essential issues. First, there is the choice of sector since five sectors in LDCs—environment, health, governance, knowledge, and peace and security—are associated with public goods. Second, provision decisions must be made among public goods whose benefits create diverse levels of spillovers. As such, support can be given to NPGs, regional public goods (RPGs), transregional public goods (TRPGs), or global public goods (GPGs). Each of these classes of public goods involves an expanding recipient pool, with GPGs, unlike many TPGs, *providing benefits worldwide*. The extent of public good spillovers has important implications not only for donor and recipient incentives but also for which donors should assume the responsibility for providing the good. Third, the nature of the public good influences the direction of income distribution and the type of transfer—cash or in-kind. Many of these issues and other discussed here are unique to public good assistance.

Public Good Aid

Public good aid takes at least two forms: the transfer of income for public good purchases and the direct provision of public goods. When income is transferred, the donor will demand a subsequent accounting to ensure that money supported public good provision. In some cases, the money will be channeled to a sector that embodies public goods, such as the health sector. In-kind transfers may consist of a vaccination program, new technology to substitute for targeted pollutants, peacekeeping forces, or assistance in financial practices. Assistance can provide NPGs, RPGs, TRPGs, and GPGs. Even traditional assistance involves the provision of NPGs. The difference today is the level of NPG support *and* the understanding that these NPGs are complementary to the recipient country's ability to assimilate TPGs with varying ranges of spillovers.

Based on the data from the Organisation of Economic Cooperation and Development (OECD), te Velde, Morrissey, and Hewitt (2002, 128) showed that aid-funded support for public goods more than doubled from 16.22 percent of assistance from 1980 to 1982 to 38.19 percent from 1996 to 1998. Much of this increase was in terms of NPGs: from 1996 to 1998, 29.40 percent of official assistance funded NPGs compared with 8.79 percent for TPGs. Raffer (1999) estimated that public good aid varied from 20 to 40 percent of official foreign assistance, depending on the definition applied. More important, Raffer indicated that the share of these public goods in foreign aid increased significantly in the 1990s. The World Bank (2001, 110–113) estimated that $5 billion is directly spent each year to support the provision of TPGs, and another $11 billion is spent annually on complementary activities (i.e., provision of NPGs) that enable LDCs to absorb these goods. These official aid figures do not reflect the provision of public goods to LDCs given by charitable foundations (e.g., Gates Foundation and Wellcome Trust), nongovernmental organizations (NGOs), and partnerships (e.g., Global Fund, Onchocerciasis Control Programme, and Medicines for Malaria Venture).

Millennium Development Goals (MDGs)

The establishment of MDGs serves as a coordination and awareness mechanism to get developed countries, other donors, and poor countries to focus on addressing crucial aspects of extreme poverty. By reporting yearly progress reports, the United Nations monitors and coordinates collective action to meet these goals. As some goals are approached, the United Nations redirects donors' efforts on laggard targets. As displayed in table 3.1, MDGs include eight basic goals as listed in the left-hand column. If explicit target dates are given for specific accomplishments, then these are displayed in parentheses. Below each of the major goals, we list specific subgoals.

In the middle column of table 3.1, the primary public good sectors are identified for each of the MDGs, while, in the right-hand column, any secondary public good sectors are also indicated. Health, knowledge, and the environment figure most prominently among the primary sectors. A greater diversity of public good sectors characterizes the secondary sectors. For the first MDG, poverty and hunger are primarily alleviated through income and private good transfers, so that no primary public good sector is indicated. Curbing poverty and hunger will, however, have a secondary influence on the health sector as populations are more resistant to diseases. Peace and security also improve because higher income levels are less associated with conflict (Collier et al. 2003). The primary education goal is closely tied to knowledge as the public good sector in the recipient country. Because a more knowledgeable population can support better governance, there are also transnational spillovers for foreign investors. Gender equality not only fosters knowledge but also promotes health, because more-educated women tend to limit family size. In fact, gender equality can have tremendous influences on reducing poverty and curbing negative spillovers by controlling population growth. Curbing child mortality of those under five years old by two-thirds supports the health sector, because such efforts create healthier populations, not weakened by severe childhood illnesses. Similarly, the promotion of maternal health makes for healthier populations as mothers are better able to nourish their children. Reducing maternal deaths will lead to fewer orphans. Efforts to combat HIV/AIDS, malaria, and other diseases of poor countries bolster health and limit the transmission of diseases abroad. The promotion of environmental sustainability can limit regional dispersion of pollutants, thereby improving the environment sector at home and abroad. In general, a better environment has secondary health

Table 3.1
Millennium development goals and targets: primary and secondary public good sectors

Goals and specified targets (date)	Primary public good sectors	Secondary public good sectors
• Eradicate abject poverty and hunger Halve hunger (2015)	Not applicable	Health, peace and security
• Obtain universal primary education Primary education for all children (2015)	Knowledge	Governance
• Foster gender equality and empower women No gender disparity in primary and secondary education (2015)	Knowledge	Health
• Curb child mortality Reduce mortality of children under age five by two-thirds (2015)	Health	
• Bolster maternal health Reduce maternal mortality ratio by three-quarters (2015)	Health	
• Combat HIV/AIDS, malaria, and other diseases Halt the spread of HIV/AIDS (2015) Halt the spread of malaria and other diseases (2015)	Health	
• Promote environmental sustainability Incorporate sustainable development in LDCs' policies Reverse losses in environmental resources Halve the proportion of people with unsafe drinking water and no basic sanitation (2015)	Environment	Health
• Achieve a global development partnership Address the particular needs of LDCs Improve the fairness of trade and financial systems Ameliorate LDCs' debt problems Provide decent work opportunities for youth Supply affordable drugs Make available new technologies	Health, governance, knowledge	Environment, peace and security

Source: United Nations (2005).

influences since air pollution leads to respiratory diseases and water pollution leads to bacteria-based diseases. The achievement of global partnerships can improve health, governance, and knowledge in the poorest LDCs through best practice and technology transfers. In addition, the elimination of unfair practices (e.g., protection of agriculture in developed countries) can provide LDCs with more viable markets for their primary exports. Improved economic conditions through debt relief, work opportunities, affordable drugs, and new technologies can further secondary public good sectors. For example, better jobs for youths raise their opportunity costs and keep them from becoming rebels, thereby promoting peace and security.

There are a number of implications for public good aid that can be drawn from these MDGs. First, MDGs are directly and indirectly tied to public goods at the national level and beyond; however, the current focus on NPGs in recipient countries is apt to limit progress on many MDGs. A greater emphasis on public goods with more obvious spillovers to the donor countries might speed attainment of some of these mileposts. Second, the recent increases in NPGs and TPGs as a portion of overseas development assistance (ODA) will continue over the next two decades as efforts are directed to achieving the MDGs. Third, there are many interrelationships among the underlying sectors that need to be stressed to augment donor incentives to give. For example, civil wars and conflicts (i.e., the absence of peace and security) lead to diseases, especially HIV/AIDS (Collier et al. 2003). Our efforts to identify secondary public good sectors are to emphasize some of these interrelationships. Fourth, the well-specified MDGs (e.g., primary education for all children) have the best chance of success in contrast to goals such as providing decent work opportunities for youth or reversing losses in environmental resources. Fifth, the MDGs' overwhelming emphasis on health and knowledge will mean that increases in public good aid in these areas, noted by recent studies, will continue into the foreseeable future (Mascarenhas and Sandler 2005; te Velde, Morrissey, and Hewitt 2002).

The progress to achieving these MDGs and TPG provision is, in part, dependent on the "Monterrey Consensus" that formed in January 2002 prior to the International Conference on Financing for Development that later took place on March 18–22, 2002, in Monterrey, Mexico. The Monterrey Consensus indicated that the World Bank, the International Monetary Fund, and the World Trade Organization would work toward financing development and meeting the MDGs. This Consensus underscored the necessity for recipient countries to implement sound policies by non-corrupt regimes. In addition, the Consensus was committed to implementing the recommendations in the World Bank's (2001) *Global Development Finance* report that called for greater funding of NPGs and TPGs in LDCs.

The Monterrey conference resulted in the Bush administration's delegation walking out in reaction to the Zedillo Report's (United Nations 2001) call for greater TPG provision by rich countries. This walkout was precipitated in part by some LDCs characterizing U.S. interest rate policy as a TPG, which they should have a say in when it adversely affected their economies. Following the Monterrey conference, Sweden and France established the International Task Force on Global Public Goods to push for greater RPG and TPG assistance that *does not reduce* traditional aid. The Task Force's report was published at the end of 2006 (Secretariat of the International Task Force on Global Public Goods 2006). Thus, there are clear efforts to promote public good aid. Although these actions have increased the percentage of aid going to public goods, they have not greatly raised the percentage of rich countries' GNP going to foreign aid.

Aggregation Technology and New Directions in Giving

As explained in chapter 1, many different aggregation technologies can influence the way in which individual contributions to a public good determine the overall level that is available for consumption. Closely related to the summation aggregator is the weighted-sum aggregator, where the public good equals a weighted total of the agents' public good contributions. In the case of acid rain, actions by countries to curb sulfur emissions differentially affect other countries depending on wind, country size, and location considerations (Murdoch, Sandler, and Sargent 1997). Large countries receive more of their own sulfur pollutants as dry and wet depositions. Countries to the east of an emitting country receive more acid rain than those to the west owing to prevailing winds. With a summation technology of public supply, each agent's contribution is a perfect substitute for that of other agents, which is not the case for weighted sum as some countries may import less or a lot of pollution from elsewhere. For weakest-link public goods, the aggregate level equals the smallest contribution level. Actions by countries in a region to keep a terrorist group from gaining a base of operations will only be as good as the country applying the smallest effort. Weaker-link public goods is a less extreme form where the smallest contribution has the greatest impact on the good's aggregate level, followed by the second smallest contribution, and so on. Limiting the spread of an agricultural pest is a weaker-link public good insofar as actions beyond the smallest can provide some additional protection. For best-shot public goods, the largest contribution determines the overall level of the good. The research team that manages the breakthrough to cure a disease makes the discovery for everyone; further contributions or actions are redundant. Finally, a better-shot public good allows effort levels below the largest to add to the public good; however, the largest contribution has the greatest influence on the good's overall level, followed by the second-largest contribution, and so on. Discovering vaccines is a better-shot public good, because equally effective vaccines may be tolerated by those who cannot take the recommended line of defense—for example, the Sabin polio vaccine for patients who could not tolerate the Salk vaccine.

Each aggregator technology has essential implications for the practice of public good aid.[3] In the case of public good aid, summation aggregators will be associated with too little action on the part of donors, even when they receive benefit spillovers. Multilateral institutions have a real role to perform in limiting free riding and suboptimality by fostering giving. The situation is more hopeful for weighted sum, especially when some donor and recipient nations obtain a large share of country-specific benefits. Because a significant share of sulfur pollutants falls on polluter nations, they have been quick to curb their sulfur emissions. A weighted-sum technology has the potential to privatize some portions of a public good's benefits, and this provides incentives for nations to act.

In the case of weakest-link public goods, two considerations come into play for public good assistance. First, matching provision levels are needed in all countries receiving the good's benefits. If, for example, one country supplies just two units, then higher provision levels elsewhere will use up resources without adding to the overall consumption of the public good. Second, income constrains the smallest level that is provided. Consider a region trying to limit the spread of a deadly plague. The poorest country will supply the smallest prophylactic measures, thereby determining the safety of the entire region. If this level is unacceptable to other countries, then they must pool their efforts to shore up the weakest link(s) or else rely on some outside donor to do so. Such shoring-up efforts may lead to a free-rider problem that can be addressed by a multilateral agency or some rich country that greatly values the good. The World Health Organization (WHO) and the U.S. Centers for Disease Control and Prevention (CDC) perform this shoring-up effort with respect to discovering, tracking, and isolating infectious diseases. Weakest-link public goods have the best prognosis when the affected countries are similar in tastes and endowments, which will *not* be the case for foreign aid scenarios in which some countries have limited financial capacity to provide the good. Charitable foundations, NGOs, and partnerships can help with the capacity concern.

Weaker-link public goods display varied implications depending upon their associated benefits and costs and the manner in which extra contributions by some countries can *offset* inadequate contributions by others. If, for example, this offset is limited, then matching behavior is again the desired outcome, with some departure where one country contributes a little more than others. When, however, this offset is an important influence, agents with greater income can make up for provision shortfalls in poorer nations. As such, weaker-link public goods may possess a good prognosis, where, for example, a weak-link RPG may be provided through greater effort by the region's richer countries.

A best-shot public good presents a different type of coordination problem in which one nation provides the good for others to avoid redundant effort. In an aid situation, the coordination issue can be addressed in one of two ways: aid is given to the best-endowed country (i.e., the most likely best shooter) or the public good is provided by the donors. In the former case, the best-endowed country in, say, a region will then acquire the capacity to provide the good with benefit spillovers to neighboring countries. Technical assistance is an instance where the donor provides the best-shot public good directly to the recipient country. Better-shot public goods present less of a coordination problem, because contributions by those other than the best shooter augment the overall level of the public good. Thus, aid does not have to be so targeted to the best-endowed countries.

Each of the six basic aggregators implies different recommendations with respect to the direction of income redistribution. In some instances, these recommendations are at odds with standard ethical intuition. For summation, there is a neutrality theorem to circumvent if the redistribution is to be effective (Cornes and Sandler 1984). The neutrality theorem indicates that income redistributed *among existing contributors* of the public good has no influence on the overall level of the public good even though money is redistributed from rich to poor countries. In essence, the increased contributions by those receiving income are canceled by the reduced contributions of those giving up income. Thus, efforts to bolster GPG provision through the aid channel may cause difficulties with respect to such goods as reduced global warming (Kanbur, Sandler, and Morrison 1999), which responds to the aggregate reductions in emissions. Neutrality is less of a concern when income infusion comes from new contributors (e.g., charitable foundations, NGOs, and partnerships). Additionally, neutrality does not apply if joint products are present and the redistribution is in the direction of those receiving a greater share of country-specific benefits. For a summation aggregator, public good provision may be augmented if richer recipients receive income transfers from non-contributors rather than spreading the transfers over a wider group of recipients (Itaya, de Meza, and Myles 1997). Thus, RPGs in a developing area are best served by channeling income to the better-off countries that can then provide benefit spillovers region-wide.

For weakest-link public goods, neutrality is not an issue if income transfers are to the poor, smaller contributors. Now, ethical intuition agrees with the most efficacious direction for income transfers. In some cases, in-kind transfers by the low-cost provider are best (Vicary and Sandler 2002). Vaccination programs may require a low-cost donor to go in and provide the services. Weaker-link public goods abide by similar principles of income transfer, except that it is no longer necessary to bring all countries up to the same standard of provision.

For best-shot public goods, the nation with the best chance to supply the good needs the income transfer. In developing regions, the likely best shooter is the wealthiest country; hence, income transfers that augment income inequality are desired to encourage regional provision of the best-shot public good. If, for example, satellite-launch capability is to be encouraged in South America, then Brazil is the country to support because the Brazilian Alcantara launch center has an advantageous equatorial position. A wider range of support will lead to duplication or failed efforts that do not surmount required thresholds. Better-shot public goods require less inequality-promoting transfers.

Table 3.2 provides a summary of the six aggregators that includes definitions, examples, income redistribution implications, and transfer recommendations. A number of novel insights are associated with public good aid. First, neutrality considerations apply for some public goods but not for others, depending in part on the aggregator. When neutrality applies, it is important to bring in participants with new sources of income to circumvent the underlying crowding-out problem. As such, charitable foundations, NGOs, and partnerships have much to offer. Second, income inequality among recipients must be bolstered for

Table 3.2
Aggregation technologies of public supply and income redistribution

Aggregation technology	Example	Income distribution implications	Recommendations
Summation: overall level of public good equals the sum of countries' contributions.	Preserving a rain forest	Neutral unless redistribute to a noncontributor	Bring in new participants, and encourage donor-specific benefits. Transfer income to richer recipients.
Weighted sum: overall level of public good equals a weighted sum of countries' contributions.	Reducing acid rain	Nonneutral	Redistribute to those countries with more country-specific impact.
Weakest link: smallest contribution determines the good's aggregate level.	Surveillance of disease outbreak	Neutral or nonneutral	Income transfers to smaller contributor or in-kind transfers by low-cost provider.
Weaker-link: smallest contribution has the greatest influence on the good's aggregate level, followed by the second smallest contribution, and so on.	Inhibiting the spread of an agricultural pest	Nonneutral	Income transfers to small contributor or in-kind transfers by low-cost provider. Less need for income-equality-promoting transfers than for weakest link.
Best shot: largest contribution determines the good's aggregate level.	Curing a disease	Nonneutral	Income transfer to best shooter, which augments inequality.
Better shot: largest contribution has the greatest influence on the good's aggregate level, followed by second largest contribution, and so on.	Discovering effective vaccines	Nonneutral	Income transfer to better shooters. Less need to augment inequality than for best-shot public goods.

summation and best-shot public goods, while income equality among recipients must be fostered for weakest-link and weaker-link public goods. Third, capacity is an essential consideration for both weakest-link and best-shot public goods. Fourth, income equality becomes less of a driver when public good aid is investigated. This follows because engineered inequality can yield some public goods whose benefits augment non-contributors' well-being.

Five Sectors of Aid

Five sectors have figured prominently in foreign aid over the last twenty-five years. Most studies of GPGs have adopted this five-sector classification in identifying and quantifying public good aid allocations (te Velde, Morrissey, and Hewitt 2002). The environment sector involves actions to preserve ecosystems and to curb all forms of pollution. Since the 1980s, there has been a focus on sustainable development that does not degrade a recipient country's environmental assets. This focus has bolstered foreign assistance and is partly motivated by donors' self-interest, because pollutants of recipient countries can be carried by air and water abroad. The environment sector received the largest share of ODA from 1980 until the mid 1990s (Mascarenhas and Sandler 2005; te Velde, Morrissey, and Hewitt 2002). With the rise of HIV/AIDS, Ebola, severe acute respiratory syndrome (SARS), and bird flu, foreign support of LDCs' health sectors has increased as a share of ODA in the 1990s. The health sector involves providing a health care infrastructure, eradicating and monitoring communicable diseases, treating the sick, vaccinating against diseases, and limiting disease transmission (e.g., provision of clean water and sanitation). The recent rise in the health sector's share of ODA is a clear reflection of donors' self-interest. The health interests of rich and poor countries are not completely aligned, because developed countries are more interested in non-infectious disease (i.e., heart disease and cancer) that do not present the same risks for LDCs in which life expectancy is shorter. Moreover, some serious diseases for LDCs—for example, malaria, tuberculosis, measles, and tropical diseases—are not a concern for most developed countries.

The knowledge sector includes education, research and development, innovations, and technical assistance. As a share of ODA, the knowledge sector grew since the 1980s, and displayed an even larger increase in the 1990s. Given that many knowledge public goods are NPGs and RPGs where donor spillovers are small, the sector's second smallest share of

ODA is understandable. The governance sector displayed the largest increase in ODA shares after the mid-1990s, following the Asian financial crises. Support for the governance sector is in the interests of developed countries with investments in emerging markets. With globalization, financial instability anywhere can have a resonance worldwide, as shown by the 2008–2009 recession.

The peace and security sector involves the smallest ODA share, which shows no trend over time. This sector includes not only restoring peace but also providing post-conflict reconstruction and assistance. The main reason for the sector's small ODA share hinges on much of the expenditure on peacekeeping coming out of the UN and NATO missions. As such, these efforts are not part of ODA.

Table 3.3 describes the five public good aid sectors and the past behavior of their ODA shares. The third column indicates the aggregator technologies primarily associated with each sector.

Insofar as each sector relies on different sets of aggregators, sectors have diverse prognoses and income redistribution needs. Free-riding concerns will plague the environment sector owing to summation public goods. Greater incentive compatibility and, thus, more efficient collective action will be associated with those pollutants adhering to a weighted-sum aggregator (e.g., sulfur). For the health sector, capacity is a concern, given the prevalence of weakest-link and best-shot public goods. For those diseases that do not affect rich countries, either the capacity of the region's wealthiest country must be bolstered or else new participants must play a financial role. The heavy reliance on summation, best-shot, and better-shot public goods in the knowledge sector means that income flows must be to those nations in a given region that have the best chance to supply the public goods with their region-wide spillovers. The governance sector is often incentive compatible, because LDCs must adopt principles acceptable to the developed countries if the former is to attract portfolio and foreign direct investment. The developed countries can establish acceptable rules— such as the Basle Accord on financial practices—for the LDCs to follow.

Finally, the peace and security sector involves summation and best-shot public goods. Peacekeeping force strength is additive, while the ability to create a stable post-conflict government is more of a best-shot effort. These forces can come from varied sources: a multilateral agency, a nearby regional power, or a rich nation. Often post-conflict reconstruction and assistance comes from a multilateral agency that collects funds from a host of donors. Spatial propinquity can motivate a neighbor to

Table 3.3
Five sectors of public good aid

Sectors	Share of ODA[1]	Aggregators[2]	Issues
Environment: actions to preserve ecosystems and to curb pollution. Recent emphasis on sustainability.	Largest from 1980 until mid 1990s	Summation, weighted sum	Free riding and incentive compatibility. Mixed prognoses.
Health: provision of health infrastructure, eradicate and monitor communicable diseases, find cures and vaccines, and limit disease transmission (clean water and sanitation).	Increasing in 1990s	Weakest link, best shot, and other aggregators	Capacity is a real issue for a weakest-link and best-shot issues. Also, rich countries may not have an interest in some LDCs' diseases.
Knowledge: provision of education, research and development, and technical assistance.	Rising since 1980s; greater increase in 1990s	Summation, best shot, better shot	Capacity is an issue. Education is a complementary activity necessary to utilize knowledge public goods of developed countries.
Governance: building economic and financial capacity. Allows LDCs to become an active participant in the globalized economy.	Largest after mid 1990s in some calculations	Best shot	Adoption of governance conventions is often incentive compatible. Capacity remains an issue and can be supplied through technical assistance.
Peace and security: eliminating conflict and ameliorating its consequences. Postconflict reconstruction and assistance.	Smallest	Summation, best shot	Nearest impacted nations have the greatest incentives to do anything. Most assistance related to peace and security is not provided as part of ODA.

1. Mascarenhas and Sandler (2005), te Velde, Morrissey, and Hewitt (2002).
2. Arce and Sandler (2002), Sandler (2004), and Sandler and Arce (2002).

restore order so as to reduce negative externalities—for example, refugee inflows and blocked resource supplies.

Prognosis for Public Goods Based on Spatial Considerations

Next, we investigate how spatial spillover considerations either promote or inhibit the provision of NPGs, RPGs, TRPGs, and GPGs for aid purposes. If not careful, one might falsely conclude that as the goods' range of spillovers grows their aid provision will be more problematic.

In table 3.4, we list factors that promote and inhibit aid-based provision of each type of public good. For every category, there are favorable and unfavorable influences; nevertheless, we draw some net prognoses. NPGs are favored by donors primarily because recipients are willing to accept loans, so that donors can be paid back. Moreover, NPGs are complementary to TPGs, thereby potentially giving benefit spillovers indirectly to donors. Aid-recipient nations are the main beneficiaries of NPGs and, thus, are motivated to supply them once they possess the means. RPGs pose, perhaps, the greatest difficulty even though the number of beneficiaries is smaller than for TRPGs and GPGs. In many cases, foreign support for RPGs is limited because *donors may not receive benefit spillovers*. Also, there may be no clear entity to secure loans to support RPGs. Why should a nation carry a loan for an RPG that largely benefits other nations? This problem can be rectified if regional development banks rely on grants to finance RPGs, but their practice has been to favor loans (Mascarenhas and Sandler 2005). Other factors—the absence of a leader nation in some regions and insufficient capacity of regional development banks—impede aid support for RPGs. To date, there is a donor culture that favors channeling aid to multilateral agencies that are more interested in TRPGs and GPGs with wider ranges of benefit spillovers.

Of the four spatial classes of public goods, TRPGs represent the second most problematic category, because they require an institutional arrangement that networks the impacted regions. Two notable inter-regional networks have been established in recent years to address environmental concerns and agricultural research. Through loans, the Global Environment Facility (GEF) rectifies regional and global commons issues. The Consultative Group on International Agricultural Research (CGIAR) fosters the creation of knowledge through a strategic alliance involving countries, multilateral institutions, and charitable foundations. Another institutional device to provide TRPGs is a partnership that draws on the

Table 3.4
Factors promoting and inhibiting NPGs, RPGs, TRPGs, and GPGs

National public goods (NPGs)
• Incentives for nations to provide (Promote)
• Loans will be taken out (Promote)
• Aid agencies and donor countries are willing to provide (Promote)
• NPGs are complementary to RPGs, TRPGs, and GPGs (Promote)
• Nations may lack finances (Inhibit)

Regional public goods (RPGs)
• Fewer nations involved than for TRPGs and GPGs (Promote)
• New regionalism and trading blocs can facilitate provision (Promote)
• Favorable characteristics of publicness (e.g., excludable benefits, joint products, weighted-sum aggregator) (Promote)
• Cultural and spatial propinquity among countries (Promote)
• Absence of donor spillovers owing to regional specificity of benefits (Inhibit)
• No clear entity to obtain loans, provide collateral, or promote a regional agenda (Inhibit)
• Possible absence of leader nation (Inhibit)
• Insufficient capacity of some regional development banks (Inhibit)
• Absence of a culture to support regional development banks (Inhibit)

Transregional public good (TRPGs)
• Donor spillovers may arise owing to more global reach (Promote)
• Multilateral aid agencies provide funding (Promote)
• Inter-regional networks can be established (e.g., Global Environment Facility [GEF]), Consultative Group for International Agricultural Research [CGIAR]) (Promote)
• Problem can have some region-specific characteristics (Inhibit)
• Large number of involved nations (Inhibit)
• Geographical dispersion of spillover recipients (Inhibit)

Global public goods (GPGs)
• Donor spillovers exist (Promote)
• Multilateral aid agencies provide funding (Promote)
• Rich leader nations heavily involved with the problem (Inhibit)
• May possess unfavorable publicness properties (Inhibit)

comparative advantage of diverse participants. For example, the Oncho-cerciasis (river blindness) Control Programme links together Merck, WHO, recipient nations, and donor nations to fight a disease that is endemic to the Arabian Peninsula, Africa, and Latin America. Another TRPG partnership is the Medicines for Malaria Venture. In many TRPG cases, linked regions confront differences that must be taken into account—for example, the prophylactics for malaria differ among regions. These differences can diminish the network's effectiveness. The large number of countries often involved may inhibit collective action. Many TRPGs, such as preventing tropical diseases, may offer no direct spillovers to donor nations, which, in turn, may inhibit action. On balance, the prognosis for TRPGs lies between that of NPGs and RPGs.

Perhaps surprising, GPGs have a better prognosis than RPGs and TRPGs for effective action because donor nations obtain benefit spill-overs from their assistance, making generosity incentive compatible. Research on many GPGs (e.g., ozone-shield depleters) provides an under-standing of the process behind the problem, which fosters collective action and the willingness of rich countries to assist poorer countries to achieve targets (Sandler 2004). Multilateral agencies are geared to coor-dinate efforts to provide GPGs. Moreover, there is a culture to support these institutions' GPG provision. Detracting factors include the absence of a rich leader nation that is heavily involved with some GPG problems. For global warming, the United States creates almost a quarter of the greenhouse gas emissions but has not yet assumed the leadership role that it played for ozone depleters. The publicness properties of some GPGs may impede action; nevertheless, donor nations have supported GPGs through foreign assistance. This support is anticipated to grow with time.

Conclusion

As we have shown, the face of foreign assistance is changing as more public goods *with diverse spillover ranges* account for an increasing proportion of aid. This changing composition has ethical implications: aid is no longer driven by either altruism *or* self-serving concerns, since some public good aid provides benefit spillovers to donor nations in addition to recipient private benefits. This collective rationale can be exploited by the international community to educate donors about how augmenting their aid budget addresses their own interests. If this aware-ness is fostered, then public good aid need not crowd out traditional aid.

(Crowding out occurs when foreign aid is not increased to fund TPGs in developing countries.) We have shown that the MDGs embrace many public goods and, as such, their prognosis hinges on considerations that motivate public good assistance.

This new form of aid requires an understanding of the factors that determine incentives of donor and recipient nations. Thus, how the three properties of publicness—benefit non-rivalry, non-excludability, and aggregator technologies—affect the actions of donors and recipients must be fathomed. The aggregator technology is particularly important since it affects not only the direction of income transfers toward greater or lesser equality, but also the identity of the appropriate donor—that is, donor nation, multilateral institution, charitable foundation, or another entity. Each of the five sectors associated with public good aid displays different aggregators and, thus, alternative policy recommendations. We have also argued that the spatial extent of public good spillovers influences the prognosis for effective collective action in the form of foreign assistance. NPGs have the best prognosis, followed by GPGs when donor nations receive spillovers. RPGs pose the greater concern, followed by TRPGs.

Public good aid will grow as a percentage of ODA with time. As this growth occurs, an understanding of the implications of public good aid for the appropriate donor, policy recommendations, and the direction of income transfers becomes essential for effective foreign assistance.

Notes

This chapter has been published originally as Sandler, T. and D. G. Arce. New face of development assistance: Public goods and changing ethics. *Journal of International Development* 19(4): 527–544. Permission granted for republication.

1. Despite the importance of altruism, donors were always motivated, in part, by self-interest. For example, the Marshall Plan, which rebuilt Europe after World War II, gave the United States strong allies and trade partners. This plan also curbed the spread of communism in Europe. Public good aid combines altruism and donor self-interest in a subtle way by providing goods whose benefits may also enrich the donor.

2. Recent books on public goods and foreign assistance include: Arce and Sandler (2002); Estevadeoral and Nguyen (2004); Ferroni and Mody (2002); Kanbur, Sandler, and Morrison (1999); Kaul, Grunberg, and Stern (1999); and Sandler (1997, 2004).

3. The theoretical results discussed in the remainder of this section come from Arce (2001); Arce and Sandler (2001); Cornes and Sandler (1984, 1996); Sandler (1992, 1997, 1998, 2004); Vicary (1990); and Vicary and Sandler (2002).

II

Designing Complex Incentive Schemes

The chapters in the second part provide arguments for designing complex incentive schemes, based on a careful examination of the influence of various instruments on the outcomes of GPG provision, and on an analysis of the complex relations between instruments. Frey's chapter is a powerful illustration of this perspective. By drawing on research findings from economics, psychology, and political science, it analyzes the complex interplay that exists between incentive instruments and the likelihood of a spontaneous contribution to public goods. The possibility of the crowding out of voluntary contributions becomes a major issue here. It depends critically on the refusal of being manipulated by those who design the incentive instruments. The next chapter, by Gunningham, links these arguments to the broader themes of public good provision and reflexive governance. Legal instruments are also affected by these complex influences on individual preferences. The last chapter in this part, by Sarr and Swanson, highlights the fact that the endowments of the various players influence their ability to exploit legal instruments, which shows the limits of solutions that do not influence the distribution of wealth and capabilities. This chapter makes the point that certain governance solutions will result in an unequal distribution of benefits in function of the capabilities of the players on the downstream markets. As shown by the example of contracts between developed and developing countries for genetic resources, the uneven initial endowments of human resources and technological capabilities lead to biases in the distribution of profits that favor the developed world.

The chapters in this second part provide an overview of the efficiency and the legitimacy challenges of mixed policy instruments that are based on monetary and nonmonetary incentive mechanisms, such as information and the influence of social norms. They directly address important innovations that have been implemented in the context of reflexive regulation in Australia, the Netherlands, and the United States, and that have also influenced governance innovations in other parts of the world. An example of these policy mixes is the role of instruments that encourage and reward corporate environmental motivation, vis à vis coercive measures. The logic of encouragement is clearly to switch from the manipulation of extrinsic motivation to the building of intrinsic motivation to adopt environmentally friendly behavior. However, the exact outcome of these new policies is still an open question.

4

Crowding Out and Crowding In of Intrinsic Preferences

Bruno Frey

Standard Microeconomics: Homo Oeconomicus

The fundamental idea of modern microeconomic theory is that individuals act rationally—that is, consistently—and are subject to external constraints. This model of humans has often been called the "homo oeconomicus," and it provides clear and empirically testable predictions about how individuals will react to changes in relative prices, controlling for income changes induced. The "price effect" when applied to demand states that a price rise reduces the quantity demanded; the demand curve is negatively sloped. Applied to supply the price effect predicts that a higher price induces an increase in supply; price and quantity are positively related. Paying a higher compensation unequivocally raises the effort and quantity of work.

This simple theory of human behavior has been extremely successful[1]. What has become known as "economic imperialism" (Stigler 1984, Hirshleifer 1985, Lazear 2000), or the "rational choice approach," is based mainly on the application of the price effect to a large number of issues and problems, as pioneered by Gary Becker (1976). The more traditional applications have been implemented in education, health, the natural environment, and politics; more unorthodox ones can be seen in such realms as the family, the arts, crime, sports, and religion. It has also been applied to global public goods such as those involving international environmental problems or issues of war and peace (see Frey 1984). This imperialism has not been without controversy both inside and outside of economics. One of the major points of criticism has been that this theory of behavior is too simplistic and does not account for human behavior especially outside the area dominated by explicit prices (e.g., Sen 1977; Lane 1991). In these applications outside the market, the term *price*—used in its broad sense as a cost— is often difficult to observe as it takes the form of opportunity cost. As the large literature on the non-market applications demonstrates, a skilful use of the price effect yields fascinating and non-trivial insights (McKenzie and Tullock 1975; Radnitzky and Bernholz 1987; Kirchgaessner 1991; Frey 1992, 2001).

Economic imperialism has had a substantial impact on other social sciences and beyond. In political science, the corresponding field is called "public choice" or "political economics"; in sociology "rational choice," in legal studies "law and economics," and in historical studies "cliometrics."

In the field of GPG provision, non-market motivations also play an important role. Therefore the simple homo oeconomicus model of man cannot account for the complex motivations that lead individuals to contribute to GPG. However, as will be seen in the other chapters of this volume, many GPG policies still very much depend on this particular economic model, because they are targeted mainly to influencing self-interest-related motivations, whether through monetary incentives or sanctions in the context of direct state regulation. To bridge the gap, this chapter reviews new models that have been developed in economics, and provides experimental evidence for a broadened approach to human behavior that underlies the analysis of intrinsic preferences and social norms in GPG provision in the subsequent chapters of this volume. Therefore, in spite of a lack of direct contribution to models of reflexive governance, it lays the groundwork for the analysis in this book of the alignment and misalignment between concepts of GPG and the complex preferences and motivations of the actors contributing to their provision. Overall, this chapter shows that new developments in behavioral and experimental economics provide a set of operational models that can be used to analyze complex preferences and thereby enrich our toolbox of institutional analysis beyond a focus on monetary incentives and sanctions only.

A Broader Set of Motivations

There has been a dramatic change over the past few years in how motivation is seen to affect behavior (cf. the contributions by Gächter, Meier, Bohnet, Benz, and Oberholzer-Gee in Frey and Stutzer [2007]). Based on results originally found in experimental social psychology (Deci 1971), an effect of a price change on behavior has been identified. This predicts the exact *opposite effect* on behavior. In particular, a price increase is predicted to *decrease*, rather than increase, the supply of work offered. This is a remarkable result; it goes much beyond the many "behavioral anomalies"[2] identified in other parts of what today constitutes "psychology and economics"[3] (sometimes also called "behavioral economics"[4]). This "crowding-out effect" is part of a larger theory including a neutral and a "crowding-in effect." As will be argued, the crowding effects lead to a generalization of the relationship between motivation and behavior; it certainly does not substitute for the price effect. Rather, the price effect is taken to always work in the way suggested by standard theory, but an additional type of motivation is added, *intrinsic motivation*, which under identifiable conditions leads to dramatically different behavioral responses to price changes.

The crowding-out effect may be illustrated by an example:

A boy on good terms with his parents willingly mows the lawn of the family home. His father then offers to pay him money each time he cuts the lawn.

The crowding-out effect suggests that the boy will lose his intrinsic motivation to cut the lawn (he may go on doing so, but now he does it because he is paid), but he will not be prepared to do any type of housework for free. The example shows that the price effect, on which economics is founded, is not valid for all conditions and under all circumstances, and that the connection between a monetary reward offered and its supply must be analyzed in a wider perspective.

The next section of this chapter develops crowding theory, discusses its basis in social psychology, integrates it into economics, and analyzes the conditions under which the crowding-out effect takes place. After that, the empirical evidence of crowding effects is explored. Conclusions are drawn in the final section: both economic theory and policy are strongly affected by the existence of crowding effects. More care should be taken when applying incentive payments in firms, or in the public sector (for example, when following new public management ideas), or when using incentive instruments in economic policy (for example, with respect to the environment).

Crowding Theory

Psychological Background
Social psychologists have empirically identified that external intervention, in the form of a reward, reduces individuals' intrinsic incentives. This relationship has been termed alternatively the "undermining effect," "overjustification effect," "the hidden costs of reward" (Lepper and

Greene 1978), "corruption effect" (Kruglanski 1978), or "cognitive evaluation theory" (Deci and Ryan 1985; Deci and Flaste 1995) by the
psychological scholars involved.

The hidden costs of rewards rest on the distinction between internal
and external motivation: "One is said to be intrinsically motivated to
perform an activity when one receives no apparent reward except the
activity itself" (Deci 1971, 105). Three psychological processes have been
identified to account for the hidden costs of rewards:

- The *loss of self-determination* shifts the locus of control from the inside
  to the outside of the person affected. When individuals perceive the
  external intervention to be controlling, in the sense of reducing the
  extent to which they can determine actions themselves, intrinsic motivation is replaced by extrinsic control.

- Outside intervention undermines the actor's intrinsic motivation, if it
  carries the notion that the actor's intrinsic motivation is not acknowledged. The person affected feels that his or her competence is not appre-
  ciated, which leads to *impaired self-esteem*, resulting in reduced effort.

- A person acting on the basis of his or her intrinsic motivation is
  deprived of the chance to exhibit this intrinsic motivation to other
  persons. As a reaction, the persons affected exhibit "altruistic anger"
  and will in turn relinquish the inner motivation and behave according
  to external motives.

Conditions

Whether rewards affect intrinsic motivation negatively or positively is
determined by the following conditions:

- External intervention *crowds out* intrinsic motivation if the individuals
  affected perceive the intervening individuals to be *controlling*. Self-
  determination, self-esteem, and the possibility for expression suffer, and
  the individuals react by reducing their intrinsic motivation in the activity controlled.

- External intervention *crowds in* intrinsic motivation if the individuals
  concerned perceive it as *supportive* (or informative in a positive way).
  Self-esteem is fostered, and individuals feel that their self-determination
  is increased, which, in turn, raises intrinsic motivation.

Integration into Economics

Crowding effects *generalize* the hidden costs of reward in three important
ways (Frey 1997):

1. Intrinsic motivation is potentially affected by *all kinds of intervention* coming from outside the person considered. Thus, not only rewards, but also *commands,* may crowd out intrinsic motivation.

2. Intrinsic motivation may be *reduced* or *raised* (crowding *out* and crowding *in*). Thus, there may not only be hidden "costs" but also hidden "gains."

3. External intervention affects the *internally held values* of individuals. Hence, they affect not only narrowly defined intrinsic motivation, but also *norms* internalized by individuals. Moreover, external intervention may induce a shift from other-regarding or group-regarding to *more selfish* preferences and behavior.

These three generalizations greatly increase the scope and applicability of crowding theory.

To successfully apply crowding theory to issues pertaining to economics, it is necessary to simultaneously take into account the price effect normally considered in economics. Here, attention is focused on crowding out, because it affects behavior contrary to the price effect.

Consider a normal, positively inclined supply function (S in figure 4.1) for an activity. At zero price, the individuals considered are prepared to supply the quantity q^{IM}. That means individuals are assumed to

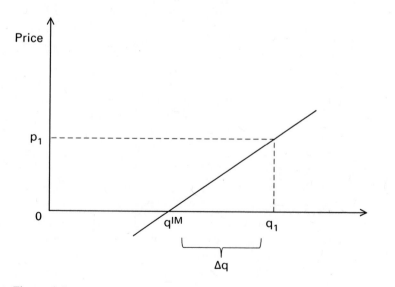

Figure 4.1
Conventional supply theory

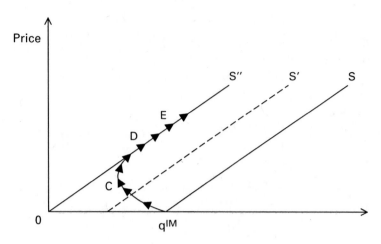

Figure 4.2
Supply including crowding-out effect

undertake the activity for its own sake, or be intrinsically motivated. Such behavior is perfectly consistent with economic theory. Following the price effect, conventional economic theory predicts that a price rise (from O to p1) raises supply from q^{IM} to q^1, moving along the supply curve.

The extrinsically induced supply increase Δq is perfectly *additive* to the intrinsically supplied quantity q^{IM}, thus $q^1 = q^{IM} + \Delta q$. In contrast, the crowding-out effect induces a shift in the supply curve to the left (figure 4.2).

The supply curve moves to the left (from S to S'), until intrinsic motivation is completely crowded out (at S") when a positive price is offered. More precisely, each supply curve is associated with a given *stock* of capital of intrinsic motivation. Once this capital stock is exhausted, or at most constant, supply only moves along S" as the price effect exists.

The supply response moves quite differently than is suggested by conventional economic theory. In the figure, it is assumed at first that the crowding-out effect prevails over the price effect, and supply *falls*: the individuals concerned reduce the extent of their activity. Beginning at point C, the price effect dominates. Only when point D is reached does the quantity supplied exceed the amount previously intrinsically supplied. At point D on supply curve S," the stock of intrinsic capital is constant (and possibly exhausted), so that the price effect determines supply behavior exclusively.

Obviously, the crowding effect also has important consequences for policy. Thus, many seemingly "modern" compensation systems have to be reconsidered. Pay-for-performance schemes negatively affect performance, in so far as they negatively affect work morale, a specific kind of intrinsic motivation. Under certain conditions, for example with volunteers who are essentially intrinsically motivated to work, it may be a mistake to introduce monetary compensation at all.

In important cases, external intervention through monetary means can transform the nature of a good or relationship fundamentally. Sometimes, the offer of a monetary reward completely destroys the existing commodity in question. Romantic love is an example: it simply cannot be bought, and if an attempt were made to buy it, the good can no longer be called unselfish love but rather, taken to the extreme, prostitution. The same is true for trust, admiration, or friendliness, which change their intrinsic nature when they are bought.

Empirical Evidence on Motivation Crowding Effects

Experiments
The hidden costs of reward have been extensively studied in laboratories by social psychologists. The number of laboratory experiments on the crowding effect is so large that it is impossible to summarize the results. Fortunately, there already have been done several formal meta-analytical studies of crowding theory. The most extensive and recent study by Deci, Koestner, and Ryan (1999) shows that the crowding-out effect is indeed a robust phenomenon of significant size under the specified conditions. Experimental economic research has also identified various crowding effects on motivation in the economic setting (for a survey, see Frey and Jegen 2000). Crowding effects have not only been identified in experiments, but also are of great importance for practical, real world problems.

Case Studies
Day care centers provide a striking example of how monetary intervention can achieve the opposite of what would be expected on the basis of the price effect. Such institutions are confronted with the problem that parents sometimes arrive late to pick up their children, which forces the employees to stay after the official closing time. To remedy the situation, economists would typically suggest imposing a monetary fine for collecting children late. Such punishment is expected to compel parents to be

on time. A study on a day care center in Israel revealed a completely different outcome (Gneezy and Rusticchini 2000a, 2000b). After the introduction of a rather hefty fine, the number of parents arriving late *increased* substantially, which is in line with the crowding-out effect. Introducing a monetary fine transforms the relationship between parents and day care employees from a mostly personal to a more monetary relationship. As a result, the parents' intrinsic motivation to keep to the time schedule was reduced or crowded out altogether, the perception being that the employees were now "paid" for the inconvenience of having to stay longer. Being late to pick up the children was no longer associated with any feeling of guilt.

Econometric Studies
Work motivation is an area where crowding theory is particularly relevant and where several econometric studies have been undertaken (Frey and Osterloh 2002, 2005; Osterloh and Frey 2000, 2004, 2006; Osterloh 2007).

Motivational Transfer Effect
External intervention may have an *indirect* damaging effect on intrinsic motivation. The crowding-out effect may spread to other areas, even into such areas where no external intervention has been applied. If intrinsic motivation is crowded out in areas where it is a major (or even the only) behavioral incentive, the overall outcome of an external intervention tends to be even more strongly against the principal's interest. There may thus be an indirect "motivational transfer effect," which has to be added to the direct crowding-out effect. Policy instruments, such as effluent charges or tradable permits, provide an additional example. They work efficiently where they are applied, but an induced substitution of environmental ethics by monetary incentives may then lead people to protect the environment less in areas for which no external incentives exist. This undesired motivational transfer effect not only takes place when monetary incentives are used, but also when rules and regulations are applied.

Conclusions

Crowding theory introduces a (thus far) disregarded but crucial and empirically well-supported psychological effect into economics. Its integration into economics shows that it certainly does not replace the conventional price effect, but rather amends it.

Crowding theory has important implications for economic theory. In particular, a systematic relationship between intrinsic and extrinsic motivation is established; a negative relationship designates the crowding-out effect, a positive relationship the crowding-in effect. Both effects are well supported by laboratory experiments under carefully controlled conditions. In order to show the relevance for current social issues, crowding theory has also been applied to pressing policy problems.

The social sciences and, in particular, economics should pay more attention to intrinsic motivation as an important incentive, and as a viable instrument for policy making. This applies to current policy, as well as to policy at the level of the constitution. It is an essential task to establish institutions, to make constitutional choices, which support individuals' own initiatives.

Notes

This chapter draws in part upon the discussion of crowding theory in Frey 2001; chapter 5.

1. However, the empirical application is not always easy especially as all other factors, except the price change, must be controlled for. For small price changes, and when only a small part of total expenditures is spent on the respective goods and services, the income effect can be disregarded because of its insignificance. This helps to identify the price effect.

2. Such as the endowment, reference point, opportunity cost, anchoring, availability, representativeness, overconfidence effects, and biases (e.g., Kahneman, Slovic, and Tversky 1982; Dawes 1988; Thaler 1992; Frey and Eichenberger 1994).

3. Important forerunners are Hirschman 1970; Scitovsky 1976; Leibenstein 1976; Schelling 1980; Akerlof 1984; Frank 1988; Schlicht 1998; Brennan and Pettit 2004. An effort to develop a "psychological economics" *independent* of neoclassical economics has, for example, been undertaken by Furnham and Lewis (1986) and Lea, Tarpy, and Webley (1987).

4. This is a misnomer because the "behavioral" school in psychology posits a mechanistic response to outside interventions which is, of course, in clear contrast to what psychological economics stands for.

5

Regulatory Reform and Reflexive Regulation: Beyond Command and Control

Neil Gunningham

The concept of reflexive governance initially emerged within the context of the discussions on sustainable development, in part because of the importance given to non-market values in this debate and the call for the development of new modes of regulation more attuned to complex motivations. As a result, many innovative practices have been developed and put into practice over the last two decades in the field of environmental governance. This chapter builds upon this literature, by constructing a typology of reflexive governance models that have been proposed as a means to overcome various insufficiencies of direct—or command and control—state regulation. By providing a systematic overview of these initiatives and by situating them in the broader context of the socio-legal studies on new modes of regulation, this chapter shows that they also contain important lessons for the reflexive governance of global public goods more generally.

Since the early 1990s, the architecture of environmental regulation in North America, Western Europe, and Australasia has changed substantially. The best-known examples include: in the United States, the Clinton-Gore Reinventing Environmental Regulation initiative; in Canada, a version of "smart regulation"; in Europe, negotiated agreements, environmental partnerships, and voluntary initiatives; and in Australia, Accredited Licensing and Environmental Improvement Plans (Gunningham and Sinclair 2002, chap. 6). In addition, many developed countries have introduced a plethora of informational regulation initiatives, various forms of industry self-management, and a variety of policy instruments built around harnessing third parties as surrogate regulators (Stewart 2001). These various "next generation" environmental instruments have substantially reconfigured the regulatory landscape.

This reconfiguration is still in process, and the next generation instruments that have emerged are diverse. Some seek out and nurture win-win solutions, some seek to replace conflict with cooperation between major stakeholders, and others seek to mitigate power imbalances, and to increase transparency and accountability, as is the case with informational regulation. Many, in stark contrast to first generation environment regulation, seek to encourage and reward enterprises for going beyond compliance with existing regulation. And the large majority exemplify the changing role of the state, which in the domestic environmental arena at least, is engaged in less direct intervention in the affairs of business than previously.

These changes have, in broad terms, been attempts to design more efficient and effective (and occasionally more legitimate) regulation. But they have been developed in an era in which neoliberalism has become the dominant political discourse (particularly in the Anglo-Saxon jurisdictions) and in which there are repeated efforts to "roll back" the regulatory state. In consequence, it is no coincidence that many second generation instruments have favored "light-handed regulation" and in some cases, the replacement of government intervention by industry self-regulation.

Nor is it surprising that many such instruments have attempted to go beyond, or replace, traditional "command and control" regulation. Indeed, command and control was both the central pillar of first generation regulation, and anathema to neoliberals. Its critics suggest that: (1) regulatory agencies, particularly in the United States, adopted an adversarial stance toward duty holders that often engendered regulatory resistance and proved counterproductive (Bardach and Kagan 2002); and (2) command and control regulation, both in the United States and elsewhere, is often inflexible and excessively costly for business to comply with. Indeed, centralized, bureaucratic standard-setting—the center piece of traditional forms of command and control—is now routinely castigated by its critics for being "inherently inefficient and cumbersome" (Elliott 1994, 1840) and for failing to deliver many of the environmental benefits it promised.

But the relative strengths and weaknesses of command and control vary substantially with the context. In broad terms, the more complex the environmental problem, the more obvious become the limitations of command and control to address it. For example, it is one thing to regulate point-source pollution caused by large readily identifiable industrial facilities operating within a single jurisdiction—and, by and large, command and control has done this reasonably well (Gunningham, Kagan, and Thornton 2003, 44–51). But it is quite another to apply the same approach to diffuse source pollution from agriculture, to biodiversity loss on private land, or to numerous natural resource management problems involving public goods—especially those that can only be addressed within a multilevel governance framework.

A particular criticism of command and control is that it lacks reflexivity and the capacity to nurture contextualized learning and mutual adjustment between stakeholders. This is not a particular problem if one simply wants a given industry sector to adopt an established environmental technology to curb its point-source pollution (a typical first generation regulatory fix), but it is a large, possibly insurmountable problem when it comes to regulating complex environmental issues such as those described above. Unsurprisingly, much of the literature on reflexive law documents the incapacity of the regulatory state to deal with such issues. As Teubner (1983) and others (Teubner, Farmer, and Murphy 1994) have argued, there is a limit to the extent to which it is possible to add more and more specific prescriptions without this resulting in counterproductive regulatory overload.

In contrast, reflexive regulation, which uses *indirect* means to achieve broad social goals, has, according to its proponents, a much greater capacity to come to terms with increasingly complex social arrangements. This is because it "focuses on enhancing the self-referential capacities of social systems and institutions outside the legal system, rather than direct intervention of the legal system itself through its agencies, highly detailed statutes, or delegation of great powers to the courts . . . [it] aims to establish self-reflective processes within businesses to encourage creative, critical, and continual thinking about how to minimize . . . harms and maximize . . . benefits" (Orts 1995, 1232). Put differently, reflexive regulation is procedure oriented rather than directly focused on a prescribed goal, and seeks to design self-regulating social systems by establishing norms of organization and procedure. At its core are participatory procedures for securing regulatory objectives and mechanisms that facilitate and encourage deliberation and mutual learning between organizations (Yeung 2007).

This chapter examines a variety of next generation policy instruments, intended to overcome, or at least to mitigate, the considerable problems associated with command and control and better address market failures in the name of the public interest. The second section examines five frameworks, or lenses, through which one might better understand this regulatory reconfiguration, the next generation mechanisms that have evolved and their relationship with reflexive law. It shows how, in stark contrast to command and control, each of these approaches seeks to achieve its environmental goals through stimulating "second order effects" on the part of actors and increases the possibilities for reflexivity. The third section takes a more critical perspective, noting that not all second generation environmental regulation adopts a reflexive approach, that policy makers do not necessarily adopt reflexive instruments primarily because they incorporate this characteristic, and that reflexive regulation is not necessarily effective in achieving its policy goals. This leads, in the final section, to an exploration of the circumstances in which reflexivity is likely to make its greatest contribution, and to a recognition of the limits of our existing knowledge as to how to design reflexive regulation to achieve best results. The chapter concludes that in situations of complexity (including those involving public goods and multilevel governance challenges) there may be no credible alternative except to invoke reflexive law; that (returning to the five frameworks) different forms of reflexive regulation may be appropriately invoked in different circumstances; and that in some circumstances, complementary combinations of reflexive regulation and other policy instruments may achieve better results than reflexive regulation alone.

The regulatory reconfiguration which this chapter describes, has taken place primarily at state, regional, and local levels rather than in the global context. It is a development closely connected with the nation-state. As such this chapter does not engage directly with questions of how best to address the environmental challenges relating to global public goods. Nevertheless, the history it describes, the insights it provides concerning how reflexive approaches play out within the nation-state, and the transition it tracks from regulation to governance, enable lessons at the national or local level to be connected to the study of public goods globally. As such it provides, in combination with chapter 4 a useful precursor to the broader discussion of those issues later in this volume.

Next Generation Regulation: Five Frameworks

Process Based and Meta-Regulation

One of the most striking changes that have taken place concerns the *type* of standards contained in environmental regulations. Traditionally, under command and control, regulators enforced either prescriptive standards (which tell duty holders precisely what measures to take) or to performance standards (which specify outcomes or the desired level of performance). In contrast, since the early 1990s, there has been an increasing reliance upon what are variously termed *process*, *systems*, and *management-based standards*. These are standards that require firms to develop internal planning and management practices designed to achieve regulatory goals. Such standards have the considerable attractions of providing flexibility to enterprises to devise their own least-cost solutions, of giving them incentives to go beyond compliance with minimum legal standards, and of being applicable to a broad range of circumstances and to heterogeneous enterprises (Coglianese and Nash 2006).

Unlike prescriptive and performance-based standards, which only require enterprises to achieve minimum standards and do not encourage reflection or provide any incentives or encouragement to go beyond the minimum, process- based standards encourage both reflection and continuous improvement. Crucially, process-based approaches have the capacity to influence the internal self-regulation and norms of organizations, to make them more responsive and reflexive (rather than merely reactive) to environmental concerns.

While this approach is increasingly embedded in environmental regulation, it is equally found in many environmental self-regulatory initiatives. Perhaps the most advanced manifestation of this form of regulation (or combination of regulation and self-regulation) is the "safety case," which was first instituted in the United Kingdom and later adopted in the European Union with regard to Major Hazard Facilities under the Seveso II Directive. What is distinctive about this approach is that responsibility is placed on the operator of a Major Hazard Facility to submit their plans to the regulator (or conceivably a third party) for approval (i.e., to "make their case" that they have addressed all hazards and ensured that the facility is as safe and capable of minimizing its environmental impact as is practicable). Those plans are then audited and, if satisfactory, form the basis for accreditation.

Such a strategy could be viewed as "enforced self-regulation" (Ayres and Braithwaite 1992) but is more usefully treated as a type of "meta-regulation" or "meta risk management," whereby government, rather than regulating directly, oversees the risk management of individual enterprises. Under such an approach, the role of regulation ceases to be primarily about government inspectors checking compliance with rules and becomes more about encouraging the industry to put in place environmental (and safety) management systems that are then scrutinized by regulators. Rather than regulating prescriptively, meta-regulation seeks by law to stimulate modes of self-organization within the firm in such a way as to encourage internal self-critical reflection about its safety, health, and environmental performance.

Meta regulation is in some respects the quintessential form of reflexive regulation. It recognizes that the capacity to deal with complex organizations and complex environmental or safety problems through rules alone is limited, and that it would be better to design a form of responsive regulation that induces companies themselves to acquire the specialized skills and knowledge to self-regulate, subject to state and third-party scrutiny. Indeed some suggest that the only viable means of achieving social goals such as environment protection is for organizations and companies, who know their own operations and facilities better than anyone, to take on the regulatory tasks themselves subject to government oversight.

Informational Regulation

An increasingly important alternative or complement to conventional regulation is what is becoming known as "informational regulation" (Sabel, Fung, and Karkkainen 2000), which has been defined as "regulation which provides to affected stakeholders information on the operations of regulated entities, usually with the expectation that such stakeholders will then exert pressure on those entities to comply with regulations in a manner which serves the interests of stakeholders" (Kleindorfer and Orts 1996, 1). In contrast to command and control, informational regulation involves the state encouraging (as in corporate environmental reporting) or requiring (as with community right to know) the provision of information about environmental impacts but *without* directly requiring a change in those practices. Rather, this approach relies upon economic markets and public opinion as the mechanisms to bring about improved corporate environmental performance. As such, informational regulation "reinforces and augments direct regulatory monitoring and enforcement through third party monitoring and incentives" (Kleindorfer and Orts 1996, 1).

Informational regulation can take a number of different forms. Probably the most successful and best known of these is the use of "community right to know" and pollution inventories such as the U.S. Toxics Release Inventory (TRI), which requires individual companies to estimate their emissions of specified hazardous substances. This information is then used to compile a publicly available inventory, which can then be interrogated by communities, the media, individuals, environmental groups, and other NGOs that can ascertain, for example, the total emission load in a particular geographical area, or the total emissions of particular companies.

A critical element of informational regulation is its capacity to stimulate reflexivity on the part of business. For example, requiring facilities to track and report their emissions (as under the TRI), not only empowers community groups, and enables markets to make more informed judgments, but it also leads to a degree of self-reflection on how things might be done differently. Dow Chemical is among those firms that freely acknowledge that they had not previously measured their wastes and as a result had no idea how much they were discharging. Once they did so, they realized that there was a business opportunity in making pollution prevention pay, through reuse, recycling, the substitution of different substances, and the use of fewer chemicals. Thus, a strategy that involved no requirement to do anything other than estimate discharges and disclose them served to generate internal organizational change, which in turn resulted in substantially improved environmental performance.

Ecological Modernization

Another paradigm that emerged in the 1990s and has since become increasingly influential is ecological modernization. In contrast to many analyses suggesting that a radical reorientation of our current economic and social arrangements will be necessary to avert ecological disaster, ecological modernization suggests that ecologically sound capitalism is not only possible, but worth working toward. This good news message may indeed be a substantial part of the attraction of the ecological modernization approach. Beyond this, the main tenets of this perspective are difficult to encapsulate, since writings under the ecological modernization banner are diverse and draw from a number of different schools of thought.

For present purposes the focus is on its core, which emphasizes how strategies such as eco-efficiency can facilitate environmental improvements in the private sector (particularly in relation to manufacturing) by simultaneously increasing efficiency and minimizing pollution and waste. This will require switching to the use of cleaner, more efficient and less resource-intensive technologies, shifting away from energy and resource-intense industries to those which are value- and knowledge-intensive, anticipatory planning processes, and the "organisational internalization of ecological responsibility" (Cohen 1997, 109).

However, this is not to suggest that markets unaided, or past environmental policy, will provide the appropriate messages and incentives to enable industry to achieve these goals. On the contrary, ecological modernization suggests that such an outcome requires action on a number of fronts, and government regulation in particular will need to promote innovation in environmental technology.

In so arguing, many proponents of ecological modernization place considerable emphasis on its reflexive capabilities, suggesting that:

Rather than dismantling the foundations of industrial societies, the only viable alternative to solve the ecological crises—the continuous burdening of the sustenance base of the planet—is to fully explore the potential of wealth creation. This would be done through the use of one central source of dynamism of modernity: the *reflexivity* of knowledge appropriation. The use of rational capabilities should allow us to install a process of continuous revaluation and redesign of modern institutions. Over time, systems production and consumption would be redefined according to ecological requirements, besides economic and technical ones. The intensification of reflexive thinking would, ultimately, allow modern societies to redefine the rules governing the economy, as well as its social extensions. (Orsato and Clegg, 2005, 262)

Thus far, the ecological modernization literature has resonance with a number of other perspectives described in this chapter. However, on one fundamental issue, ecological modernization departs substantially from other perspectives, namely in its assumption that by following the precepts of ecological modernization there will be a "dissolution of the conflict between economic progress and responsible environmental management because it will be possible to achieve both objectives simultaneously" (Cohen 1997, 109).

In arguing that the business community could successfully combine the objectives of environmental protection and economic growth, ecological modernization resonates with the views of a variety of business strategists, environmental commentators, and corporations arguing that by preventing pollution and thereby cutting costs and avoiding waste directly, by more effective risk management, and by developing the environmental technology to compete effectively in the global environmental market, businesses can achieve win-win outcomes, gaining economically from environmental improvements (Smart 1992; Schmidheiny 1992).

A number of next generation instruments are consistent with this general approach. For example, instruments that harness market forces, so as to encourage rather than inhibit commercial drive and innovation (including many economic instruments and performance standards), meet with approval. And various other flexible and arguably cost-efficient mechanisms for curbing environmental degradation such as self-regulation, information-based strategies, the use of liability rules, and other financial instruments, are also consistent with this approach. In this perspective, government's role includes nudging firms toward cleaner production, heightening their awareness of environmental issues, providing them with financial incentives (which at the margin may be crucial), and encouraging the reordering of corporate priorities to reap the benefits of improved environmental performance.

The proponents of ecological modernization assume that these aspirations will be achieved through a reflexive process whereby enterprises respond strategically to programs and institution building based on the above precepts. This in turn will result "in the construction of new actors and environmental perceptions in the industry, a new technological selection milieu, and the building of new competencies within the enterprises" (Sondergard, Hansen, and Holm 2004, 337). Thus modern societies are seen as going through a process of institutional reflexivity and in so doing developing the institutional capacity to handle their ecological crisis (Mol 1995).

Smart Regulation

Gunningham and Grabosky (1998) advocate the concept of "smart regulation," a term they use to refer to an emerging form of regulatory pluralism that embraces flexible, imaginative, and innovative forms of social control, which seek to harness not just governments but also business and third parties. For example, it is concerned with self-regulation and co-regulation, with using both commercial interests and NGOs, and with finding surrogates for direct government regulation, as well as with improving the effectiveness and efficiency of more conventional forms of direct government regulation.

The central argument is that, in the majority of circumstances, the use of multiple rather than single policy instruments, and a broader range of regulatory actors, will produce better regulation. Further, that this will allow the implementation of complementary combinations of instruments and participants tailored to meet the imperatives of specific environmental issues. By implication, this means a far more imaginative, flexible, and pluralistic approach to environmental regulation than has so far been adopted in most jurisdictions (see generally Gunningham and Grabosky 1998). However, as Scott (2004) points out, it is an approach that privileges state law rather than treating the state as simply one of a number of governance institutions.

This approach seeks to engage regulators to reflect on the most appropriate policy instruments to impose, on the intensity with which those instruments should be enforced, and on the potential to develop new instruments that may be better tailored to achieve their environmental goals (see in particular Gunningham and Grabosky 1998, chap. 6). It also encourages and rewards reflection on the part of duty holders, both directly and by facilitating a wide range of stakeholders to exchange information and engage in dialogue to achieve their purposes.

Such insights have led some policy makers to investigate how public agencies may harness institutions and resources residing *outside* the public sector to further policy objectives in specific concrete situations. It resonates with the broader transition in the role of governments internationally, from "rowing the boat to steering it" (Osborne and Gaebler 1992) or choosing to "regulate at a distance," by acting as facilitators of self- and co-regulation rather than regulating directly. Thus for "smart regulation," environmental policy making involves government harnessing the capacities of markets, civil society, and other institutions to accomplish its policy goals more effectively, with greater social acceptance and at less cost to the state (Gunningham, Grabosky, and Phillipson 1999).

A substantial number of next generation instruments are consistent with the precepts of smart regulation, including the Canadian government's regulatory reform program under this banner (Government of Canada 2005). Others, such as the regulatory flexibility initiatives established under the Clinton-Gore Reinventing Environmental Regulation initiative, were directly inspired by Osborne and Gaebler's (1992) concept of "steering not rowing." Both incorporate the quintessentially reflexive strategy of seeking to embed environmental values and processes within the corporate culture in such a way that it becomes self-regulating, relying upon oversight from local communities and perhaps third-party auditors, to supplement or even replace direct regulation. Similarly, the approach adopted in Victoria, Australia, under Environment Improvement Plans (Holley and Gunningham 2006) also follows the precepts of smart regulation and is reflexive in both conception and execution. More recently the European Community Regulation on chemicals and their safe use (European Community 2006c), which deals with the Registration, Evaluation, Authorisation and Restriction of Chemical substances (REACH), is also built very much in the mode of smart regulation.

The New Environmental Governance

A more recent and far reaching form of "next generation" regulation is what is commonly referred to as the "new environmental governance" (a shift in terminology that recognizes the decentered role of the state). This is an enterprise that involves collaboration between a diversity of private, public, and nongovernment stakeholders who, acting together toward commonly agreed goals, hope to achieve far more collectively than individually.

"New governance" in this context involves a cluster of characteristics: participatory dialogue and deliberation, devolved decision making, flexibility rather than uniformity, inclusiveness, transparency, institutionalized consensus-building practices, and a shift from hierarchy to heterarchy. This definition embraces the broad spirit of the new governance literature that recognizes a shift is taking place in the role of the nation-state, which has moved substantially away from top-down command-and-control regulation to a much more decentralized and consensual approach that seeks to coordinate at multiple levels and is distinctively polycentric (see generally Trubek and Trubek 2007, 542). This approach in turn provides greater scope for non-state actors to assume administrative, regulatory, managerial, and mediating functions previously undertaken by the state.

Since the new environmental governance is still evolving, its precise architecture remains open to debate and numerous versions of "democratic experimentalism" arguably fall under this heading (Dorf and Sabel 1998). For illustrative purposes, attention will focus on an ambitious new governance experiment that is taking place in the sphere of natural resource management (NRM) in Australia, which is commonly referred to as the new regional-based approach to NRM (regional NRM). This involves multiple stakeholders, multiple levels of government, and industry and civil society engagement on a broad geographical scale. This experiment connects with many of the central themes of this book, not least that it is an attempt to engage with public goods problems within a multilevel governance framework.

The context for this new development is the twin recognition that (1) NRM in Australia is in crisis, with massive problems relating to rising water tables, increasing salinity, water scarcity, land clearing, loss of topsoil, diffuse pollution from broad scale rural land use and biodiversity loss; and (2) that traditional approaches (and indeed some nontraditional approaches such as Landcare), which purported to address this environmental challenge, have manifestly failed. In part this failure is attributable to the fact that many natural resources are public in nature and generally available for society at large. Biodiversity, for example, is a public good because we all benefit from it, although we largely rely on others (mostly private landowners) to provide it, and we don't give them much incentive to provide it. This is equally the case with the protection of eco-services and the prevention of widespread land degradation (for example, through dry land salinity).

The challenge is to successfully engage with complex NRM problems—particularly those involving public goods. In the early years of the new millennium the Australian federal government approached this challenge through a far-reaching new approach to NRM that involves devolving NRM decision-making power to the regional level. Fifty-six regional NRM bodies have been created across Australia at the initiative of the federal government. These bodies generally include a mix of community, rural, and other stakeholders, along with government officials, and have responsibility for undertaking NRM consultation, planning, and priority setting. They must each develop a regional plan and regional investment strategy and implement these under a collaborative partnership-based decision-making process. These plans and strategies are subject to performance indicators and other controls imposed by the federal government.

This collaborative regional approach involves a style of governance that seeks wide-ranging partnerships between landholders (including Indigenous Australians); regional communities; industry; local, state, territory, and commonwealth governments, and the wider community in which power (in terms of priority setting and how to achieve those priorities, as well as program delivery) is exercised through multi-stakeholder participation in decision making (including local land managers, local communities, NGOs, and other ground-level stakeholders), coupled with monitoring, evaluation, and oversight by the regional bodies themselves, by Commonwealth/State Steering Committees, the NRM Ministerial Council and (through the relevant ministers themselves) the state and federal government itself. There is an emphasis on "joined–up" institutional arrangements, networks and knowledge exchange. Crucially, the federal government, which is providing the money without which these initiatives could not operate, maintains tight control over the purse strings, and regional bodies are well aware that should they depart substantially from the parameters laid down by the commonwealth, they risk losing their funding, dissolution and replacement by a new entity.

Central to the architecture of the new regional NRM is recognition that different regions/ecosystems raise very different environmental challenges, that NRM in each of these regions involves multiple stakeholders and that the resources, capacities, and institutions necessary to address the NRM challenges can themselves vary significantly. Like the Open Method of Coordination (OMC) in the European Union, it is a means of reconciling the pursuit of common objectives while respecting the need for diversity at lower levels and fostering collective learning "on the ground" in a manner that is arguably a prerequisite for the advancement of sustainable policies (Dryzek 1997).

This approach assumes that the state has very limited ability to achieve its NRM objectives directly and that only by enlisting non-state actors with local capacities and local knowledge are substantial gains likely to be achieved. To borrow Julia Black's description of other versions of the regulation of self-regulation, what is involved is "a process of co-ordination, steering, influencing and balancing interactions between actors/systems, and of creating new patterns of interaction which enable social actors/systems to organize themselves, using such techniques as procedurisation, calibration, feedback loop, redundancy and above, all, countering variety with variety" (Black 2001, 111).

New governance encourages reflexivity because deliberation, coopera-tion, and learning at local level may lead to responses that better take account of local circumstances, build on local knowledge and capacities, and result in greater stakeholder ownership and "buy in." For example, the collaborative approach encourages the exchange of information and enables stakeholder to develop better knowledge of the consequences of their actions. This in turn leads to policy learning and adaptation. Dia-logue similarly facilitates stakeholders to consider the environmental impact of their actions and to learn from shared knowledge and experi-ence. Deliberation, crucially, is seen as a "(self) reflective debate by which participants reason about proposals and are open to changing their initial preferences (Cohen and Sabel 2003, 346). The fundamental assumption is that deliberation will stimulate learning and behavioral change.

This approach can also be thought of in terms of an exchange in which lower-level actors are "granted autonomy to experiment with solutions of their own to common problems, within broadly defined parameters. In return, they furnish 'rich information' concerning solutions to the central bodies (De Schutter and Deakin 2005, 9.

Another form of reflexivity that is often encouraged by new gover-nance initiatives is the capacity for program learning by sharing experi-ences. For example, the pooling of information and experience about what generates success may lead to the identification of best practice (although at this stage at least, this is seriously underdeveloped in RNRM). How this might be achieved is seen most clearly in the Open Method of

Coordination which "is a way of encouraging co-operation, the exchange of best practice and agreeing common targets and guidelines for Member States . . . It relies on regulator monitoring of progress to meet those targets, allowing Member States to compare their efforts and learn from the experience of others" (European Commission 2001, 21).

In summary, the new regional NRM is a substantial departure from most previous NRM strategies, although some of the changes that have been introduced are less radical than might first appear (in particular, the state retains more substantial control and continues to provide a steering mechanism). It is nevertheless an ambitious experiment in engaging multiple stakeholders through collaborative approaches to address complex, contested, and hitherto intractable NRM problems in a reflexive manner.

Reflexive Regulation in Perspective

How should the relationship between "next generation" environmental regulation and reflexivity best be understood? This section examines a number of limitations of reflexive regulation in order to provide a context for the final section that seeks to assess the circumstances in which reflexive regulation and governance are likely to make its greatest contributions.

Not all next generation instruments facilitate reflexivity. Even proponents of reflexive regulation commonly acknowledge that it is a substantial component of some but by no means all viable policy options. Hirsch (2005), for example, provides a threefold classification of environmental policy instruments in terms of negotiated compliance arrangements, market-based approaches, and reflexive law, while conceding that these categories involve some overlap. Even within a category of policy instruments the degree of reflexivity may vary substantially. Take economic instruments. A financial assurance involves little if any reflexivity. In contrast, marketable permits, such as emissions trading and acid rain allowance-trading programs in the United States, "induce reflection by specifying a goal and allowing firms to decide how to achieve it, given their circumstances" (Fiorino 1999, 450). And in some cases, there is no element of reflexivity whatsoever. Thus regulation by architecture (e.g., software as an instrument of control of information technology, or a traffic bollard) could hardly be less reflexive (Scott 2004, 164).

Even when instruments are introduced that are substantively reflexive in nature, they are not necessarily introduced with these reflexive features in mind, and their potential for reflexivity may not be harnessed in practice. For example skeptics argue that the Australian regional NRM initiative described earlier, was introduced more because it provided a convenient means for a federal Liberal government to bypass the states (all of which currently have Labour governments) than because its reflexivity promised better results that the status quo, while other critics argue that the devolution of responsibility to local groups was perceived as a mechanism whereby the federal government could "pass the buck" for what is widely perceived as an intractable problem. Thus Whelan and Lyons (2005, 600) argue that "deliberative governance may entail a sleight of hand whereby government agencies avoid both the cost of and responsibility for environmental protection. Indeed, natural resource management partnerships have been criticized as 'greenwash' to allow governments to shirk their responsibilities by abrogating to civil society and business."

More important, even when policy instruments are introduced with intent to take advantage of their reflexive nature, this reflexivity by no means guarantees success. For example, empirical evaluations of process and meta-regulation (the first of the five frames described earlier), has so far produced very mixed results. There is some evidence to suggest that environmental management systems (which are central to this form of procedural regulation), like other process-based tools, are just that—tools—which can only be effective when implemented with genuine commitment on the part of management. For example, Gunningham, Kagan, and Thorton (2003, chap. 5) found that management style and motivation are more important in shaping the environmental performance of firms than the system itself. In essence, management matters far more than management systems. Or as Parker and Nielson (2006) have argued, it is the *quality* of action taken to manage environmental performance that makes a difference to outcomes and not just particular procedures or systems. This suggests that mandatory imposition of process-based requirements—systems, plans and risk management more generally—may only have a limited influence on environmental outcomes and that policy makers are mistaken in their belief that those who are required to jump over various hurdles (developing and implementing plans and systems, adopting a safety case) will necessarily become more reflexive and, as a result, improve both their attitudes and performance.

Two particular challenges that reflexive regulation needs to overcome to achieve success concern: conflicts of interest and disparities of power, and implementation deficits. In terms of the former, some of the literature (particularly that which focuses on voluntary environmental management mechanisms and negotiated agreements, ecological modernization, and new governance) implicitly relegates conflict of interest and the antagonism between interests groups, to the periphery. Tacitly, it assumes win-win solutions, that most problems can be resolved through deliberation, and/or that the majority of citizens will behave responsibly even in the absence of government intervention (Doyle 2000). But there is little empirical support for such assumptions in the frequently war-torn terrain of environmental protection and NRM. At least on the limited evidence available so far, deliberation and reflexivity have not necessarily led to mutual understanding and consensus solutions as each side comes to better understand the other's position and search for compromises (Whelan and Lyons 2005). Indeed, some environmental groups have concluded that the available modes of reflexive governance are inadequate and that better outcomes are likely to be achieved by active lobbying for direct government intervention.

In terms of implementation, there is often a substantial gap between theory and practice. For example, the broader literature on environmental partnerships such as regional NRM suggests that they frequently fail to live up to their promise to work as "non-hierarchical multi-actor governance because in implementation and design, actors and arrangements hang still too strong on conventional ideas of state governance, frustrating a fundamental shift to 'real' environmental partnerships" (Mol 2007, 224). Similarly, although the U.S. Endangered Species Act's Habitat Conservation Plan program is sometimes viewed as a successful example of reflexive governance experimentation, Camacho shows how this regulatory experiment is failing because the agencies charged with administering it have never seriously treated it like an experiment because of resistance at the level of "on ground" agents (Camacho 2007). Couple this with a dearth of resources to carry through experiments in reflexive regulation, and a failure to redress power imbalances that leads civil society organizations to be rendered ineffective, and the often large gap between aspirations and achievements becomes more readily explicable.

Conclusion

From the above discussion, it will be apparent that sometimes "next generation" policy instruments that are not reflexive play an important role in policy making, and that where reflexive policy instruments are invoked, there is no guarantee of success. From here, the obvious next questions are: When is it likely that reflexive policy instruments have a comparative advantage? In what circumstances should instruments that fall within one or more of the five frameworks identified earlier, be preferred to other policy instruments? And how can they be designed and implemented to maximize their chances of success?

Certainly there are circumstances in which instruments that involve little or no reflexivity can effectively (and even efficiently) achieve the desired environmental outcomes, as with direct regulation and some economic instruments referred to above. But there are likely substantial limitations on the circumstances in which such instruments can appropriately be invoked. For example, financial assurances are generally effective, but only where there is just one source of potential environmental damage and where the damage can be reasonably estimated. Again, property rights approaches such as those advocated by free market economists tend to work best when there are only a small number of players and free rider problems are limited. And returning to "first generation" instruments, command and control remains a viable option to deal with large point source polluters, particularly where "one size fits all" (as for example, when a single appropriate environmental technology is available) but is not well suited to dealing with the cumulative pollution caused by a myriad of small- and medium-sized enterprises, or with diffuse source pollution.

The clue to the appropriate role of reflexive instruments may be that in all the above examples in which *un*reflexive approaches seem credible, the environmental challenge they address is a relatively straightforward one. But the more complex the challenge becomes (e.g., the greater the number of players, the higher the transactions costs, the larger the asymmetries of information between regulator and regulated) the less plausible it is to invoke such unreflexive policy instruments. As Fiorino (1999, 464) puts it: "the increased complexity, dynamism, diversity, and interdependence of contemporary society" requires more flexible, adaptive, and reflexive policy technologies and patterns of governance. Indeed, it is partly in response to the perceived shortcomings of many unreflexive policy options in this more challenging policy environment that each of these five conceptual frameworks described earlier evolved.

The greatest contribution of reflexive instruments in their various forms may be their capacity to achieve outcomes in circumstances that are beyond the capacity of other approaches to engage. Thus it is no coincidence that many of the examples provided in the second section of this chapter (where one or more of the five frames were invoked) concerned such challenging problems as regulating Major Hazard Facilities (where asymmetry of information between regulator and regulate is a major issue), natural resource management (e.g., multilevel governance challenges, multiple stakeholders, public goods problems, large geographical scale) or achieving shifts in technology and ecological modernization on an ambitious scale. Going further, Voß, Bauknecht, and Kemp (2006, ch. 1) suggest that system analysis and complexity, heterogeneous interactions, uncertainty, and path dependency are particular challenges that perhaps reflexive governance alone can address.

These conclusions raise two further questions: Which particular type of reflexive regulation is appropriate to which particular contexts; and should reflexive regulation be used in combinations with other, non-reflexive instruments, and if so, which ones?

The first question leads us back to the earlier discussion and analysis of five particular forms of reflexive regulation and governance. It will be apparent from the discussion in section two that each of these frameworks has something valuable to offer and none of them is "right" or "wrong" in the abstract. Rather, they make differing contributions depending upon the nature and context of the environmental policy issue to be addressed. Meta-regulation is demonstrably effective in dealing with complex technologies at individual identifiable enterprises, particularly when there is likely to be a substantial asymmetry of information between regulator and regulatee. Informational regulation has particular attraction in empowering civil society, which in turn operates as a surrogate regulator, and both the requirement on targeted enterprises to generate information and the subsequent pressure from civil society serve to stimulate reflexivity. New environmental governance is particularly geared to deal with problems involving (all or most of) the following: scientific uncertainty, challenges of scale and multilevel governance, public goods problems, multiple stakeholders, and uncertain solutions.

In terms of the second question, as an increasing number of commentators are coming to recognize (Stewart 2001, 133–134), there is no reason to assume that forms of reflexive regulation work best as "stand alone" policy instruments or as substitutes for other forms of regulation (although in some cases they do). There will certainly be circumstances where, consistent with the precepts of smart regulation, complementary combinations of policy instruments are likely to work better than individual policy instruments, with each instrument in the policy mix making a contribution that others cannot.

For example some forms of reflexive regulation are more likely to succeed if they are underpinned by direct regulation. Thus under process or meta-regulation, some enterprises may be tempted to develop "paper systems" and tokenistic responses that "independent" third-party auditors may fail to detect (O'Rourke 2000). However, the threat of sanctions if enterprises fail to deliver on performance targets set by the state will substantially reduce the risk of free riding. Again there is evidence that informational regulation does not necessarily replace traditional regulation and enforcement practices but rather that the two instruments work best when they are used in a complementary combination (Foulon, Lanouie, and Lapante 1999). Equally, emissions trading systems may be implemented in the context of technology requirements, thereby involving a combination of substantive and reflexive law. Having said this, it must be emphasized that not all combinations are complementary. Some indeed are counterproductive (Gunningham and Grabosky 1998, chap. 6).

Unfortunately, much of our knowledge about reflexive policy instruments and their relationship with other policy instruments, and in particular about what works and when, is tentative, contingent, and uncertain. Reflexive regulation scholarship has not yet been capable of specifying the conditions under which a reflexive process may succeed and whether such conditions can be affirmatively created. As De Schutter and Deakin (2005) point out, the key challenge for reflexive regulation is to identify exactly how and when law can apply procedural and reflexive mechanisms to catalyze changes in environmental behavior—and, we might add, in what combinations with other policy instruments.

Recognizing that there is still much we do not know, there is particular virtue in one form of reflexivity—adaptive learning, and in treating policies as experiments from which we can learn and which in turn can help shape the next generation of instruments.

But notwithstanding our limited knowledge, it should be emphasized that there may often be little choice but to persevere with forms of reflexive law. For example, "reliance on a firm's internal management controls [meta-regulation] to implement regulatory norms and objectives is inevitable; regulators have to rely on firms' ability to regulate themselves. They do not have the resources to do anything else." (Black 2006, 22). The reality may be that, notwithstanding its limitations, reflexive regulation still represents the best way forward, albeit that, where practicable, it should be complemented by other mechanisms.

This chapter has focused on reflexive regulation in the domestic sphere where the state, although in retreat, is far from being entirely "decentered." The central argument has been about the strengths and limitations of reflexivity rather than with how best to engage with public goods problems per se. But at least some of the insights provided by the five frameworks discussed earlier resonate with the challenges presented by global public goods in the international sphere—not least because the challenge of engaging with complexity is common to both spheres. There are also a number of other common threads. For example, the arguments that can be made in favor of a network model of decentralized global governance are in many respects similar to the arguments in favor of the new environmental governance at domestic level. And smart regulation, which recognizes that in dealing with complexity, *context specific* combinations of actors and instruments will work better than stand-alone solutions also has application to the context of global public goods. So too, ecological modernization's emphasis on the market rather than the state (think carbon trading) and on harnessing business as part of the solution rather than part of the problem (think the World Business Council for Sustainable Development) is as much an international as domestic application. Again, information regulation's concern with transparency and accountability is equally salient in the international sphere while process and meta-regulation are mechanisms that enable us to better think through the options for "regulating at a distance," particularly in circumstances where, given a disaggregation of power, public goods problems are particularly difficult to engage with. But these, like the related roles of reflexivity, are issues that will be explored in considerably greater depth in subsequent chapters.

6

Governance of the Research and Development Sector for Biotechnology: Intellectual Property Rights and Bioprospecting

Mare Sarr and Timothy Swanson

Bioprospecting is a form of research and development (R&D) used by pharmaceutical or biotechnology firms to find and collect natural compounds necessary for the development of new drugs. It requires cooperation between the bioprospecting firm and the community hosting the genetic resources and/or traditional knowledge. The host community provides basic or pure information on potential solution concepts, while the R&D firm supplies the practical capabilities for developing these solution concepts into marketable compounds and products. In this manner, primary biological information is generated and channeled through a secondary R&D sector to become commercial products capable of addressing consumer needs.

An important issue concerns the nature of the governance mechanism that should manage the production of innovation within this R&D sector. One possibility is for the sector to operate by means of intellectual property rights (IPR) and contracting. In this setup, each stage of the R&D sector is incentivized by reason of property rights, and then coordination and transfers between them are managed by means of contracts. The difficulty in this situation is in providing adequate incentives at appropriate levels for a service as complex as joint R&D. Information production is difficult to compensate correctly, and the development of multiple property rights and contracts regarding them is a complicated endeavor.

The current arrangement in this industry is indicative of the complexity of the problem. Current laws usually provide for a single property right at the secondary stage of R&D, and thus require contracting between the two independent entities. That is, most current IPR regimes fail to recognize the rights of producers of primary information in this area (often termed "traditional knowledge"), but will recognize rights in innovative products developed out of this primary information. Thus, the bioprospecting firm will be able to claim intellectual property rights in the pharmaceuticals or plant varieties it markets, but the community that produces the original information or genetic resource will have no rights of any kind to either initial information or final product.

This approach is particularly problematic as it requires that the downstream firm contract with its predecessor for the provision of the correct amount of information (about biological activity or distinctive genetic resource). This places a lot of emphasis upon the capabilities of the upstream firm for the creation of downstream incentive mechanisms. In addition, this firm must attempt to achieve this efficient information production via arms-length contracting. This is a difficult problem in mechanism design. How can a downstream firm generate incentives for upstream entities to develop information it might use when it has little knowledge regarding its production or little capacity to restrict competing producers? (Other primary producers of the same information will be able to compete away the rents of the first innovator, irrespective of the contract.) This problem requires something more on the order of a state governance mechanism than a bilateral contract.

If the state does not act, what can the upstream firm do? When contractual complexity becomes too great, there may be incentives to integrate the two entities à la Coase's transactions cost theory of the firm (Coase 1937). Under this theory, governance is best accomplished by the vertical structure that is best able to minimize the costs of transaction within the vertical industry. If the transaction costs are too great when operating independently, the separate stages of the industry should vertically integrate (Williamson 1985). The upstream user of information would then apply its property-right mechanism directly to the purpose of generating primary information.

In this chapter we set out our analysis of the bioprospecting industry within this framework. Its aim is to contribute through an in-depth case study to the analysis of the complex impact of market incentives on GPG provision, in the specific case of using intellectual property as an incentive for generating investment in research based on in situ and ex situ biodiversity. It adds to the analysis of the effect of monetary incentives in chapter 5, however, by showing how information asymmetries might modify the equity of the resulting outcomes. We observe the costliness and inefficiency of attempting to coordinate the industry under existing rights structures and explore the means for integration. We find that the introduction of a second property right at the primary stage is necessary to provide the basis for integrating the two sectors into a single integrated entity. Although this property right is critical to achieving efficient integration in the industry, it does not appear that it will impact upon the distribution of benefits significantly. For this reason, a second property right and integration within the industry is probably more important for efficiency reasons than it is for equity.

Economic Analysis of Cumulative Innovation

We have already suggested that bioprospecting is best viewed as an example of information production, in which the first stage generates pure or primary information and the second stage develops this into a marketable (and patentable) product. This manner of interaction between the primary and secondary stages of an R&D industry is a good fit with the cumulative research framework developed within the industrial organization literature in economic theory, in which abstract basic research is built upon by developers to generate concrete innovations. (Scotchmer 1996; Green and Scotchmer 1995). In this section we wish to set out the general implications of this literature for the management of R&D in this biotechnology sector.

R&D Governance and Bioprospecting
The industrial organization literature has analyzed the cumulative nature of innovation and its implications for the design of intellectual property rights policy. Emphasis there is placed on giving first-stage innovators adequate incentives to invest and innovate, because no inventions or discovery would be possible without their contribution. It is therefore argued that first innovators should be protected via patents while the second innovator can be denied patent protection if licensing can be relied upon (Green and Scotchmer 1995). It is striking that in practice in the biological sector, the opposite result has obtained. Only the secondary stage of the research process is granted property rights protection in this sector, while the primary traditional stage is left unrewarded despite its crucial contribution to innovation. This raises two problems, one of efficiency and one of equity.

First, if traditional knowledge is not protected, it may first remain unknown and then may even become lost forever, which would lead to a relatively lower rate of innovation and therefore reduced levels of social welfare. Secondly, in this particular area of R&D, there is a North-South (or distributional) aspect to the I/O problem as well as an efficiency aspect. This is because we can assume here that the R&D firm will nearly always come from the stylized "North" (where the North is possessed of unique technological capability as well as access to important markets). In contrast, the stylized "South" can be assumed to be uniquely possessed of rich stocks of genetic resources and accumulated traditional knowledge (know-how, remedies, practices), without access to technological capability to develop marketable or patentable products.

Because the patent system exclusively rewards the North for its innovation, despite the South's undeniable contribution, concern about a fair division of benefits has led some observers to make the case for protecting genetic resource owners or traditional knowledge owners with intellectual property rights. In this chapter, we set out to explore the questions of the number and placement of patents within the entire vertical industry (i.e., the suppliers of genetic resources as well as the manufacturers). In particular we wish to examine how the creation of additional property rights might help to enable the transformation of this sequential, diverse, and divisive industry into one that might instead be unitary, integrated, and efficient. What would this transformation look like? How would it occur?

Innovation and the Internalization of Information Externalities

The economic rationale for granting property rights to innovations was first explained by Nelson (1959) and Arrow (1962). Their argument proceeds as follows. Because innovation or knowledge is a public good (non rival and non-excludable), it is likely to be undersupplied as its social value exceeds its private value. A mechanism ensuring that positive externalities are internalized is therefore necessary. The implementation of an intellectual property rights regime is one such mechanism. By granting a temporary monopoly over the use and exploitation of an innovation, intellectual property regimes give innovators the incentive to invest by ensuring that they capture part of the social value they have generated. However, the creation of such a property right is only one means for internalizing the externalities of information production. When there are several entities cooperating in the production of information, one possibility for governance is the use of property rights and contracting while another possibility is integration and internal coordination.

Earlier economic analysis considered R&D innovations as a stand-alone process; that is, innovations were not based to any important extent on preexisting research. However, in many instances information is passed down through a chain of innovators as it is processed toward marketability. For example, it is not uncommon for some entities to be specialized in basic research while others are focused on the development of products based upon the primary knowledge supplied by the former. Thus, the end product results from the accumulation of information across both stages of these types of R&D industries.

An important problem noted in the sequential research literature is that, when innovation is sequential, early innovators in a nonintegrated vertical industry may lack the incentive to invest if they do not hold a distinct property right (Scotchmer 1996). This point, raised earlier, is fundamental in the literature and indicative of the presumption in favor of primary property rights in sequential R&D. In the context of bioprospecting, this would imply the addition of a second property right within the industry, as a clear right exists to innovations occurring at the secondary stage.

This raises another important issue regarding the efficiency of the governance structure. If both innovators are granted patents and continue to operate independently, then the double monopoly distortion within the vertical industry may induce a welfare loss. When successive monopolies operate in the same vertical industry, the impact is to impose successive margins within the chain of production. This implies distortions to efficient resource allocation, even greater than those emanating from a single monopoly (Graham and Vernon 1971). This distortion would create incentives for closer coordination or integration.

To this point we have argued that the current governance structure is inefficient, since contracting upstream to create information-generation mechanisms is usually not possible. A second property right at the primary stage might enable better incentives at that stage, but at the cost of double distortions within the vertical sector. These considerations indicate that integration within the industry is the likely way forward for incentivizing information production at both levels. Integration would enable full coordination in information production, and in revenue generation, so there would be no need for multiple distortions.

The question now concerns how integration could proceed. On what basis would efficient integration occur, and how would each level be compensated to create incentives for efficient information generation?

We will investigate how property rights in bioprospecting can and will determine the outcome of negotiations over the structure of this industry. In particular, we wish to ask how the recognition of a second property right in the primary stage of R&D in bioprospecting and the willingness of the courts in the North to enforce it might impact upon the efficiency and equity impacts of the creation of a unitary, integrated industrial structure for R&D.

Economics of Cumulative Research in Biotech

In this section we wish to demonstrate how the property right (and judicial) framework determines how the successive levels of R&D might be integrated. We wish to use this framework to assess both the efficiency and the distributional implications of governance within this R&D sector.

Informational Assumptions behind the Modeling of the Industry

Traditional Knowledge as Tacit Information   Gehl Sampath (2005) argues that biological information may be viewed on a continuum from highly uncodified (or tacit information) to highly codified (tangible information). The codified information represents information processed by the biological sector with the view to develop a marketable end product. Biotechnology or pharmaceutical companies commonly use basic information as input for further research. For example, it is not uncommon for small- and medium-sized biotechnology firms to act as suppliers of information to larger firms that process the final product. The supply of traditional knowledge to these R&D firms may play a similar role as the provision of tacit information. Biotechnology and pharmaceutical companies, through bioprospecting, may attempt to identify new principles or approaches for curing existing diseases. A particular plant or fungus might contain an active ingredient that gives a clue or an idea on how to initiate new lines of research (Swanson 1995). On the other hand, traditional knowledge accumulated over the centuries may be particularly useful in the screening process for potential inputs and may help increase the rate of discovery while decreasing substantially the research costs required to make it (Rausser and Small 2000). There is substantial evidence that traditional knowledge makes a significant contribution to the innovation process (Evenson and Gollin 1998). Thus, both flows of biological information and stocks of previously accumulated information can be important parts of the R&D process. For instance, the rosy periwinkle from Madagascar—traditionally used for treating diabetes—was used by the pharmaceutical manufacturer Eli Lilly to develop two anticancer drugs, vincristine (against childhood leukemia) and vinblastine (against Hodgkin's disease). The drugs ensured Eli Lilly annual sales of more than $100 million by

1985 (Farnsworth 1988) and more than \$180 million by 1997 (Hunter 1997). Similarly, the tranquilizer reserpine is derived from the Asian rauwolfia plant—traditionally used in Southeast Asia to treat mental health disorders and snakebites. Its annual market was estimated at \$260 million (Kloppenburg 1991).

Vertical Structure of the R&D Industry   From these assumptions on the nature of the informational flows within this sector, we model the R&D industry (in the biological sector) as a nonintegrated vertical industry of two stages. In the primary stage, a flow of information (originating within the natural environment and requiring a diverse stock of natural capital—namely land) is captured by virtue of investment in traditional human capital—in settings where human populations interact with the natural environment through observation and selection. The combination of the two factors results in a primary sector output of pure information. In the next stage of this vertical industry, the secondary stage biological R&D process collects these informational flows (from the primary R&D stage), and invests in physical and human capital (laboratory equipment and scientists) to produce innovations—new products designed to meet consumers' wants and needs.

Definitions: Regions, Endowments, Efficiency

The current property rights regime rewards only the North and fails to reward the South. This chapter addresses the distribution problem and suggests a possible way to allow the South to be rewarded for its contribution within the vertical industry. Economic theory posits that the most efficient way to do that is to let the two parties integrate and then protect the whole industry and let them share the joint profit. Efficiency here is considered from the producer point of view only. However, the sharing of profit is also of importance. Is it more efficient to grant the property right either to the North or to the South? What is the optimal breadth? How is the division of profit affected?

Industrial Structure of the Economy   Consider an economy populated by two agents in the South and North, specialized in two different sectors. The South is endowed with genetic capital and has a comparative advantage in the production of pure information (R). The North is endowed with human capital and has a comparative advantage in developing innovations (D) based on information (R). In the first stage of the R&D industry, the South produces pure information (R). The combination of this information

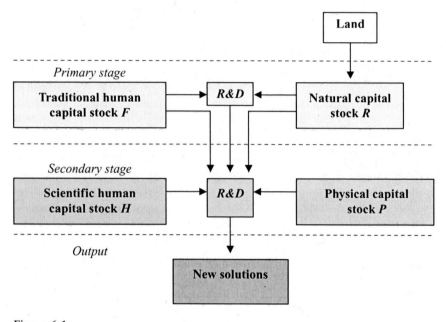

Figure 6.1
R&D stages in the biological sector

with the human capital from the North results in the second-stage innovation (D) incorporating (R). The innovation (D) is able to be patented and is consumed by individuals to generate welfare.

For example, we can think of an industry in which the South produces an herbal medicine that has natural curative properties. In such industry, the information encapsulated within the herbal medicine is extracted and used by the pharmaceutical or biotechnology firms from the North to develop new drugs as (D). The issues we address here relate to how well the North and South cooperate in this R&D industry, and how they share the benefits. The North might or might not compensate the South for the information used to develop (D). Then the South might compete with the North by attempting to develop and market the herb (integration into D).

We now wish to define the efficiency objective for an industry of this nature.

Proposition 1   From the perspective of the producers North and South, the first best solution requires a single property right, complete specialization, and a joint venture.

In a vertical industry, it is well-known that integration brings efficiency from the producer's point of view since the joint profit is maximized. By forming a joint venture North and South integrate into a single entity able to develop new products using the comparative expertise of both partners. A single property right is then sufficient to protect the innovations made by this entity. Besides, given the complementarity of the two partners, comparative advantage will dictate full specialization within the joint venture.

Any departure from the conditions stated in proposition 1 results in loss of efficiency. The allocation of two property rights in the vertical industry leads to the problem of multiple distortionary IPR regimes, and possibly to double marginalization that decreases the joint profit. In addition, competition erodes the profit of each party. An all-out competition at both stages of the industry is even more wasteful from the producers' perspective: not only does it reduce each profit, it also causes a large loss of specialization since North and South invest in the sector where they have no comparative advantage. The opportunity cost of such behavior is therefore particularly high. This case represents the worst possible outcome for the producers.

Institutional Status Quo   We now wish to describe the status quo ante in which the IPR system protects innovations developed by firms in the North but fails to protect information from genetic resources held by communities in the South.

Proposition 2   If there is a single property right at the development level D and no property right is available in the information R, then either (a) the North uses information R at price of zero resulting in lack of investment in R; or (b) the South invests in sector D, which results in a loss of comparative advantage.

In short, in the absence of a well-formulated property right in R, either there is little incentive to invest in the production of R or there is a loss of comparative advantage. This implies that the first best cannot be attained by the current status quo property right regime.

Now, the purpose of our chapter is to contrast the status quo with the case where a property right in R is afforded to the South. We examine the potential for this to achieve the first best and explore the implications for the division of surplus in that instance.

A Model a of Second Property Right in the R&D Industry

In this section we now establish the means by which the establishment of a property right in R together with a procedure for its enforcement determines the prospects for efficient integration and benefit sharing.

Description of the Game

We use a game theoretical framework in which three players interact:

- North whose actions are (offer contract, invest, not invest, license if infringement, compete if no infringement).
- South whose actions are (accept, reject, license if infringement, compete if no infringement)
- Court that decides upon infringement of D

The sequence of the decisions and the interaction between the players is as follows:

1. As the first mover, the North offers the South to integrate and gives a share of the joint profit.
2. The South decides:
   (a) to accept the offer, then they form a joint venture that is able to make innovation using both R and D
   (b) or to reject the offer and makes use of its property right on R.
3. The North decides:
   (a) not to invest and the game is over
   (b) or to invest in which case the Court has to intervene.
4. The makes an enforceable decision upon infringement based on the breadth of the property right.
   (a) in case of infringement the North needs a license to market the new product
   (b) if there is no infringement North and South compete.

Specification of the Model

Suppose the South is granted a property right protecting its traditional knowledge, and suppose that the North has an idea to develop a new product using this information. Since the North needs the knowledge from the South, it offers the South to integrate by forming a joint venture, against the payment of a royalty on the joint profit. If the ex ante negotiation succeeds then a joint venture is formed and will

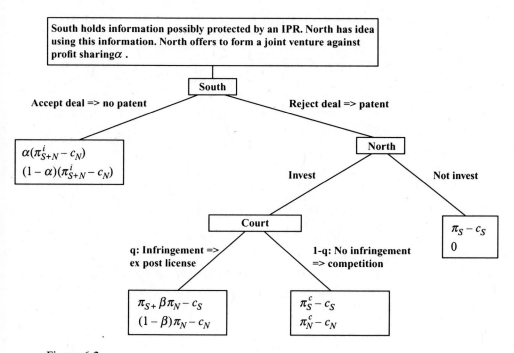

Figure 6.2
Game tree

develop a new product that can be patented. The South receives a payoff:

$$\Pi_S^i = \alpha(\pi_{N+S}^i - c_N)$$

and the North receives:

$$\Pi_N^i = (1 - \alpha)(\pi_{N+S}^i - c_N)$$

where π_{N+S}^i is the integrated joint monopoly revenue earned by the joint venture, α is the share of profit offered by the North, and c_N is the total development costs incurred by the North given the South has exclusively revealed its information.

However, if the ex ante agreement fails, the South will patent its traditional knowledge. The North has to decide whether or not to invest in research and development given that information is diffused via the property right held by the South. If the North decides to invest, then a court decides whether it infringes the right, in which case an ex post license is required. If the North does not infringe then its innovation is patented and competes with the South. Following Green and Scotchmer (1995), we formalize the product developed by the North as being of quality d. The breadth of the original property right of the South r^* is defined as the minimum improvement required to avoid infringement. Provided $d > r^*$ the North does not infringe. The North infringes with probability q, and does not infringe with probability $1 - q$. The South receives an expected profit equal to:

$$\Pi_S^{ni} = q(\pi_S + \beta\pi_N) + (1 - q)\pi_S^c - c_S$$

and the North expected profit is:

$$\Pi_N^{ni} = q(1 - \beta)\pi_N + (1 - q)\pi_N^c - c_N$$

Note that β is the share of the North profit captured by the South through ex post licensing.

In contrast if the North decides not to invest in the research at all, the South receives a profit of $\pi_S - c_S$ and the North gets nothing.

Further assumptions:

(1) The joint revenue when there is a joint venture is larger than the non-integrated profit in the whole industry: $\pi_{N+S}^i \geq \pi_N + \pi_S = \pi_{N+S}^{ni}$

(2) Competition erodes the revenue of both parties: $\pi_S^c < \pi_S$ and $\pi_N^c < \pi_N$.

(3) Investment increases the overall profit in the vertical industry, i.e., $\pi_S^c - c_S + \pi_N^c - c_N \geq \pi_S - c_S$, which implies that $\pi_N^c - c_N \geq \pi_S - \pi_S^c > 0$.

Equilibrium When the South Provides Information of Equal Quality

We will now examine the basic nature of the outcome of this setup, given that the members of the bargaining entity South always offer information of the same quality. This allows us to derive a unique outcome to this bargaining situation, in which an integrated entity will result in making use of a single property right, and sharing profits in a uniquely determined manner.

Proposition 3 In an industry where the North and the South each possess important information for the production of successive innovations, if the South provides information of equal quality and transaction costs are low, then there is a unique equilibrium involving profit sharing through a joint venture where the South obtains a share α^* of the joint profit. This equilibrium reaches the first best and requires the existence of a single property right allocated to the joint venture.

First, note that because the assumption that investment increases the industry profit implies that $\pi_N^c - c_N$, there cannot be an equilibrium in which the North does not invest. In our setup, the North has the first move and proposes to the South a contract that maximizes its own profit subject to the South participation constraint.

The problem of the North is:

$$\max_{\alpha} (1 - \alpha)(\pi_{N+S}^i - c_N)$$
$$s.t. \quad \alpha(\pi_{N+S}^i - c_N) \geq q[\pi_S + \beta\pi_N] + (1 - q)\pi_S^c - c_S$$

In equilibrium, the participation constraint is binding. If that were not the case then the North could slightly decrease α, satisfy the constraint and increase its profit. This contradicts the fact that we are in the equilibrium. Therefore the participation constraint must be binding. We then obtain:

$$\alpha^* = \frac{q[\pi_S + \beta\pi_N] + (1 - q)\pi_S^c - c_S}{\pi_{N+S}^i - c_N}$$

The North chooses a profit share α^* that gives the South the rent that makes it indifferent between accepting and rejecting the offer contingent on the breadth of the original property right. As a result, the North captures the entire surplus generated by the joint venture. This is due, under our assumptions, to the North's current (and ongoing) control over the rights to the important final markets for the product. This control determines the basis upon which the entities bargain over integration, and give the North the unique ability to offer the terms on which integration may proceed.

Then, when the quality of the information held by the South is homogeneous, a joint venture is formed along the terms offered by the North. Note that when the joint venture is formed, the South reveals its information exclusively to its partner. Both North and South specialize according to their comparative advantage to produce a new product protected by a property right, which induces a single monopoly pricing. Hence, this vertical integration achieves the first best outcome for the producers.[1]

Distributional Considerations

We have seen that the North and South immediately agree to integrate their information-generating processes into a single R&D sector. We have also seen that there is a unique equilibrium in this framework, in which the North pays the South the amount required for its participation within the integrated firm. There are several important factors that determine the amount that the South will receive.

First, the court plays an important role in the determination of the magnitude of profit sharing because it makes decisions regarding infringement. In other words the decision of the court determining the breadth of the property rights determines the distribution of benefits between North and South. The share of profit offered to the South is related to the probability of infringement. The North has to pay license fees to the South, only if the latter decides to reject the former's offer and the court enforces its rights.

Because of the uniqueness of the equilibrium (which is also efficient), the informational rights of the South can be substantially protected without inducing any loss of efficiency. Therefore, the maximum share received by the South (α^{*S}) in this framework is where the property right is very broad; that is, where $r^* \to \infty$, or equivalently the probability of infringement $q \to 1$.

$$\alpha^{*S}(i.e. \quad at \quad q=1) = \frac{\pi_S + \beta\pi_N - c_S}{\pi_{N+S}^i - c_N}$$

Moreover, the larger the outside option—the profit obtained by the South by patenting (the larger π_S, β or π_N and smaller c_S)—the larger α will be. In addition, because the outside option value to the South is fixed, a greater joint venture profit (larger π_{N+S}^i and smaller c_N) will lead to a lower *share* of the profit for the South. This implies that the more efficient integration is relative to nonintegration (in terms of enhanced profitability), the more inequitable profit sharing becomes. This clearly shows that a second property right addresses the distributional issues only to an extent. Although the South's right enables efficiency to emerge, it may benefit little from the outcome. It gets some reward through the assignment of a broad patent ensuring the highest possible profit, but it does not earn much of the surplus generated by the integration this helps to achieve.

Proposition 4   The optimal share of profit offered to the South (a) increases in the South's outside option; and (b) decreases with the joint venture profit. Because of (a) the initial patent granted to the South for its information R must be very broad to enable any profit sharing by the South. Despite this improvement the sharing involves payment to the South only that amount required to secure its participation (i.e., the amount of the value of its outside option) and the North receives any residual.

Conclusion

This chapter has surveyed the considerations important for determining the efficient governance structure for successive R&D in the biotechnology sector. We have argued that multiple property rights and contracting mechanisms are probably inappropriate in this context, due to the complexity of information generation at successive levels. For this reason we have focused on the idea of an integrated vertical industry, in which both levels of R&D coordinate carefully within a single entity. We have examined here how the introduction of a second property right might be capable of generating this integrated outcome, and what would determine the precise nature of that outcome.

In order to do this, the chapter analyzes a simple model of the interactions between North and South in relation to traditional knowledge and bioprospecting. Here we have assumed that the North is rich in human capital but needs essential genetic resources and knowledge that are available only in the South—in order to generate innovations in the biological sector. We use the cumulative research framework developed in the industrial organization literature to examine the possibility of assigning a property right to the basic information held by the South. In doing so, we investigate whether this can achieve efficiency and discuss the implications for the division of the profit. We find that such a move is efficient from the producers' perspective because it is conducive to integration and therefore to the maximization of the joint profit.

However, although there may be improvement (compared to the current status quo) when the South is afforded broad protection of its property rights, the benefit sharing still largely favors the North. Indeed the latter captures all the surplus generated by the efficient outcome although the South has contributed to the emergence of the first best. This is due to the fact that the North retains control over the final markets and marketing of the product, and hence remains in control of the bargaining framework for integrating the two producers.

In conclusion, the governance mechanism appropriate in this context requires careful coordination between successive levels of R&D. The definition of a second property right in primary R&D may be an important step toward making efficient integration possible, and thus achieving efficient governance. Such a property right is more important for efficiency reasons than it is for equity purposes.

Notes

We wish to acknowledge support from the EU RefGov Programme in the undertaking of this research. We are grateful to the following individuals for the comments they provided: Tom Dedeurwaredere, Erwin Bulte, Christine Frison, Zhou Jidong, participants in various RefGov and BioEcon workshops, and three anonymous reviewers.

1. It is nevertheless important to note that such an outcome can occur only if transaction costs are low enough; that is, if the benefits of information revelation from the first innovator exceed the costs of bargaining.

III

Compliance: From Legal Tools to Moral Norms

This third part of the book addresses the role of informal compliance measures, such as social norms, moral pressure, and long-term change in core policy beliefs. Addressing global public good provision at regional and transnational levels necessitates a departure from the more formal instruments of the state. Sovereign states have their own agendas and can be constrained by short-term electoral politics, which explains why they are often reluctant to comply with cooperative agreements on GPGs that only provide diffuse, long-term benefits. The chapter by Godard shows that the voice of worldwide citizen movements and the threat of a loss of moral standing in the international debate provide a way to influence national decision making on sustainable development issues. Another means of putting pressure on states exploits the opportunities offered by the multilevel governance system. As Borges, Walter, and Rey show, the multilevel climate regime offers innovative ways to bypass the conventional and often over-formalized rule making of the state. This can be done, for instance, by building regional policy networks for taking local initiatives, or by directly integrating regional activities with initiatives at the international level. The main effect of these informal mechanisms is to enrich the toolbox of measures for implementing international agreements. These lessons for compliance are also in line with the more general message (developed in the first part of the book) on the importance of including both state and non-state actors in the provision of global public goods.

In some cases the change in social norms is based on a long-term change in core policy beliefs. The chapter by Feindt contributes to the already well-established literature in this field, by showing how the learning process on core beliefs is influenced by the interrelatedness of various global public goods. Many collective goods are overlapping. By acting on the provision of one, the provision of other GPGs may also be improved. This was clearly established in the chapter by Sandler in the first part. Feindt's chapter nicely shows that this leads to interactions in the social learning processes between different sectoral policies that deal with interrelated public goods. An example is the case of the common agricultural policy in the EU, which for a long time was dedicated to increasing productivity. Now, through long-term changes in policy in the European Commission, it plays an increasing part in environmental policy. The interrelatedness of the GPGs provides an interesting way of analyzing the fact that concepts of public goods and their provision systems change over time.

7

Managing Global Risks through "Proportionate" Precaution: The Interplay between States, Civil Society, and International Regulation

Olivier Godard

Among the risk management concepts that the twenty-first century inherited from the last two decades of the twentieth , the precautionary principle (PP) has been an especially critical breakthrough. The concept was first introduced in the 1980s and has been built incrementally into environmental law ever since. In spite of undeniable achievements, the status of the PP as a tool for tackling major environmental issues of global scope remains surprisingly weak. This is due in part to the temptation by many to rely on a less legally-demanding precautionary approach (PA); but more fundamental and problematic explanations are also involved. In fact, the meaning of the PP has been critically ambivalent: even when it has gained recognition in the international arena, it has often been called upon as a means to reinforce sovereign unilateral decisions of states and claim exceptions from previously agreed international rules. This is a far cry from the expectation that the PP instead would enhance coordination of international action in the spirit of the conventions adopted in Rio in 1992 regarding climate change and biodiversity.

This evolution points to the fact that in the international arena, the PP exhibits the contradiction inherent in the current status of international governance—between, on the one hand, international regulations called for by global and urgent environmental issues, and on the other hand, institutions that bear political responsibility for managing risks and ensuring the safety of their citizens (i.e., nation-states.) As risks turn ever more threatening, although science cannot fully ascertain their scope, origins, or consequences, states increasingly resort to their sovereign authority to confront them and prove reluctant to commit to binding international agreements, in spite of apparent pronouncements to the contrary. Thus the PA-PP, though conceived in the initial phase as a means to promote early collective action even in the absence of scientific certainty, paradoxically tends to hinder progress in international efforts toward the global regulations that are most needed—for example, climate change. If anything, in the current phase the concept contributes to collective failure in the face of global threats: in an economist's jargon, a very inefficient "Nash equilibrium."

This chapter aims to explore this contradiction and the ways in which it can be overcome, then bringing about a "third phase" in the history of the PP concept. We envision two main routes that would enable us to do so. The first is to strengthen global environmental governance by increasing legal enforcement mechanisms and the democratic legitimacy of dedicated international organizations, with an uncertain outcome (Held 1995; Dahl 1999a; Keohane 2006). Alternatively, we could bet on a longer feedback loop based on the transformation of international market mechanisms on the premise that business, under the actual or potential pressure of NGOs and consumers, will push for new environmental standards regarding the quality of goods and will regard their implementation as a precondition for inclusion in trade flows. These two options are not mutually exclusive. In fact, real progress will likely occur when both directions are explored jointly (Karkkainen 2004) or through alternative phases: although market pressures can usefully complement interstate relations for a while, they can only be deeply effective provided states come eventually to agree on new rules of the game for all competitors.

Climate change is a case in point. Voluntary commitments from the business community have been triggered by the prospect of a new international public regime for the carbon economy; when interstate cooperation seemingly reaches an impasse, initiatives from business, NGOs, and local governments provide a way out and put additional pressure on nation-states. But voluntary action of business cannot become the primary channel to achieve appropriate worldwide regulation of global greenhouse gas (GHG) emissions: due to economic competition, private initiatives will have difficulties to overcome limitations raised by incompleteness of the climate regime and poor enforcement of commitments or agreements.

The focus on the precautionary principle allows revisiting the important debate on the governance of global risks that lay at the basis of the historical concept of reflexive governance proposed by Ulrich Beck (1992, 1994), and which was further developed in his work on cosmopolitan citizenship (2007). The framework of cosmopolitan citizenship fails however to catch the strong link between issues of management of collective risks and sovereignty of nation-states and to address the important influence of national collective preferences in the debate around the implementation of the precautionary principle, as can be seen in the conflicts over the regulation of genetically modified organisms and growth hormones in bovines between the European Union (EU) and the United States, for example. Therefore, the analysis in this chapter, while building upon the work on new modes of legitimacy in the global context, aims to broaden the debate on reflexive governance as understood by Beck through including layers of governance that allow the expression of national and regional collective preferences regarding global risks by citizen and consumer movements.

The first section lays out the basic EU doctrine of the PP to prevent common confusions between the PP and a principle of abstention that asks to forbid an activity or a technology every time there are scientific doubts on possible impacts on health and the environment (Godard 1997, 2006; Godard et al. 2002). This principle of abstention seems to have been dignified by the 1998 Wingspread Statement on the Precautionary Principle in the United States (Raffensperger and Ticknell 1999), which introduced much confusion in the U.S.-EU dialogue on the PP. The second section goes back to the basic contradiction that we have identified in the PP concept regarding its international status. The third explores the implications of national collective preferences for the implementation of international trade laws and explains why the PP is affected by collective preferences. The fourth section considers recent trends that have expanded the meaning of "quality of commodities" in commercial transactions, to include social conditions of production and environmental impacts at all stages of the production chain. This evolution has challenged the traditional distinction between processes and products which used to restrain the legitimate perimeter of state intervention under World Trade Organization (WTO) rules, thereby affecting traditional limits of direct interstate relations. Before concluding, the fifth section underlines the need to develop a new, hybrid notion of sovereignty, combining bottom-up and top-down sources of legitimacy, such as will promote the development of new forms of public concern and political accountability in the management of global environmental risks.

The True Meaning of the Precautionary Principle

Historical Landmarks
Notable years in the development of the PP include 1992, with the Earth Summit in Rio de Janeiro and the Maastricht Treaty that created the

European Union; and 2000, when several EU bodies made crucial doc-
trinal contributions to the effort, such as the Communication on the
Precautionary Principle by the European Commission, and a Resolution
on the Precautionary Principle adopted by the European Council held in
Nice in December of that year.

Inclusion of the concept in domestic law has varied among regions
worldwide. The European Union clearly has been at the forefront of
efforts to incorporate the PP into law, since the PP has been turned into
a legal norm for environmental protection as early as 1992. Later on,
EU regulation of food safety in 2002 confirmed the relevance of the PP
in the field of public health and food safety, following 1998 legal decisions by the European Court of Justice in the specific context of the BSE
(bovine spongiform encephalopathy or "mad cow disease") crisis. In
October 2003 this court enshrined the PP as a general principle of European law (in the Solvay case).

France underwent a similar process from ad hoc to general recognition
of the concept. In an initial phase, the PP was first acknowledged in 1995
by Law # 95-101, aimed at enhancing environmental protection; but it
was endowed with direct constitutional validity in 2005, when it was
written into a major article of the new Environmental Charter that laid
out rights and duties of the public and government in this respect.

By contrast, international law has been slower at recognizing the PP
(Kiss and Shelton 2000). Outside Europe, many countries still appear
reluctant to give it legal force, although core ideas in the PP are in some
way echoed in the WTO sanitary and phytosanitary (SPS) agreement, as
well as the current implementation of WTO rules (Noiville 2000; McDonald 2006). Therefore, in the international arena, the PP has been watered
down into a "precautionary approach".

What the PP Is and Is Not

According to the European public doctrine, the PP does not claim that
any technology whose potential environmental impact is merely unclear
should be forbidden. As a general principle, it does not reverse the burden
of proof, meaning that it does not require that the absence of any short-
or long-term risk be established before a technology can be approved.

Reversing burden of proof or not is, in fact, one crucial difference
between the PP and the "principle of abstention," with which it is sometimes mistakenly confused. Arguments in favor of abstention before risk
are often adduced from the work of the German philosopher Hans Jonas
(1984), who talked of an "Imperative of Responsibility" that impels

present generations to preserve the ultimate possibility of maintaining physically and morally a human life on Earth. For Jonas, this would imply absolutely avoiding any risk of giving birth to potentially apocalyptic courses, whatever the envisaged benefits. Although many premises of Jonas's thinking are undeniably relevant, the conclusion he reached with respect to judicious management of risks suffers from logical inconsistency (Godard et al. 2002): it is impossible to prove of anything that it will not cause *any* "apocalyptic" or even "harmful" effects whatsoever now or in the future. It is equally impossible to draw practically at an early stage a clear-cut distinction between "apocalyptic" and "non-apocalyptic" kinds of risks. This apocalyptic vision of the PP has not been adopted by the U.S. authorities since "the precautionary principle as an independent legal concept is not applied in the United States" (Zander 2010) , has been rightly rejected by scholars like Cass Sunstein (2005), and is at odds with EU doctrine.

The PP's essential contribution is to call upon authorities to take potential hazards into account as early as possible. The main innovation is to promote a change in the timing of risk management: public authorities should not wait for full scientific evidence before considering control of a suspected threat to public health or environmental quality. Then the leading concept that must inform all precautionary measures is *proportionality*, which involves an assessment of four sorts of variables: (a) the level of safety that should be reached by technologies and products according to stated collective values and policy goals; (b) the extent of potential damage that can be anticipated through various scenarios in the present state of our incomplete knowledge, which leaves room for lingering uncertainty; (c) the direct and opportunity costs of the various precautionary measures that can be envisaged, including the option to do nothing; (d) the weight of scientific work and evidence supporting the plausibility of hypotheses that there may indeed be significant risks.

The shift in timing that the PP brings, in turn, affects the profile of preventive actions. In fact authorities can choose among a large range of measures, from specific research programs and information dissemination to economic incentives (taxes or emission trading), partial restrictions of use, suspension of an authorization, and ultimately pure and simple bans. Moreover, while the PP calls for early intervention, this is balanced by the notion that initial decisions must be seen as temporary and flexible, so they can be revised as new evidence and information comes to light. Specifically, the PP calls for sustained scientific monitoring of technologies and products that it has provisionally authorized based on the current state of scientific knowledge. Experience-based information feedback and dedicated research are therefore crucial components in its implementation.

The Use of the Precautionary Principle and Approach in International Affairs

Use of the PP in international relations has been strangely ambivalent. On the one hand, it has been instrumental in major advances in international cooperation, such as the main agreements and texts adopted by the international community at the Earth Summit held in Rio de Janeiro in June 1992.

On the other hand, the PP has also been used to suspend previously agreed international rules, specifically trade rules. A typical case is the dispute between the EU and the United States and other countries regarding imports into the EU of beef produced with growth-enhancing hormones. Such measures have been justified by potential threats to human or animal health, even though science had yet to reach a final verdict on the nature and scale of these threats at the time the decisions were initially made. In this and other cases, the PP has been used as a means to justify sovereign unilateral judgments; that is, to claim exemption from agreed international trade rules. In fact, the disputing parties initiated legal procedures, an action that makes it clear that no internationally agreed framework for use of the PP as a risk management tool was actually in existence. The PP, rather than bringing about more harmonious international governance, can actually turn into a wedge that splits international relations asunder.

In this context, the Cartagena Protocol on Biosafety (January 2000) is especially interesting, because it combines both uses of the PP. The Protocol develops organizational means to improve international exchange of information regarding risks related to the dissemination of living modified organisms (LMOs). At the same time it defines agreed procedures and conditions under which states can protect their border through unilateral measures that derogate from ordinary rules of trade for this specific class of goods. Some have claimed this agreement as a victory for the PA, as the protocol enables a country to block imports of specific LMOs on the basis of alleged potential risks that are not yet confirmed by scientific investigations. However, it is doubtful whether this provision is in fact the best possible way to preserve biodiversity on Earth—which is a crucial goal of the convention that produced the

Protocol. We could have expected the PP to found the creation of a new, integrated regime for preserving biodiversity hot spots and set a common management of the issue of LMOs. On the contrary, the PP in fact has been turned into a concession to sovereign national preferences within the system ruling international trade.

It is clear, then, that the counterintuitive tendency for nation-states to use the PP to enhance or reaffirm their right to sovereign unilateral measures is not a one-off aberration, but a trend: the PP has become the toy for legitimizing unilateral judgments and actions. This is all the more so when global environmental public goods are apprehended through categories of risks and threats. Clearly risk management, in the present state of international governance, is still first and foremost the province of politically legitimate sovereign bodies—that is, nation-state governments. Sovereignty and paradoxically the PA-PP itself (to the extent that it is linked to it), hinder the emergence of an appropriate framework for the management of global environmental risks.

The Links between Collective Preferences and the Precautionary Principle

Collective Preferences, an Emergent Issue in the Context of Globalization

Since 1992, as global risks have become a major issue in international affairs, requiring increased international cooperation, a growing demand has emerged that national collective preferences be acknowledged in the implementation of various international agreements. This dual-track, contradictory movement has been observed in several contexts, but most notably for trade agreements, to the extent that Pascal Lamy, before becoming director of the WTO, outlined potential mechanisms aiming to increase awareness of "certified" national collective preferences in international trade rules (Lamy 2004).

Lamy argued in favor of showing increased consideration for the opinions and preferences of a country's people and citizens regarding major trade-offs between health safety, local and global environmental protection, free trade, and improvements in welfare. He saw this "decent respect to the opinions" of citizens as critical to the democratic processes of political communities, and to prevent a deleterious conflict between an ever-expanding free trade and democracy.

This proposal from an influential figure of the international scene shows that we have only just begun thinking through mechanisms that would allow a better equilibrium between "one-size-fits-all" international rules and a diversity of collective preferences expressed at the national level and fixed in national institutions and procedures.

Many observers already have expressed their skepticism regarding the introduction of an explicit status for collective preferences (Charnowitz 2005). However, in what follows I accept the premise that collective preferences remain an open-ended issue for international trade, as I focus on the links between them and the implementation of the PP.

Although conceived as an intellectual tool to address situations of scientific uncertainty, the PP also exhibits subtle but strong links with the issue of collective preferences. First, the PP is not by itself a criterion for decision making. It calls for a case-by-case judgment under imperfect and piecemeal information. Consequently implementing the PP requires more than scientific expertise. This is why the concept is often associated with demands for public deliberation and consultation with stakeholders. Second, proportionality is a key feature of the PP that raises the question of collective preferences. In a European context, discussions of trade and public health risks often refer to "other legitimate factors" mentioned, for example, in Article 7 of Regulation 178/2002 relative to food safety (European Parliament and Council of the European Community 2002; Belvèze 2003). On the whole, "it is generally agreed that defining the level of acceptable risk is a decision that belongs to the democratically elected and accountable institutions of a state" (Christoforou 2002, 216). It is difficult to underscore more clearly that the PP relates to democracy, national collective preferences, and ultimately sovereignty, in relation to the management of collective risks, be they national or global.

Opening the "Black Box" of Collective Preferences

The notion of "collective preferences" encapsulates a great variety of issues and should be examined in more detail, in order to identify what is relevant to the PP and what is not.

Preferences for Specific Goods or for National Rules versus International Rule   Collective rules belong to the realm of politics and sovereignty, provided the latter has not been delegated to supranational entities. Autonomy in the setting of rules lies at the core of democratic polities, and this holds true also of rules that concern the management of risks: in other words, there is no a priori basis for objecting to a country's choice of its rules as long as those do not violate previous commitments and basic human rights.

In case sovereignty in some respects has been transferred to supranational bodies, new democratic procedures must also be put into place at this higher level. The accusation most often heard against the present state of affairs is that transfers of power and sovereignty to international bodies have not been balanced by a commensurate expansion of democratic control on these new institutions (Held 1995). In such circumstances, rising claims on behalf of collective preferences also express frustration at the insufficient democratic legitimacy of international organizations such as the WTO, whose governing bodies represent nation-states rather than peoples.

The situation of preferences for goods is quite different and opens on two main subcases.

Private versus Public Goods   Private goods absolutely independent of any public oversight—no externalities and no public good dimensions—are subject to the rules of competitive markets. Then corresponding "collective preferences" are no more than a statistical aggregate of market equilibriums. They offer no basis for state intervention at the borders and have no connection with the PP. Not so with public goods produced or maintained by public authorities: by virtue of their dependency on public institutions, they inevitably enter a public arena where political discourse rules, and decisions must be justified before the greater public (Boltanski and Thévenot 2006). In this context, procedures and institutions tasked in each country with providing those goods inevitably reflect collective preferences regarding the most prominent social values, for instance in favor of consensus-based decision making, or standards ensuring the equitable (re)distribution of goods and risks. Thus organizational forms of supplying public goods may belong to the block of a country's sovereignty, although choices of a given regime can alter conditions of competition on the market.

Aggregation of Individual Preferences of Consumers, or Preferences of the Political Community As Such?   "Preferences" vis-à-vis goods might refer either to consumers as such, or to a polity's citizens: the normative background for these two types of judgment is not identical. In the former case, trade relations and market equilibriums are devoid of direct political meaning, except for the freedom of choice guaranteed to consumers. Distributive issues can be addressed through ad hoc lump sum transfers without altering markets. However, preferences expressed by citizens, rather than consumers, are more genuinely "collective"; they involve democratic and political processes, and therefore issues of representation and deliberation.

These pairs of concepts show that the crucial distinction that must be drawn to refine our understanding of collective preferences lies between the economic and the political realms. Considerable differences between the two belie the superficial overlap implied by the common use of the word *preferences* in both cases. We have the market on the one hand, and deliberation, representation, voting, and arbitration on the other. More fundamentally, only when used in a political rather than a consumer setting does the expression *collective preferences* have any analytical substance.

Among consumers, what is therefore aggregated is simply contingent personal tastes aiming to fulfill self-centered needs. By contrast, among citizens, it is individual, reflexive views on the common good, which they can only develop by thinking above and beyond their personal circumstances and local attachments (e.g., family links, geographical origin, and vested interest). This is why Rousseau, in his analysis of the general interest, called for downgrading all intermediate communities and guilds, perceived as obstacles that hindered the expression of a common will by the national community as a whole. Rawls' "veil of ignorance" aimed to achieve the same result, namely to transcend individual peculiarities (Rawls 1971).

The conclusion is straightforward: the only collective preferences truly relevant to our analysis are those that are expressed in the political realm, and affect the choice of collective rules and the provision of public goods when the latter embodies some community values beyond the satisfaction of consumers' tastes.

Proportionality of the PP and Collective Preferences

Four criteria define whether precautionary measures are indeed "proportionate": possible damage, safety goals, direct and opportunity costs of the proposed measures, and last but not least, the scientific plausibility of the hypothesis that damage will in fact occur. The first three among these variables ultimately depend on collective preferences, though on slightly different aspects of the concept. Thus, "damage" will first be anticipated based on the aggregation of individual (dis) utilities, which do not concern collective preferences as such, except in case of significant externalities calling for public policies. But assessment of damage also depends on social values aiming to ensure an equitable sharing of damage and benefits. Similarly desirable "safety goals" will be defined based both on individual choices and collective preferences, in relation to political considerations such as the acceptable distribution of exposure to hazards among social groups (Beck 1992). Finally, "costs" will include private but also collective expenditures, for instance those incurred by democratically managed public funds. There is no reason why different countries should share the same values, or come to identical results when rating these three variables or making trade-offs among them, given unavoidable differences in their respective goals and political circumstances. An especially striking example is the uneven value accorded to statistical human life in different polities.

Turning to the fourth variable, conclusions as to the credibility of a given hypothetical risk will vary according to the scenario that is chosen as a framework of reference in assessing its likelihood and seriousness. For instance, depending on whether LMOs are set over against modern intensive agricultural practices or only organic agriculture, a different impression will ensue as to their own dangerousness. In addition, however, processes that determine the scientific credibility of a risk will also reflect national specificities with regard to the organization of expertise, and the patterns of interaction among experts, stakeholders, and decision makers (Stirling, Renn, and van Zwanenberg 2006). While science is supposed to rely on universal procedures aiming to develop universal knowledge, outcomes of expertise inescapably are influenced by the context in which expertise is organized. This "framing effect" in turn depends on the specific features of public life in the country (or in the national or international arena) in which experts operate (Fisher, Jones, and von Schomberg 2006).

Therefore, all four determinants of proportionality are to some extent affected by political processes that involve collective preferences; they cannot be abstracted from the realm of state sovereignty. The PP implementation vary from one country to the next and these differences emphatically do not imply that some are right and others wrong, provided that collective preferences are given strict limits of risk management. This is precisely the reason why, as we have seen, the PP fits uneasily with (and indeed often runs counter to) monolithic and binding international rules.

Concluding his disquisition of the appropriate influence that collective preferences should wield upon trade rules, Pascal Lamy (2004) argued that while they should be acknowledged and granted legitimate standing, they should still be held to reasonable limits; he suggested that states mobilizing their collective preference to take measures at their borders against imports should pay compensation to affected states when it proved impossible to find a voluntary agreement with them. With respect to implementation of the PP, I suggest taking a different track. When considering collective preferences, a distinction should be made between those that apply to domestic issues, and those that concern policies addressing global risks and the interests of humankind as such. By now, the implications of the former are well known but the meaning of the latter, and their incorporation into international rules and behavior, are still being worked out. The dichotomy between these two types of objects for collective preferences can be boiled down to two conflicting philosophies of international relations: the "sanctity" of national preferences ("this is nobody else's business but mine") versus the more proactive approach ("your business is also my concern") that results from the PP insofar as it is informed by "globally-minded" collective preferences. This second perspective in fact has already begun gaining ground, though not in the setting that might have been expected.

Environmental and Health Risks, Factors of Change for Trade Rules

Two Parallel Developments of International Law

Since the United Nations Conference on the Human Environment held in Stockholm in 1972, health and environmental protection policies, on the one hand, and competition and international trade rules, on the other, have developed along largely separate lines, in spite of the formulation of principles such as the polluter-pays principle (OECD 1975). This period saw two parallel developments: first, the emergence of global environmental problems, and second, a gradual liberalization of world trade framed by GATT-WTO rules, and growing financial and economic interdependency of activities worldwide. These two trends have been accompanied by new institutional developments, particularly on the international scene, including the Montreal Protocol, the United Nations Framework Convention on Climate Change, the UN Convention on Biodiversity, and Agenda 21, on the one hand; and the conclusions of the Uruguay Round, notably the SPS agreement and the creation of the WTO, on the other.

These two developments imply different equilibriums between state sovereignty and international coordination. This led to growing frictions, which the PP-PA only amplified. New questions arose, as to which objective should come first, and consequently, which branch of international law should prevail. In less black-and-white terms, the resulting challenge was how to integrate these two fundamental developments into a coherent and balanced overall regime.

Although the expansion of world trade is not intrinsically incompatible with health and environmental protection, under modern technological conditions, with market and state failures in regulating environmental externalities and the huge dependency of transportation on fossil fuels, commercial globalization has multiform impacts on the environment. Beyond the specific GHG emissions of transports, growing opportunities for the valorization of local resources on world markets increase pressure on nonmarketable goods and services provided by ecosystems. For instance the expansion of land superficies dedicated to growing sugarcane or palm trees for biofuels contributes to tropical deforestation and biodiversity loss.

How can we see a road to convergence between the two objectives of increasing welfare through the expansion of trade and enhancing environmental protections in the wake of incredible ecological threats on a global level? It is worthwhile, at the onset of a discussion of the "trade versus environment" dilemma, to introduce a few basic distinctions to enlighten claims about who is to take measures addressing environmental problems.

Basic Economic Distinctions

Some environmental issues are essentially local (most cases of water pollution initially have local effects); others are regional (for instance acid rain and sustainable forest management in Europe, Asia, and Africa); still others are global (climate change). Another relevant distinction must be made depending on the economic processes at the origin of the problems: some arise because of production processes, while others stem from consumption and waste.

From a general economic standpoint, the management of local environmental problems generated by production activities must take into account preferences of affected groups and populations in the producing country. In this case imposing worldwide, uniform standards are beside the point, except insofar as global economies of scale can facilitate production of green equipment.

When problems are generated by consumption, the same standpoint suggests that it behooves public authorities of the state where consumption or waste management are at issue to take measures in accordance with the collective preferences of their own citizens. There is no economic reason why these states should renounce their own authentic collective preferences and align with those of exporting countries. The only incentive that could prevent a splitting of standards across consumer countries would be the mutual benefits brought about by a standardization of requirements—again due to economies of scale in the production and distribution of internationally traded goods. For instance, with respect to the design of an appropriate regime for the treatment of packaging waste (selective collection and sorting to facilitate recycling, reduction at the source, disposal in landfills), it is perfectly legitimate that the preferences of the consumer country should determine incentives, requirements, and standards about packaging, regardless of the difficulties this might cause for exporters wishing to enter the market with packaged products, as long as the approach remains nondiscriminatory.

However, for a global risk such as threats raised by climate change, the issue is framed differently: ideally, a global institutional framework is needed to set up a unified worldwide economic regime that can neutralize the temptation of individual free riding, and that can allocate responsibilities to reduce net emissions in a cost-effective manner. However, not all countries will be affected by climate change in the same way, nor will they share identical priorities and trade-offs between immediate consumption and protection of climate. This makes it especially difficult to ensure that effectiveness and equity are not achieved at one another's expense. Entanglement of both aspects in turn increases the level of cooperation required in order to set up an operational regime. "Simply" setting a single price for carbon on the world market through emissions trading or an international tax would not succeed in maximizing global welfare in the face of climate change; cooperation should also extend to the choice of a global cap on emissions and the initial allocation of obligations and rights in order to take into account varying expositions to climatic hazards and diverging priorities between immediate consumption, saving for investment, and environmental protection (Chichilnisky and Heal 2000). National collective preferences would then impose their own constraints on the negotiation of a multilateral environmental agreement.

Environmental Globalization at Work

These analytical distinctions are useful, but it must be acknowledged that real-world phenomena restrict the validity of this overly neat framework. Most notably, the distinction between local and global problems has become increasingly blurred, as globalization has spread to our perception of the main environmental issues. Two concomitant evolutions are evident in this respect. One of the strategic tricks underlying action by NGOs devoted to environmental protection is to give the largest possible scope and meaning to local crises and events by connecting them with issues of planetary significance, be it the preservation of biodiversity, the prevention of climate-related risks, the fight against desertification, or the growing global scarcity of critical natural resources (e.g., agricultural land, water, and oil). The concept of an ecological footprint is a useful tool to this regard. These organizations also strive to give the greatest possible publicity worldwide to local practices of international businesses that they believe run afoul of the requirements of sustainable development or environmental protection. In response, to safeguard their reputation and legitimacy, multinational companies now increasingly take notice of the extra-local implications of accidents for which they might be held liable and strive to root out of environmental carelessness in their production units, even when their behavior in fact abides by the local regulations of the host country. For various reasons, most transnational companies have decided to work toward achieving convergence of their environmental management rules at their industrial facilities worldwide. In this context, environmental policies tend to broaden and transcend local contexts to become regional or global. This contributes to expanding the relevance of global international efforts towards the definition of common or at least harmonized environmental rules. This is where the risk perspective tends to put up a barrier by raising concerns for sovereign judgment based on national collective preferences.

New Concerns Lead to a Broader "Quality of Goods" Concept

Consumers, NGOs, and major retailers (most notably in Europe) have expressed growing concern vis-à-vis the health risks incurred through consumption of certain foods, as well as the environmental impact brought about by the industrial world's inordinate use of natural resources and mass importations from developing countries. This had resulted in a new approach towards the notion of "quality of goods." Criteria that define quality have been considerably extended in some cases. For instance, suppliers now must certify that the wood used in furnishings comes from forests managed according to the rules of sustainability; they must offer indirect guarantees that beef does not contain pathogenic prions, by certifying that the cattle was raised at a given farm in a given region, where the animals' diet demonstrably did not include recycled beef waste; and they must certify that peas were grown in fields that have not been fertilized with liquid or urban manure over a period of at least five years.

Thus the distinction between process and product in relation to trade rules is especially challenged in two distinct set of circumstances. First, this is the case whenever the quality of goods at the border is in doubt and can only be ascertained by scrutinizing the entire production chain in the country of origin. Second, among consumers some increasingly exhibit "ethical awareness" in their purchasing behavior, taking into account social and environmental conditions in producing countries. In both respects, the ability to certify the quality of production chains according to safety and environmental criteria tends to become critical.

Because of this new approach toward the quality of goods, information flows underlying trade relations have increased and become more complex. In the dawning "age of precaution," sensitive products can only be traded internationally if large amounts of corresponding information are also available: for example, analyses of life cycles, proof that components meet various threshold standards, disquisition of what is or is not included in the product, environmental certificates, and traceability indicators enabling identification of economic and geographical origins. Similar demands for detailed information have also emerged with respect to ethical norms and working conditions in producing countries.

As an economic institution, the marketplace had often been hailed as an efficient mechanism with minimum informational requirements, based on the notion that prices synthesize all the data that buyers might need to know, since they reflect all facets of production costs. This view can only be supported by forgetting various sorts of external costs, including environmental ones. Seen in this light, however, standard markets come across as "amnesiac" institutions, as they draw a veil on the exact nature of conditions of productions in distant lands. This is precisely what is being put into question by the emergence of consumer-citizens, exhibiting concerns about health hazards, environmental problems, and human rights records.

The gradual inclusion of the PP in international law will necessarily modify the technical and political foundations of trade, since each region of the world will most likely come up with a different evaluation of acceptable risks, different standards for credible expertise, or even different definitions of the scientific data that legitimate expertise should take into account. Today, therefore, we are facing the prospect of a split of trade rules into various regimes specific to different classes of goods. This in turn will contribute to the dynamics that today hinder the homogeneous expansion of free trade.

A Projected Differentiation of Trade Rules

This leads us to a counter-intuitive conjecture. Contrary to what is often forecast —namely that we are heading towards a massive process of convergence, resulting in one-size-fits-all liberal trade rules and a single world market—the future in fact could bring about a differentiation among several regimes for the international circulation of goods. There are two conditions for this to happen: environmental and health issues continue to catch huge interest of consumers, and the latter increasingly cast a citizen's look on consumer choices. Consumer and governmental concern for environmental and health issues would then add to other obstacles that restrict trading of certain goods, such as national security considerations for defense-sensitive technologies.

For products carrying a health risk or resulting from an environmentally sensitive manufacturing process, trade networks will be called upon to abide by new information requirements and to accept a basic alternative: either they can find ways to provide the information required to certify quality without compromising a mass manufacturing approach based on interconnected and far-reaching trade channels, or they will have to move toward shorter and specialized production and distribution chains with precise specifications. If the latter, the spread of trade channels will become commensurate with the producer's capacity to exhibit environmental and health certifications acceptable in a greater or smaller number of importing countries.

Based on these premises, we can identify three "ideal-typical" regimes in relation to health and environmental safety:

• Ordinary goods of undoubted quality, which pose no health or environmental issue; they will be subjected to free trade rules provided that they meet commonly agreed technical standards (e.g., computers, books, clothes).

- Specific goods characterized by obvious dangerousness or problematic environmental impact (e.g., toxic waste or animals belonging to protected natural species). Stringent limitations and control on trade flows will inevitably come into effect; for instance, a principle of geographical proximity of treatment for toxic waste has been adopted by the EU law.
- Finally, goods of undetermined but potentially problematic quality regarding health and environmental impacts of production will be subject to the new, broader concept of quality described above. Their circulation will depend on the producers' ability to produce all required information and guarantees with respect to the health and environmental characteristics of the entire production chain. Because of potential risks, precautionary requirements will apply, reflecting consumers' and citizens' concerns. Varying views on "acceptable" levels of risks will define circulation areas in which all agree on a common assessment in this regard, just as commercialization of LMOs today is subjected to a distinction between regions in which their cultivation is permitted and those for which that is not the case (mainly the EU). In some cases, new opportunities for alternative trade patterns will develop through the emergence of short chains of distribution that ensure that producers and consumers know and trust each other. This third category of goods will elicit new information requirements, as well as changes in production and distribution techniques. Most notably, it will challenge the mass, undifferentiated pooling of raw materials, because this compromises the quality of information available on a product, which will prove crucial for its commercialization.

Such a differentiation of trade rules would fit well into the new equilibrium now emerging between strong global coordination aiming to tackle environmental risks and maintain the order of international trade and the sustained sovereignty of nation-states, derived from their status as the most appropriate and natural context for democratic expression and implementation of collective preferences regarding threats for health and the environment.

The overall context of this new equilibrium is one in which issues of risks management take on increasing importance, as the world is characterized by growing and multifaceted uncertainty in regard to such factors as access to natural resources, the impact of new technologies, human migration flows, financial stability, or geopolitical balance.

Contribution of the PP to a Hybrid Concept of Sovereignty

Ambivalent, "inward-looking" use of the PP in international relations can be attributed to the strong link that exists within democracies between the concept of risk and the responsibility of nation-states' governments to ensure the safety and health of their people and of their natural environment, which is seen as a common heritage. Therefore, regarding these types of collective risks, states remain reluctant to set up strong international regimes to coordinate their actions, as this would limit their sovereignty. Therefore, the "risk society" is inherently contradictory: the emergence of concerns for environmental risks at once calls for improved global governance and creates the obstacles that impede it.

However, therein lies a surprising solution to this dilemma. States might reject any curtailment of their sovereignty; they might wish to retain control over the management of poorly understood and controversial risks, and most notably use the PP as a means to impose inward-looking, unilateral approaches. Yet, the link between the PP and collective preferences, together with governments' need to ensure extended societal "buy-in" to confront these complex risks in a politically accepted way, has paved the way for an increase in the direct implication of civil society in risk management. Though initially this might have resulted in more inward-looking, defensive reactions vis-à-vis threats and dangers from abroad, this civil involvement has now expanded to include heightened concern for global issues. As a result, through this "raising of consciousness," the limits of interstate relations tend in fact to be circumvented by collective action and initiatives of consumer-citizens, environmental NGOs, as well as retailers and producers that take anticipatory action to prevent future crises and consumer disaffection. For instance, specifications imposed by Walmart or Carrefour on their suppliers abroad may turn out to be just as significant as what states may (or may not) decide on the issue of ecological dumping in the context of the Doha cycle of negotiations under the WTO aiming at lowering trade barriers and improving market access of developing countries.

Thus we can outline an evolution of the PA-PP concept as a governance tool through four stages, in the course of which the national versus international dichotomy has fluctuated. Born initially from a movement toward international cooperation for the protection of regional (North Sea) and global (climate) public goods being at risk, the notion was instead forced back into a framework of unilateral action by nations-states concerned with the rise of poorly understood new threats, aiming to ensure the safety of their own citizens as well as to respond to their specific preferences. However, a third phase would see the concerns of consumer-citizens expanding beyond purely domestic issues, leading to market-induced shifts in quality standards for traded goods. Finally, completing the loop, this could lead to disseminating new standards and facilitating new steps in international regulation, thus reflecting the heightened global concerns of the collective citizenry.

We are seeing the dawn of a new era in which reflexive governance implies that the greater public be granted the right to take into account the behavior of foreign producers and states the right to hold one another accountable for their respective impact on the global commons. This latter development can be described as an expansion of sovereignty, since a state's sovereignty now extends, in a sense, to other states' internal affairs to the extent that they have international effects through commercial relations. After an initial phase when it was mostly used to justify unilateral measures, the PP may revert to its original purpose, by conferring upon states a right to cross examine one another's activities insofar as they touch universal values or have a global dimension.

Being reciprocal, such an extension can also be seen as a restriction of the traditional concept of sovereignty: a concern for humankind and basic cosmopolitan rights erode absolute concepts of sovereignty at the same time when this extension opens new fields of action to national governments through international cooperation. Therefore, the PP will bring its own contribution to the current change of understanding of the concept of state sovereignty (Strange 1996; Dahl 1999b; Krasner 1999; Held and McGrew 2002; Nagan and Hammer 2005).

International governance of global environmental risks is unlikely to make progress as long as states fail to reform their conception of sovereignty toward a more balanced and hybrid concept of rights and obligations. Only by acknowledging the transnational concerns of civil society, NGOs and foreign governments can states lay the ground for a new regime in which more issues could be managed in common.

Judging by the experience gained in the 1990s and the 2000s, these evolutions will not exclusively or even primarily stem from interstate negotiations, be it the Doha cycle or the project to create a World Environment Organization, but will instead come about first through commercial relationships among consumers, retailers, and producers worldwide.

Conclusion

Though the first effect of the PP has been to reinforce sovereign judgment on risk management and raise new obstacles on the road toward efficient regulation of global environmental risks, the emergence of national collective preferences as a background of sovereignty in democracies also opened the way for an active contribution of civil society and business for matters linked to the management of collective risks. Thereafter, dissemination of privately defined standards for internationally traded goods began to give an incentive for states to negotiate new international regimes that allow a better response to global risks.

Recent progress in this regard remains fragile: the PP can only complete its dialectical loop back to its original, globally minded purpose, and global environmental governance can only become a reality, if consumers and civil society sustain and expand their concern for the common interest of humankind, beyond short-term consumerism. This process cannot be prodded by Adam Smith's invisible hand: it must be anchored in adequate support from national institutions, and international rules regarding socioeconomic and legal rights. In addition, governments, business, and NGOS will have to exhibit considerable wisdom and restraint to defuse the tensions that are sure to arise, because assertion of their right to examine one another's internal affairs is sure to be condemned in some instances as excessively intrusive or aggressive interference, or even as a poor smokescreen for new forms of domination and colonialism.

Notes

The author thanks Erwan Lagadec, Foreign Policy Institute Fellow, School of Advanced International Studies, Johns Hopkins University, for precious assistance during the preparation of the English manuscript. All mistakes remain mine.

8

Subnational Climate-Friendly Governance Initiatives in the Developing World: A Case Study of the State of São Paulo, Brazil

Kamyla Borges Cunha, Fernando Rei, and Arnaldo César Walter

The recognition of global environmental issues, such as climate change, along with other challenges that call for rapid and effective responses from society has turned the attention of policy makers to the international spheres of political decision making. More and more nation-state governments are starting to incorporate actions aimed at reducing the impacts of climate change into their strategic decisions.

However, from the perspective of legitimacy and effectiveness, other challenges are added to that of the changing climate regime, in particular the complexity of international laws governing the adoption and implementation of effective measures to combat global warming, and the interaction that must prevail between international proclimate policies and other governance spheres.

The goal of this chapter is to discuss the extent to which these two challenges can be understood as a factor watering down the perception of the legitimacy and effectiveness of the climate regime, and how the introduction of the concept of environmental governance could minimize this impact. In line with this aim, the present study focuses on the experience of the state of São Paulo, Brazil.

The first section discusses the role of developing countries in the evolution of the climate regime, pointing out the reluctance of major emitters in assuming broader commitments in the international climate regime. It is also argued that, in view of the difficulty to develop the climate regime amid a lack of supportive climate-friendly attitudes by nation-states, thinking about alternative and complementary actions is probably a good idea.

The second section highlights the emergence of alternative environmental policy structures, mainly governmental measures originating from local and state institutions. It shows that such initiatives could have important positive effects at the state level, such as encouraging governments to promote climate-friendly measures, taking on the role of centerpiece in environmental education and awareness-raising programs, influencing the position of nation-states, and exerting pressure at international forums and summits.

The last section shows that such structures can result in important benefits for the developing world, and discusses the experience of some Brazilian states, particularly the state of São Paulo. The position of Brazil's federal government within the context of climate change negotiations is outlined, and some climate-friendly measures that are currently in the process of implementation at state levels are described in more detail.

By addressing the problem of GPG provision in the context of multilevel governance systems, this chapter addresses a central point of the analysis in this book, which is the fact that many global goods can be split in locally provided goods and therefore governed at an infra-national basis, even if coordination needs have to be addressed at a higher level. However, even if an important part of the analysis is based on this literature on multilevel governance, the chapter also clearly contributes to the analysis in the previous chapter of the role of citizen and consumer movements, and other civil society initiatives, in building national and regional collective preferences that play an important role in collective decision making over GPGs.

The Challenge of Consensus in Negotiations on the Climate Regime: Toward Policy and Politics

The recognition that climate change is one of the most dramatic global environmental problems—reinforced by *Climate Change 2007* (Intergovernmental Panel on Climate Change 2007), the IPCC's Fourth Assessment Report—has instigated the international community to discuss further measures commensurate with the issue. The problem is that after the Kyoto Protocol ends in 2012 an effective climate change regime implies the challenge of engaging all the world's major greenhouse gas (GHG) emitters, notably the United States and the so-called key developing countries (China, India, and Brazil) in a long-term effort that fairly and effectively mobilizes resources needed to protect the global climate (Diringer 2003).

From the perspective of the principle of common but differentiated responsibility, it is imperative that Annex I Parties take the lead in combating climate change, what does not exempt developing parties to act.

From the environmental perspective, a broader participation of the developing countries in mitigation efforts is an important condition to bring effectiveness to the international climate regime.

However, the developing countries, united around the G-77 and China, have almost unanimously held the position of refusing to discuss any specific mitigation commitments. They argue that their historic emissions are still lower than those of developed countries (NAE 2005). They also try to make their participation in the climatic regime conditional on the discussion about vulnerability, adaptation, promotion of sustainable development, resource and technology transfers, and capacity building (Girardin and Bouille 2003).

Thus, the main challenge facing the international climate regime lies in reconciling the effectiveness of its measures with the assurance that equity is the presiding parameter in apportioning responsibilities among countries for the implementation of these measures. In practical terms, what matters most is distributing responsibilities for the major emitters.

To achieve an agreement able to embrace all these often conflicting factors, a complex political negotiation process is inevitable (Ott et al. 2004). In the context of the post-2012 regime negotiations, this means that the possibility cannot be dismissed that important countries will refuse to cooperate, impose conditions to their adherence to the regime, or even participate in an ineffectual way (Höhne et al 2003).

By ignoring that climate balance is a common good, and by prioritizing short-term interests often corresponding to specific economic interests, the positions of nation-state governments in international negotiations fail to reflect that of the societies they represent, resulting in a loss of authority (Litfin 2000). As a key component to authority, the legitimacy of a nation-state is dependent upon the perception among its citizens that the government is performing its ascribed roles (Frickel and Davidson 2004). Thus, legitimacy requires a reflective subject capable of judging whether an action, rule, or proposal is in accordance either with its interests or else with established rules or principles (Litfin 2000).

Thus, in a context of inherently complex political decisions requiring consensus, and of prevalence of diverging interests of the national governments, implementation of the climate regime raises issues of legitimacy and effectiveness. These issues also may surface in a context of weak domestic actions developed by federal governments, where citizens cannot see consistency between official talk and real governance, and where there is a lack of public policies focused on climate change or where these policies do not lead to concrete results. In view of this, it is to be expected that alternative and complementary mechanisms will emerge as more legitimate ways to effectively address the global environmental problem.

New Forms of Addressing Climate Change and Their Role in the Developing World

By ignoring territorial boundaries, global environmental problems such as climate change give rise to the need for effective cooperation, leading to the understanding that such problems are ultimately those of a global common (Rei 1994), concretely felt in subnational levels (Bodansky 1999). When contrasted with the complexity of a response through the action of national governments within the framework of international law, the idea of global commons inculcates a sense of intergenerational responsibility at all levels of social organization (Litfin 2000), signifying the emergence of new and complementary structures to face global environmental problems.

These new structures originate from the recognition that facing global environmental issues requires the cooperative and coordinated action of governance systems based on multilevel environmental governance (national, supranational, subnational and international) and composed of multilevel environmental policy structures (international, national, state, and local), each performing a variety of roles (Olsson 2003). In this way, these networks become embedded in a logic that demands coordination, solidarity, definition of common objectives, and reduction of friction and conflicts, making the integration of demands a horizontal process (Jacobi 2000).

Proactive initiatives in subnational spheres—even if driven by demands from abroad—when established within the structure of national governments whose environmental actions are ineffective or lack flexibility, have two values. First, they become a means to press against the inertia of national governments, and according to Bulkeley (2005) the significance of nongovernmental or state and local actors lies in the extent to which they shape, facilitate, or change the behavior of nation-states within international regimes. And second, they constitute an alternative path to face environmental problems: subnational initiatives are deemed more responsive to pressures of inter-locality economic competition and continuous policy innovation, on the one hand, and citizen demands for proactive measures, on the other (Jonas and Pincetl 2006).

The idea of multilevel environmental governance has been initially fostered by the call in Agenda 21 (Bulkele, 2005). In the domain of climatic change, subnational governance initiatives began to gain strength as international negotiations, performed under the coordination of the UN and carried out by national governments, became increasingly complex, leading to ineffective practical results and falling short of the requirements for a real combat of climate change. In addition to the emergence of essentially scientific networks, which yield a strong influence over international decisions, and to the expansion of the activities of nongovernmental organizations, state and local governance initiatives have emerged as new forms of reinforcing the legitimation and effectiveness of climate-friendly measures.

The common aspect about these local and state actions is to rescale climate change as an issue with local causes and consequences, while at the same time reframing issues that are institutionalized and imagined as local, when in fact they also have global dimensions. In doing so, these initiatives increase the importance of state and local institutions and practices as an arena of influence and reduce the role of international and national scales of governance, giving them the opportunity to highlight the role of local and state authorities in addressing climate change (Engel and Orbach 2008).

From the perspective of the developing world, these initiatives could be viewed as an alternative way to address climate change challenges in which the official position of nation-states is still one of reluctance to take early action. As previously mentioned, these initiatives could bring important positive effects at the subnational level: encouraging states to promote climate-friendly measures, influencing the position of nation-states and putting pressure at the international negotiations arena, particularly on the developing world.

However, the legitimacy and effectiveness of subnational initiatives in tackling climate change depends, to a large extent, on how the interaction between the global problem of climate change and the state and local problems and environmental impacts is dealt with. Assuming that the main anthropogenic sources of GHG are also at the basis of important subnational and local environmental problems, mitigation and adaptation measures that acknowledge global-local relationships have better chances of succeeding, not only because they lead to real global and local environmental benefits, but also because they place the issue of global warming on a level closer to the everyday reality of people. The common citizen begins to see more easily the correlation between his or her direct actions and the global environmental problems (Bulkeley and Betsill 2003). Environmental governance, in this sense, means to conjugate the causes and consequences of environmental problems, and their construction as such, with practices and policies taking place at a multitude of sites and scales of governance (Bulkeley 2005).

If, on the contrary, actions to combat global environmental problems, such as climate change, focus exclusively on the national/global perspective, ignoring local effects of such measures, then other economic, environmental, and social problems may arise on these levels. A conflict between global-local solutions can bring about a lack of effectiveness and a diminished perception of the legitimacy of those measures.

The experience of Brazil is a case in point. Considering the reluctant position of Brazil's federal government in assuming specific mitigation international commitments to protect the climate, many possible proactive measures in the state sphere have been contemplated. The positive results of such measures, and their ensuing legitimacy and effectiveness, depend on whether they will be implemented as part of an environmental governance focus.

Climate-Friendly Governance Initiatives at the State Level in Brazil

Federal Reluctance versus State Proactive Action
Brazil has played a decisive role in international negotiations, putting forward important proposals within the context of the Kyoto Protocol framework relative to further regulations, in addition to advocating the general interests of other developing countries. The Brazilian government shares the same viewpoint of other developing countries, stating that incentives are necessary and should encompass the provision of new and additional financial resources and technology transference, as well as capacity building. As stated in the UNFCCC Dialogue working paper submitted by the Brazilian government: "the Federal Government of Brazil believes that efforts undertaken by developing countries to reduce emissions in different sectors within their territories can only be characterized as voluntary and, therefore, cannot be linked or associated to goals, targets or timeframes" (UNFCCC 2006b).

The reluctance to assume more specific commitments under the climate regime might be due to the fact that Brazil is currently one of the major emitters in the world: it currently holds nineteenth position in the ranking of CO_2 emissions from the energy sector. However, since its main emission source is deforestation, which accounts for 75 percent of all domestic CO_2 emissions (MCT 2004), the country's position in a total emission ranking is actually much higher: it occupies the fifth place (UNFCCC 2006a).

At the domestic level, the Brazilian government's performance has been characterized by lack of coordination and consistency. Climate change has not been inserted as a matter of state, as the governmental agenda remains focused on actions to promote economic growth and social policies. This facilitates incoherence among government ministries' positions on the subject, contributing to a distorted view of the matter.

At the federal level, there are no governmental bodies which comprise, and centralize decisions and measures on the issue. Three separate ministries—those of Science and Technology, Foreign Affairs, and Environment—have been directly involved in climate change discussions both in the international and domestic arena, but not always demonstrating consensus positions.

There are two federal commissions created to deal with climate change issues. The first one is the Interministerial Commission on Climate Change (CIMGC) established in 1999 with the purpose of assisting the presidency with technical advice and to act as the Brazilian National Designated Authority. It is composed of the main ministries and executive agencies related to the issue—including Foreign Affairs, Office of the President's Chief of Staff, Transports, Agriculture Livestock and Food Supply, Development Industry and Foreign Trade. The second commission is the Interministerial Committee on Climate Change (CIM) created in 2007 with the purpose of elaborating, managing, and monitoring the National Climate Change Plan (PNMC). It is also composed of the relevant ministries and is coordinated by the Executive Office of the President. An Executive Group has been instituted to assist CIM.

PNMC shows evidence of inconsistencies and lack of coordination at the federal level. Officially launched during COP 14 in Poznan, Poland, PNMC seems to have been tailored to please international players but, from a domestic implementation perspective, it is a collection of isolated actions that are being developed in different governmental and nongovernmental spheres.

Even considering the efforts of the federal government, it is not possible to know for sure whether the reduction in deforestation rates recorded since 2005 is the result of governmental policies or a consequence of low or declining international market prices for agricultural products (mainly soybean and meat) (Salati, Santos, and Kablin 2006). Moreover, the reinforcement of existing energy efficiency and renewable energy programs has not yet led to effective results. Consequently, domestic emissions are expected to continue growing. Furthermore, extreme climate events that occurred in the last few years, such as the drought in the Amazon region in 2005 and the Catarina cyclone that hit the southern states of Brazil in 2004, demonstrated that the extent of Brazil's vulnerability to climate change is actually still unknown.

As pointed out above, although on one hand the federal government's reluctance is seen as an obstacle to taking early action against climate change, on the other it has spurred a reaction from society at both local and state levels. Such is the case in some Brazilian states.

Since 2008, perception of the importance of climate change in Brazilian society has grown considerably. This perception translates into proactive actions by civil society organizations or individuals, and also by state and local governments. The range of these actions is extensive, and although not always fully implemented, they can at least be regarded as a valid point of departure.

At least eight of the twenty-seven Brazilian states (Rio Grande do Sul, Santa Catarina, Paraná, São Paulo, Minas Gerais, Rio de Janeiro, Espírito Santo, and Bahia) have already instituted a climate change forum composed of representatives of government institutions, civil society organizations, universities, and private sector companies and/or membership organizations. The idea behind these initiatives is to turn the forum into an arena for the exchange and discussion of experiences and good practices related to climate change mitigation and adaptation. In some states, São Paulo included, the efforts have evolved to include the preparation of a GHG emissions inventory by source, vulnerability studies, and the implementation of economic instruments to improve mitigation measures.

Climate-Friendly Governance Initiatives in the State of São Paulo

The state of São Paulo, located in the Southeast of Brazil, is the most populous and urbanized in the country: it has a population of 41 million, or 21 percent of the country's entire population (IBGE 2008). The state has the largest economy of Brazil, representing 31 percent of the total national GDP (US$235 billion in 2003) and with strong participation of industry and service sectors (IBGE 2008). As a result of its economic profile, in 2000 the energy consumption of São Paulo accounted to 27 percent of the national consumption (SMA 2002). In 2005, the industrial and transport sectors were the most significant energy consumers, with 39 percent and 26 percent of the state total, respectively. Most of the energy consumed by the industrial sector comes from biomass (44 percent), particularly sugarcane bagasse (36.5 percent); this is due to the high concentration of sugarcane industry in the São Paulo. In contrast, the major energy sources of the transport sector were fossil fuels, especially diesel (44 percent) (BEESP 2006).

Due to the energy matrix in São Paulo, the transport and industrial sectors are the most important sources of CO_2 emissions in the state, accounting for 45.8 percent and 37.3 percent of the total of 67.9 $MtCO_2$ emitted in 2005 (BEESP, 2006). If ranked alongside nations on the basis of CO_2 emissions (excluding land use change), the state would be the thirty-ninth largest source of net GHG emissions in the world (SMA 2005).

Aware of its role as the main contributor to Brazil's energy emissions, the state of São Paulo began to pay attention to climate change as far back as 1995, when the state government enacted its Climate Change Prevention Program—PROCLIMA. Under this program, the state created a special administrative department, the Global Issues Division, with the tasks of producing information for the general public regarding climate change, promoting seminars and conferences to introduce the problem and discuss mitigation alternatives, promoting capacity development, and cooperating with federal climate change activities (SMA 2008). The PROCLIMA team is one of the main technical bodies responsible for preparing Brazil's National Communication Strategy and Action Plan.

In 2002, the state published its Agenda 21, in which climate change figures prominently. In the same year, the state government and other countries' state authorities launched the Network of Regional Governments for Sustainable Development (NRG4SD), with the purpose of sharing climate mitigation and other sustainable development experiences, and acting as the main vehicle of representative participation in international negotiations (NRG4SD 2008). The state of São Paulo is also an active member of ABEMA—the Brazilian association congregating state environmental agencies (ABEMA 2008).

In 2005, the São Paulo State Forum on Global Climate Change and Biodiversity (Fórum Paulista de Mudanças Climáticas Globais e de Biodiversidade—FPMC) was created to raise awareness and mobilize society to discuss and take a stance about climate change, acting as a forum for all stakeholders in society. FPMC includes representatives of the state government, civil society organizations and also, as invited participants, representatives of the federal government, of the municipalities of São

Paulo state, the state legislature and the Brazilian Forum on Climate Change (FBMC 2008).

Also in 2005 the state government signed a cooperation agreement with the state of California in the United States to identify and implement actions that can further reduce GHG emissions, increase energy efficiency, and reduce emissions of other pollutants (SMA 2008).

In the beginning of 2007, the state of São Paulo launched a wide portfolio of twenty-one environmental projects, including a future environmental scenario study. The main goals of these projects are evaluation of climate change impacts at the state level, improvement of deforestation control mechanisms, reforestation activities in riparian areas, measures to control the demand for illegal wood, and renewable energy promotion (mainly biomass cogeneration and sugarcane ethanol production) (SMA 2008).

The government is also working with the private sector to define emission targets for the industries with the highest emissions in the state. The first action was to prepare and publicize a state inventory of CO_2 emissions from specific industrial sources. This inventory was based on information on fuel consumption and industrial processes obtained from questionnaires (371 sent; 329 or 89 percent answered) (SMA 2008).

The state government also started, through the State Department of Environmental Protection, the formulation of a State Policy on Climate Change. In early 2008 its proposals were submitted to public opinion on the Internet, and the government promoted public discussion involving different sectors of civil society: universities, private companies, and civil society organizations. FPMC had an important role in this process, acting as a coalescing forum for the discussions. The government proposal was being revised in order to take into account the results of public discussion and consultation (SMA 2008). In 2009, the final proposal was approved by the State Assembly and then promulgated as the State Policy on Climate Change (Law 13798/2009).

This State Policy on Climate Change might be seen as innovative in the context of the developing countries, since it establishes that the state of São Paulo shall define real, measurable, and verifiable actions to reduce its GHG emissions by adopting: (1) emission reduction targets, both individually and in cooperation with other subnational governments of the country and the world; (2) sector efficiency targets, based on GHG emissions; and (3) additional mechanisms to exchange acquired rights. The proposed policy also requires the state to update and improve its GHG Communication every five years (including an inventory in accordance with IPCC guidelines), and to create and maintain a Public Register of Emissions to establish measurable criteria and transparent monitoring of the results of GHG mitigation measures.

All the above mentioned activities in the state of São Paulo are carried out to a greater or lesser extent through a number of coordinated actions both inside and outside the state. Within the state, the work of the FPMC is gaining relevance. It promotes public discussions about climate change across all sectors of society, and not only amalgamates different perspectives on the matter but also acts as a channel to bring them to the decision forums, making it a center of proclimate pressure. Its multi-sector composition adds legitimacy to its work, allowing it to cross state frontiers. Therefore, FPMC is part of the Brazilian Forum on Climate Change, with direct participation in the preparation of the National Climate Change Plan.

As a forum for the exchange of experiences on environmental and climatic matters at the subnational level of different countries, NRG4SD has been acting both as a channel to exert pressure on the states and as a means of international promotion of those states with a more proactive behavior in climatic and environmental matters. The participation of states in NRG4SD also increases their prominence in the international arena, which is positive for both the environment and economic competitiveness. In global markets the incorporation of proclimate strategies has been gaining importance as an opportunity for companies to do business and survive in the market (Hamilton 2006).

This market perspective may also be regarded as a contribution to larger negotiation flexibility and the incorporation of proclimate measures by the state government. Whereas in most of Brazil deforestation is the main emission source, in the state of São Paulo the primary GHG emission sources are the industrial and transport sectors. Therefore, the main mitigation actions should be directed toward efficient energy use in factories, modernization of industrial process, and changes in urban mobility planning and systems.

The GHG emission profile of the state of São Paulo is similar to that of developed countries, and the state is the home of many industrial manufacturing units in the country, most of them owned and operated by transnational companies. Taken together, these facts have facilitated the adoption of mitigation actions by these companies, reinforcing governmental actions.

Contrasting once more with the federal government's neutral attitude concerning the encouragement of clean development mechanism (CDM) projects in Brazil, mitigation actions and proposals from the state of São

Paulo reinforce the state's role as a forum to encourage such activities, a fact that has an influence on the international carbon market. Commercial opportunities are also behind bilateral agreements formalized by the state. The São Paulo–California agreement is an example of this, with both states working together on developing more efficient technology transfer mechanisms and, probably in the future, on launching joint initiatives related to the carbon market.

The proclimate actions undertaken within the state boundaries have found resonance in other parts of the country, mainly as a result of state government's proactive role as an ABEMA member. This association has served as a forum for the exchange of proclimate experiences among Brazilian states, stimulating coordinated action at the subnational level, helping fill the void left by the federal government's position at international climate negotiation table.

The state of São Paulo has been flexible and successful in developing cooperative proclimate arrangements and measures in consonance with the needs and potentialities of both the public and private sectors (including those of the economic sphere) at the state and interstate levels, but not at the federal level. At that level, the role of São Paulo state remains limited to the providing of technical support, the preparation of the national GHG emission inventory through PROCLIMA, and acting as a technical advisor to the Brazilian delegation at international negotiation meetings.

In spite of their modest scope so far, climate change mitigation measures at a state level can be regarded as examples of attempts to implement environmental governance actions. In the process of formulation and implementation of these programs, there has been direct participation of the third sector and other social actors. Whether as a strategy to gain wider adherence and social acceptance among the population (legitimacy), or as a means to make such programs economically viable, the partnership initiatives between public authorities, citizen groups, and other social sectors are already an established reality.

However, it must be noted that the many proactive measures at the state level in Brazil cannot be taken as a sign of robust mitigation and adaptation results. Just as in any other sector of the Brazilian public administration, sufficient financial and technical capability resources do not back the deployment of environmental initiatives by governments.

From the perspective of effectiveness and legitimacy, all the proactive state measures mentioned above must be seen as subnational initiatives capable of introducing the climate change issue into the state decision-making agenda, and thus allowing the development of public policies more in tune with local realities. Moreover, these initiatives gain importance when perceived in the context of the federal government's reluctance and difficulty to effectively develop national climate change mitigation and adaptation policies and take on a proactive position in the international arena.

Conclusions

The facts and plans compiled in this chapter suggest that, even though nation-states may remain reluctant to assume early climate change mitigation measures, thus making the international arena a complex and difficult path for the convergence of climate-friendly initiatives, there is enough scope for alternative structures and approaches in both developing and developed countries.

Local and state initiatives, though praiseworthy, can hardly gain access to the international agenda of the climate change regime and show their contribution, because international relations are still the prerogative of sovereign nation-states. Nevertheless, the spread of environmental networks at local and state levels is an interesting example of governance, which legitimates subnational climate-friendly actions, enhancing closer interregional cooperation and acting as a vital voice capable of positive impact at the national and international level. Implementing climate-friendly measures and publicizing their benefits can be used to pressure nation-states to change their positions.

Such alternative multilevel environmental approaches are particularly important to the developing world. Countries such as Brazil, China, and India are already among the major GHG emitters, and thus their broader participation in the international climate regime is necessary to achieve more effective results in fighting climate change. However, the reluctance of these nation-states (including Brazil) to take on formal international mitigation obligations may be seen as a factor that reduces the effectiveness of international environmental law. In this context, subnational proactive initiatives within these countries can contribute both effective results against global warming and legitimate options for combating this global environmental problem.

The experience of the state of São Paulo illustrates that early action toward climate change mitigation can yield alternative means of environmental governance—a fact that is particularly meaningful for developing countries.

9

Reflexive Governance and Multilevel Decision Making in Agricultural Policy: Conceptual Reflections and Empirical Evidence

Peter H. Feindt

The concept of *reflexive governance* has gained much attention in the discussion about science policy (Wynne 1993), network governance (Rhodes 1997), sustainability governance (Voß, Bauknecht, and Kemp 2006), and multilevel decision making (Lenoble 2005; Rogowski 2006). It denotes a mode of governance in which cognitive procedures are designed to create feedback on multiple regulatory frameworks to influence actors' beliefs and norms (Dedeurwaerdere 2009). In reflexive governance, cognitive and normative beliefs complement the political-administrative hierarchy and economic incentives as mechanisms for coordination.

Different aspects of reflexive governance have been accentuated in the various fields of research. In the context of multilevel governance, reflexive governance denotes institutional arrangements in which the upper level sets guidelines, principles, and sometimes policy aims and the lower level decides about the precise programs and instruments (Lenoble 2005; Rogowski 2006). Network governance becomes reflexive when flexible actor arrangements complement the more static and compartmentalized working of the state apparatus in ways that use the capacities of various modes of coordination (Jessop 2003); it requires meta-governance to achieve the desired social, policy, and knowledge integration (Sørensen 2006; Sørensen and Torfing 2009). In the context of science policy, reflexive governance points to a mode of policy making which takes into account that knowledge claims are intrinsically bound to social and professional identities (Wynne 1993); governance therefore needs to reflect on the plurality of referential contexts, some of which are highly specialized scientific and administrative discourses. Finally, the notion of sustainability governance (e.g., Petschow, Rosenau, and von Weizsäcker 2005), with its normatively tuned call for temporal, cross-scale, and cross-departmental policy integration, links both dimensions—multilevel and multireferential governance—to which reflexivity should then refer.

Dedeurwaerdere (2009) distinguishes between reflexive governance as design problem in which rules for reflexive learning are created within a given normative framework (a case of first order learning), and a normative perspective that aims at reflexive capacity building, which finally leads to new design rules (a case of second order learning). The latter, normative aspect resonates with conceptual developments in the field of environmental democracy (Fischer 2003) and interpretive policy analysis (Fischer and Forester 1993), in particular an interest in procedural arrangements that encourage the reframing of policy discourses in order to overcome intractable controversies (Rein and Schön 1993; Laws and Rein 2003). Reflexive capacity building is also at the core of an understanding of reflexive governance as "a mode of steering that encourages actors to scrutinize and reconsider their underlying assumptions, institutional arrangements and practices" (Hendriks and Grin 2007).

These accounts suggest that reflexive governance occurs when institutional and procedural arrangements involve actors from various levels of governance and/or various epistemic backgrounds

• in an effort to reflect on and possibly adapt their cognitive and normative beliefs;
• in ways that take into account and acknowledge alternative understandings of the problems;
• in an attempt to integrate multiple approaches to problem solution.

Reflexive governance is an important concept with regard to global public goods (Kaul, Grunberg, and Stern 1999; International Task Force on Global Public Goods 2006). Pointing to the problem of fit between institutions and problems (Young, Schroeder, and King 2008), the very notion of a public good implies a call for a new, global layer of governance. The global public good discourse has been institutionalized in a new layer of international bodies and practices, for example the United Nations Conventions on Biological Diversity (UNCBD), Climate Change (UNFCCC), and Desertification (UNCCD). At the same time, the globality of these goods has been constituted through scientifically saturated discourses; governing global public goods therefore requires the integration of information across variegated realms of knowledge, including science, local practices, and international relations. This generates issues of multireferentiality. As a result, the governance of global public goods implies both multilevel and multireferential governance.

Against this background, the aim of this chapter is twofold: to embed the notion of multireferential governance in theories of structural differentiation and deliberative democracy to add conceptual strength to the concept, and to demonstrate the usefulness of this concept for the analysis of policy change in multilevel governance systems. Therefore, in line with the analysis of the principle of precaution in chapter 7, this chapter focuses on the way new types of collective actors. such as civil society groups and sectoral organizations, participate in the reframing of policy concepts in the field of environmental policy at various levels of collective decision making. It adds to the latter analysis, however, by situating the examination of multilevel governance in the context of a review of the broader literature on reframing in interpretative political science, which shows how learning on common understandings can be envisioned within such a multilevel architecture.

The second section of the chapter reviews conceptual contributions to the reflexive governance debate that are based on theories of structural differentiation, reflexive modernity, ecological economics, and deliberative democracy. From this emerges an understanding of "reflexivity" as a normative-practical concept that circumscribes a mode of governance to help overcome structurally embedded ignorance of specialized organizations and institutions with regard to the external effects of their own operations. The third section discusses how shifts in the Common Agricultural Policy (CAP) of the European Union (EU) qualify as a move toward reflexive governance. The CAP has been selected because it constitutes a case in which multilevel governance has tended to work as a barrier against more reflexive modes of governance. The final section draws the conclusions and discusses the relevance of the findings beyond the case.

Concepts of Reflexive Governance

Theories of Functional Differentiation

Sociologists have heavily drawn on the observation that in modern society individual and organizational specialization on certain activities is one of the most prominent structural features. Early sociologists like Durkheim ([1893] 1967) explained this phenomenon through the principle of division of labor. Mid-twentieth-century sociologists like Talcott Parsons assumed underlying functionalities. Parson's famous AGIL model claimed that any society needed to ensure that the four basic functions of adaptation, goal attainment, integration, and latency (pattern maintenance) are maintained, which in modern societies would be the task of four society-wide functional subsystems: the economic, political, social, and cultural system (e.g., Parsons 1966). Theories of functional differentiation (Rueschemeyer 1974; Luhmann 1977) assume that modern societies are structured in a specific way that separates them from premodern societies. Although traditional societies were mainly divided into clans or families, and the main structural dividing line was kinship, feudal societies of early modernity were stratified; that is, the prime structural principle was based on different societal strata such as the nobility, clergy, and peasantry. Modern societies, in contrast, are primarily differentiated along functional divisions. They are composed of specialized subsystems such as law, science, economy, and sports. An important instance of these subsystems is the establishment of professional communities like lawyers, economists, or engineers. Each of the subsystems produces special goods and values that system theorists take great effort to portray in a somewhat stylized manner. According to Luhmann (1986, 2000) the political system produces collectively binding decisions, the scientific system produces truth, and so on.

In the Luhmann type of differentiation theory, society is constituted through communication. Communication in the subsystems is highly specialized and focused on the functions the subsystem is expected to fulfill. From these functions arise specific criteria of relevance which then structure the systemic communication. In the most stylized version of his theory of differentiation, Luhmann (1986) holds that systemic communication is binary coded. For example, in the economic subsystem, information is processed with regard to the binary code revenue/expenditures, in the legal subsystem the code is legal/illegal, in the political system power/no power. Therefore an event contains information for the economic system only if it has an impact on revenues or expenditures somewhere in the system, for the legal system only if it implies a norm violation or norm compliance, and so on. For example, the spillover of the wastewater treatment system of a chemical production plant will trigger further communication in the legal system only if it constitutes a norm violation, and in the economic system only if this violation possibly results in a fine or if users of the affected waters, such as fishermen, suffer from financial losses. However, the incidence will be ignored by the political system unless issues like lenient control procedures by state agencies or legal loopholes enter the agenda. In any case, the incidence will probably be completely irrelevant for the sports or the arts subsystems and not be noted at all in their communication. As this example illustrates, functionally specialized subsystems communicate according to their different relevance criteria, and as a result they produce different

kinds of knowledge. Knowledge in this theoretical framework is understood as "any operational schema applied in order to observe and
describe the world, including the observing episteme itself" (Bora 2006,
6). Highly specialized knowledge results in increased performance of the
specific function and in narrowed perception. Because events are observed
with regard to the specific relevance criteria, subsystems regularly neglect
side effects from their operations—side effects in terms of the subsystem's
own relevance criteria. Hence, functionally specialized communication
tends to follow narrowly defined instrumental rationalities (cf. Habermas
1981). Since functional subsystems tend to ignore the influence of their
observational schemes on what they observe, they are in need of "supervision" (Willke 1997).

Subsystems are, however, only one layer of societal structure. As long
as the analysis remains on the level of multiple, society-wide subsystems
with partial and incompatible schemas of observation, it is difficult to
achieve more than a somehow stylized analysis that limits itself to explain
one reason for plurality and multireferentiality in modern societies. If we
conceive organizations and the actors that take roles in them as another—
or two other—layers, we gain a more complex and pragmatic picture.
According to the "actor centered institutionalism" approach (Mayntz
et al. 1988; Braun 1993; Mayntz and Scharpf 1995; Schimank 2005),
subsystems provide actors with evaluative criteria (e.g., profit, power, or
truth) and select the types of goals they are expected to achieve in their
roles, whereas the organizational context specifies the normative expectations (rights and duties) and the resources that come with specific roles.
This multilayer concept allows us to describe the paradox that although
the "logic of action" (March and Olsen 1989) in an organization is
usually guided by a functionally specified rationality and the respective
evaluative criteria, organizations often incorporate subunits that mirror
other functionally specified logics. For example, business corporations
usually include a legal unit that has the task of observing the legal environment of the organization and the organization's activities with regard
to their relevance to legal norms as well as dealing with external legal
interventions that arise from the corporation's activities being observed
by others in the operational schema of law. In other words, even inside
functionally specialized organizations peculiar fields of "multireferentiality" (Bora 2006) can be found in which multiple types of knowledge are
processed.

Multireferentiality becomes even more pertinent when it comes to
the organizational fields or networks in which multiple organizations

interact (Kenis and Knoke 2002). While this meso-level concept depicts the more stable features of interorganizational constellations, the concept of a governance situation (Stirling 2006) focuses on the situational instances. From the point of view of differentiation theory, governance situations are at the nodal points of observation of one or more functionally differentiated systems. Whether and how this plurality of observational schemas is taken into account and becomes effective is then at the heart of the quest for reflexive governance.

In the context of this debate, Stirling (2006, 226–229) discerns three types of governance situations: unreflectiveness, reflection, and reflexivity. "Unreflectiveness is ... a governance situation in which representations, understanding and interventions are effectively restricted to whatever are held to be the most obvious operational, or instrumentally pertinent attributes of the object under attention" (Stirling 2006, 226). In the context of differentiation theory, the strictly mono-functional operational mode of subsystems would qualify as unreflective. Hence, system theorists see a need to make subsystems reflect on their effects on other subsystems. Japp (1997), for example, calls for "inter-systemic discourses," and Willke (1997) for "supervision." The intended effect is that in a certain governance situation a plurality of perspectives would be considered, creating reflectiveness that "refers to a mode of representation, understanding and intervention by governance systems in which attention extends to a 'full range' of whatever are held to be broadly salient attributes of the object in question" (Stirling 2006, 227).

Yet governance problems arise not only from multiple representations of the governance object but also from differences in the operational modes of the governing and the governed system. Steering theories based on differentiation theory stress that if the target system's operational logic differs from that of the steering system, steering efforts are doomed to be either irrelevant, to over-regulate, or to trigger excessive side effects. Hence, the theory of "reflexive law" (Teubner 1989) concludes that any steering effort needs to be linked to processes of self-organization in the target system to achieve the desired effects (Rogowski 2006). Reflexivity thus demands more than taking into account different viewpoints. With reflexivity, "attention simultaneously encompasses and helps constitute both subject and object," it constitutes a "recursive mutual contingency of subjective representations and interventions" (Stirling 2006, 229).

Processes of this kind are difficult to describe in the terms offered by the theory of functional differentiation. However, this perspective provides us with a caveat that some sectors of society have rigid internal schema of observation, along with highly selective criteria of relevance, often tightened through the establishment of professional communities (Abbott 1988). Another important aspect is that in functionally differentiated societies everyone is a layperson in most fields of life and has to rely on expert judgments. Hence, trust in expertise and in experts has become a precondition for the acceptance of expert judgments (Giddens 1990). If expertise becomes contested, trust needs to be restored through procedural provisions.

Theory of Reflexive Modernity

According to Ulrich Beck's theory of reflexive modernization, reflexivity and consideration of effects can be and are indeed enforced through the politicization of "side-effects" (Beck, Bonss, and Lau 2003). Institutions and practices of the "first modernity" work toward the standardization of agents and objects. They presuppose the existence of core institutions: the nation-state, individualization, employment societies, exploitable nature, instrumental control, and functional differentiation (Beck, Bonss, and Lau 2003). Under conditions of second modernity, the institutions of first modernity are weakened and questioned as a result of their own success. For example, in the field of agriculture, it is exactly the success of the modernist paradigm of productivism that undercuts the ecological foundations of production. In the transition to second modernity the environmental side effects are no longer accepted. Food safety crises have shattered the trust that modernist farming has the expertise to provide safe and healthy food (Wilkinson, Lowe, and Donaldson 2010). While change was part of life in first modernity, we now face what Beck calls "meta-change."

John Grin (2006) argues that the institutions of first or simple modernity (parliaments, agricultural research centers, farmers' organizations) are increasingly complemented by institutions of reflexive modernity. Model projects, participatory arrangements, stakeholder bodies, research programs for system transition management or transdisciplinary advisory boards are expected to bring new ideas to established practices. To become effective, they need to take into account the plurality of actors' logics. They open up hybrid places where, for example, farmers, consumers and environmentalists meet and create new approaches and solutions. To gain legitimacy under conditions of network governance, they turn to reflexive arrangements that do not prescribe certain outcomes but instead make sure that different views are taken into consideration. These arrangements also take into account the plurality of internal organizational logics. For example, the meaning of sustainable development will be spelled out differently by and for small organic farmers than by and for large-scale specialized holdings. Also, power and vested interests will trigger strategic behavior, and the normative ambition of reflexive governance might find limited acceptance, being in tension with the perception of actors in the field and the knowledge and norms implicit in their practices (Grin 2006).

Evolutionary Economics

A third approach to the discussion of reflexive governance has been formulated by Tom Dedeurwaerdere (2005). Building on ideas from evolutionary economics and criticizing shortcomings of transaction cost economics, he addresses the problem that policy instruments that are designed to protect public goods often have the reverse effect when established in the context of specific local logics of action. For example, under the UN Convention on Biological Diversity access and benefit-sharing schemes were implemented to provide incentives for protecting biodiversity in countries of origin. However, in practice they crowded out intrinsic motivations to preserve natural resources. The new benefit schemes redefined these resources as private goods, and the communities lost their motivation to treat them as public on the basis of mutual trust and social control. The main question would then be how reflexive governance can contribute to the formation of collective preferences and the generation of knowledge for (global) public goods such as biodiversity and climate change.

Deliberative Democracy

The theory of deliberative democracy as developed by Jürgen Habermas opens another road to reflexive governance. Habermas's original intention was a critique of technocratic policy making and planning (Habermas 1968). This he staged as a critique of instrumental rationality that optimizes means to given ends without reflecting the rationality of the ends. Optimizing agricultural productivity under conditions of overproduction would be a good example. But value rationality (cf. Weber 1922) also falls short of what is needed if the value reflection is limited to the normative horizon of one particular community or one functional subsystem while effects concern others.

Habermas (1981) introduces the concept of communicative rationality as a logic of action that allows reflection of validity claims about what is true, authentic, right, and just. Here rationality is understood as practical reason that comes to life through processes of inter-subjective communication that allow validity claims to be made and tested. If different actors introduce different logics of action to a communication, the concept of communicative rationality requires that their pre-assumptions and implications can be thematized as the object of debate. Such processes of communication allow for the creation of reflexivity on multiple value horizons and logics of action. The communicative space where plural viewpoints meet is not governed by specialized instrumental rationality but constitutes a realm of practical reason in which arguments from divergent provenances are balanced against each other in the medium of deliberation; that is, the pondering argumentation about the desirable and the possible guided by rules of practical reason. Ensuring that validity claims of all sorts can be tested implies that all affected and interested parties should be able to participate. Hence, deliberation and participation are both indispensable prerequisites for uninhibited reflexivity.

However, Fischer (2005) insists that there can be no general theory of participatory design because the rules and meanings of what is going on in a specific arena are continuously renegotiated among participants. Because participants bring their discourses and experiences to the table, the web of meanings that constitute the social space of such arrangements is intertwined with threads of those discourses which are part of the practices outside—practices that such reflexive arrangements are set up to change. Participants thus have to take a reflexive stance toward the discourses and practices in which they and their social activities are embedded. Deliberative participation therefore requires a political culture that allows actors to acquire and practice the corresponding skills and attitudes.

The processes of meaning-making that emerge in such reflexive, participatory and deliberative arrangements have been described as reframing (Rein and Schön 1993; Schön and Rein 1994). According to this concept the logic of action for organizations and groups forms an interpretive frame for the understanding of such factors as events, proposals, and initiatives. If in participatory and deliberative arrangements several of these frames are articulated by participants, the interactive communication can be used to develop new interpretive frames in order to reframe controversial or novel issues and facilitate collaboration. Empirical case studies show that such participatory and deliberative arrangements can help to reflect not only on the effects but also on the inner logic of established practices and thus allow development of more integrative approaches (e.g., Forester 2009). Therefore, it is crucial to begin with the definitions of the situation that the actors bring along: "The scope for reframing is strongest when the ideas, concepts and theories that reframing draws on derive from the experience, understanding and active involvement of actors in concrete social situations" (Laws and Rein 2003, 173).

In conclusion, a multitude of theories—ranging from system theoretical interpretation of functional differentiation to theories of modernity, ecological, and evolutionary economics, as well as theories of deliberative democracy—converge on the diagnosis that not only consideration of the effects of societal routines and practices must be improved (moving from unreflectedness to reflectiveness), but also that reflexive arrangements are needed to encourage participants to gain a reflexive stance toward the construction of governance objects through the operational schemes of observation, thereby moving toward reflexivity.

Reframing Agricultural Policy toward Reflexive Modernity and Reflectedness

This section uses the various concepts of reflexive governance to discuss shifts in agriculture policies that are crucially important for the delivery of global public goods. Beginning with the notion of a paradigm shift in agriculture policy as evidence of reframing and a focus on the shifting notions of the relevant public goods, the discussion then moves on to assess the degree to which this reflects a move toward reflexive modernization, to more reflectedness and reflexivity, and a reflexive notion of sustainable development.

Reframing Agricultural Policy and Shifting Notions of the Public Good

Within countries that are members of the Organisation for Economic Co-operation and Development (OECD) agriculture policies have been widely reframed since the mid-1980s. This has been captured by the notion of a paradigm shift (Coleman, Skogstad,, and Atkinson 1997; Daugbjerg 2003). According to Peter Hall's (1993) concept—which is based on Thomas Kuhn's work on "scientific revolutions" (Kuhn 1962)—a policy paradigm is an "interpretive frame" for the formulation and implementation of a policy. It includes normative and cognitive ideas, policy goals, theories about the world, and preferable policy instruments and practices.

The interpretive framework that dominated agriculture policies in all Western countries from the 1930s to the 1980s (Tracy 1989) has been termed the *developmental or state-assisted paradigm* (Coleman and Grant 1998, 636), *state assistance paradigm* (Skogstad 1998) or *dependent agriculture paradigm* (Moyer and Josling 2002). It is based on the assumption that the key public good that agriculture provides is food security, which is threatened by market failure, especially volatile markets and ruinous prices in years of good harvest. The state must help to stabilize markets and control supply through import controls, surplus buying, state trading, and state aid for exports (Moyer and Josling 2002, 33). Environmental goods as such are not a concern. Rather, the agrarian landscape is seen as a productive resource that needs to be optimized, and farmers are intrinsically motivated to preserve the productivity of natural resources (Feindt et al. 2008, 289). Based on an ideology of "agricultural exceptionalism" (Skogstad 1998) and a range of "agricultural myths" (Browne et al. 1992), the sector is perceived and treated as different from others, isolating the policy discourse from external criticism.

The *competitive* or *market liberal agriculture paradigm* (Moyer and Josling 2002), which was embraced by the Reagan administration during the 1980s, assumes that the market can best provide cheap and abundant food. Product-related market policies should be reduced to a safety net with minimum prices; for a transitional period direct payments can be made but should be decoupled from production. Environmental concerns are not addressed as provision of public goods but rather through regulation that limits negative external effects from production. Because of congressional resistance, the market liberal paradigm had limited impact in the United States (Orden, Paarlberg, and Roe 1999), but it was broadly implemented in Australia and New Zealand during the 1990s.

The *multifunctional agriculture paradigm* (Coleman 1998) embraces a broad range of public goods that are perceived as being coupled to farming activities, including the "cultural landscape," natural resources such as groundwater, biodiversity, and the viability of rural spaces. The state has to ensure that agriculture continues to fulfill its social and ecological functions, and that the cultural landscape and the family farm remain viable. Since farmers are insufficiently rewarded for the nonmarketable goods they produce through the price they receive for their sellable goods, the state should prevent dominance of "mono-functional" agriculture and remunerate farmers for the environmental benefits they produce (Moyer and Josling 2002, 34–36). Apart from the EU, the multifunctionality paradigm has been adopted by Norway, Switzerland, Korea, and Japan (OECD 2001; Feindt and Lange 2007), who even formed a group called the "friends of multifunctionality" at WTO negotiations (World Trade Organization 2004).

The *globalised production paradigm* (Josling 2002, 94–99; Coleman, Grant, and Josling 2004, 98–110) moves from a national to a global perspective and comes closer to the notion of *global* public goods. Markets for food, feed, and agricultural raw materials are globalizing, and mainstream agriculture is becoming part of complex transnational networks of production and distribution (Higgins and Lawrence 2005; Morgan, Marsden, and Murdoch 2006). This allows producers and retailers to exploit regulatory differentiation and evade costs for the provision of public goods or the mitigation of negative externalities. However, a more global perspective on public goods is also evolving. Consequently, domestic environmental improvements are no longer viewed as satisfying and efficient if they are achieved through the export of "dirty" or environmentally inefficient processes of production. These developments call for international harmonization of standards on a high level of ambition (Harl 2003) to avoid a "race to the bottom" (Vogel 1995). Another feature of the globalized production paradigm is the notion that markets have become more demand driven and differentiated. The provision of global public goods can be enhanced through "ethical consumerism," for which consumer trust is critical. Hence the state should guarantee transparency and consumer safety through quality and safety standards, labeling, and control schemes. Examples include traceability rules and the labeling of genetically modified organisms, organic products, and products of regional origin.

In sum, over the last two decades, as part of a continuous reframing of agriculture policies in OECD countries, environmental concerns are taken into account as being threatened by negative externalities of competitive agriculture, as a public good provided by multifunctional agriculture, or a quality that adds value in the eye of the cosmopolitan consumer. Depending on the frame, the necessary policies are regulation of minimum standards, remuneration of public goods, or differentiated standards and harmonization.

Through a series of reforms—the 1992 MacSherry reform, Agenda 2000, and the 2003 Fischler reform (see Coleman, Skogstad, and Atkinson 1997; Ackrill 2005; Greer 2005)—the EU's Common Agricultural Policy (CAP) has taken up idea elements from all four policy paradigms:

- In line with the market liberal paradigm, most market price policies were reduced to a safety-net level. Instead, farmers now receive an area-based "Single Farm Payment," which is decoupled from production. This has eliminated state incentives to increase production and specialize in a few subsidized products.

- In line with the multifunctionality paradigm, agro-environmental programs compensate farmers for the higher costs they incur from providing public goods, especially environmental benefits. The Single Farm Payment requires recipient farmers to comply with environmental, consumer protection, and animal welfare standards (cross-compliance regulations). In some member states a "regional premium" has been introduced from which more extensive farms benefit. Modulation—the capping of payments above €5,000 by several percent and redirection of the saved funds to rural development, structural, and agro-environmental policies—diminishes the concentration of payments flowing to large and productive farms (European Commission 2006, 3).

- The salience of standards highly resonates with the global agricultural production paradigm. The conditionality of the Single Farm Payment to "cross compliance" rules uses the financial resources as leverage to implement environmental and food safety standards and traceability systems. The EU also tries to anchor these systems and rules in the WTO system and make them the global standard (Vincent 2007), especially in the context of the Agreement on the Application of Sanitary and Phytosanitary Measures (SPS) and Codex Alimentarius.

- Justification and results of the CAP reform are still in line with the state-dependent agriculture paradigm. Cross compliance implies that farmers are paid for obeying the law. Agricultural exceptionalism still seems to be alive. Decoupling farm payments from production has also stressed the income function of these payments.

As a result of these shifts the CAP now embraces a wider range of ideas. But does this constitute a move toward reflexive governance?

Toward Reflexive Modernity

The state-dependent agriculture paradigm fits well with the core institutions of first modernity, and evolves as its manifestation in the sector. The nation-state is the key actor that strives for food sovereignty and protects domestic producers from outside threats, most prominently import competitors. Farmers are also shielded against natural disasters—constituting nature as an "other" of society that needs to be controlled.

Natural hazards are transformed into manageable risks through variegated institutions ranging from public weather forecasts to hail insur-
ance. Nature is also constituted as exploitable. The quest for increasing
productivity requires mechanical, biological, and chemical control over
nature. Even during periods of unsalable surplus production, technical
progress is never questioned but continuously advanced through gener-
ous funding for research and development, outreach, and education.
Farmers' identities are constituted around the notion of production and
a productivist use of the countryside (Marsden 1993). This creates
various policy inconsistencies. For example, the 1933 U.S. Agriculture
Act introduced set aside programs to lower surplus and stabilize market
prices, while another program in the law authorized government money
to be spent on buying and storing surplus, providing incentives to increase
production (Tweeten 1989, 325). The massive use of interventionist
policy instruments displays a trust in instrumental control that is characteristic to first modernity. During the following decades, market intervention effectively provided a floor market price, kept marginal producers
in the market, and gave incentives to increase production. The costs were
partly shifted to "third countries" (those not in the European Union)
through import controls and export subsidies, following the nationalist
policy approach characteristic for first modernity institutions. Coupling
support to production, rather than focusing on income, mirrors the
prominence of the employment society as a core institution of first
modernity in which the welfare state prefers policies that link benefits
to work and production (like the coupling of social benefits to income
from dependent work). Finally, the commodity programs further contributed to the individualization and disembedding of farmers, who increasingly produced staple crops for anonymous mass markets (or the state
intervention system) rather than for local communities, specific consumer
groups, or regional markets. Production processes were reorganized
according to the principle of functional differentiation; specialized companies for seeds, machinery, fertilizers, and other inputs, as well as for
distribution and processing, took over functions that used to be located
on the farm.

The interventionist and productivist agriculture policies were continuously surrounded by notions of crisis (e.g., Tracy 1989) that have increasingly politicized side effects of modern agriculture and farm policies. In
the EU, recurrent budget crises indicated an unsustainable need for
external financial resources. The rural crisis brought to attention an
increasing disconnection between disembedded modes of production and

the rural economy. Environmental impacts have been registered with alarm. A series of food scares and animal diseases triggered questions about the controllability of biological processes and the treatment of animals, while also creating widespread consciousness about the blurring boundaries between knowledge and ignorance as well as the natural and the artificial in modern agriculture (Dressel 2002).

Over time, the institutional boundaries shifted, too. The state is now complemented by all sorts of professional and standards organizations as a guarantor of sound practice (Feindt and Flynn 2009; Marsden et al. 2009). With the emerging WTO and intellectual property regimes (Tansey and Rajotte 2008), the location of control has moved partly from the national to the international and transnational arena. The idea of controlling nature is contested by the organic and traditional agriculture movements. Spending on agriculture research decreased, which has been cited as one of the reasons for the global food crisis in 2008. The dominant ideas about the rural space shifted from productivist to consumptionist countryside (Marsden 1993; Frouws 1998). Paralleling the crisis of the employment society the focus of agriculture policy moved from supporting farming per se to governing the effects of farming. The local food movement, supported by regulation on traditional and geographical products, strives to reconnect agriculture and food production to a wider notion of locality (Sonnino and Marsden 2006; Feagan 2007).

Toward Reflectedness

Traditional agriculture policies were characterized by an astonishing degree of unreflectedness. Since the late 1970s, these policies have encouraged overproduction and triggered budget problems. Since the late 1970s they were criticized for harming the environment and for failing to prevent rural decline, at least in peripheral areas. Facing structural and ever-rising surpluses of grain and beef, as well as high costs for public budgets, the state-assisted paradigm came into disrepute. The governance situation became increasingly reflected (e.g., Commission of the European Communities 1985). Since 1987 the OECD started to build up a monitoring system for the agricultural policies of its member states (OECD 1987). Consented indicators were developed that showed the costs of the dependent agriculture paradigm were borne not only by taxpayers but also by consumers and processors who faced higher prices for raw materials and consumer goods (OECD 2005b). Further costs, it was shown, arose for producers in third countries who lost market shares through import restrictions and export subsidies. Arising trade conflicts and foregone trade liberalization put costs on the trading industries.

In the EU, new budget procedures introduced through the Single European Act 1987 and the Inter-Institutional Agreements between the European Parliament, Commission, and Council on budgetary discipline and budgetary procedure since 1988 have changed the dynamics of the budget process from an annual bargaining over support prices to the design of agricultural programs over a period of five (and later seven) years, in tune with the EU budget period (Laffan 1997). These new procedures have improved the conditions for policy learning, allowing the Commission to strategically develop innovative policy schemes over a preparatory and discussion period of several years. In addition, the process now encompasses several levels of decision making, calling for broader consideration of issues beyond the narrow horizon of the policy field. Finance ministers and heads of state need to agree on the spending limits. Agricultural ministers then have to develop programs within the financial confines. Consequently, the budget limits force the Agriculture Council and the Commission to set policy priorities.

The more reflected governance situation for policy formulation was mirrored by shifting policy paradigms. The market liberal paradigm, while deeply rooted in economic thinking (Moyer and Josling 2002) and framing governance situations in terms of economic costs and benefits, still requires more deliberation than the state-assisted agriculture paradigm. First, with agriculture no longer considered "exceptional," lobbyists and politicians cannot fully disregard calls for comparing costs and benefits of agriculture policy with those of other policies. Second, to the degree that the market liberal paradigm takes a global rather than a national perspective, reasoning extends to international policy effects. Third, through the calculation of costs not only to taxpayers, but also to consumers (OECD 2007), broader distributive effects enter the horizon. Fourth, environmental issues, as long as they can be economically valued, enter the deliberation. While this allows for a relatively high degree of reflectedness, all arguments have to be translated into economic terms. Reflexivity as attention to "recursive mutual contingency of subjective representations and interventions" (Stirling 2006, 229; discussed above) is not encouraged. Reframing in the market liberal paradigm requires translating all other frames into the economic one.

The multifunctional agriculture paradigm seems to be more appropriate in relation to concepts of reflexive governance. The very term indicates the acknowledgment of multiple goals and value dimensions. Yet not every account of multifunctionality is inductive to reflexivity. The term as such leaves open which functions are considered and how they are valued. It is only when the concept of multifunctionality is linked to ideas about value pluralism and the regular appearance of non-commensurate values in public deliberation, that the road is open to a more reflexive governance approach.

At first glance, the globalized production paradigm seems to suffer from similar limitations as those that face the market liberal paradigm. It is often presented in economic terms that appear not conducive for reflexive deliberation (Josling 2002a; Harl 2003); however, the paradigm is political from the start. The underlying problem in the description puts market power and rivaling standards at the core. On the level of instruments, standards like the EU's labels for protected designation of origin, protected geographical indication, or traditional specialties (European Community 2006a, 2006b) embody cultural ideas about food, landscape, and the environment. Harmonizing standards on a global scale, therefore, requires negotiations that are not limited to power-based bargaining but must also include arguing on the reasons for different concepts (on arguing versus bargaining, see Elster 1998). The kind of reflexive practical reasoning needed here resembles ethical arguments in an intercultural setting, calling for the reflection of the issue at hand from the partial points of view of the various cultural standpoints as well as from a global perspective. In this sense, the globalized production paradigm with its focus on the internationalization of regulatory issues in a globalized marketplace then calls for a "cosmopolitan" perspective (cf. Beck 2007; Zierhofer 2007).

Conclusions: Toward Reflexivity and Sustainability?

In a globalizing marketplace the character of public goods that are coupled to or threatened by different kinds of agricultural production becomes increasingly global. For example, food security and food safety are traded globally with the food. Achieving domestic environmental goals increasingly depends on developments in transnational markets. Other environmental goods such as biodiversity, prevention of desertification, and biosecurity are increasingly framed in global arenas and addressed by global regimes. The provision of global public goods will often require reforms of deeply entrenched, functionally differentiated, highly specialized, and narrow-minded policies and routines in production and consumption. As the example of agriculture policy illustrates, such entrenched policies and routines are typically characterized by unreflectedness. Institutional changes in the policy environment that enhance the reflectedness of the decision-making process can help to reframe policies. But only enriched interpretive frameworks create perceived governance situations that are more integrated and allow more viewpoints from global to local and corporate to be taken into account.

Regarding the CAP specifically, a sequence of reforms has transformed the governance situation in which it operates from unreflectiveness toward reflectedness. This move is underpinned by the fact that all programs are now continuously evaluated. But does the CAP qualify as moving toward reflexive governance? Methodologically, attributing degrees of reflexivity to a governance situation is to assess situations that are constructed by actors through interpretive frames. In this regard, most policy makers agree that the CAP after 2003 rests on a set of diverse policy ideas (Feindt and Lange 2007) and insofar has become multireferential. Over time new policies have been layered on top of the older ones. Old policies and goals like reliable and affordable food supply then need to be reinterpreted in the light of new ones like environmental goals or climate change (Feindt and Flynn 2009). As a result, multiple policy goals are translated into normative tensions between various layers of policy. This creates opportunities for reflexivity, albeit vulnerable to closure when the logic of resource-based bargaining takes over. But altogether the institutional framework of agriculture and food policy has moved toward multireferentiality.

As with European politics in general, this process has been paved by the emerging multilevel architecture of decision making, which encourages the articulation of perspectives that are pitched at different scales of concern. According to the "community method" the Commission acts as representative of the community while the Council represents the member states. In practice this unfortunately implies a division of labor in which the conceptual work and the policy-learning (arguing) is left to the Commission while the member states in the Council concentrate on distributive bargaining (Gehring 2000). While the Commission combines the roles of knowledge broker and agenda-setter (Peters 1996), the dominance of distributive bargaining in the Council tends to limit the scope of considerations, encourages a status quo orientation, and is one of the explanations for path dependency in agriculture policy (Kay 2003; Ackrill 2005), putting a break on reflexivity. At the same time, however, the continuity of negotiations and consultations in an EU-like regime helps to develop common perspectives, shared understandings, and mutual solidarity (Kohler-Koch 2005), which also facilitate the social construction of common, transnational public goods. In the EU, the existence of two institutions, the Commission and the Parliament, which ideally embody the common political community, is important. Further moves toward reflexivity will depend as much on continuing investments in political culture as on policy design.

Agriculture is only one example of a wide sectoral policy arena (which includes energy, transport, housing, and chemicals) with neo-corporatist governance patterns, in which side effects outside the sector tend to be ignored or downplayed. In such policy environments, reflexive governance cannot be equated with a purely sectoral bottom-up approach. Instead, a reflexive governance perspective pays due attention to the interplay among wider institutional arrangements, deliberative preference building in specialized sectors, and processes of framing and reframing in a fragmented and pluralist world. As the example of the CAP demonstrates, reflexive governance is needed to address the joint challenges of multilevel and multireferential governance in providing global public goods; it emerges from ongoing parallel attempts to build multilevel policies and cope with the side effects from practices and institutions of the first modernity type; and if well identified, it is an important force for the progressive reframing of monoreferential and narrow-minded policies and practices.

IV

Multi-Stakeholder Coordination: How to Manage Heterogeneity

The fourth part of the book explores the general call for multi-stakeholder and deliberative methods to manage the new interdependencies of actors on a global scale. Since the initial enthusiasm in the 1990s for these innovations in governance, many experiments have been run and systematic analysis has been carried out. This allows some first lessons for GPG provision to be drawn. First, there are some important trade-offs, such as between increasing the effectiveness of agreements and complying with higher environmental standards. The research also shows the need to combine multi-stakeholder coordination with other tools, such as learning about legal and social norms, and the complex systems of incentives that have been discussed in other parts of the book. Further, the comparative strengths and weaknesses of multi-stakeholder coordination, international norm setting and complex incentives have to be assessed.

The chapters in this part explore alternative ways of involving and coordinating various stakeholders in collective decision making. From the survey of cases and methods in the chapter by Fritsch and Newig, it becomes clear that these methods also have problems and drawbacks. Although it is clear that participatory methods have the potential to improve the legitimacy and the implementation of decisions, they do not always improve the quality of the policy that is adopted. Further, participatory methods do not automatically help to generate more usable and adequate knowledge on GPG issues and solutions. Finally, all these processes are highly context dependent.

The combination of various mechanisms can help to overcome some of these drawbacks. The chapter by Dedeurwaerdere shows how the combination of multi-stakeholder coordination and economic incentives provides a supplementary element for increasing the effectiveness of the implementation and the scaling up of environmental standards. The

detailed case study in this chapter is a good example of the environmental network governance that has emphasized the shifting role of the state from powering to steering. As argued in the chapter, multi-stakeholder networks can be especially effective for addressing the non-use values of environmental services, such as the existence values of plants and animals, and landscape values. The chapter by Stagl builds further on these arguments, by showing how the effectiveness of deliberative methods can be increased by combining them with quantitative appraisal of the value of ecosystem services. This chapter shows some interesting trade-offs between the more instrumentally oriented forms of participatory assessment (which often try to provide monetary estimates), and the more exploratory forms (such as multi-criteria mapping). In general, this chapter shows how hybrid methods provide opportunities for learning during the assessment and increasing transparency in social choice on the ranking of sustainability targets.

10

Participatory Governance and Sustainability: Findings of a Meta-Analysis of Stakeholder Involvement in Environmental Decision Making

Oliver Fritsch and Jens Newig

Environmental governance on both sides of the Atlantic increasingly relies on the participation of non-state actors such as citizens and organized interest groups (Kagan, Gunningham, and Thornton 2003). Prompted by the U.S. Negotiated Rulemaking Act of 1990 and the Rio Declaration of 1992 (which demands in principle 10 that "environmental issues are best handled with the participation of all concerned citizens"), followed by the Aarhus Convention of 1998, four recent European Union directives[1] have legally institutionalized access to information and public participation in environmental decisions.

Among the motives and rationales for public participation, which have traditionally centered around emancipatory and legitimacy aspects, it is now an increased *effectiveness of governance* that is being discussed—and aimed at (Heinelt 2002; Hunold and Dryzek 2005; Koontz and Thomas 2006). In the face of continuing implementation deficits of environmental policy (Knill and Lenschow 2000) and increasingly complex societal structures, participatory decision modes that are suited to foster collective learning are indeed regarded as a prerequisite for the advancement of sustainable policies (Dryzek 1997). Focusing on substantive outcomes rather than on fairness or other aspects, participation thus becomes a means to achieve environmental goals in a more targeted, swift, and effective way (Bulkeley and Mol 2003). For example, there is the claim of the guidance document on public participation relative to the EC Water Framework Directive that "public participation is not an end in itself but a tool to achieve the environmental objectives of the Water Framework Directive" (European Union 2002, 6). Specifically, participatory governance relies on the expectation that participation improves the "quality" of decisions by incorporating the knowledge of local actors (Steele 2001; Pellizzoni 2003). Moreover, it is expected that the involvement of non-state actors leads to a higher acceptance of decisions and thus improves implementation and compliance (Macnaghten and Jacobs 1997). Both mechanisms are assumed to ultimately lead to better environmental outcomes as opposed to more hierarchical modes of steering (Newig 2007).

However, this "instrumental claim", which focuses on substantive outcomes, has not remained undisputed. Scholars have pointed out multiple dangers and trade-offs that Dahl (1994) has termed a "democratic dilemma" between effectiveness and participation. From a rational choice perspective, the collective use of resources regularly implies social dilemma situations (Hardin 1968), which call for institutional arrangements on scales large enough to internalize the negative externalities. Participatory decision making, however, is typically located on local or regional scales (Ostrom, Gardner, and Walker 2003; Kastens and Newig 2007), and, contrary to sustainability goals, the interests of local actors tend to focus on shorter time horizons. Accordingly, more and more authors have recently been asking whether participatory modes of implementation actually improve substantive policy outcomes. Even if one does not embrace the notion of participation as the "new tyranny" (Cooke and Kothari 2001), "there is something of a dilemma if participation turns out, empirically, not to improve outcomes" (Lee and Abbot 2003, 87–88).

Although the whole field of participation research has now reached a welcome degree of differentiation and variety, the issue of the ecological outcomes of participatory governance has received surprisingly little attention (Beierle and Cayford 2002; Koontz and Thomas 2006). Accordingly, the empirical basis is still weak and, above all, fragmented (see Diduck and Sinclair 2002). Although a considerable body of empirical and theoretical knowledge exists, this lies scattered throughout a large number of single (case) studies, most of which—if at all—only touch upon aspects of outcome effectiveness; the underlying mechanisms are often only implicitly assumed. Thus, Beierle and Cayford in their seminal study on public participation demand that "more research on implementation is needed. The value of public participation will ultimately be judged by its ability to enhance implementation and show demonstrable benefits for environmental quality. Understanding the links between participation and actions on the ground is a high priority" (Beierle and Cayford 2002, 76).

The present chapter seeks to critically assess the potential of participatory and reflexive governance for attaining sustainability goals. We aim to elucidate the conditions as well as the reflexive and participatory mechanisms that are favorable (or less favorable) to foster the generation of local knowledge, collective learning, and eventually the attainment of environmental goals. As a first step, we formulate three clusters of hypotheses regarding causal mechanisms. Next, we present early findings from a meta-analysis of thirty-five case studies on participatory environmental decision processes, drawing on the set of hypotheses as an analytical framework. The last section is devoted to our conclusions.

Conceptual Framework: Influencing Factors and Hypotheses

Participatory governance embraces a wide array of forms and settings; "participation," as such, even more so. In this chapter, we focus on those instances of public participation that have been initiated in order to agree on collectively binding public decisions. These include hearings, citizen juries, environmental mediation, public deliberative forums, consensus conferences (Renn 2005), or other forms as long as they serve to include actors that are not routinely engaged in the decision at stake. Participatory processes without aiming at binding decisions, such as Local Agenda 21, are excluded from our analysis.

Since participatory governance is embedded in a larger political context, we call for a "global" perspective linking sociopolitical *context,* decision *process,* actor *characteristics,* and—as dependent variables— decision *results* such as decision quality (output), implementation, and improvements of the ecological state of natural resources (outcome). A first account of such a perspective has been developed in Newig (2007), including more than forty-five influencing factors. This section presents a brief summary of the main hypotheses on the effects of participatory environmental governance put forward in the literature. We group these into three clusters. While the first cluster covers hypotheses explaining decision *output* by process characteristics, the second relates to explanations of decision *outcome* (implementation) by process characteristics. The importance of *context* factors is dealt with in the third cluster.

Mechanisms I: Improved Decisions through Participation?
Scholarly literature promoting participatory and reflexive governance as an instrument to more effectively attain sustainability goals (see Voß et al. 2008) puts forward three distinct causal mechanisms leading to more ecological decisions. These are: a modified power structure, an improved information basis, and emergent effects of collective learning.

According to the first argument, current environmental managers are captured by interests less supportive of pollution control, nature preservation, or sustainable lifestyles, such as business or development advocates. Furthermore, government environmental decision-making bodies and administering agencies are subject to party politics leading to compromises on their ecological goals for competing social or economic objectives. To implement policies in line with ecological goals once agreed upon, these groups of decision makers have to be opened to include civil society actors, nongovernmental organization representatives, and experts who have not been involved so far (Smith 2003). Conversely, in societal contexts characterized by a highly committed environmental administration and a less environmentally friendly citizenship, participatory decision making is likely to water-down high ecological goals (Layzer 2008). Whether or not participation will improve environmental standards most likely depends on the kind of actors that exist and the respective interests they pursue (Dryzek et al. 2005).

A second argument emphasizes the potential of participation to generate factual information that would otherwise not be available for the decision maker. This holds true in particular for very local issues (see chapter 13 in this volume). The involvement of informed lay persons may help to provide detailed knowledge of special local characteristics and conditions (Pellizzoni 2003). However, in other cases this information deficit of public authorities can be overcome by the mobilization of experts, the more so as many decisions in environmental governance are highly technical in nature and thus call for expert knowledge instead of lay contributions (Thomas 1995).

A third strand of arguments discusses in how far public involvement fosters processes of social learning. This line of reasoning goes beyond the mere acquisition of factual knowledge and underlines that group interactions might be the starting point for collectively and creatively developing new solutions due to genuine deliberation and reflection, an inspiring group atmosphere, and the multiplicity of perspectives involved (Pahl-Wostl and Hare 2004; Siebenhüner and Suplie 2005). Many authors identified mutual trust among the participants as a precondition for social learning (Leach and Sabatier 2005). Yet, social psychologists call attention to potential adverse effects such as groups making risky decisions or group closure (Cooke 2001).

In sum, the challenge is to empirically test whether public participation will increase the chance for non-state actors to break open political in-groups, improve the knowledge base of environmental decisions, and foster social learning. Finally, it has to be explored whether these mechanisms are in fact likely to enhance ecological standards of decisions.

Mechanisms II: Improved Implementation of Decisions through Participation?

Implementation research in environmental politics has provided ample evidence that traditional top-down modes of governance face serious implementation problems, which are a principal reason for low performances in reducing pollution or protecting natural resources (Knill and Lenschow 2000). Often, these deficits can be attributed to low rates of acceptance among implementing agencies, competing state actors, and affected citizens who can delay and prevent policy implementation or take legal action in order to preserve their interests. Citizen involvement is assumed to have the potential to effectively respond to these concerns (Macnaghten and Jacobs 1997; Bulkeley and Mol 2003).

First and foremost, it can be argued that the effective inclusion of actor groups with their respective preferences and interests into decision making will enhance acceptance on their part for the final decision and thus improve implementation and compliance, just because the decision also reflects their interests. However, the validity of this hypothesis depends to a considerable degree on the representation of legitimate interests; if this is not the case, acceptance by third party groups is likely to remain low.

Second, scholars of procedural justice argue that this increase of acceptance can even be observed when the final decision contradicts stakeholders' interests, so long as the procedure is perceived as fair and legitimate (Lind and Tyler 1988). However, scholarly literature has produced quite a diverse set of assumptions on how procedural legitimacy can be attained in a participatory process. While some scholars stress the equal chance to have a say and to represent one's own interests (Webler 1995), others emphasize the transparency of the process, open communication structures, early participation in all stages of policy making, consensus vote, and a neutral and professional moderation between all involved actors (Susskind, Bacow, and Wheeler 1983). Many authors argue that rules of fairness are effective only if the actors involved can have an impact on the final decision. Hence, acceptance rates are likely to decrease if important parts of the decisions have already been made elsewhere (Diduck and Sinclair 2002). Coglianese (1997) challenges these claims, maintaining that the pitfalls of conventional rule making are strongly overemphasized. He argues, on the contrary, that participatory modes of governance could increase acceptance problems because dis-agreements on who shall given right to participate can never be fully resolved. Furthermore, participatory processes shed light on disadvanta-geous aspects of the decision at hand that affected persons might have been previously unaware of, hence reducing acceptance.

Given the prevailing contradicting theoretical assertions and the lack of empirical underpinning, it will be crucial to examine how forms of public participation have an impact on acceptance, implementation, and compliance of environmental policies.

Mechanisms III: Influence of the Context

While research on participatory governance has predominantly been focusing on processes, scholars have also been paying attention to the societal context and actor constellations (Delli Carpini, Cook, and Jacobs 2004).

Processes with considerable power asymmetries tend to suppress the interests of weaker actors compared to formalized top-down processes. This is likely to impact on the substance of a decision as well as on its acceptance, because disadvantaged actors might choose to delay or prevent implementation after the process by appealing to court (Cupps 1977; Turner and Weninger 2005).

As argued above, consensual decision making can contribute to legiti-macy and, thus, to acceptance and improved implementation. However, contextual characteristics such as specific problem constellations might render a consensus vote almost impossible, particularly in social dilemma situations (e.g., NIMBY) that are virtually irresolvable in consensus without one actor taking a large part of the costs (Elliott 1984; Thomas 1995). On the other hand, when problems can be framed as win-win situations, participatory decision making is more likely to foster high-quality decisions and swift implementation (Susskind, Bacow, and Wheeler 1983).

Many of the causal mechanisms presented so far have been claimed—implicitly or explicitly—for participatory implementations of higher-order policies. However, a considerable number of case studies is available that examine citizen involvement in local policy making or the collabora-tive interplay of different public agencies and non-state actors in complex multilevel systems. Although the participatory instruments employed in both types of settings are often the same, it is reasonable to assume that the causal mechanisms outlined above will work differently. The absence of a given policy goal transforms the rationale of a participatory process from collaborative adaptation to local conditions and improved implementation toward a more power-dominated and interest-based struggle for the general direction of policy. Accordingly, we assume that the political context the decision process is embedded in is likely to have a major impact on the relevance of some causal assumptions discussed and, as a consequence, on policy outputs and outcomes.

Findings of a Meta-Analysis of Case Studies

Methodology

In this section, we will put the hypotheses outlined above to an empirical test by conducting a meta-analysis of thirty-five well-documented cases of environmental governance (see table 10.1). These samples were taken from a larger database of 200 case studies of—more or less—collaborative environmental management in Western democracies, elaborated by political scientists, geographers, and legal scholars and published in the last thirty years in journals or edited volumes. The sample cases have been selected according to the comprehensiveness of provided information and mainly stem from North America, reflecting the popularity of participatory governance in the United States and Canada. Statistical analysis has shown virtually no significant correlations between the continent and country of the case study with other variables, implying that both structural and process characteristics are well comparable across the Atlantic.

The case-survey method (Bullock and Tubbs 1987; Larsson 1993; Newig and Fritsch 2009) employed for this study combines qualitative and quantitative techniques. Based on a coding scheme that comprises some 100 theoretically relevant variables, all cases were read and coded on a 0- to 4-point semi-quantitative scale, thus quantifying all relevant information. Half of the selected studies were coded by at least two researchers with an intercoder reliability of 75 percent. Across all cases, we were able to code on average 87 percent of variables.

In a third step, we calculated Pearson correlation coefficients among variables. To this end, we aggregated some of the original variables. To assess whether public participation improved decision quality (output) and implementation in terms of ecological outcomes, we assumed a hypothetical top-down situation for each individual case and asked to what extent we can assume public participation to have contributed to improving environmental outcomes. The comparison is based on a careful reconstruction of the case history that enabled us to establish

Table 10.1
Overview of case studies analyzed

Case	Country	Year*	Reference
301h Water Regulation	USA	1977	Burgess, Hoffman, and Lucci 1983
Aargau Landfill Siting	Switzerland	1993	Renn and Webler1998
Albemarle-Pamlico Estuarine Study	USA	1990	Koontz et al. 2004
Animas River Stakeholder Group	USA	1998	Koontz et al. 2004
Belmont Open Space Controversy	USA	1998	Layzer 2002
Brayton Point Coal Conversion	USA	1977	Burgess and Smith 1983
Cold Lake Large-Scale Bitumen Extraction	Canada	1978	Elder 1982
Colstrip Power Plant Mediation	USA	1978	Sullivan 1983
Colorado Grand Canyon River Management Plan	USA	2001	Orton 2005
Foothills Water Management Case	USA	1976	Burgess 1983
Frankfurt Airport Airstrip Extension	Germany	1999	Geis 2005
Holston River Chemical Plant Mediation	USA	1974	Jaegerman 1983
Hudson River Power Station Settlement	USA	1980	Talbot 1984
Inland Northwest Field Burning Summit	USA	1990	Mangerich and Luton 1995
Interstate 90 Extension	USA	1976	Talbot 1984
Jackson Sewage Treatment Plant	USA	1978	Hill 1983
Lübeck Waste Management Proposal	Germany	1995	Wiedemann,. Claus, and Gremler, 1995
Münchehagen Hazardous Waste Siting	Germany	1992	Müller-Erwig 1995
Neuss Waste Management Plan	Germany	1993	Fietkau and Weidner 1998

Table 10.1
(continued)

Case	Country	Year*	Reference
Pig's Eye Mississippi River and Wetlands Case	USA	1980	Nelson 1990a
Portage Island Park Management Case	USA	1979	Talbot 1984
Sand Lakes Quiet Area Oil Drilling Negotiation	USA	1981	Nelson 1990b
Sandspit Harbour Mediation	Canada	1992	Sigurdson 1998
San Juan National Forest Mediation	USA	1983	Tableman 1990
Snoqualmie River Flood Protection Mediation	USA	1974	Dembart and Kwartler 1980
Spreewald Riparian Land Project	Germany	2002	Baranek and Günther 2005
Sugarbush Water Withdrawal Mediation	USA	1992	Fitzhugh and Dozier 1996
Swan Lake Hydroelectric Powerplant Conflict	USA	1979	Talbot 1984
Three Rivers Watershed	USA	1972	Mazmanian 1979
Umatilla Basin Mediation	USA	1992	Neuman 1996
Upper Narragansett Bay Waste Water Treatment	USA	1996	Burroughs 1999
Wildcat and San Pablo Creek Flood Management	USA	1972	Mazmanian 1979
Winfield Locks Toxic Waste Case	USA	1992	Langton 1996
Wisconsin Groundwater Commission	USA	1982	Edgar 1990
Yukon Wolf Management Team	USA	1992	Todd 2002

*Average year of participatory process

initial agency goals and an assessment of probable implementation deficits.

Finally, we controlled for a number of moderator variables, which allowed us to specify the conditions under which participatory governance is conducive to sustainability and when it is not.

Results I: Better Decisions Through Participation?

In the previous section we referred to the widely held view within participation research that participatory forms of governance increase the (ecological) quality of decisions. We operationalize the "quality" of decisions as (1) the amount of new and useful information generated in the process through the involvement of non-state actors (*information gain*); (2) the extent to which there has been *collective learning* in the sense of more creative solutions or the exploitation of win-win potentials through group interaction; and (3) ultimately, the degree to which a decision takes into account ecological issues, sets environmental standards and is suitable to *enhance environmental quality* compared to the reference scenario.

Information Gain   In most of the thirty-five cases, new and useful information was in fact generated. The variable *information gain* received an average score of 1.9 points out of 4.0 (with a standard deviation of 0.9). However, information gain is only loosely correlated with process-related variables (see table 10.2). Only variables related to the type of participants show significant correlations. Participation of a governmental authority appears to foster information gain, while the involvement of individual citizens tends to hamper it. This suggests that—contrary to theory—private citizens have (at least on average) little specific knowledge to offer compared with that of governmental agencies, which holds true for cases such as the Animas stakeholder group, but clearly not for others such as the Albemarle-Pamlico estuarine study, in which dedicated citizens contributed much relevant information. Other variables relating to the intensity of participation show no significant statistical relation with information gain. On the level of the whole data set, this finding clearly contradicts the hypothesis of the importance of lay local knowledge.

Indeed, in many of the cases in which much useful information was generated, issues were very technical, leaving little room for citizens to contribute. In the Holston River case, for instance, citizens and grassroots groups left the negotiations over water quality standards with a large

Table 10.2
Correlates of process with "quality of decision" variables

	Information, reflection, and learning		Environmental outputs	
	Information gain	Collective learning	Decision goal— stakeholder goal	Decision goal—govt. goal
Grassroots involved		–	.30	
Citizens involved	–.32			
Government participates	.36 *			
Spokespersons		.44**		
Controlled participant select.				.46**
Face-to-face		.36*	.47**	.60***
Mediation/ facilitation		.50**	−.30	.58***
Representation		.47**		
Fairness		.53**		
Communication		.55***		.32
Consultation		.43*		
Participation		.61***		

Note: Only significant correlations with $p < .1$ are depicted. * $p < .05$, ** $p < .01$, *** $p < .001$.

chemical plant entirely to the U.S. Environmental Protection Agency (U.S. EPA). Similarly, in the Animas stakeholder group, which worked on a remediation plan for heavily polluted mining sites to improve water quality, citizens and representatives of environmental organizations could contribute little to solving the very technical issues. Likewise, both in the Lübeck and the Neuss waste management cases, much useful information was generated, albeit mainly through the involvement of technical experts. Environmental groups and engaged citizens, on the other hand, worked closely together with experts in the Albemarle-Pamlico estuarine process, generating a highly improved scientific basis for an estuarine conservation and management plan.

Overall, although there is a considerable gain of useful information in the cases analyzed, we find hardly any evidence that this gain crucially depends on the way the decision process is conducted and to what extent it is participatory.

Collective Learning   With *collective learning*—defined as the extent to which collectively new and creative ideas and solutions were developed and win-win potentials were discovered within the decision process—we find considerably more evidence of the role of participation. The variable obtains an average score of 2.1 (with a standard deviation of 1.0). It is positively correlated with many process-related variables (see table 10.2) such as the degree of stakeholder interaction and the intensity of communication and information flows, but also aspects of process fairness and legitimate representation of stakeholders influence collective learning. The high correlation of information-flow-related variables suggests that an effective information flow presupposes deliberation, reflection, and the development of creative solutions. Legitimacy-related variables (spokespersons, representation, fairness), consistent with theory, appear to influence the willingness of stakeholders to actually cooperate and thus learn collectively.

Two positive examples are the Aargau and Snoqualmie cases. In a rather formalized, highly deliberative process, citizen representatives of nine Swiss communities in the Kanton Aargau, which were considered as potential waste sites, successfully (and consensually) developed a ranking of waste sites based on ecological criteria. In the first environmental mediation in the United States, environmentalists, farmers, residents, and the U.S. Army Corps of Engineers discussed flood protection at the Snoqualmie River. In a controversial, but fair and highly participatory mediation process, stakeholders discovered common interests and win-win potentials, which led to an innovative compromise benefiting both ecological and flood-protection interests. Conversely, the involvement of citizens and groups opposed to economic development was clearly insufficient in the Belmont hospital case, which was one factor why hardly any innovative solutions could be developed, although an enormous amount of technical information was generated.

Comparing the results regarding *collective learning* with those of *information gain* leads us to draw two conclusions. First, both information gain and collective learning happen in the analyzed cases to an approximately equal degree and with similar variance. Second, collective learning to a much larger extent than information gain appears to depend on the way the process is conducted. Information and technical data, it seems, can be generated without having to rely on participation; creative new solutions and win-win-potentials, on the other hand, appear to presuppose high degrees of participation.

Effects on Environmental Quality   Ultimately, we are interested to see whether participation not only improves the knowledge base of the decisions but also actually leads to more ecological decisions. Measured on a scale from -4 to 4, the ecological standard of decisions averages at 0.2 (standard deviation: 1.8); that is, in some cases, environmental programs were enacted, while in others, large development projects, harmful to the environment, were decided upon. Taking this output variable (decision goal) as the relevant measure, we find that by far the highest correlation is with the variable *mean actor goals* (0.89, p < 0.001). This clearly suggests it is the interests of the stakeholders that more than any other factor determine the output. Although it does not come as a surprise that stakeholder interests affect governance outputs, the predominance of this factor is indeed stunning. It suggests that regardless of how the process is actually shaped, the societal interests will determine the output. In order to examine the effect of participation more closely, we first calculated the difference of the output and the mean actor goals. The key variables that statistically correlate with this measure of difference are the involvement of grassroots actors, face-to-face settings, and a mediated process (table 10.2).

One example is the Colstrip mediation case, in which a tribe of Indians opposed the upgrading of a power plant close to their homelands. Through active participation the group achieved additional measures of air pollution control as a precondition for the upgrading. This participatory process is particularly typical because those actors taking an ecological perspective preferred to put forward economic, quality of life, and health-related arguments to support their case instead of employing ecological or even eco-centric reasons. Obviously, emphasizing personal harm and affection was key for success. In other cases, the decision output was ecologically inferior to the mean stakeholder goals, largely due to the noninvolvement of an environmentally oriented grassroots initiative. This was the case in Belmont, where a private hospital and a nearby municipality negotiated the future use of ecologically valuable property that had been declared for sale by the former. As the participatory process excluded green NGOs and conservation-oriented citizen groups, ecological arguments met with no response. As a consequence, the agreement allowed for the sale of the estate and also its commercial use leading to a major deterioration of nature. Contrary to the Colstrip case, though, green actors could not refer to direct negative impacts for those they represented, considerably weakening their general position.

To determine whether participatory governance—as opposed to "top-down" administrative or governmental decisions—actually makes a difference, we calculated the difference between decision output and the governmental goal (average of policy goal and agency goal). Assuming that without participation, the pure government goal would have been decided, this difference gives us a measure of the deviation of the hypothetical, counterfactual top-down alternative. As table 10.3 shows, in a slight majority of cases, outputs were ecologically inferior to the counterfactual top-down alternative. In particular, this is observable when environmental agencies, such as the U.S. EPA, initiated public participation processes. Their ambitious ecological approach is regularly watered down by participants who neither share the agency's environmental awareness nor the will for rigorous implementation of ecological measures. In a sense, this can be interpreted as the reversal of the "modified power structure" argument discussed above. Consequently, a participatory agreement is closer to a compromise between competing interests than to a collective search for ecologically optimal solutions. For instance, in the Spreewald riparian land project, local actors from tourism, agriculture, forestry, and fishery opposed strict ecological measures, fearing expropriation and loss of incomes. In other instances, such as the mentioned Yukon or Snoqualmie cases, participation led to ecologically superior decisions.

Contrary to theory, the learning-related variables *information gain* and *collective learning* are not significantly correlated with either of the

Table 10.3
Differences of environmental output and outcome variables regarding the hypothetical top-down alternative (governmental environmental goal).

	Improvement	Deterioration	No difference	No data	Sum
Output	12	15	4	4	35
Outcome	16	5	11	3	35

Note: Output denotes the substantial quality of a policy decision towards environmental protection, outcome the degree of policy implementation.

environmental output variables. This suggests that both are really two different matters. Improved ecological standards do not require an improved knowledge base; conversely, learning effects need not lead to ecologically better decisions.

Results II: Better Implementation through Participation?
The two main lines of reasoning elaborated in this section suggest that (1) participatory and reflexive decision making helps to resolve conflicts, increases trust among the participants, builds social capital and leads to an improved acceptance of decisions. (2) This, in turn, is supposed to enhance the implementation of decisions and thus, ultimately, improve environmental outcomes or impacts.

Participatory and Reflexive Decision Making Table 10.4 gives an overview of the multiple correlates between process variables and output variables relating to conflict resolution, trust building, and acceptance. The six output variables obtain average scores of 2.2 to 3.1 with standard deviations around 1.0, indicating relatively high levels of conflict resolution, trust building, and acceptance in the analyzed case studies, but with considerable variance. Three of the supposedly independent variables show the most important correlations: the existence of legitimate spokespersons, representation, and, foremost, fairness. Interestingly, all three are dimensions of the *legitimacy* of the decision process, thus strongly supporting the claims of procedural justice theory. Furthermore, fairness is the only variable correlating with the acceptance of third-party actors. All in all, the legitimacy of the process appears even more important for the acceptance of results than the structural process characteristics, although the latter do play a significant role. Some process variables appear to have quite particular effects, such as the importance of government (agencies) for the final decision; this decreases trust building but, quite plausibly, increases the acceptance of the decision by government (agency) itself. Remarkably and unexpectedly, methods of facilitated and structured information elicitation, although they contribute to an education of stakeholders (correlation 0.36, $p < 0.05$), seem to impede acceptance.

The Snoqualmie River mediation may serve to illustrate a case of a highly participatory process with a well-accepted decision. The mediated process served both to resolve a year-old conflict and to produce a solution that was accepted by stakeholders and government. Conversely, decisions made in the Albemarle-Pamlico process, while highly

Table 10.4
Correlates of process with "acceptance" variables

	Conflict resolution	Trust building inter-NSA	Trust building NSA-govt.	Acceptance NSA	Acceptance govt.	Acceptance third parties
Government decision		-.46*	-.38*		.32	
Identifiable actors				.35*		
Spokespersons	.36*	.39*	.34	.51**	.30	
Facilitated inform. elicit.				-.46**	-.33	
Face-to-face			.31	.42*		
Mediation / facilitation			.38*	.45**	.39*	
Representation	.33	.53**	.47**			
Fairness	.57***	.77***	.72***	.51**		.50
Number participants (lg)				-.43*		
Communication			.50**			
Consultation		.42*	.40*			
Participation			.30			

Notes: Only significant correlations with $p < .1$ are depicted. * $p < .05$, ** $p < .01$, *** $p < .001$.
Trust building inter-NSA = trust building among nonstate actors
Trust building NSA-govt. = trust building between state and nonstate actors
Acceptance NSA = acceptance by nonstate actors of policy decisions
Acceptance govt = acceptance by state actors of policy decisions
Acceptance third parties = acceptance by third parties of policy decisions

participatory as well—although not mediated—was on the whole less accepted, largely because of the voluntary nonparticipation of a certain actor group. In a different setting, the agreement in the Holston River case was well accepted by the one stakeholder, a large chemical company, without any broad participation in the classical sense; mere technical bargaining with the U.S. EPA sufficed.

Implementation of Decisions   While the examined cases generally provided thorough material on decision outputs, much less information was given on their implementation. This is mainly due to the fact that the case descriptions typically end with a successfully completed decision, partly because case studies were published before implementation could even have taken place. About a dozen case studies do, however, supply sufficient information on implementation; another twenty cases allowed at least reasonable guesses about what would happen. When, for instance, in the San Juan National Forest mediation case it was agreed that in a certain area there will be no tree cutting, then it is reasonable to assume that this will most likely be implemented, given the fact that implementation equals "doing nothing," plus the obvious possibility of detecting any violation. For several of the published case studies, additional information on implementation could be found online at the Web sites of citizen advisory committees or other organizations.

As table 10.2 shows, there was an (apparent) improvement of implementation in most cases. It should be noted that what we refer to is implementation of environmental measures, not necessarily a larger project as such. In the Foothills case, for instance, the construction of a major water reservoir—which is expected to negatively affect water quality and sustainable urban planning in the city of Denver, Colorado—is facilitated through a complex, mediated process, whereas the construction of recreational areas (i.e., the "ecological" part of the agreement) had not even started two years after the agreement.

Statistically, acceptance of non-state actors correlates with implementation (environmental outcomes) at 0.34 (with $p = 0.06$), while all other "acceptance" variables show no significant correlations. Improved implementation through a negotiated settlement can be exemplified in the Holston River case. Following the interpretation of the author, negotiations produced an environmentally less stringent agreement as compared to a hypothetical top-down solutions, but with a higher chance of actual implementation due to the reduced risk of a court trial with an uncertain decision. Similarly, without the participatory agreement in the Spreewald case, federal funds for the large nature conservation project would not even have been granted; given the local opposition to the project, the participatory agreement constituted virtually a prerequisite for implementation.

Results III: Influence of the Context

The context of the analyzed cases apparently has (1) a considerable *direct* influence both on the process design as well as on outputs and outcomes. Due to space restrictions, we will concentrate on the latter aspects. (2) Context variables also have important *indirect* consequences in that they affect the correlations between process and result variables.

Direct Influences   *Direct* effects of context variables are summarized in table 10.5. As expected, the degree of conflict among the relevant parties correlates negatively both with quality of decision as well as with acceptance variables, indicating that less conflictual settings are more likely to produce desired outputs and outcomes. For instance, in the Upper Narragansett Bay process, a rather technical problem of wastewater treatment is collaboratively tackled in a little conflictual setting; rational collaboration yields considerable information and a broadly accepted agreement with a rather high ecological standard. Likewise, the existence of solutions (e.g., technical, legal, organizational) appears to have a positive influence on ecological decision standards as well as on conflict resolution and overall trust building, albeit not on acceptance. Again, Upper Narragansett Bay is a typical example of a case with a high potential of (technical) solutions. The existence of win-win potentials shows similar effects. A typical case of a high win-win potential and resulting conflict resolution, trust building and acceptance is the *San Juan* National Forest mediation. Whereas the U.S. Department of Agriculture's Forest Service sought to clear-cut a certain forested area in a touristy region, local stakeholders opposed this plan for economic and ecological reasons. The fact that the area under consideration, originally viewed as a unit, could be split up in a part with high touristy value with no tree cutting and another, more distant part with tree cutting, constituted an important win-win potential that was successfully used for a consensual agreement. As expected, the variable social capital correlates positively with the acceptance of decisions by non-state actors, indicating a more consensual decision environment, and even with the environmental quality of decisions. Finally, the degree to which the issue of the decision

Table 10.5
Correlates of context with results variables

	Information gain	Decision goal	Decision goal— govt. goal	Conflict resolution	Trust building Inter- NSA-NSA govt.	Acceptance NSA govt.
Degree of conflict	-.31	-.36*				-.34* -.30
Existence of solutions		.35*		.37*	.39*	
Win-win potential				.37*	.43*	.41*
Social capital			.33		.32	.45***
Defined issue						.42*

Note: Only significant correlations with p < .1 are depicted. * p < .05, ** p < .01, *** p < .001.

process was clearly defined contributed positively to the acceptance of decisions. Here, again, the more technical cases such as Upper Narragansett Bay or the Holston River case provide examples of very clearly defined issues, as opposed to the complex setting of the Albemarle-Pamlico estuarine study that produced very low acceptance on the part of certain non-state actor groups.

Indirect Influences   Context variables show *indirect* effects by affecting the way process variables correlate with result variables. Thus, they function as "third variables," specifying the conditions under which the above described relationships exist or do not exist. By assessing their impact, we understand the conditions under which participation fosters sustainability and those under which it does not. Overall, we find considerable effects of context variables on correlations between process and result variables.

We first considered variables that characterize whether the decision (process) is driven by government or by non-state actors. One variable measures agenda-setting by government or by non-state actors, another measures whether or not a higher-order policy goal exists that needs to be implemented. For those cases with a given higher-order policy goal we find even more positive correlations between "decision goal" minus "government goal" and process variables as compared to those depicted in table 10.3; cases *without* given higher-order policy goal show no such correlations whatsoever. Very similarly, in the subset of cases in which government is the leading agenda-setter, multiple strong correlations between "decision goal" minus "government goal" and process variables exist, whereas those cases with non-state actors as primary agenda-setters show hardly any such correlations. Furthermore, learning-related variables correlate much higher with process-related variables in the cases with given-policy goals and with government as agenda setter. On the other hand, "fairness" and "legitimate representation" correlate much higher with learning, trust building and acceptance variables in those cases without higher-order policy goal and in which non-state actors are the dominant agenda setters. Both findings lead us to conclude that different mechanisms are at work in governmental policy implementation settings as opposed to those in which local actors seek to resolve local conflicts and set their own policy goals. In the latter, fairness and legitimacy aspects appear to play a principal role for conflict resolution, trust building, and acceptance. However, this has hardly any effects on ecological outputs or outcomes. In the former, we find many of the hypotheses regarding the effects of participation and learning on ecological outputs and outcomes to be confirmed.

Second, we examined the effect of (un) favorable context conditions such as the degree of conflict present among the relevant actors. For cases with high levels of conflict we found distinctive and high correlations between process variables—including those characterizing information flows—with information gain, (collective) learning, building of trust, and acceptance by non-state actors; much less so for cases with low levels of conflict. Regardless of this, process variables in both subsets correlate very similarly with "decision goal"—"government goal." Therefore, not surprisingly, the building of trust and the resolution of conflict plays a much more important role in highly conflictual settings. On the other hand, this does not appear to affect environmental outcomes, suggesting that the resolution of conflicts is more a preliminary to sustainable decision making than an actual success factor.

Conclusions and Outlook

Will participatory and reflexive governance foster (collective) learning, build and utilize local knowledge, and ultimately produce more ecological and sustainable outcomes, as compared to classical top-down administrative decision making? In this chapter, we have sought to contribute to responding to this question by presenting findings from a meta-analysis of thirty-five case studies of—more or less—participatory environmental governance.

With respect to our main hypotheses, we find a divided result. The analysis provides, on the one hand, evidence that many of those mechanisms discussed in the literature can indeed be observed, yet only in certain cases and only to a certain extent.

- The main hypothesis according to which participation improves the quality of environmental decisions cannot generally be confirmed. Only in one third of all cases new perspectives involved, information-generated or social-learning processes initiated lead to a better consideration of environmental perspectives in the final agreement. In 43 percent of all cases, the involvement of non-state actors accounts for less stringent environmental decisions.

- However, we were able to clearly identify improvements of environmental policy implementation as to litigation rates and compliance due to the involvement of non-state actors. While public participation obstructed environmental outcomes in only 16 percent, it improved outcomes in 46 percent.

- The single most important factor for environmental outputs and outcomes are the interests and goals of the involved actors. Although it is not surprising that these do play a role, the strength of the correlations (coefficients around 0.85 with $p < 0.001$, stable for almost all controlled third variables) is indeed striking.

- Even though the scholarly literature on participation tends to emphasize process characteristics as important influencing factors, our analysis highlights the importance of the societal and ecological *context*. While a number of context variables such as the existence of win-win potentials or of social capital directly influence outcomes, the context also affects the way process variables affect outcomes. Remarkably, the influence of participatory and reflexive forms of governance is most evident in settings with external policy goals and/or governmental agenda setting, while in the opposite cases (no external policy goal, civil society agenda setting) participation hardly makes any difference for the attainment of sustainable outputs and outcomes.

- While information gains and collective learning play considerable roles in the analyzed cases, these do not necessarily imply more sustainable outputs and outcomes. Apparently, improved ecological standards do not require an improved knowledge base, and conversely, learning effects need not lead to ecologically better decisions.

Our analysis has focused on local or regional forms of decision making, allowing for an intensive involvement of concerned actor groups. Here, participatory approaches appear to be most fruitful in *policy implementation* settings. Further integration of existing case study knowledge will be crucial to deepen our understanding of the mechanisms at work. Because there is, up to now, little experience with participatory and reflexive approaches to govern global sustainability, policy makers will be well advised to carefully consider the plethora of empirical results gained on regional decision scales. Accordingly, advantages of deliberation and reflexivity in governing global public goods, which have also been voiced in this volume, have to be carefully confronted with possible pitfalls. Participatory forms of environmental governance, thus, are a two-edged sword with the potential to both support or hamper the attainment of sustainability goals, depending on the societal and environmental context.

Notes

1. These are the Water Framework Directive (2000/60/EC), the Strategic Environmental Assessment Directive (2001/42/EC), the new Environmental Information Directive (RL 2003/4/EC) and the Public Participation Directive (2003/35/EC).

11

Social Learning in the Governance of Forest Ecosystem Services

Tom Dedeurwaerdere

A lot of work on institutions has focused on the design of well-adapted systems of rules, which best fit to the biophysical and social environment. In such a static approach the goal is to look for the most optimal institutional design given a certain model of the actor situation. However, in spite of the obvious operational strengths of this approach, it fails to address important dynamic features of complex systems—particularly in the case of environmental governance, in which the relatively slow natural evolution of ecological systems is at present confronted with new rapidly evolving, human-induced constraints such as the biodiversity crisis, climate change, and global market pressures on the exploitation of natural resources.

As a result, dynamic governance issues, such as knowledge generation and social learning among a range of new actors and stakeholders that are bearing the consequences of the rapid change, become increasingly important. Nevertheless, there is still a lack of empirical analysis that would allow for better understanding of the possible role and function of various governance mechanisms in fostering such social learning. To help bridge the gap, this chapter presents an in-depth case study analysis of such mechanisms by focusing on a specific governance experiment with social learning in the field of biodiversity governance.

The case of managed forest landscapes seems an appropriate test field for analyzing the contribution of social learning to dynamic efficiency. Indeed, to encourage forest owners to adopt multifunctional forest management, policy makers have used not only a wide range of regulatory and economic instruments, but also experimented with mechanisms based on processes of social learning.

In the case of the forest groups in Flanders, Belgium, which will be the focus of this case study, social learning has lead to quite impressive outcomes in a relatively short period, in a policy field in which regulatory and economic incentive policies were well established, but were not able to produce the expected outcomes. One of the challenges in studying social learning (as highlighted in chapter 10) is to combine an analysis of its impact on effectiveness and on the normative legitimacy of the adopted rules, especially in situations of rapidly changing social and ecological systems. Therefore, this case study focuses in particular on three mechanisms of social learning that have been widely used in the management of social-ecological systems: (1) the recourse to monitoring based on sustainability criteria and indicators as an open-ended learning device, allowing for redefinition of the current beliefs around sustainable development; (2) the experimentation with disruptive action strategies to put the new beliefs into practice; and (3) the involvement of new stakeholders and users in the learning process with the view toward building new forms of social cooperation around these new beliefs and practices. The hypothesis behind this analysis is that a combination of cognitive and social mechanisms of social learning is needed to generate effective and legitimate institutional change.

Theoretical Perspectives on Institutional Dynamics and Social Learning

The conditions for organizing social learning through a mechanism of monitoring have been studied in more detail by Charles Sabel (1994), both in the context of firm behavior (in the "non-standard firm"), and in the context of public policy (in "deliberative polyarchies"). Because our interest is in social learning among private forest owners, we will mainly focus here on the theory of the non-standard firm. In his approach, Sabel highlights two conditions for open-ended learning: first, the role of practical incentives for promoting the exploration of "disruptive possibilities" (Dorf and Sabel 1998, 286) and, second, a set of institutional rules that define the engagement in the cooperative enterprise. First, to establish initial product designs and production methods, firms turn to benchmarking: an exacting survey of current or promising products and processes that identifies products and processes superior to those the company presently uses, but which are within its capacity to emulate and eventually surpass. Benchmarking thus allows a comparative evaluation with possible improvements, and, as such, provides an incentive to disrupt the current routines and representations of possible outcomes. Further incentives for promoting the exploration of disruptive possibilities are simultaneous engineering based on the initial benchmarking and correction of errors revealed by the new action possibilities. Second, beyond these practical incentives, generating collaboration and change in the non-standard firm also depends on an institutional context that defines a set of rules of engagement of the actors in the joint enterprise. These rules require mutual monitoring of each participant's contribution, information sharing and the mutual assessment of each participant's reliability in relation to the joint activity.

Based on these two conditions, the practical incentives and the rules of engagement, we can expect increased productive learning in the forest groups to occur when the monitoring process generates: (1) a process of joint investigation and comparative evaluation of disruptive possibilities, and (2) a process of mutual comparison to verify the reliability of the outcomes proposed by different groups. In the cases in which these conditions are realized, one expects a broadening of the set of possible productive action strategies beyond the current routines and representations of the organization.

The institutional dynamics, in situations of open-ended learning on sustainable forestry, does not only depend however on the opening of new perspectives within the forest groups through the mechanisms highlighted by Sabel. It also depends on the interaction with stakeholders and users in the broader social and political environment, who can be mutually supportive, neutral, or antagonistic. In particular, the concept of multifunctional forest management implies taking into account important components that impact on the broader user communities of the forest ecosystems services.

From the point of view of governance theory, the contribution of the interaction with the broader user communities to forest governance can be modeled as a situation in which cooperation is built through a combination of instrumental trust, based on reciprocity and enforced by increased transparency and means of verification, and social trust, based on symbols (e.g., languages, rituals, and gestures) and enforced by creating respect and esteem (Tyler 1998). Indeed lack of trust in one of the major challenges that forest policy has to face in building cooperation; private forest owners do not trust the government, and there exists a lack of trust among different categories of forest owners as well. As demonstrated through an extensive survey in Flanders, the forest owners show a high degree of distrust in the government and place the highest trust in technical engineers from the forest administration. To build trust with the government and among the forest owners, the forest groups have focused on both instrumental and social trust; the former by enhancing transparency and mutual monitoring through the criteria and indicator

(C&I) process, and the latter by enforcing the social identities of the forest owners—generating respect for the owners' ideas and interests and bringing owners back to their forest and stimulating a sense of forest stewardship (Bosgroepen 2005).

Multi-Stakeholder Coordination for Governing Managed Forest Landscapes

In Europe, forests have all been altered by man to some extent, with the exception of the boreal zone on the European side of the Russian Federation and some scattered relics in mountainous areas of the Balkan, Alpine, and Carpathian regions (Frank et al. 2005, 378). Moreover, the majority of forest owners own small or fragmented forests, and hence small-scale forest owners are an important target group for any forest policy in Europe. This typical patchwork of forests has some peculiar characteristics such as low commercial value of the wood, diverse collective preferences, and levels of understanding of sustainability and high transaction costs in the monitoring of the management practices of the different actors. In these managed forest landscapes, collaborative management organizations such as the forest groups play an important role in the provision of forest-related services. Through social learning, forest owners and users can compromise and build consensus on common objectives and collectively manage services such as selling of wood in a cost-effective manner.

Forest Groups as New Policy Instruments in Multifunctional Forest Management

In densely populated regions such as Flanders, multifunctional forest management appears to be the most direct means of extending the forest-related services. Because non-industrial private forest (NIPF) owners in Europe and the United States own more than half of the forests (up to 70 percent in Flanders), the promotion of multifunctional management depends strongly on the cooperation of NIPF owners. To encourage NIPF owners to adopt the government policy of multifunctional forest management, policy makers have used a wide range of regulatory, economic, and informational instruments. The NIPF owners mostly do not support these instruments because the underlying ideas conflict with their opinions, harvest rights are not protected, and there is too much interference from the federal government (Brunson et al. 1996). More successful instruments should inform and educate forest owners, allow wood trade, involve the owners of neighboring forests, and be independent of government. Forest groups (forest cooperatives, forest owner associations, or cooperative forest management arrangements) exhibit these characteristics and are used in more than fifteen European countries (Kittredge 2005).

In the case of Flanders, the creation of forest groups led to quite impressive outcomes in a relatively short period. The overall region that is covered by the forest groups recognized in 2006 is an estimated 100 hectares, which amounts for 75 percent of the forest cover in Flanders. Each of the forest groups (called *bosgroepen*) focuses on sub-areas within these regions, where forest degradation is progressing most rapidly or where dispersed ownership is highest. (Forest groups do not deal with big public forests or, in principle, with private forests above 5 hectares.) In the focus sub-areas the forest groups have been able to involve private forest owners in extensive coordination on forest management and in common stewardship for the various values of the forest landscape.

Why is this innovative scheme successful in a policy field in which the regulatory and economic incentive policies, already in place from 1990 to 1996, were not able to convince the private forest owners and produce the expected outcomes? The failure of the transition to sustainable forest management in this first phase of implementation of the 1990 Forest Decree cannot be explained by an insufficient level of economic incentives such as cost-share policies (Serbruyns and Luyssaert 2006). For example, as pointed out by an in-depth study of forest conversion that includes the Bosgroep Zuiderkempen (BZK) working area, the economic incentive scheme covers more than the lost revenue of forest conversion to the forest owner (Verheyen et al. 2006, 73). The lost revenue is estimated to be between €45 and €96 per hectare annually for conversion from a Corsican pine stand to pedunculate oak under a rotation period of 77 years (Verheyen et al. 2006, 71), while the direct subsidies are around €150 per hectare yearly. Nevertheless, between 1990 and 1999 only 200 to 250 owners per year applied and received the reforestation subsidy, while owners of only 317 hectares applied and received the subsidy for forest management plans and owners of 317 hectares for opening up their land for private use (Serbruyns and Luyssaerts 2006, 287). From an ecological point of view, the 1990 Forest Decree was already based on the detailed set of criteria and indicators for multifunctional forest use and management, which had been agreed upon in the Pan-European Forestry Process, in which both forest interests and nature movements were represented (Ministerial Conference on the Protection of Forests in Europe 1998). Hence. it seems that the issue at stake here is not the lack of economic incentive policies or inappropriate legal concepts from an ecological point of view.

The main innovation introduced from 1996 on, through the progressive creation of the forest groups, is the explicit organization of processes of social learning among the forest owners and stakeholders. Even if other factors more generally contributed to raising awareness on sustainable forest management in the same period, such as the introduction of forest certification and civil society/market pressures, none of these trends had any direct significant influence on small-scale forest owners. That is why learning new social preferences, or "crowding in" (in the language of chapter 4), through combining the economic incentive politics with mechanisms of social learning seemed an appropriate way forward.

The forest groups introduce elements of joint information processing and social learning both between the forest owners and the government officials and among the forest owners and the various stakeholders. The main decision-making body of the forest group is the general assembly of forest owners, assisted by a forest group coordinator and one administrative staff member. All decisions on forest management, felling, and negotiations with user organizations are taken by the general assembly, on the basis of "one man, one vote," independent of the forest surface of the owner. The forest groups also strive to achieve a balanced membership among small public and private forest owners, requiring a majority of private forest owners in the general assembly. The drafting of the forest management plans is realized through the help of the forest group coordinator, whose main role is to involve the owners in the organization of the information coming from the different forest plots. The general assembly of forest owners discusses and approves the specific organization of wood selling and intervention in the forest landscapes, based on the common knowledge base that is built for the specific forest landscape that is managed by the group.

The Bosgroep Zuiderkempen (BZK), a well-established forest group, illustrates the results of combining the incentive and regulatory policy tools with tools for organizing social learning. This forest group operates in a landscape containing about 8000 hectares of forest. Within this landscape a priority working area of 1,134 hectares of highly scattered forests has been selected for building cooperative forest services in the period 2003–2006, with the management plan for 2007–2010 calling for another 801 hectares to be added. In the working area, meetings with forest owners are organized, membership to the Forest Group proposed, and forest management plans discussed. As a result of this process, a 513-hectare private forest has been integrated into detailed common forest management plans (45 percent of the working area), involving a total of 462 different small private forest owners (an estimated 30 percent of the total number of owners in the working area). Moreover, through the negotiation of access plans among the forest group, user representatives, and the local authorities, a total area of 342 hectares of private forest has been opened up to different user groups (30 percent of the working area). If similar results could be accomplished in the other forest groups in Flanders, then an expected total area of 5,909 hectares could be opened up for walking and recreation in the nearby future, which is more than the total area of the largest remaining public forest in Flanders.

Social Learning through the Use of Sustainability Criteria and Indicators

The methodology for the organization of social learning adopted by the forest groups in Flanders is based on a process of gradual change in understanding by the different stakeholders—from the opposition between nature conservation and timber interests to an ecosystem services approach that broadens the debate to the overall determinants of the sustainability of the forest ecosystem (Hassan, Scholes, and Ash 2005, 29; Perrings and Touza-Montero 2004, 16). Three components are central to this process as it is described in the vision document of the forest groups. First, the project starts from the interests and needs of the forest owners, rather than from their position and discourse in regard to nature conservation. Second, the forest group organizes a learning process on the definition of the sustainability targets. Third, the design of the learning process itself is evaluated at regular intervals by the participants to adapt it to the local circumstances and stakes at hand.

The use of indicators by the forest group provides a useful yardstick to measure the progress of the learning process. Indeed, we can compare these indicators, which are the result of a social learning process within the organization, to the set of formal targets in the legislation on "criteria for sustainable forest management" (CSFM). The formal targets, which came out of the Pan-European Forestry Process and have been adopted by the Flemish government, are compulsory—wherever relevant—for all private forests that are more than 5 hectares, and for all public forests and all forests in the Flemish ecological network. Their adoption is voluntary for the private forests that are less than 5 hectares, but they are considered to be the official reference standards to be used by the forest groups. In practice, however, both for the public and private forests, compliance with the CSFM criteria is still extremely weak (Dumortier et al. 2006, 30).

The forest group has been conceived by its initiators as a process in which: management objectives are confronted by the perceptions of opportunities by forest owners, and the generated information is used to adapt the operational objectives of the forest group. The forest group receives support by the government, as long as the operational objectives, formulated through a clear set of indicators, are met and if the indicators show a progress in moving toward the government targets.

The CSFM are a clear expression of what the concept of multifunctional forest management would look like in the ideal case. It defines clear targets organized around six main sets of criteria of sustainable forestry. Each set of criteria is measured through a set of legally specified indicators, leading to a total set of twenty-four criteria and fifty-two indicators. The six main sets of criteria cover:

1. Implementation of the existing legislation
2. Maintenance of the social and cultural functions of the forest
3. Maintenance of the economic and productive functions of the forest
4. Contribution to the protection of the environment
5. Contribution to biodiversity conservation
6. Monitoring and planning the forest management

To analyze the gap between these sets of legal criteria and the indicators and targets elaborated in the forest group, we can use the available data of the BZK, considered a reference case by the Flemish government one in which the learning process for the translation of the CSFM criteria has already been going on for a fairly long period (from 1999 to 2006). The subsidies to the forest group by the Flemish government are conditioned by the adoption, at regular periods in time, of a management plan with clear indicators. Once adopted by the forest group, these operational targets have to be implemented within the time frame of the management plan. The comparison between the legal criteria and indicators and the operational targets results in a matrix of correspondences and gaps. Below, we will use this matrix to analyze: (a) what has been learned in the forest group (self-evaluation), and (b) what are the remaining challenges in the learning process. We use here the indicators and targets adopted by the General Assembly of BZK for their operational management plan for 2007–2012.

The main lessons drawn from this matrix are:

- Correspondences between CSFM and BZK: mainly within the criteria set 2 (social and cultural functions) and 6 (monitoring and planning); some indicators of criteria set 3 (economic functions) and 5 (forest diversity)
- Gaps between CSFM and BZK: no clear reference in BZK to criteria set 4 (environmental services) and very few to criteria set 5 (forest diversity)

The main sustainability indicators and targets that have been adopted by the forest owners' organization concern the social and cultural functions of the forests and the protection of habitat (forest borders and heath landscapes). A clear target of 690 hectares of forest area with selective access of the population to the forest (35 percent of the extended working area) and an information and reporting system of the local population's wishes have been put into place (target audience of 350 persons filing questions and complaints per year). Forest management measures for fragile or biodiversity rich habitats have been planned with the use of detailed geographic information system (GIS) maps for an area of 150 hectares per year. Further action for combating invasive species (e.g., *prunus serotina*—the American black cherry) will be pursued in the priority working area. These sustainability targets set by the forest owners are the result of awareness building and discussion and negotiation around experimental test cases.

The comparison also reveals some important gaps. For instance, it is interesting to see that the diversity of tree species as such is not taken over as an explicit measure of sustainability by the forest owners. Beyond the habitat protection mentioned previously, most of the indicators within the forest biodiversity category (criteria 5) are not taken into account. Also the indicators for contribution to environmental protection (criteria 4) do not appear in the targets of the management plan.

What kind of limitations does this comparison reveal from a dynamic institutional perspective? First, from the ecological perspective, the forest group has clearly shown a gap between the expert-built criteria for sustainable forestry and the way that these criteria can be coherently applied in concrete action settings. This gap is shown to be a permanent critical challenge for the forest group. The decentralization of the decision-making power on the real management decisions has allowed for building an effective context for the translation of some of the sustainability indicators. The selling of timber, resulting from the joint management, is of course an important driver for the activities of the forest groups—albeit with direct impact on more healthy forests—but this is balanced with a concern for other eco-services such as clear targets for access agreements and combating invasive species.

Second, the comparison shows some of the remaining challenges to be tackled by the forestry group. In particular, the conservation of tree species diversity remains a difficult issue. A pilot project started in 2009 aims to develop a different methodology for "limited sustainable forest management plans," which includes a concern for tree diversity. The forest legislation has created a frame for the development of these plans, but, again, very few of these have been implemented. The pilot project will reconsider the basic concepts of these plans with the stakeholders in the field.

In summary, the use of indicators allows for the creation of a flexible framework for implementing the forest legislation and for coordinating and monitoring the use of different subsidy and economic incentives from different authorities (both regional and European). The legal framework leaves the different forest groups room to build their own operational management plan by selecting the set of indicators that they consider most relevant for their own forest landscape. As such, the use of indicators allows a process of internal self-evaluation around feasible and evolving targets in the collective management organization and a process of feedback to the government, leading to the design of new incentives schemes or adjustment of its policy.

Learning by Mutual Monitoring

The decentralized implementation of the Forest Decree through the creation of the collective management organizations has proved to be an effective tool in fostering social learning. However, important aspects of sustainable forestry, such as access to private forests in Flanders and biodiversity conservation, still remain underrepresented in this learning process. Moreover broadening the scope of the representation of forest owners in the forest groups, which are based on voluntary membership, remains an important challenge to be addressed.

A second mechanism of social learning in the forest groups focuses on the social learning generated by the interaction of different subgroups within the organization. This latter mechanism has played an important role in overcoming some of the obstacles related to experimenting with forest access management plans in private forests and is expected to help to foster learning on new issues, such as biodiversity. The main difference with the previous mechanism is that learning by monitoring is especially appropriate for more experimental forms of learning, so-called disruptive forms of learning (Sabel 1994). Disruptive learning processes lead to actions that cannot be framed within the current representations of the forest groups. If these experiments lead to successful outcomes, they provide, in turn, an incentive for the revision of the current representations.

An example of incremental learning in the forest management regime is the increase in the level of direct and indirect subsidies to the forest owners in the implementation of the 1990 Forest Decree. This adjustment of the strategies for implementation was based on extensive socioeconomic research, but did not reconsidering the basic premises of the economic incentive politics that prevailed in the first phase of the implementation of the Decree. An example of disruptive learning can be found within the first 1996 pilot forest group. Here, the learning has lead to new strategies and a new representation of the priorities to be addressed in sustainable forest management.

Within BZK, the learning that has lead to the adoption of the quinquennial management plan in 2006 can be qualified as incremental learning. The main belief is the same that of the 1996 pilot project—the need for organizing cooperative learning among private forest owners. For example, incremental learning within the frame of this belief played a role in the definition of the operational targets in terms of the criteria and indicators that were discussed previously. However, this incremental process failed to generate progress on important remaining challenges, such as the access of hikers and cyclers to private forests and forest conversion from planted pine forests to mixed broadleaf forests.

One of the main reasons for poor progress on these issues is the lack of consensus among the different subgroups that compose the forest group and the different constraints faced by small, medium, and larger forest owners. Consequently, in 2006, an experiment was organized within a subgroup that outsourced the drafting of the management plan to an independent consultant in the case of larger forest owners

(Bosgroep Zuiderkempen 2006). This experiment produced some positive outcomes, and further experiments will be organized to improve partnerships with independent consultants for dealing with large private forest owners. However, the current sustainable forest management plans are probably too demanding for small forest owners and are often not considered to be a legitimate objective for small private forest owners. In particular, the conservation of tree species diversity, beyond the direct social, cultural, and economic roles of the forest, remains a difficult issue. The pilot project that started in 2009, which works with some specific subgroups to develop a specific methodology adapted to small forest owners, includes a discussion on the owners' understanding of forest diversity. The explicit goal of the pilot project is to reconsider the basic concepts of these plans with the stakeholders in the field and to foster the development of new initiatives that do not directly fall under the current conceptions of sustainable forest management. These and other experiments illustrate the organization of open-ended initiatives by some subgroups, in an attempt to go beyond the insufficiencies of the incremental learning by questioning the legitimacy of the current conceptions of sustainable forestry in the forest groups.

The learning processes in the forest groups have been able to generate both innovation in strategies and diversification of representation within and between the forest groups. Some of these experiments have led to a change in action strategies and operational targets approved by the general assembly. Others resulted in the rejection of the new proposed action strategies, because they did not lead to improved outcomes. All these changes were the result not only of the communication process in the context of existing beliefs, but also of a process of experimentation that aims to broaden the set of workable strategies and objectives considered by the forest group.

The Institutional Dynamics of Change in Social Norms

The third mechanism for organizing social learning in the forest groups goes beyond the learning within the groups. It addresses the second condition for generating institutional change, which is the social embedding of the new proposed institutional rules and policies. Its main focus is on building trust between different categories of forest owners to broaden the membership of the forest groups, and on building trust between the members of the forest groups and other stakeholders— primarily the various forest user groups.

Progress in building new norms of cooperation has been achieved mainly in the involvement of passive forest owners in the forest group. The three main divisions among social groups, as revealed by sociological analysis among forest owners in Flanders, are: active exploitation (owners involved in use and management), active use (owners involved only in use, not management), and passive ownership (ownership only for investment or from heritage) of the forest (Verheyen et al. 2006). Owners in the active exploitation category are the most concerned about their forests and inclined to participate in the forest management plans; the passive owners are the least involved.

Among the passive forest owners only between 3 percent and 13 percent initially had a positive attitude toward collaborative forest management. This situation corresponds to the one that prevailed between 1990 and 1999, when no joint forest management organization existed (except for the 1996 pilot project). Self-organized forest groupings could already apply for subsidies, but with very low success rates (with subsidies going mainly to the environmentalists and the active forest owners). Without social learning, the forest group would at best represent the active forest exploiters and some public forest owners who own small forests, which would mean a membership rate of around 10 percent in the BZK priority areas. Since the creation of the forest groups, the average involvement rate has been between 17 percent and 34 percent (in the initial phase) and 41 percent and 76 percent (after some years) in the selected focus working areas (*boscomplexen*). Hence, the BZK organization was able to involve part of the active users and passive owners in the activities of the joint forest management.

A second case in which cooperative learning has been built around the forest groups is demonstrated by the creation of cooperation between nature associations and forest owners. These two groups traditionally have very different positions, the first favoring such strategies as buy-back policies of forest to nonprofit organizations or to government, allowing implementation of a strict biodiversity protection policy, and the second favoring economic incentives and market mechanisms. However, through building collaborative dialogue around issues of common concern in adjacent forest areas, trust and increasing levels of cooperation have been established in the core working areas of the BZK forest group.

The main characteristic of the methodology used in the forest group for rebuilding trust is that all the actors are considered and treated from the perspective of forest owners and forest managers. Indeed, that is the common thread in the way in which nature associations and private owners are brought together and the way cooperation is built between active forest owners and recreationists. However, in these activities, no new action identity is built by the different owners around the concept of multifunctional management. Instead, the old identities are simply reproduced within the new framework. Hence, the limit of this methodology for building social trust stems from the fact that it is incapable of identifying the need for a more profound transformation of the identity of the forest groups, in relation to the remaining challenges for addressing the issues raised by users of the forest related ecosystems services and the building of cooperation with local communities.

Within the forest groups, there is also a second approach, which takes into account the limits of this first approach and attempts to address the challenge of broadening cooperative learning with the users as a third party, without subordinating this cooperation to the current identity of the forest groups understood as representing forest managers. Indications for such a second approach are clearly present in initiatives such as the experiment with the access negotiations in the Bosgroep Zuiderkempen and the integration of the complaints of the local population in the workings of the forest groups (Bosgroepen Zuiderkempen 2006). This is also reflected in some position statements by the forest groups on the cultural and social values of the forests, and the concern frequently expressed about the remaining gap between the interests of the nature associations on one hand and the inhabitants and the forest owners on the other (Bosgroep Zuiderkempen 2006; Bosgroepen 2005). Hence, instead of the reproduction of the old social identities, within the context of a new cognitive frame, as is the case in the first approach, this second approach points to a more profound transformation that is going on at the same time, which is a more fundamental transformation of the identity of the forest group as the basis of the cooperative orientation that promotes further productive learning.

By addressing the reconstruction of the collective identity of the forest groups, through experimenting with the association of the forest user groups to its activities, BZK has been able to address the failure of the cognitive approach to social learning; that is, its incapacity to take into account the interaction with the changes in the social domain. BZK has been one of the few forest groups to explicitly design experiments for developing new methodologies beyond the issues identified within the forest owner groups. Based on the success of this limited test, BZK launched a second experiment (which runs from 2007 to 2012) to develop a methodology for addressing the problem of increasing the species richness in the overall structure of the forest landscape (Perrings and Touza-Montero 2004), an issue that has also led to defensive reactions from both the forest owners and the inhabitants (Interview with W. De Maeyer, Agentschap voor Natuur en Bos [Agency for Nature and Forest], Brussels, 2007).

The Role of the Forest Group Coordinator in the Process of Change

In hypothesizing that joint forest management can address some of the collective action problems that are encountered in the management of forest complexes with multiple small owners, we have reviewed two types of collective action problems: coordination in providing ecosystem services and cooperation between owners and intermediaries in building a market for products of small-scale forestry. The various explanations of the role of the forest groups in addressing these problems point to the existence of different potential roles of the forest group coordinator in managing the process of transitioning to sustainable forest management. This section draws some implications of this analysis for the evaluation of the role of the forest group coordinator and the members of the forest groups in the process of change.

The analysis of the mechanisms of social learning in this chapter leads to distinguishing three different models of the role of the forest group: first, gathering information and coordinating plans; second, generating change in beliefs; and third, generating change in social norms. In the first model, the role of the forest coordinator can be understood as an external monitor of teamwork, as developed in several game-theory approaches to free riding in teams (Alchian and Demsetz 1972; Holmstrom 1982). Indeed, in this first model, the operation of the forest groups is characterized by organizing joint information processing between the owners and the forest administration on one hand and among the forest owners on the other. The role of the forest group coordinator is to organize these joint processes in an efficient way, especially through drafting the joint forest management plans and coordinating wood-selling activities. In this first model, the role of the forest group members is restricted to their contribution of information to the management and coordination process.

Because of the important role of the forest groups in organizing the process of change in beliefs and norms, the forest group coordinator also has to go beyond the role of monitoring the work of the team—taking on two other important roles: as a political entrepreneur who organizes the process of experimentating with new beliefs, and as a trusted intermediary.

Political entrepreneurship has been at the heart of the forest groups from their beginning. The 1996 pilot project received early recognition for experimenting with new ways of dealing with forest management. In a demonstration of political entrepreneurship, the first forest group coordinator showed the feasibility of combining economic and environmental objectives, by organizing collective selling of the wood that had been generated through management activities. Hence, the coordinator has played a key role in initiating strategies for building a market in small-scale forest products, going well beyond the original intent of the 1990 Forest Decree on multifunctional forestry and taking on responsibilities that did not exist before the operation of the forest groups. The new 1999 forest law was inspired mainly by the lessons that were learned from the 1996 pilot project. This sequence of experimentation and change in the policy framework has been reiterated in the subsequent development of the forest groups.

Finally, the case of the forest groups also establishes the role of the forest coordinator as a non-state actor who plays the role of a trusted intermediary in building the renewed confidence of forest owners in the government's forest policy. Indeed, throughout the process of change, a clear division of tasks was established: the control function of compliance with government regulation remained with the executive bodies (e.g., the forest administration, the forest rangers, and the local authorities), while social learning was the specific task of the forest group.

Possible Governance Frameworks for Collaborative Natural Resource Management

The case of the forest groups provides an important example of how decentralized networks can work in environmental governance. The emerging networks of state and non-state actors offer innovative answers to the present difficulties of the multilateral environmental governance system (Kanie and Haas 2004; Delmas and Young 2009). These new forms of governance can be characterized by an attempt to take into account the increasing importance of non-hierarchical forms of governance based on the negotiated interaction between a plurality of public, semi-public, and private actors (Sørensen and Torfing 2007). In this context the state is increasingly evolving into a role by which it steers autonomous network dynamics (Ibid.). The aim of network governance is to create a synergy between different competences and sources of knowledge to deal with complex and interlinked problems. This section draws some implications about decentralized forest management in forest groups in the broader context of natural resources governance.

Recent reforms in environmental governance worldwide show some important efforts that recognize the need for transferring decision making to new actor networks and a correlative need for state authorities to support social learning processes and build adaptive competences, beyond their traditional role in regulating network externalities. This approach seems especially appropriate in governance of local environmental goods, which has both local and global impacts, but where mechanisms to deal with global ecological interdependencies are often lacking. In those cases the mobilization of new types of non-state collective actors in different functions of governance has proven to be a necessary complement to the state's regulation and economic incentive politics.

In the field of natural resource management in human-dominated ecological landscapes, two forms of network governance have emerged. The first is based on the creation of new collective management entities, while the second is based on the decentralized coordination between existing constituencies. To situate the case of the forest groups in the broader discussion on new modes of governance, this section briefly gives some salient examples of each of these forms.

The new regional natural resource management approach in Australia exemplifies the first approach, with important similarities to the forest groups in Flanders. In this ambitious new governance experiment, fifty-six regional natural resource management bodies have been created (see chapter 5). These bodies generally include a mix of community, rural, and other stakeholders and have formal office holders and responsibility for planning and setting priority. In this approach, each region develops its own regional plan and regional investment strategy for addressing management challenges within parameters set nationally. These activities are coupled with monitoring, evaluation, and oversight by the regional bodies themselves and by state-led steering committees. Crucially, these bodies are aware that should they depart substantially from the parameters laid down by the federal government, they risk losing their funding, dissolution, and replacement by a new entity.

A more far-reaching example of this first type of network governance can be found in cases in which the history of state intervention is less prominent. A clear-cut example concerns groundwater management in the Los Angeles metropolitan area (Ostrom 2008), where a water association composed of cities, industrial users, and farmers was able to gradually build a local public economy around the allocation and management of groundwater rights. Similar to the cases of new environmental governance, this process received support from the government to facilitate the interaction among the different water producers. Indeed, the appointment of a watermaster played an important role in making reliable information available, and also led to the establishment of new regional entity, the Water Replenishment District of Southern Los Angeles County.

The second approach to network governance focuses on the coordination and cooperation between existing constituencies, without delegating new decision-making powers on resource management to regional collective entities. Illustrating this approach in the field of small-scale forestry, the New Forest in southern England (Rydin and Matar 2006) presents an interesting case history. With a landscape of 37,500 hectares, the New Forest includes a mixture of forest and heathland surrounded by large urban areas. Two networks for establishing collective action in this area have been created: the first a consultative panel, with seventy member organizations, including town and parish councils, NGOs, government agencies and local interest groups; and the second, the more formal New Forest Committee, with nine member organizations, all of which have an already-existing statutory role in the management of the New Forest. The consultative panel has performed a useful function in bringing new issues to public attention, such as the declining economic viability of grazing in the heathland and the conflict between landscape conservation by the "commoners"—farmers with common grazing rights on the heathland—and timber and tourism interests. However, the New Forest Committee has been the key network for promoting collective action. The committee has been able to establish concrete projects based on partnerships between the different actors, such as developing a Forest Friendly Farming Accreditation Scheme and drafting a New Forest Strategy published in 2003 based on intensive public consultation.

These examples are, of course, brief illustrations among many, showing the wide variety of potential forms of network governance in the management of human-dominated ecological landscapes. However, they all point to the importance of mechanisms of social learning in the networks creating normative and cognitive change and the new role of the government in facilitating the network dynamics. Developing more empirical research remains a crucial issue, because such research would allow specifying the conditions under which different forms of network governance may succeed in accomplishing these functions and whether such conditions can be affirmatively created.

Conclusion

Based on an in-depth case study and insights from theories of governance, this chapter established the contribution of three different mechanisms to foster social learning on sustainable forest management, respectively through: (1) the use of sustainability criteria and indicators as an open-ended learning device, (2) experimentation with disruptive action strategies to put new beliefs into practice and (3) building new forms of social cooperation around this new beliefs and practices.

The main finding of the chapter is the need to combine different mechanisms of social learning, including both mechanisms based on in-group learning processes and learning processes with external stakeholders. It is only by combining these different mechanisms that it is possible to go beyond the resistance to of the new regulatory and economic incentive policies of the first years of implementation of the new 1990 Forest Decree in Flanders. Indeed, the case study on forest groups has shown that, in the absence of these mechanisms, the learning process was restricted by concerns over timber exploitation and independence from government intervention.

From the point of view of the contribution to the provision of global and local ecosystems services, the case study on joint forest management has also shown the effective contribution of this governance mechanism to more integrated ecosystems-based management. In particular, the case study has demonstrated that open-ended and disruptive learning in the forest groups allowed to integrate important non-market values such as the landscape diversity, spatial externalities (through the joint forest management plans), and some concern for species diversity (through combating invasive species), in the forest management practices. However, the adaptation to new social demands such as recreation in private forests or conservation of tree species diversity as such remains a difficult issue in the small-scale nonindustrial forest landscapes in Flanders.

Note

This chapter draws in part upon the case study discussed in Dedeurwaerdere, T. 2009. Social learning as a basis for cooperative small-scale forest management. *Small-Scale Forestry* 8:193–209.

12

Value Articulating Institutions and Changing Social Preferences

Sigrid Stagl

Governance for sustainable development struggles with complexity, uncertainty, path-dependence, ambivalence, and distributed control. Reflexive governance is societal steering that is embedded in ongoing dynamics of socio-ecological change and that focuses on interactions and feedback relations for open-ended systemic learning rather than achieving defined ends and striving for control. Strategies for implementing reflexive governance include: integrated knowledge production; iterative, participatory goal formulation; appraising options by anticipation of their possible indirect and long-term effects on system dynamics; and interactive strategy development and adaptive strategies and experimentation. Reflexive governance requires opening up governance processes for interaction and feedback, with closing down of these processes needed for collective action (Voß, Bauknecht, and Kemp 2006).

For the task of appraising and comparing sustainable options, traditional economic techniques such as cost–benefit analysis have turned out to be unsuitable (Munda 1996). Consequently, there has been a call for new tools and methods because of: (1) the need to address uncertainty and to account for multiple framings resulting from the characteristics of complex adaptive systems; and (2) the increasing acceptance of the idea that preferences and institutions are intertwined; formal and informal institutions influence actors and shape preferences.

This chapter illustrates how the reflexive governance approach can be applied to innovative institutional design of the science-policy interface in the field of global and local public good provision. To this purpose, it will discuss methodological options for sustainability appraisal that address uncertainty, capture the decision process as well as the outcome, and account for social influence on decision making. Viewing appraisal methods as value-articulating institutions moves them from technical detail to crucial policy choice (Vatn 2004).

For environmental governance we need institutions that are inclusive and deliberative, allowing preferences to form and change; and we need to be reflective about the designs of value-articulating institutions. Although participatory, integrated appraisal tools are still being further developed, they have been shown to be suitable for more broadly informing policy processes and governance for sustainable development.

This chapter maps different valuation and appraisal methods that have been used in multiple real-world applications. The methods highlighted in this chapter are conceptually and practically particularly suited for appraising policies, programs, and projects for which sustainability is an important component. The next section of the chapter explores the implications of a complex systems perspective on appraisal methods and recent findings on the relationship between institutions and preferences. It is followed by a review of sustainability appraisal methods that combine analytical and participatory methods, account for different types of knowledge, provide opportunities for learning during the appraisal process, and have a process that is completely transparent. The methods discussed are: deliberative monetary valuation, social multi-criteria evaluation, three-stage multi-criteria analysis, multi-criteria mapping, deliberative mapping, and stakeholder decision/dialogue analysis. The final section points to methodological and practical opportunities and challenges for the reflective governance approach.

Appraising the Sustainability of Complex Systems

As climate change and poverty rise in importance on the political agenda, and the appraisal of policies, programs, and projects based on sustainability criteria becomes more widespread, theorists and practitioners ask the following fundamental questions about the nature of appraisal and its role in the political process:

1. Sustainable development is a multidimensional concept: How can potentially conflicting impacts that are measured in different units (monetary/nonmonetary) and in different ways (quantitative / qualitative) be brought together to aid decision making (Martinez-Alier, Munda, and O'Neill 1998)?

2. The interface between science and policy is complex: How can appraisal tools aid decision making when the field of policy analysis increasingly rejects the concept of neutral, objective advice (Owens, Raynor, and Bina 2004)?

3. Natural and human systems are adaptive: How can valuation and appraisal tools account for the dynamic and uncertain nature of natural and human systems (Folke et al. 2005)?

Hence, the aim of sustainable development puts special demands on valuation and appraisal methods, which makes it necessary to test the applicability of existing valuation and appraisal tools in this context.

It is often argued that for the environment to be taken seriously in government and business decisions, it must be assigned a monetary value. Environmental economists have developed and used a range of methods including travel cost, hedonic pricing, production function analysis, contingent valuation, and choice modeling (Hanley and Spash 1993) to attribute monetary values to the "environment" in decision-making processes. This approach has been successful in that many national and international agencies are performing monetary valuation exercises as part of their overall assessment of projects. However, there has also been criticism of the monetary valuation of environmental goods and services. Critiques can be broadly grouped into those concerned with the theoretical foundations of economic valuation, and those looking at the validity of the specific numbers produced and the tools employed.

Cost–benefit analysis claims that benefits and costs can be expressed in monetary terms and hence made comparable or commensurable. A significant literature in ethics, political philosophy, and economics has arisen which doubts this assumption. If the surrogate markets of cost–benefit analysis are regarded as unacceptable for political decisions concerning say, abortion policy, then it is argued to be inappropriate for much environmental policy, too (Anderson 1993; O'Neill 1993; Vatn and Bromley 1994; Sunstein 1997). Another strand of academic literature argues that incommensurability arises when a rational agent is unable to attach a monetary value to certain "goods" (e.g., environmental assets) for legitimate reasons (see Aldred 2006 for a more comprehensive review of these issues). David Pearce acknowledged, "the issue of 'incommensurables' grew to be the single most controversial issue in cost–benefit analysis, and it remains so today" (Pearce 1998, 86. Furthermore, there are concerns that cost–benefit analysis builds on axioms of choice that are inconsistent with theories of modern psychology and empirical evidence (Kahneman and Tversky 1979; Knetsch 1995). Practical matters (e.g., an interviewer wearing either formal or more casual clothing) were shown to have undue impact on the stated willingness-to-pay for an environmental good (Bateman and Mawby 2004). Another challenge to cost-benefit analysis arises from the long-term perspective that is necessary in sustainability valuation. It has been argued that with all but very small discount rates, long-term consequences are left out of decisions (Stern 2006, esp. section 2A.2).

Researchers and policy makers are increasingly recognizing that the interface between science and policy is complex. The old technical-rational model of appraisal, in which "objective assessment" was assumed to lead straightforwardly to better decisions, has proved theoretically, politically, and practically inadequate. Instead, attention has been drawn to the complexities of appraisal practices, and to the different, sometimes subtle, ways in which they might secure legitimacy, influence outcomes, and lead to the adjustment of policies. Owens, Raynor, and Bina (2004) argue that an important objective for appraisal should be to foster learning of more than one type and, potentially, to modify the belief systems and behavior of individuals and organizations over time. Hence, valuation and appraisal tools that support social learning processes have more potential to aid decision making for sustainable development.

Natural and human systems are adaptive, and impacts of changes in the systems are characterized by uncertainty (Pimm 1984; Anderson, Arrow, and Pines,1988; Allen 2001; Folke 2005). All these factors redefine the role of experts, the meaning of knowledge and how decision processes need to be designed to make more effective policy. Post-normal science argues that under these circumstances we should shift away from the sole focus on outcome toward the quality of decision processes (Funtowicz and Ravetz 1990). They have also called for more transparent, deliberative, and inclusive processes for informing policy and decisions. Hence, valuation and appraisal tools that include public and stakeholder engagement and that are transparent tend to perform better in decision making for sustainable development.

The characteristics of adaptiveness and uncertainty also lead to difficulties in the measurement of all impacts in quantitative terms. In situations where important impacts can only be measured in qualitative terms, methods are needed that can make use of both types of knowledge and bring them together in a systematic way. Hence, valuation and appraisal tools that can draw on both quantitative and qualitative data and bring them together in a systematic way are more suitable for issues of sustainable development.

Since the mid 1990s, researchers and practitioners working in the fields of ecological economics, institutional economics, sustainability science, decision analysis, and policy appraisal have sought to address the various challenges laid out above and developed an alternative toolbox to aid more sustainable decision-making and the articulation of public values. Most prominently, the "hybrid methodologies" combine interpersonal deliberation and quantitative methods.

However, sustainability appraisal is not merely a methodological issue. The type of evaluation and the institutional structures in which the appraisal is embedded influences the outcome. Therefore the choice of valuation and appraisal methods is a process one of "institutionalizing social choice." The method of inclusion of environmental resources and ecosystem services in decision processes determines how far the environment is taken into account with results affecting the quality of our lives and those of future generations; the same applies to social aspects of sustainability. Valuation and appraisal methods determine who participates in the decision-making process, how they participate and in what capacity (consumer, stakeholder, citizen), what counts as data, and which data processing and aggregation procedures are used. Therefore valuation methods can be seen as "value-articulating institutions" (Jacobs 1997; Vatn 2004).

All the methods reviewed in this chapter build on the following principles: (1) accounting for different types of knowledge (monetary and nonmonetary, quantitative and qualitative data); (2) considering seriously the issue of intergenerational equity; (3) providing opportunities for learning during the appraisal process; (4) ensuring transparency of each step of the appraisal process; and (5) having a strong element of public and stakeholder engagement.

Sustainability Appraisal Methods

Deliberative Monetary Valuation

Cost-benefit analysis was developed for the appraisal of infrastructure projects. Deliberative monetary valuation primarily differs from cost-benefit analysis in that preferences are constructed during the deliberation process. Deliberative monetary valuation is most suitable for the appraisal of projects whose impacts are rather well understood, when the impacts are relatively short term, and which do not affect complex ecosystem services such as biodiversity. The results of a monetary valuation study can be presented with a focus on the calculated net present value or with a focus on explaining the underlying ethics, belief structures, and conflicts that were potentially explored in the deliberative process.

The combination of monetary valuation with deliberative processes was advocated by several authors (Brown, Peterson, and Tonn 1995; Jacobs 1997; Ward 1999; Kenyon and Nevin 2001; MacMillan et al. 2002; McDaniels et al. 2003) to account within monetary valuation more explicitly for the fact that preferences are socially constructed. The notion of value construction suggests that respondents do not have well-defined preferences for many complex environmental goods prior to the elicitation process, but that these preferences are constructed during this elicitation process itself (Gregory et al. 1997; Payne and Bettman 1999; O'Connor 2000). Otherwise the assumptions are similar to those of cost-benefit analysis.

A group of citizens are selected and meet to discuss information about environmental damages associated with the proposed development. Known costs and benefits (discounted) are presented, while those pertaining to environmental damages are deliberated. The citizens form a jury aiming to provide a monetary value for environmental damages that might be in terms of an individual willingness-to-accept to allow the project to proceed. The result would then be incorporated into a net present-value calculation to determine the viability of the project.

Alternatively, deliberative processes can be used to complement monetary valuation techniques. For example, (1) group deliberation can help test the monetary valuation survey design (e.g., wording and comprehension of questions), validate the information content, and help identify design biases; (2) deliberative methods can be used for determining the policy options or the institutional context, upon which the valuation survey will be based; or (3) outcomes of an environmental valuation can be validated by a participatory process (Kallis et al. 2004).

A criticism of deliberative monetary valuation, which applies in particular to the combined use (rather than the complementary use) of deliberative and monetary techniques, refers to the fundamental differences between deliberative forums (e.g., citizens' juries) and monetary valuation (e.g., contingent valuation) (Niemeyer and Spash 2001). These include the different approaches taken to theoretical foundations (individual and social ontology, preference basis, rationality theory), practical issues (justification, framing, value representation, institutional setting), and political issues (manipulation, representation, social impact). In short, there are significant difficulties in incorporating the views of the public from the deliberative process into the monetary valuation part of the exercise. Whether the combined version of deliberative monetary valuation could therefore be described as an improvement on the contingent valuation approach is currently contested (O'Brien 2003).

Social Multi-Criteria Evaluation

Social multi-criteria evaluation was developed to address complex issues and to deal with uncertainty in the context of sustainable development. It is the combined use of participatory techniques and multi-criteria analysis (MCA) to aid decision making about a number of policy options while taking conflicting interests and multiple criteria into account. It highlights transparency and social learning during the appraisal process (Munda 2004). This method is most suitable for the appraisal of policies, programs or projects whose impacts are not yet well understood and therefore benefit from a multidisciplinary modeling of impacts. The results include a ranking of options (policies, projects, or technologies) as well as an analysis of the different perspectives about the options held among respondents. Depending on the application and requirements of decision makers, the ranking may be complete or partial; the latter includes the natural avowal of incomparable alternatives (e.g., one policy option being much better in the social criteria than another that is much better in the environmental criteria).

A social multi-criteria evaluation consists of six main steps: (1) characterizing a wide range of relevant alternative ways to achieve a particular policy aim (options); here, social multi-criteria evaluation emphasizes the need for institutional analyses to fully understand the decision-making context and the need for stakeholder and public participation to cover the main option as well as ensuring "buy-in" from relevant groups of society; (2) developing a set of criteria to represent different viewpoints on the issues that are relevant to the appraising of those options; (3) evaluating options against each criterion based on models or expert judgment from various disciplines (impact matrix) and specifying the preference function for each criterion; (4) assigning a quantitative weighting to each criterion, to reflect its relative importance under the viewpoint in question; (5) calculating an overall performance rank for each option under all the criteria, which can be presented either as an overall ranking based on group weights or as separate rankings for particular viewpoints or individuals; and (6) analyzing the potential for conflicts and coalitions between participating stakeholders (equity matrix).

Deliberation among citizens or stakeholders over alternative development options has the potential to generate new ideas. The iterative process of social multi-criteria evaluation is flexible and allows for new options to be added as the social learning process proceeds.

There are a number of multi-criteria algorithms and corresponding software packages available. (For a discussion of the different types of algorithms and their respective advantages and disadvantages, see Dodgson et al. 2000 or De Montis et al. 2005). Most algorithms require the definition of indifference or gradual degrees of preference, and these have to be associated to the deviations observed between the evaluations. This is a challenging task for which it is difficult to obtain evidence. Another challenge that is common to most multi-criteria algorithms is the establishment of criteria weights; a range of interpretations of weights and corresponding weighting procedures exist (Choo et al. 1999).

The main weakness of sophisticated methods such as NAIADE[1] is their lack of transparency, which may lead to difficulties in acceptance among the citizens and stakeholders participating in the MCA process.

Three-Stage Multi-Criteria Analysis

Three-stage multi-criteria analysis is the combined use of participatory techniques and multi-criteria analysis to aid decision making about policy options while taking conflicting interests and multiple criteria into account. Stakeholders select the evaluation criteria, experts present information and measure impacts, and citizens explore values (Renn et al. 1993; Renn and Webler1998). The results include a ranking of policy options as well as an analysis of the different perspectives about the options held among citizen participants and possibly among stakeholders and experts. The calculated ranking is complete, but this result is compared with a more holistic appraisal. The final recommendations are always based on a holistic judgment by individuals or groups and include a ranking and the reasoning for this ranking.

Developed for the social appraisal of technologies with particular emphasis on the role of risk and uncertainty, three-stage multi-criteria analysis is most suitable for the appraisal of policies, programs, or projects whose impacts are reasonably well understood by experts and which contain a signficant technical element.

The sequencing and choice of participants is based on the Renn and Webler (1993; 1998) "cooperative discourse" model. First, concerns and evaluative criteria are identified and selected. All relevant stakeholder groups are asked to reveal their values and criteria for judging different options. A value-tree analysis is used to elicit the values and evaluative criteria used for judging different options (von Winterfeldt 1987). The purpose of a value-tree is to elicit and represent the concerns of all relevant stakeholder groups.

Second, the impacts and consequences related to different policy options are identified and measured. The research team or an external expert group operationalizes and transforms the evaluative criteria derived from the value-tree into indicators. The participating stakeholder groups review these operational definitions and indicators. Once approved by all parties, the indicators are used to evaluate the performance of each policy option on all value dimensions. Experts from relevant academic disciplines and with diverse perspectives on the topic of the discourse are asked to judge the performance of each policy option on each indicator.

Third, a discourse is conducted with randomly selected citizens as jurors and representation of interest groups as witnesses. The final step is the evaluation of potential solutions by one group or several groups of randomly selected citizens (Dienel 1989; Dienel and Renn 1995). These panels are asked to evaluate and design policy options based on knowledge of the likely consequences and their own values and preferences. The participating citizens are informed about the options, evaluative criteria, and performance profiles of options. Their involvement helps to elicit values and assign relative weights to the different value dimensions. The procedures used for this purpose are derived from multi-attribute utility theory (von Winterfeldt and Edwards 1986).

The main strengths of utility-based multi-criteria appraisal methods are their simplicity and strong theoretical grounding. However, being based on utility theory and rational expectations, these algorithms are subject to the same critique as the theories on which they are built (strong assumptions about preference functions and commensurability of values). Initially, utility-based MCA algorithms were applied for production planning and financial portfolio choices and geared toward individual decision makers. More recently they have also been applied in environmental decision making and extended to group decision making (Beinat and Nijkamp 1998).

Multi-Criteria Mapping
Multi-criteria mapping is an interview-based multi-criteria analysis whereby individual specialists and stakeholders are invited to appraise the performance of core and discretionary options against their own sets of criteria. It focuses on eliciting and documenting detailed technical and evaluative judgments concerning the performance of alternative policy

options. It devotes particular attention to the systematic exploration of uncertainties and the sources of variability between diverse viewpoints (Stirling 1997). The results include rankings of options either per stakeholder, per perspectives (i.e., groups of participants), or averages of all pessimistic (left-hand end of bar) and of all optimistic (right-hand end of bar) ranks (i.e., combined weighted scores for all criteria) for core options and for additional options. The interpretation of the rankings is helped by the textual analysis of statements recorded in the software during the interview and from the interview transcripts.

Developed to address complex issues and to deal with uncertainty in the context of sustainable development, multi-criteria mapping is most suitable for the appraisal of policies, programs, or projects to which stakeholders had some exposure and when views about data, as well as about options and criteria, are controversial.

Multi-criteria mapping consists of six main steps: (1) characterizing a wide range of relevant alternative ways to achieve a particular policy aim (options); (2) developing a set of criteria to represent different viewpoints on the issues that are relevant to the appraisal of those options; (3) evaluating each criterion in turn with numerical scores, to reflect the performance of each option under each criterion for a given viewpoint; (4) exploring uncertainties in the data (by asking respondents for scores under optimistic and pessimistic conditions) and ambiguities in the assumptions (by analyzing qualitative data collected during the interviews); (5) assigning a quantitative weighting to each criterion that reflects the relative importance of their criteria to the interviewee. In contrast to the relatively technical business of scoring, this weighting process reflects intrinsically subjective judgments over priorities and values; (6) calculating an overall performance rank for each option under all the criteria taken together for a particular viewpoint.

Multi-criteria mapping uses the "linear additive weighting" procedure, in which the rank simply represents the weighted sum of normalized scores. After seeing the ranking of options, participants are free to alter their weightings or scores in the light of this, with the objective of arriving at a final overall pattern of ranks, which they feel comfortable accurately represents their personal perspective. Sometimes, this review prompts participants to define new options or criteria, or even to reconsider aspects of scoring. In such cases, the interviewer should encourage the participants to justify their reasons for any changes.

One of the advantages of multi-criteria mapping is the simplicity of the algorithm and the subsequent transparency of the analysis process.

Multi-criteria mapping avoids the distinction between impacts and preference functions, which simplifies the algorithm and might increase the buy-in of participants.

Rather than seeking to produce a single aggregate answer, the multi-criteria mapping tool is used to explore how differing assumptions, priorities, and value judgments shape participants' individual appraisals. Depending on the viewpoint, this additional feature of multi-criteria mapping may be seen as an advantage or as a disadvantage.

Deliberative Mapping

Deliberative mapping is the combined use of participatory techniques and multi-criteria analysis to aid decision making about policy options while taking conflicting interests and multiple criteria into account. Besides measuring the specific performance of each option against the criteria, it highlights the need for exploring the arguments that participants used to justify their judgments. Specialists and small groups of citizens follow the same assessment process (Davies, Burgess, and Stirling 2003). The results include a ranking of policy options as well as an analysis of the different perspectives about the options held among citizen participants and among experts. The interpretation of the rankings is helped by the textual analysis of statements recorded in the software during the interview and from the interview and group transcripts. Developed to address complex issues and to deal with uncertainty in the context of sustainable development, deliberative mapping is most suitable for the appraisal of policies, programs, or projects where views are controversial and value judgments are particularly important.

First, the team of researchers conducts open-ended interviews with specialists and stakeholders for being able to understand the biophysical system and the socioeconomic context of the proposed project. The team of researchers develops a set of core evaluation criteria and core options, which all participants are asked to consider. Then, facilitated group discussions with small groups of citizens help to clarify, discuss, and then agree on the meanings, definitions, and implications of the options to be appraised. The groups discuss and agree on a shared set of criteria to be used by the citizen panel to judge the pros and cons of the different options. Citizens score options under the chosen criteria; the panel then reviews the performance patterns and decides what issues to take to a joint workshop. At the same time, criteria mapping interviews are conducted with specialists who are guided by a researcher through their own individual analysis in separate two- to three-hour sessions. As part of this session, the specialists are asked if they would like to add any criteria or options that might be relevant for them for appraising the project under consideration. During the session the researcher works interactively with a piece of computer software to explore the performance of options against their criteria under different assumptions. In addition to the quantitative and textual documentation recorded using the software package, the interviews are also audio-recorded for later transcription and analysis. In a joint workshop, specialists exchange views with citizens and respond to questions. In a follow-up group meeting, panelists discuss workshop outcomes, rescore options, weigh criteria to reflect priorities, and discuss individual and full panel results. The specialists go through a second multi-criteria mapping interview after the joint workshop to elicit any changes in their appraisals. In a later workshop, specialists reflect on the various per-spectives and emerging findings and evaluate the process. From the outset, the aim is not to achieve a consensus on how to proceed on the proposal, but to expose the variety of views among and between special-ists and citizens and to try to understand where the differences are most marked and why.

Like multi-criteria mapping it does not seek to primarily deliver a ranking of options, which may be viewed as an advantage or a disadvantage.

Stakeholder Decision/Dialogue Analysis

The combined use of group deliberation techniques and (a qualitative form of) multi-criteria analysis aids decision making about policy options while taking conflicting interests and multiple criteria into account. It highlights the framing of problems, scoping options, eliciting criteria, and making judgments through facilitated deliberation (Burgess 2000). The results include a ranking of (groups of) policy options as well as an analysis of the different perspectives about the options held among stakeholders. The interpretation of the rankings is helped by the analysis of the qualitative data collected during the workshops. The results should also include a sensitivity analysis and a clear view of the conflict-ing character of the criteria and the influence of a particular set of weights. Developed to address complex issues and to deal with uncer-tainty in the context of sustainable development, stakeholder decision analysis is most suitable for the appraisal of policies, programs, or proj-ects in which it is important to work first on a common problem under-standing and when a rough impact assessment is sufficient as input in the decision process.

In a series of four workshops stakeholders are provided with relevant information about the proposed project and asked to go through a carefully designed combination of individual and collective processes to rank options. The main steps (e.g., final rankings) must be agreed on by all group members. The process allows for reconsideration and revision of results in a transparent manner.

Clark et al. (1998) recommends using this method on no more than twenty-four issues/options and to involve the stakeholders in the process as early as possible. When feasible, they should be involved in the generation of the list of issues/options to be prioritized.

Stakeholder decision/dialogue analysis uses a range of qualitative tools for facilitating and interpreting in-depth discussion groups, enabling consultation to transcend conventional emphasis on scientific knowledge and rational, utilitarian argument and to complement this with moral, aesthetic, emotional, and local ways of knowing and valuing.

The group members work interactively with one another and use low-tech pen and paper techniques to record their judgments about the performance of options against criteria. The focus is more on empowering participants and less on using latest modeling and presentation techniques.

Methodological and Practical Implications for Governance Approach

The aim of sustainable development puts special demands on valuation and appraisal methods. Given that sustainable development is a multi-dimensional concept, crucial for human survival, and a long-term issue, it is necessary to test currently used valuation and appraisal tools for their fitness for this context. A range of new sustainability valuation and appraisal methods have been developed and road-tested over the last ten years. They combine interpersonal deliberation with quantitative methods. These methods build on the following principles: accounting for different types of knowledge (monetary and nonmonetary; quantitative and qualitative data); taking intergenerational equity seriously; providing opportunities for learning during the appraisal process; ensuring transparency of each step of the appraisal process; and having a strong element of public and stakeholder engagement. While the new sustainability valuation and appraisal methods vary somewhat and their application is suitable for slightly different problems, the main distinction lies between this group of methods and monetary environmental valuation on the one hand and deliberative methods on the other hand. An overview of the various methods covered in this chapter is given in table 12.1.

Table 12.1

Summary of the six appraisal methods and their main features (weakly relevant (•), moderately relevant(••), highly relevant (•••) and very highly relevant (••••))

Name	Criteria come from[1]	Transparency[2]	Public and stakeholder engagement[3]	Focus on opening up[4]	Focus on closing down[6]	Robustness[5]	Uncertainty[6,7]	Types of outcomes that the approach is good at producing[7]
Deliberative monetary valuation	Citizens panel/s and researchers	••	•	•	•••	••	Sensitivity or scenario analysis	Monetary value
Social multi-criteria evaluation	Stakeholders and / or research team	•••	••	••	•••	•••	Fuzzy numbers; sensitivity or scenario analysis	Complete or partial ranking
Three-stage multi-criteria analysis	Stakeholders	•••	••	••	•••	•••	Sensitivity or scenario analysis	Complete ranking
Multi-criteria mapping	Stakeholders and research team	••••	••	•••	••	•••	Optimistic and pessimistic scores; sensitivity or scenario analysis	Map of perspectives and ranking, plus qualitative discourse analysis
Deliberative mapping	Stakeholders and research team	•••	•••	•••	••	•••	Optimistic and pessimistic scores; sensitivity or scenario analysis	Map of perspectives and ranking, plus qualitative discourse analysis

Table 12.1
(continued)

Name	Criteria come from[1]	Transparency[2]	Public and stakeholder engagement[3]	Focus on opening up[4]	Focus on closing down[6]	Robustness[5]	Uncertainty[6,7]	Types of outcomes that the approach is good at producing[7]
Stakeholder decision analysis	Stakeholders	••••	•••	•••	•••	•••	Qualitative analysis	Complete or partial ranking

1. An initial list of criteria is often suggested by the research team, which can then be altered by participants. Some methods (MCM, DM) allow each individual participant to add criteria to the common list, but most methods require a common list of criteria to be used by all participants.

2. Transparency is rated higher, if participants have the opportunity to go through the whole process and if the tools applied are simple and can be easily explained in a workshop.

3. All reviewed methods include a substantial amount of citizen, expert and/or stakeholder engagement. However, with some methods a wider range of elements (e.g., criteria, options, weights, policy suggestions) is drawn from the deliberations than in others.

4. As with public and stakeholder engagement, all methods reviewed include processes of opening up the issues and then supporting closing down and arriving at recommendations. However, in some methods the focus rests more on one particular aspect.

5. Robustness—being rigorous about data as well as framing assumptions—includes "social robustness" by involving a variety of participants.

6. The way the methods address uncertainty is briefly characterized; for most methods this includes some form of sensitivity/scenario analysis, but several go further than this.

7. The types of outputs produced effectively by the approaches are briefly characterized; a ranking of options is complete if no such incomparabilities (are assumed to) arise; the stronger the assumptions on which the algorithm is based, the more likely that a complete ranking can be calculated.

The type of evaluation and the institutional structures in which the appraisal is embedded influences the outcome. Therefore, the choice of valuation and appraisal methods is not wholly a technical question but rather one of "institutionalising social choice."

Because there is no one method that is best suitable for appraising all types of policies, programs, and projects, a more differentiated approach would produce better outcomes. Developing cultures, which support the search for the best suitable methods for specific applications, requires that departments are familiar with the different methods at hand and provide if-then type guidance to appraisers for choosing the most appropriate method.

Although significant advances in the fields of decision analysis, ecological economics, psychology, science and technology studies, and sustainability science have led to novel methods of sustainability appraisal that are ready for use, significant challenges remain. First, in the interface between participatory decision aid and policy making, we have found that participatory workshops offer an excellent opportunity for social learning, which participants tend to use effectively. However, the link from these workshops to the policy arena is weak. Second, the challenges for implementing high quality participatory workshops have been acknowledged and many initial pitfalls and problems of early applications eliminated. However, the rigor of applications still varies enormously, and quality standards for participatory processes are only slowly being developed. Third, very few studies so far have compared different appraisal methods systematically for specific areas of application. Finally, knowledge about new appraisal methods is only slowly making its way into the policy arena. The dissemination of this information is as important a task for researchers to untertake as it is for policy makers and civil servants to acquire new skills.

Notes

1. NAIADE was developed by Munda 1995. NAIADE stands for "Novel Approach to Imprecise Assessment and Decision Environments" and is a discrete multi-criteria method, based on the partial comparability axiom and uses pairwise linguistic evaluation of alternatives.

V
Knowledge Generation on Global Issues

One of the cross-cutting issues in the analysis of new governance tools in this book is the generation of knowledge. Knowledge of global public goods influences individual and social preferences and informs the democratic deliberation processes discussed in the previous parts of the book. However, lack of knowledge on solutions and on collective preferences is a serious practical challenge in any problem of GPG provision.

The importance of knowledge generation is explicitly addressed in the chapters in this part of the book. They show that institutional mechanisms for global governance should be analyzed from the perspective of knowledge generation and not only from the perspective of effectiveness and legitimacy. The analysis in the chapter by Brousseau, Dedeurwaerdere, and Siebenhüner shows that there are clearly mechanisms that do not generate adequate knowledge, even when they are based on democratic deliberation. There are trade-offs between mechanisms that are better at knowledge generation, and those that are better at effectiveness or democratic legitimacy. In particular, this chapter shows that the inclusiveness of the learning process has a positive impact on the generation of knowledge about implementation. This has already been highlighted in Part IV on multi-stakeholder coordination, but here knowledge generation in various communities is explored from a comparative perspective. Inclusiveness may lead to better knowledge, but this has to be combined with mechanisms that ensure credibility and the widespread availability of the knowledge (e.g., in science communities and the umbrella organizations of nongovernmental organizations). This point is well taken in the chapter by Lawrence and Molteno, who show that knowledge generation processes are not exempt from standard conflicts of interest between various organizations, competition for leadership, and power issues in national bureaucracies.

Finally, the contribution by Grothmann and Siebenhüner points out that specific competencies are needed to manage the governance mechanisms that are specifically oriented to the generation of knowledge. Building upon the work of an interdisciplinary OECD project, their chapter shows the importance of the competency for social interaction in heterogeneous groups, the competency for deliberation and the ability to learn, and that for the ability to revise previous thoughts, decisions and practices. Taken together, these competencies are shown to be important micro-level fundamentals for reflexive governance processes.

The main challenge which is highlighted in this part of the book is that, in order to develop effective and legitimate methods of governance, there is a need for further improvement in the current means of knowledge generation on both the various GPGs and the preferences of the various communities involved. This challenge also reflects the fact, emphasized throughout this book, that the provision of global public goods is basically a question of governance. This is because the public nature of the goods has to be collectively defined in the process of clarifying the issues at hand, and in the elaboration of solutions.

13

Knowledge Matters: Institutional Frameworks to Govern the Provision of Global Public Goods

Eric Brousseau, Tom Dedeurwaerdere, and Bernd Siebenhüner

The provision of global public goods (GPGs) has been extensively discussed in recent years. This chapter focuses on institutional frameworks for generating the knowledge that is needed to make decisions about the provision of these goods. Currently, there is a lack of knowledge about both needs and solutions. Collective goals are unknown because individuals and communities can only form preferences if they are conscious of the actual issues at stake, and of the way they impact on their own individual situation, the situations of others, and those of future members of the society. Hence, this lack of knowledge is not only linked to a revelation problem as in traditional problems in public good provision. It is due to the fact that most citizens and economic agents do not have an explicit preference for goods as "conceptual" as global biodiversity, global public health, peace, and global economic security. This is partly because it is complex to assess how these GPGs impact on individual situations. The solutions are also unknown, both because the most efficient means of dealing with an issue are unclear, and because diffusion of the relevant knowledge is problematic. This is due to the limited scientific understanding of the problems and of the design and implementation of relevant institutional and organizational solutions, as well as to the limited diffusion of existing knowledge. It also occurs because the provision of these goods is interrelated and partly conflicting (e.g., development and biodiversity), leading to conflicts among interests. Such conflicts may hinder the revelation of information and the circulation of knowledge.

Thus, this chapter seeks to analyze the specific coordination needs of the generation of knowledge about global problems of GPG provision, and their possible solutions, by focusing on the involvement of different types of organized communities at different levels of governance. The chapter is structured as follows. In the next section, we develop an analytical framework aimed at establishing a link between the processes of collective decision making (in matters of GPGs) and performance in terms of knowledge generation. This leads us to highlight the various trade-offs among alternatives in matter of governance. We point out in particular that the various processes of decision making—which can be chosen for reasons other than their performance in terms of knowledge generation—have different abilities to generate knowledge in general, and also different abilities to produce the various categories of knowledge. We discuss, in particular, the production of knowledge aimed at delimiting and weighting issues and knowledge about socio-technical solutions to address these issues. Our framework is then used in a normative way to identify the institutional solutions that will best ensure the production of the various types of knowledge needed to ensure the efficient provision of GPGs. We also develop our analysis and show how our framework can be operationalized, both to be tested, and to yield real world recommendations. In the final sections, we apply our analysis to a set of case studies from the field of environmental governance.

A Knowledge-Generation Perspective on Alternative Decision-Making Mechanisms

What is needed is a framework for the assessment of alternative forms of decision making that focuses on their ability to generate knowledge so as to make more balanced choices thanks to a better knowledge of stakeholders' preferences, and to make more efficient choices thanks to a better knowledge of available solutions and of their conditions of implementation.

Our aim is to remain realistic by being able to compare the actual decision/governance principles that are under debate, while remaining parsimonious in not making our analytical categories excessively complex. For that purpose, our approach in this chapter will be based on a total cost approach, in the spirit of Ronald Coase's (1937) attempt to take into account not only the costs of production but also the costs of coordination. We therefore attempt to assess the relative efficiency/cost performance of alternative knowledge-generation processes, including a broad set of indirect costs generated by the creation and functioning of both formal and informal social and political institutions. First, we propose criteria to assess the efficiency and the quality of the knowledge-generation processes. Then, we categorize alternative processes of decision making (alternative governance regimes) in global governance.

Criteria for Assessing Knowledge-Generation Processes

As Foray (2004) has pointed out, knowledge is a good characterized by three main features. The first is uncontrollability, which means that knowledge is not available for one purpose only. The future uses of knowledge cannot usually be anticipated. Even if it emerged by targeting a goal, different users can employ a piece of knowledge in different ways. Second, knowledge is cumulative. New knowledge draws from the recombination of ideas and/or the criticism of past ideas. Third, knowledge is a non-rival good. From this vision we can highlight four dimensions that will enable us to assess the performance of an institutional arrangement in the generation of knowledge:

1. Knowledge generation can be evaluated on the basis of the *adequacy* of the resulting knowledge for the specific purpose of providing solutions to GPG-related problems. Adequacy can be understood as the degree to which the knowledge allows actors to solve actual problems. In addition, adequacy is a quality of knowledge that is perceived by actors as relevant—salient in the sense of Mitchell et al. (2006, 15)— to their decision making.

2. The ability of a process of knowledge generation to encourage *disclosure* and/or revelation is essential, because this enables the production or new knowledge (by a combination of uncontrollability and cumulativeness). In this respect, for instance, the obligation to disclose information publicly (either in the scientific world of in the realm of industrial property [patents]) can be considered efficient, given that other users can benefit from this knowledge.

3. The *speed of knowledge generation* matters, because it levers the production of knowledge (due to cumulative effects) and therefore increases the stock of available knowledge.

4. Like any other non-rival good, *access to knowledge* once it has been produced is essential. Thus, the ability of a process of knowledge generation to make knowledge available to the widest number of potential users (and therefore its costs of access, which encompass both the price of the knowledge and the costs incurred in using it, such as learning efforts and complementary investments) have to be considered.

These four criteria refer to potential benefits. However, an assessment should also consider the balance between costs and benefits. Two sources of costs differentiate the alternative decision making processes. First, there are the costs of the resources dedicated to the generation of knowledge.

These include, in particular, whether the process leads to a duplication of effort, and whether it relies on the existing stock of knowledge. Second, the costs of coordination among the parties involved in the process of generating knowledge should be taken into account.

Thus we will assess alternative ways of making decisions about global public goods on the basis of six criteria, namely their ability to: (i) generate adequate knowledge, (ii) encourage disclosure and revelation (to maximize spillovers), (iii) speed up the generation of knowledge, (iv) allow widespread access to knowledge, (v) use the available cognitive resources efficiently, and (vi) reduce the costs of coordination among those involved in the production of knowledge.

The Key Dimensions of Collective Decision-Making Mechanisms

A governance mechanism consists of a decision-making mechanism and enforcement capabilities. Because we are focusing on knowledge generation we will only consider the properties of the decision-making element. Our typology of governance mechanisms relies on two classical dichotomies that have been extensively studied in the social sciences. First, we compare centralized and decentralized decision-making mechanisms. This distinction is relevant in both a national and an international context, in which each level of governance has particular advantages and disadvantages (Karahan, Razzolini, and Shughart 2002; Bache and Flinders 2004). The second dichotomy is between contract-type mechanisms based on self-interested individuals (exclusive interests) and mechanisms that are based on social and communitarian logics with individuals oriented toward a collective outcome (inclusive interest). This dichotomy between actors' orientations has also been studied previously, for instance by Scharpf (2000) in his overview of actor-centered institutionalism. As discussed in chapter 1, these alternative principles of the orientation and delegation of decision making lead to four models of collective interaction, which have long been recognized in the social sciences (see Figure 13.1).

This characterization of the possible decision-making mechanisms (covered in more detail in chapter 1) should be broadened to include two other issues key to the GPG debate: the influence of the scope of the decision-making process and the organization of decision making. These dimensions lead to alternative modes of accountability between decision makers and stakeholders. The first issue is important because of the global character of the problems being considered, and the fact that individuals are already organized in many types of communities, although the global community is not yet fully organized. Therefore, various types of sub-global communities exist in which individuals develop their strategies to have an impact on the provision of public goods in general and global ones in particular. The second issue is important because of the increasing role of non-state actors in the global arena (see Bohman 2004 and chapter 2 of this volume), and the existence of various processes by which either isolated individuals—that is, citizens—or members/representatives of various types of organized communities interact in decision-making processes related to public goods. This leads to various patterns of knowledge generation. The following four dimensions allow us to compare the principles according to which collective decision making is or can be organized at the level of the "global society":

1. *Scope* refers to the size of the community affected by the resulting order or decision. More precisely it refers to the community whose interests are (primarily) taken into account when decisions are made or when regulatory principles are decided. This community can tend toward openness and globalism (i.e., wide scope), or it can be local and closed (i.e., narrow scope).

2. The notion of *orientation* refers to the (primary) motivations of individuals who interact to make collective decisions and/or to implement an order. Does the mechanism aim at dealing with individuals who consider above all their own individual interests (exclusive) or with individuals who also take the collective interest into account (inclusive)?

3. The *organization* of the decision making refers to the explicit design of a collective decision-making process. When the decision-making process is not explicitly designed, collective decisions simply result from the spontaneous aggregation of individual choices and from social adjustments among individuals. Organization increases the efficiency with which interdependences are managed. Moreover, it increases the accountability of the decision makers because, as stakeholders or the representatives of stakeholders (who delegate decision-making powers to them), the relative role of each decision maker is clear. When interdependences are managed spontaneously, the accountability of the actors is expected to be less. Indeed, their actual impact on the decision making is unclear, and the relationship between them and the stakeholders is not easy to establish. Their actions result in facts and information, not in collective choices and organized knowledge

4. The notion of *delegation* refers to the fact that collective decisions can be either centralized in the hands of a limited number of individuals, or decentralized in the sense that each individual is able to express an opinion and have an impact on the final decision. In the first case there is either explicit delegation of decision making (as in hierarchies and constitutional states) or a kind of spontaneous delegation by which leaders emerge who are followed by other members of a community (without any explicit attribution of the right to make collective decisions). In the second case, there is neither explicit nor implicit delegation of the rights of decision making, and the process remains decentralized in the hands of members of the communities.

These four dimensions are all continuums: scope can concern communities of any size from two people to all of humankind. However, their main features can be distinguished on a dichotomous basis by considering the two extremes of each of them. It must be clear, however, that this is just for didactic purposes. When actual decision-making mechanisms are considered, it is more meaningful to speak of more and less centralized processes than of centralization and decentralization.

These four categories refer to different trade-offs between costs and benefits:

• The scope dimension covers mechanisms that have to manage more (wide) or less (narrow) heterogeneity, and therefore result in higher or lower costs of decision making. These mechanisms lead to solutions that have larger or smaller possible economies of scale, and more or less consistency, due to the appropriate management of interdependencies (see Brousseau and Raynaud 2011).

• The orientation dimension compares the maximization of individual (exclusive) and collective (inclusive) welfare as drivers of decision making.

• Along the organization dimension we suggest that organized decision making guarantees accountability and is cheaper, faster, and more conclusive (in the sense that a decision is clearly made). However, spontaneous processes can lead to more innovative decisions and more efficient adaptations to heterogeneous and evolving needs, since they allow more freedom.

• The delegation dimension contrasts decentralized mechanisms that economize on agency costs with centralized mechanisms that minimize the duplication of effort and allow decision makers to specialize.

This way of describing alternative (de facto) decision-making mechanisms in matters of global governance allows us to compare sixteen different models of coordination. Table 13.1 shows how the combination works, and we provide examples of decision mechanisms that illustrate each of these options. Note, however, that the nickname column in this table does not correspond to actors, but rather to processes of decision making. For instance, the third line, nicknamed "global self regulation," represents a situation in which global regulations result from knowledge generated through negotiations among interest groups organized in lobbies dealing with each other on a quid pro quo basis. The fifth line, nicknamed "NGO coordination," indicates a situation in which regulation results from coordination among nongovernmental organizations each promoting their own vision of the collective interest. The nicknames given to each type of governance mechanisms are used in the discussion of their relative performance below. The examples given in the last column of Table 13.1 are discussed in the second part of the chapter.

The Capacity of Alternative Institutional Frameworks to Generate Knowledge

To analyze how the various mechanisms of governance and decision making affect on the process of knowledge generation, we now review how the characteristics of a process of collective decision making (presented in table 13.1) impact on the various criteria of performance discussed above. Being interested in the analysis of actual governance issues, we find it useful to consider the generation of knowledge as a process composed of two different analytical steps: the identification and framing of problems and issues (Argyris and Schön 1996, Schön and Rein 1994); and the innovation, testing, and filtering of operational solutions. These two steps refer to the contradictory requirements of opening up and closing down in social problem-solving processes (Voß, Bauknecht, and Kemp 2006). On the one hand, problem-oriented interactions need to be opened up to take account of the interaction of diverse factors, preferences, and interests. This is necessary to produce robust knowledge and strategies. On the other hand, the selection of relevant factors, choices about ambiguous preference rankings, and a convergence of interests are necessary to make decisions and to act (compare the discussion of exploration and exploitation in March 1991). We will label the knowledge resulting from each of these steps as "framework knowledge" and "operational knowledge" respectively. Knowledge about issues tends to be more oriented toward the establishment of collective preferences than is knowledge about solutions (which includes knowledge of the most

Table 13.1
A typology of modes of governance for dealing with global governance issues

Dimension				Mode of Governance	
Scope	Orientation	Organization	Delegation	Nickname	Example
Wide	Exclusive	Organized	Centralized	Global confederation	Global Environment Outlook (UN Environment Programme)
			Decentralized	Global direct democracy	NGO involvement in the UN Framework Convention on Climate Change and Commission on Sustainable Development
		Spontaneous	Centralized	Global self-regulation	European Culture Collections standard contract
			Decentralized	Global free market	Bioprospecting
	Inclusive	Organized	Centralized	NGO coordination	Intergovernmental Panel on Climate Change (IPCC)
			Decentralized	Republic of science	Earth System Science Partnership
		Spontaneous	Centralized	Global activism	Greenpeace
			Decentralized	Emotional collective action	Al Gore's climate campaign

Table 13.1
(continued)

Dimension				Mode of Governance	
Scope	Orientation	Organization	Delegation	Nickname	Example
Narrow	Exclusive	Organized	Centralized	National government	UK Biodiversity Action Plan
			Decentralized	Local direct democracy	Local Agenda 21
		Spontaneous	Centralized	Local self-regulation	Responsible Care Initiative in the chemical industry
			Decentralized	Legal activism	Kani model of benefit sharing
	Inclusive	Organized	Centralized	Service-providing nongovernmental organizations	Carbon compensating agencies
			Decentralized	Community management organizations	Kristianstadt watershed management
		Spontaneous	Centralized	Local activist networks	Danish windmill industry
			Decentralized	Neighborhood action	Self-supplying, carbon-free communities

effective, and least costly, ways of addressing these issues); consequently, we will analyze the influence of the various characteristics of governance on the two types of knowledge separately.

Framework Knowledge

Framework knowledge is defined as the broad conceptual, epistemological, and normative perception of a problem or an issue that determines the way actors approach and think of it (Schön 1983). To go beyond this definition, we need to discuss how the characteristics of governance mechanisms can affect the various criteria of performance in matters of knowledge generation. We will therefore consider successively the influence of the scope, orientation, organization, and delegation on our six criteria of efficiency (i to vi) (see table 13.2).

The scope refers to the size of the community considered by the decision-making mechanism and therefore to its diversity: a community of wider scope will generally include more heterogeneous stakeholders. It is obvious that the wider the scope, the greater its adequacy for the global aspects of GPGs (i). Moreover, the wider the scope, the more interests and the interdependencies can be taken into account. It should therefore lead to the production of more knowledge (ii) than similar processes with a narrower scope. Here we are not taking the incentives of individuals to hide information and ideas into account, because this is not directly linked to scope, but rather to the other criteria (orientation, organization, and delegation). There is also no reason to postulate that individuals will have fewer incentives to reveal their own needs or the collective problems they identify in a wider community. Wide scope should, however, have negative effects on the speed and costs of coordination: the wider the scope, the greater the complexity of the decision, and so the slower the decision and knowledge generation processes (iii). In the same vein, the larger number and diversity of stakeholders involved in the decision-making process, the higher the costs of coordination (vi). The number and diversity of stakeholders does not impact directly on accessibility (iv) or duplication (v), since both these criteria depend on the organization of the decision.

Orientation refers to the logic on which the governance mechanism is built. The more the decision making is oriented toward the inclusion of the interest of all stakeholders in the society, the better its adequacy with respect to the collective aspect of GPGs (i), and the greater its ability to identify relevant interdependencies among individuals and issues (ii)

Table 13.2
The performance of various governance mechanisms on generating knowledge about issues

Dimensions				Criteria					
Scope	Orientation	Organization	Delegation	Adequacy (i)	Revelation (ii)	Speed (iii)	Accessibility (iv)	Efficient use of cognitive resources (v)	Low costs of coordination (vi)
Wide	Exclusive	Organized	Centralized	+ − = =	+ − + −	− + = +	= − + −	= + + +	− = − +
			Decentralized	+ − = =	+ − + +	− + = −	= − + +	= + + −	− = − −
		Spontaneous	Centralized	+ − = =	+ − − −	− + = +	= − − −	= + − +	− = + +
			Decentralized	+ − = =	+ − − +	− + = −	= − − +	= + − −	− = + −
	Inclusive	Organized	Centralized	+ + + =	+ + + −	− − = +	= + + −	= − + +	− = − +
			Decentralized	+ + + =	+ + + +	− − = −	= + + +	= + − −	− = − −
		Spontaneous	Centralized	+ + + =	+ + − −	− − = +	= + − −	= − − +	− = + +
			Decentralized	+ + + =	+ + − +	− − = −	= + − +	= − − −	− = + −
Narrow	Exclusive	Organized	Centralized	− − = =	− − + −	+ + = +	= − + −	= + + +	+ = − +
			Decentralized	− − = =	− − + +	+ + = −	= − + +	= + + −	+ = − −
		Spontaneous	Centralized	− − = =	− − − −	+ + = +	= − − −	= + − +	+ = + +
			Decentralized	− − = =	− − − +	+ + = −	= − − +	= + − −	+ = + −
	Inclusive	Organized	Centralized	− + = =	− + + −	+ − = +	= + + −	= − + +	+ = − +
			Decentralized	− + = =	− + + +	+ − = −	= + + +	= + − −	+ = − −
		Spontaneous	Centralized	− + = =	− + − −	+ − = +	= + − −	= − − +	+ = + +
			Decentralized	− + = =	− + − +	+ − = −	= + − +	= − − −	+ = + −

+: positive impact; −: negative impact; =: neutral impact

(because revelation is facilitated). Orientation toward inclusion should also favor accessibility (iv), since decision makers presumably attach greater importance to this factor. However, more inclusiveness leads to more complex decisions because more interdependencies have to be taken into account, which tends to reduce the speed of decision making and hence knowledge generation (iii). The impact of a more inclusive orientation on the costs of knowledge generation is more questionable. Inclusiveness means that the needs and preferences of more stakeholders have to be assessed, which might raise costs. However, it could be argued that these costs are essentially dependent upon the organization of the decision making, not its orientation. A well-designed decision-making process should be able to control for most of the waste due to the potentially inefficient use of cognitive capacities and coordination costs. Because what is needed from stakeholders is information about their needs and issues, well-designed surveys and information-gathering mechanisms can easily provide the necessary information without involving all the stakeholders. Nevertheless, other things being equal, inclusiveness does demand more information gathering than exclusiveness. Moreover, those who make decisions have to absorb the knowledge and information derived from a variety of individuals and groups with differences that include divergent cognitive frameworks. This implies not only gathering and synthesizing more heterogeneous information, it also means that learning abilities have to be dedicated to the process. We therefore consider that an orientation toward more inclusion should raise the amount of resources necessary to produce the relevant knowledge to identify issues (v), although it should not directly impact on the cost of coordination (iv).

The organization of the decision making refers to the fact that collective decision making is achieved by a process in which stakeholders explicitly aggregate their individual wishes or ideas. Alternatively, collective decisions can simply result from a process of the spontaneous aggregation of individual decisions, which cannot guarantee the consideration of all individuals' preferences or contributions. Whether collective decision making is organized or spontaneous should not affect the quality of the knowledge generated (i). An organized approach allows interdependencies to be taken into account, but spontaneity enables local specificities and needs to be considered. The same type of trade-off between trends applies to speed (iii). Organized decision making relies on specialization and the development of information networks that allow quick sharing of information and knowledge and so increase the speed at which decisions can be made; but organization does not encourage mutual adjustments and tends to rely on routines that reduce the likelihood of local innovation (unless this is explicitly the purpose of the organization), and this may reduce the reactivity, creativity, and—as a result—the speed of knowledge generation. We therefore assume that the organization criterion is neutral with respect to the speed of generating knowledge about issues and needs (iii).

However, the explicit organization of a collective decision-making process should impact positively on three other criteria: revelation (ii), accessibility (iv), and efficiency in the use of cognitive resources (v). There is a trade-off between revelation (unconventional knowledge is more likely to be revealed in a spontaneous process) and accumulation (encouraged by an organized decision-making process). But the accumulation of knowledge on the needs and interdependencies of wide and heterogeneous communities is impossible without a certain degree of organization, and on this basis we assume that greater organization of the decision-making process encourages the revelation and production of knowledge (ii). Moreover, organized decision-making relies on the specialization and development of information networks that allow information and knowledge to be shared, and so organization increases accessibility (iv). In addition, organized processes of decision making are, by definition, designed to encourage more efficient use of the existing knowledge base and of cognitive resources (v). However, organized decisions are more costly in terms of coordination (vi), because spontaneous decisions do not require coordination (but spontaneous decisions lead to poorer results in terms of generating of knowledge).

Whether collective decisions are centralized (i.e., delegated) or based on direct interactions and agreements among stakeholders should be neutral with respect to the adequacy of the knowledge generated (i), since contradictory factors come into play. On the one hand, centralization allows interdependencies to be taken into account. On the other hand, decentralization allows local specificities and needs to be considered. However, centralization has a clear negative impact on two issues. It reduces the ability to reveal and produce relevant knowledge (ii) because information asymmetries between the decision makers and stakeholders create problems of revelation and may encourage decision makers to follow their private agendas. It also reduces accessibility (iv), because only decentralization relies on knowledge sharing and mutual understanding and so requires and provides incentives for greater accessibility. The positive impacts of centralization are threefold. It accelerates the speed of decision-making processes and, therefore, knowledge generation (iii). Indeed, it relies on formal mechanisms to gather information and make decisions quickly. In addition, the center can accumulate information and learn, and it is encouraged to develop its abilities to do this. Centralization also reduces the cost of making decisions (provided a relevant organization exists). By definition, it avoids the duplication of effort and tries to optimize the use of cognitive resources (v). In addition, centralization reduces coordination costs because there are fewer links to manage in a star network than in a mesh network (vi).

Operational Knowledge and Solutions

As in the previous section, we will discuss systematically how the various characteristics of governance mechanisms can have an impact on the criterion of performance with respect to the generation of knowledge about solutions to problems in the provision of GPGs. In many cases the arguments are similar to those applying to the generation of knowledge about issues. However, there are two differences. First, solutions have a more direct impact than issues on the distribution of the costs of providing GPGs among agents and on the constraints they face in accessing and using resources. Decisions and knowledge about solutions therefore have a greater effect on their individual interests. Agents' behavior thus becomes more strategic, and there are fewer incentives to reveal information that could be used against their interests or to share knowledge about solutions (since the exclusive use of this knowledge may benefit them). Second, the need to adapt solutions to their implementation contexts requires, other things being equal, more information about local contexts. This, together with the more selfish orientation of agents, creates a tension. To put it another way, when dealing with the creation of knowledge about solutions, individual interests play a greater role, and local information and individual involvement are more crucial. These factors have an impact on the properties of some dimensions of governance mechanisms (see table 13.3).

As for framework knowledge, the scope of the decision-making process has a positive influence on the adequacy (i) of the knowledge generated, and has a negative impact on speed (iii) and coordination costs (vi). Scope is neutral for accessibility (iv) and duplication of effort (v). However, it is negative for revelation (ii), for the reasons explained above. The less the scope and the closer the context of implementation (provided

Table 13.3
The performance of various governance mechanisms on generating knowledge about solutions

Dimensions				Criteria					
								Efficient use of cognitive resources	Low costs of coordination
Scope	Orientation	Organization	Delegation	Adequacy (i)	Revelation (ii)	Speed (iii)	Accessibility (iv)	(v)	(vi)
Wide	Exclusive	Organized	Centralized	+ − = =	− − = −	− + − −	= − + =	= = + +	− + − +
			Decentralized	+ − = =	− − = +	− + − +	= − + =	= = + −	− + − −
		Spontaneous	Centralized	+ − = =	− − = −	− + + +	= − − =	= = − +	− + + +
			Decentralized	+ − = =	− − = +	− + + +	= − − =	= = − −	− + + −
	Inclusive	Organized	Centralized	+ + = =	− + = −	− − − −	= + + =	= = + +	− − − +
			Decentralized	+ + = =	− + = +	− − − +	= + + =	= = + −	− − − −
		Spontaneous	Centralized	+ + = =	− + = −	− − + −	= + − =	= = − +	− − + +
			Decentralized	+ + = =	− + = +	− − + +	= + − =	= = − −	− − + −
Narrow	Exclusive	Organized	Centralized	− − = =	+ − = −	+ + − −	= − + =	= = + +	+ + − +
			Decentralized	− − = =	+ − = +	+ + − +	= − + =	= = + −	+ + − −
		Spontaneous	Centralized	− − = =	+ − = −	+ + + −	= − − =	= = − +	+ + + +
			Decentralized	− − = =	+ − = +	+ + + +	= − − =	= = − −	+ + + −
	Inclusive	Organized	Centralized	− + = =	+ + = −	+ − − −	= + + =	= = + +	+ − − +
			Decentralized	− + = =	+ + = +	+ − − +	= + + =	= = + −	+ − − −
		Spontaneous	Centralized	− + = =	+ + = −	+ − + −	= + − =	= = − +	+ − + +
			Decentralized	− + = =	+ + = +	+ − + +	= + − =	= = − −	+ − + −

+: positive impact; −: negative impact; =: neutral impact

that the global problem is well framed), the better the knowledge generated.

The orientation of the decision-making process for knowledge about solutions is similar to that for knowledge about issues on four criteria. Inclusiveness has a positive effect on adequacy (i), revelation (ii), and accessibility (iv) and a negative effect on speed (iii). The positive effects on revelation and accessibility are strengthened in the case of knowledge about solutions, because there are strong incentives to analyze the side effects of the solutions in detail and to spread knowledge about possible solutions. There are, however, significant differences between the two analyses in the matter of costs. Inclusiveness should be neutral with respect to the efficiency of using cognitive resources (v). On the one hand, duplication tends to occur because there are similarities among local situations, while, on the other hand, marginal adaptations are required to take the specificities of local contexts into account. By contrast, inclusiveness tends to increase coordination costs (vi). At the implementation stage, it leads to the involvement of the largest possible number of heterogeneous stakeholders as they appropriate the solutions and adapt them to their own ends and preferences.

The organization of the decision-making process on solutions impacts positively on accessibility (iv) and efficiency in using cognitive resources (v). It has a negative effect on coordination costs (vi), and is neutral with respect to adequacy (i) for the reasons discussed in the previous section on the generation of knowledge about issues. However, there is a difference when the issues of revelation (ii) and speed (iii) are considered. The degree of organization in the decision-making process should be irrelevant for revelation because organization makes the identification of interdependencies more efficient (which contributes to the design of better solutions and related knowledge), while spontaneity encourages information about implementation specificities to be revealed and also favors local innovation. In fact, the trade-off is the same as that discussed above for revelation in respect to knowledge about the issues. However, since local adaptation is highly valued in the design of implementable solutions, the weight of the second dimension in the trade-off is higher for solutions than for issues. This explains why the overall effect of organization on knowledge of solutions is seen as neutral, whereas it is seen as positive for knowledge of the issues. The same reasoning applies to the speed of solutions, which should be greater with spontaneous implementation than with organized coordination. Since operational decisions require quick adjustments and adaptation to the local context, spontaneous implementation could speed up decision making and the related generation of knowledge.

The delegation of decision making has a positive impact on the costs (v, vi), a negative one on revelation (ii) due to information asymmetries, and none on adequacy (i), as argued in the case of knowledge generation on issues and preferences. However delegation has a different impact on the speed (iii) and accessibility (iv) of knowledge about solutions than knowledge about issues. Centralization should have a negative impact on the speed of knowledge generation about solutions, while it is positive for issues. Centralization involves formal mechanisms to gather information and make decisions quickly. However, decentralized decisions can allow better adaptation of operational decisions. By the end there is less need for back-and-forth exchanges of information about implementation decisions, and so the process is quicker. The degree of centralization is neutral for accessibility (iv). On the one hand, decentralization requires and provides incentives for greater accessibility. On the other hand, centralization encourages the distribution of knowledge to end-users and its appropriate packaging.

Building an Efficient Governance Framework for the Generation of Knowledge

The analysis developed above shows how various principles in the organization of the decision-making process on the provision of GPGs may impact the ways in which knowledge generation relies on various criteria of quality and costs. The following tables sum up the analysis, showing how our four dimensions of organizational characteristics (scope, orientation, organization, and delegation) affect performance according to each of our six criteria of performance (i to vi). We use a plus sign to indicate that a dimension has a positive impact on a criterion, a minus sign to indicate a negative impact, and an equal sign when there is no specific impact. Each box contains four signs; the first shows the effect of scope, the second orientation, the third organization, and the fourth delegation. Table 13.2 presents the analysis for the framework knowledge of issues, and table 13.3 shows the analysis of knowledge about solutions.

These tables help us to synthesize the conclusions of the analysis in the previous section. Reading them column by column allows the impact of the various dimensions on each of our criteria of performance to be seen at a glance, while reading them line by line summarizes the main effects of the sixteen governance mechanisms identified by our typology (with each line corresponding to one of these mechanisms). We will start our discussion by making some general comments on the impacts of the organizational dimensions, before describing the comparative analysis of the mechanisms.

Before going into the details, it is important to stress the limits of our analysis. We establish our comparisons by summing the positive and negative impacts on the various criteria. This implies that we are giving equal weight to each of the organizational dimensions when comparing columns, and giving equal weight to each of the criteria (i to vi) when comparing mechanisms lines. This approach is obviously open to criticism, since neither the relative importance of the various organizational dimensions nor the relative importance of the various criteria has been assessed. At this stage of the analysis of knowledge generation in decision making, we feel that nothing would be gained, either theoretically or empirically, by a systematic analysis of the production function of knowledge related to governance mechanisms. Our analysis is merely exploratory; nevertheless, we think it provides useful insights into the relative performance of alternative principles of governance. It is clear, however, that further theoretical and empirical work will be needed to confirm and refine our provisional conclusions.

Analysis of the Trade-offs

At first glance, tables 13.2 and 13.3 show clearly that there is no single best way of generating knowledge on the provision of GPGs. None of the governance mechanisms has positive ratings on all the identified criteria. A reading of the tables line by line shows that there are trade-offs among criteria of performance and that all the possible governance approaches have drawbacks. Reading the tables column by column highlights the dimensions of some of these trade-offs. It also allows the combination of organizational dimensions that gives the best performance on each criterion to be identified. These can be grouped into three categories: adequacy (i) and revelation (ii) refer to the relevancy of the knowledge produced; speed (iii) and accessibility (iv) refer to its availability; and efficient use of cognitive resources (v) and low cost of coordination (vi) cover the costs of producing knowledge.

On the basis of our categories for evaluating the knowledge generation processes (see tables 13.4 and 13.5), two general organizational effects that are independent of the type of knowledge can be identified. First, the orientation of relationships has a strong influence on the relevancy (i and ii) of the knowledge produced: inclusiveness enhances quality. Second, the delegation of the decision impacts on its costs (v and vi): centralization is cheaper than decentralization. There are also three effects that vary, depending on the nature of the knowledge. Scope has a strong influence on the relevancy (i and ii) of knowledge on issues in which wideness favors quality, but is neutral for knowledge on solutions. The same holds for the organization of the decision-making mechanism, when high levels of organization increase the availability (iii and iv) of knowledge of issues but not knowledge of solutions. However, the degree of centralization influences the availability (iii and iv) of knowledge of solutions more than that of issues, with more centralization leading to less availability.

Mechanisms of governance that are both inclusive and decentralized seem to favor the production of adequate knowledge and revelation (i and iii). However, there is clearly a quality versus cost dilemma, since the mechanisms that produce the most relevant knowledge about the provision of GPGs are the most costly. This is true for both knowledge about issues and knowledge about solutions, although the scope has to be wide to result in relevant knowledge about issues. There does not seem to be the same dilemma over availability and costs, or relevance and availability.

Generally speaking, when considering the organizational dimensions that induce the best performance, the three categories of performance seem to demand the following different organizational characteristics:

- The best mechanisms for generating relevant knowledge (i and ii) about issues have both wide scope and inclusiveness. However, the best solutions for generating relevant knowledge about solutions are inclusive and decentralized.
- The best mechanisms for producing knowledge of issues that becomes available quickly and widely (iii and iv) combine narrowness and organization. For knowledge of solutions, narrowness and decentralization should be combined.
- The best way to minimize costs is to rely on mechanisms with a narrow scope, based on exclusive interests and centralization.

It is therefore clear that the design of efficient governance mechanisms should rely on a logic of hybridization among organizational principles

based on either single governance mechanisms combining various organizational characteristics or the combination of alternative mechanisms
in the same process of governance.

Comparative Analysis of the Governance Frameworks

The last step in our analysis is to proceed to a line-by-line discussion of
the tables so as to compare the performance of the sixteen mechanisms
of governance. A general reading of tables 13.4 and 13.5 shows that
there is no single best way to generate knowledge on the provision of
GPGs. Some mechanisms that are efficient in dealing with issues perform
poorly on solutions, and vice versa. Moreover, some perform better
according to some criteria, while being weak at others. Our categories
provide a useful tool for analyzing these patterns. In the discussion that
follows, we present some general features of the overall performance of
the various mechanisms. Then we consider the application of our framework to a set of case studies from the field of global environmental
governance.

The results of our analysis of governance mechanisms have been summarized in figure 13.1. The evaluations of each mechanism's performance
over the six criteria in tables 13.4 and 13.5 were added to give a score
between –2 and +2 for both knowledge generation about issues and
about solutions. The figure shows the position of each mechanism on
these two criteria, with issues on the horizontal axis and solutions on
the vertical axis.

The basic types of governance mechanisms can be grouped into four
clusters to facilitate the discussion of these general findings. Each cluster
groups mechanisms with similar organizational characteristics and
similar performances in knowledge generation on issues or on solutions:
community-based processes (best for solutions), national and local
democracy (moderately good for both issues and solutions), global organized debates (best for issues, poor for solutions) and spontaneous market-like coordination (worst for issues, poor or only moderately good
for solutions). Based on these distinctions, we first discuss the cluster of
global organized debates, which have been prominent in the debates on
global governance. Then we turn to the clusters that show the best balanced performance for issues and solutions—that is, community-based
processes, and national and local democracy. Finally, we highlight some
of the features of spontaneous market-like coordination mechanisms,
which seem to have the worst overall performance.

Table 13.4
An evaluation of governance mechanisms for knowledge generation on issues

Dimensions				Evaluation		
Scope	Orientation	Organization	Delegation	Relevancy (Adequacy + Revelation)	Availability (Speed + Accessibility)	Costs (Efficient use of cognitive resources + low coordination costs)
Wide	Exclusive	Organized	Centralized	0	0	+2
			Decentralized	+2	0	-2
		Spontaneous	Centralized	-2	-2	+2
			Decentralized	0	-2	-2
	Inclusive	Organized	Centralized	+4	0	0
			Decentralized	+5	0	-4
		Spontaneous	Centralized	+2	-2	0
			Decentralized	+4	-2	-4
Narrow	Exclusive	Organized	Centralized	-4	+2	+4
			Decentralized	-2	+2	0
		Spontaneous	Centralized	-6	0	+4
			Decentralized	-4	0	0
	Inclusive	Organized	Centralized	0	+2	+2
			Decentralized	+2	+2	-2
		Spontaneous	Centralized	-2	0	+2
			Decentralized	0	0	-2

Table 13.5
An evaluation of governance mechanisms for knowledge generation on solutions

Dimensions				Evaluation		
Scope	Orientation	Organization	Delegation	Relevancy (Adequacy + Revelation)	Availability (Speed + Accessibility)	Costs (Efficient use of cognitive resources + low coordination costs)
Wide	Exclusive	Organized	Centralized	-3	-2	+2
			Decentralized	-1	0	-2
		Spontaneous	Centralized	-3	-2	+2
			Decentralized	-1	0	-2
	Inclusive	Organized	Centralized	+1	-2	0
			Decentralized	+3	0	-4
		Spontaneous	Centralized	+1	-2	0
			Decentralized	+3	0	-4
Narrow	Exclusive	Organized	Centralized	-3	0	+4
			Decentralized	-1	+2	0
		Spontaneous	Centralized	-3	0	+4
			Decentralized	-1	+2	0
	Inclusive	Organized	Centralized	+1	0	+2
			Decentralized	+3	+2	-2
		Spontaneous	Centralized	+1	0	+2
			Decentralized	+3	+2	-2

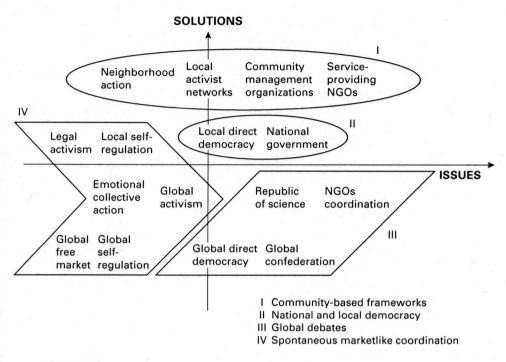

SOLUTIONS

Figure 13.1
Performance of the basic governance mechanisms in generating knowledge on issues and solutions for GPG provision

Our results indicate that global organized debates have a positive effect on the generation of knowledge about the issues involved in the production of GPGs. Indeed, the cluster of mechanisms that are wide and organized are generally the best at providing knowledge about issues. This is true for NGO coordination, republic of science, and global confederation. However global direct democracy, which is also global and wide, only performs moderately well on issues, mainly due to its high coordination costs. The NGO coordination mechanism has the best overall performance on issues in this cluster. This result is especially relevant because of the prominence of this type of mechanism in global governance (for example, the Intergovernmental Panel on Climate Change, which we will discuss in more depth below).

The main weakness of global organized debates is their generally poor performance on knowledge about solutions. This weakness is also one of the major concerns raised in assessments of global debates in the literature. Key problems relating to this weakness are the difficulty of

involving citizens and communities in the debate over the more operational aspects of possible solutions to GPG provision, and the difficulty
that global debates have in integrating the diversity of collective preferences at a national level when implementing worldwide agreements.
National and local democracy mechanisms, which involve national governments, citizens, and communities in the debates, may therefore also
be relevant to GPG provision, especially because they perform better than
global debates with respect to knowledge about solutions.

Our analysis shows that two clusters of mechanisms perform equally
well overall on issues and solutions. The first is the cluster of community-
based mechanisms (service-providing NGOs, community-management
organizations, local activist networks, and neighborhood action) in the
upper part of figure 13.1. These mechanisms are based on the involvement of local communities and citizens in the debates about GPGs, and
they are among the best-performing mechanisms for solutions. Community-management organizations and service-providing NGOs are particularly interesting, because they also are among the best for issues. They
therefore represent the most effective governance mechanisms when the
two dimensions are considered together. The second balanced cluster of
mechanisms is that based on national and local democracy. These mechanisms are usually addressed in association with global mechanisms in the
literature on multilevel governance. Both local direct democracy and
national government are exclusive, and their main strength is their efficient use of cognitive resources and the speed of the cumulative knowledge-generation process. They perform rather weakly on revelation and
adequacy when compared to global debates, but they are moderately
good at issues, and perform well on solutions, so that their overall performance is balanced.

Finally, our analysis shows the weakness of spontaneous market-like
coordination mechanisms for generating knowledge on global public
goods. The subgroup of mechanisms embodying the principles of markets
and competition and based on exclusive interests (global free markets,
global and local self-regulation, and legal activism), performs among the
worst on issues. The subgroup of global spontaneous and inclusive
mechanisms (emotional collective action and global activism) performs
badly on both solutions and issues. They are not organized in a way
that encourages structured, cumulative knowledge generation, and they
have major inefficiencies in the use of cognitive resources. The only
spontaneous mechanisms that perform comparatively well are the local
and inclusive mechanisms that we discussed above (neighborhood action

and local activist networks). Their strength on solutions stems from their proximity to direct user communities and stakeholder groups concerned with GPGs. This is a major incentive for testing the effectiveness of solutions in a way that is fine-tuned to the specificities of particular contexts.

Case Studies on Climate Change, Biodiversity, and Sustainable Develpment

In this section, we apply our theoretical argument to a set of case studies from global environmental governance, taken from the implementation of the conventions and action programs that came out of the 1992 Rio Summit. The Rio Summit was characterized by major innovations in global governance, the most prominent of which was the massive participation of civil society organizations, international federations, and other nonprofit associations in the debates. After the summit, new organizations for more systematic knowledge gathering were created, such as the Multi-Stakeholder Forum of the Commission on Sustainable Development. Three conventions, the UN Framework Convention on Climate Change, the UN Convention to Combat Desertification, and the Convention on Biological Diversity, as well as an action plan on sustainable development, Agenda 21, were the main outcomes of the Rio Summit. The issues of climate change, biodiversity, and sustainable development are all issues characterized by intense debates, conflicting and often absent collective preferences, and great uncertainty about the most appropriate solutions. Consequently, the Rio Summit and its subsequent implementation provide an appropriate collection of cases for testing our arguments.

Case Studies on Global Organized Debates on Climate Change
The **Intergovernmental Panel on Climate Change** (IPCC) and related initiatives such as the Earth System Science Partnership and the Multi-Stakeholder Forum of the Commission on Sustainable Development are examples of governance mechanisms corresponding to our category "global debate."

With the Nobel Peace Prize of 2007 awarded to the IPCC, the panel's activities have been widely acknowledged as effective and forceful in global policies (Alfsen and Skodvin, 1998; Siebenhüner 2002). Within the framework advanced in this study, the IPCC can be viewed as an NGO coordination mechanism characterized by a global, centralized, and organized process relying on an inclusive logic (due to the prominence of scientists). Launched in 1988 by a joint initiative of the World Meteorological Organization (WMO) and the UN Environment Programme (UNEP), the IPCC's central objective is to assess the current state of knowledge on climate change, and to condense it into reports that are reviewed and approved by scientific reviewers and governmental experts. Since its beginning, the IPCC has produced four major assessment reports (concluded in 1990, 1995, 2001, and 2007) and a sizeable number of special reports and technical chapters as well as supporting materials such as guidelines and documentary material (see www.ipcc.ch). In particular the 2007 report (Intergovernmental Panel on Climate Change 2007) has been widely utilized in the media and public debates. Even political outcomes such as a decision by the heads of state of the G8 in 2007 and the EU can be linked to the findings of this report.

The outcomes of the IPCC processes are focused on the specific issues at hand, but are significantly limited in generating solutions-oriented knowledge. This reflects on the adequacy of the knowledge generated in the process. The IPCC is organized into three working groups that focus on the science of climate change (Working Group I), the impact of, and adaptation to, climate change (Working Group II) and mitigation options (Working Group III) with highly disparate processes. While the first group is dominated by physicists and atmospheric chemists, it is biologists, geographers, and ecologists who form the core of Working Group II. Working Group III is composed mostly of economists and political scientists who analyze the policy instruments for reducing CO_2 emissions. Over the four assessment reports, the products of Working Group I have gained the strongest acknowledgment and attention in the public debates. Its reports present recent research about the actual changes in the climate system and the increase in global mean temperature and sea level rise. This knowledge relates to the dimensions and characterization of the problem rather than to solutions. By contrast, solutions-oriented knowledge can mostly be found in the reports of Working Group III, and these are traditionally the most contentious of the three Working Groups' reports. Since Working Group III directly addresses governments' decision making and measures to achieve ambitious policy goals, governments have been critical of its work. In addition, different ethical and paradigmatic positions among the authors have furthered a tendency toward the lowest common denominator. The disagreements among scientific experts, and in particular among those who are in the government, has lead to weak formulations and a tendency to describe policy options rather than to be prescriptive. In contrast to most national assessments (and other global assessment processes such as the Global Environment Outlook), IPCC's Working Group III has refrained from any clear suggestions or recommendations for the international negotiation process or for domestic climate policies. It restricts its reports merely to the description and analysis of possible policy instruments. In this respect, IPCC is a good illustration of the scores for the NGO coordination model in our theoretical framework.

In 2001 the **Earth System Science Partnership** (ESSP) brought together four formerly separate international research programs—the World Climate Research Programme (WCRP); the International Geosphere-Biosphere Programme (IGBP); DIVERSITAS, an international program of biodiversity science; and the International Human Dimensions Programme on Global Environmental Change (IHDP)—which exemplify our model of republic of science decision making. The aim was to acknowledge the systemic linkages between the subsystems of the Earth, namely the climate, the biosphere, the oceans, and socioeconomic systems, as one large interconnected system. The ESSP structures the related research fields by formulating science plans, organizing research programs, and exchanging information with funding agencies. It clearly illustrates the republic of science model that is characterized as wide, inclusive, organized, and decentralized. While its constituent programs have clear governance structures, the ESSP itself is loosely centralized: there is only a weak central coordination unit, and most research activities are conducted and coordinated in a decentralized manner.

The adequacy of the ESSP's knowledge-generating process can be described as good in raising issues and in analyzing problem dimensions. However, it is weak with regard to solutions. Its programs concentrate on original research that focuses on understanding the functions of the earth system and the influence of humans on them. However, solutions-oriented research is almost absent from all the constituent programs except the IHDP (where human actors are analyzed with regard to their ability to solve global environmental problems). Thus the documents produced by the ESSP are mostly analytical and rarely address solutions; nor do they formulate policy recommendations. More generally, the link to the policy world is difficult, and few of the projects have well-developed science-policy interactions or a wide audience in the policy realm.

In addition, the ESSP processes are comparatively slow. Most of its core projects operate with a time horizon of about ten years. A full project cycle starts with a scientific plan that formulates central research questions and describes crucial avenues for research in the field. The drafting, review, and adoption of such a plan usually takes about eighteen months before the project itself is officially launched. In subsequent years, researchers are called upon to contribute to answering the questions through individual research projects. In addition, the plans are communicated to funding agencies to raise interest and give an impetus to the formulation of funding strategies. The intention is that, at the end of the ten-year period, the final results of individual research projects will be presented and synthesized with respect to the overall research questions.

The **Global Environment Outlook** (GEO) reports, published by the UN Environment Programme every two to five years, provides an example of a global confederation (UNEP 1997, 2000, 2002, 2007). It gives an overview of the environmental problems of the world and formulates directions for future policy action in fields of particular need. With this objective, it is global in scale, even though it is structured according to geopolitical regions with their own specific structures and policy challenges. The reports are drafted by a limited number of researchers and UNEP staff located in the different regions. In addition, UNEP and its experts strive to include external expertise in the process of drafting the chapters and in the review process. While the core authors invite some other scientists to articulate their views in regional workshops and try to include them in the report, a larger number of external experts are approached to review and comment on the final drafts of the report. However, when compared to the IPCC, the number of authors and reviewers involved (about 200) is low. These authors include scientists, experts nominated by governments, policy practitioners, and representatives of UN organizations. Since the process is monitored by UNEP, the preparatory team is not free of the exclusive interests of the national governments represented in UNEP's Governing Council.

Knowledge generation within the GEO process is well organized, since it consists of a well-defined sequence of consultancy workshops with governments and other experts to identify crucial questions and information needs in the policy world, followed by intense drafting and assessment work by the authors, and the review and publication process. It is also centralized since UNEP serves as the focal organization that pulls together all the contributions and regional chapters and forms it into one document.

UNEP's Global Environment Outlook provides a comprehensive insight into the most pressing environmental problems on Earth, and provides directions and policy options for policy makers. It is a document that contains knowledge that is considered highly relevant not only for policy makers but also for NGOs, scientists, interested individuals, and open-minded business representatives. While it has had considerable success in highlighting specific environmental problems and the need for action, the GEO also contains stronger statements about political decision-making needs. The authors clearly mark their key messages and use much stronger language about solutions and the political action required than the IPCC documents. Like the IPCC reports, however, the GEO avoids formulating policy recommendations. The smaller number of authors leads to less revealed knowledge than is found in the IPCC reports.

It is worth pointing out that the GEO documents are accessible to all interested groups. They are written not only for scientific audiences but also for informed lay citizens, policy makers, and other interested people. In addition, they are made broadly available through the Internet and book publishers, as well as in a shortened version particularly aimed at children. This level of accessibility partly contradicts the predictions drawn from our conceptual framework. Low accessibility was expected due to the exclusive character of the process. However, the partly inclusive character of the UNEP process (which has a mandate to raise awareness of environmental problems) explains this.

The **Multi-Stakeholder Dialogue** (MSD) in the Commission on Sustainable Development (CSD) illustrates the global democracy model. The CSD was set up after the 1992 Rio Convention to implement the objectives of the Agenda 21, the action plan for implementing sustainable development. In 1997 the MSD was created as a unique participatory model that allowed major groups and governments to engage in a global dialogue on specific sustainable development issues. In 2001 a total of 3,000 organizations (and thus many more individual representatives) were accredited as "observers," with the right to participate in CSD meetings, to submit written statements at their own expense, and to set up informal events and meetings at the discretion of the chair.

An overall assessment of the MSD shows rather weak performance in knowledge generation on GPGs, but some strengths in the revelation of issues, although there is a tendency for NGOs to compete for attention and access to the decision-making arenas (Mori 2004). In particular, established NGOs attempt to exclude newcomers, because it might decrease their influence. Moreover, the various NGOs and associations have very different objectives in participating in the forum, ranging from lobbying by business associations to more open exchanges of views on issues of collective interest to find common ground. This has led to a process of negotiation and compromise rather than to a cooperative process aimed at creating better knowledge. It also has a negative impact on the speed and accessibility of the outcome. The main strength of the model is the capacity to reveal new knowledge on issues. Involvement in the MSD is highly organized and aims at the greatest possible representativeness. Equal participation is ensured by the steering group. Hence a lot of new issues can be brought to the attention of decision makers, and the MSD has been assessed as a unique way to involve major groups in reviewing the progress that is being made on sustainable development in the different member countries. However, the propositions made at the MSD are not guaranteed to be included in the chair's summary. Hence the connection with final decisions remains weak.

Case Studies on Multilevel Governance for Sustainable Development

The global debates discussed in the previous section have been criticized for their weakness in dealing with major differences in national collective preferences and for excluding nonprofit organizations and citizens from the effective decision-making and the more operational phases of the implementation. Multilevel governance frameworks involving national and local democracy and community-based frameworks have been proposed as alternative approaches, and we discuss how they are able to cope with these criticisms from the knowledge-generation perspective we have adopted.

Agenda 21 resulted in a multi-stakeholder process under the umbrella of the CSD. It was conceived from the outset as a multilevel initiative, and it had an important local component: **Local Agenda 21** (LA21) is generally considered a major innovation because it is one of the few international processes that also addresses governance at the local municipality and community level. One of its goals is the direct involvement of citizens and citizens' groups in decision making about sustainable development. As such, this innovative process is a good illustration of a systematic attempt to implement local direct democracy.

One example is LA21 in the United Kingdom, which was conceived as an essential component of the UK Biodiversity Action Plan. Here we will discuss the particular case of LA21 in Norwich, a rural town of around 130,000 inhabitants in in eastern England (O'Riordan 2001).

The adequacy of the knowledge produced by LA21 in Norwich has been much criticized: a large proportion of it reflected the contributions of the different vested interests, especially the local authorities, who framed the process in terms of the need for continued and reliable economic growth rather than sustainability per se. Some of the environmental issues, including a reduction in traffic in the town center and preserving the town's heritage, were primarily considered under a "quality of life" heading. The process therefore only highlighted a narrow range of issues.

However, the LA21 process in Norwich did have a positive impact on the accumulation of knowledge and on improving access to knowledge, thanks to the involvement of citizens. Even though it was narrowly framed, it did massively increase the opportunities for deliberation on sustainable development. Moreover, the LA21 action plan has been reviewed each year through the development of sustainability indicators and through an annual conference at which progress is reported and assessed, and new issues are raised. Overall, it can therefore be said that LA21 increased the speed and accessibility of the knowledge-generation process.

The **UK Biodiversity Action Plan** (UKBAP), mentioned above and discussed in more depth in chapter 14, is a good illustration of the characteristics of national government initiatives. Under UKBAP, data on species and habitats in the United Kingdom has been gathered in a systematic way since 1994, and target-based action plans based on the data have been developed. UKBAP is considered a prime example of a modernist (reductionist and rationalist) approach to environmental management (Adams 1997), and, as such, it is a good example of our category of centralized and organized governance devices.

From a knowledge-generation perspective, the main drawback of UKBAP is the adequacy of the knowledge it produces on GPGs. It has adopted a narrow view, focused mostly on separate species and habitats, which can easily be reported by individual information providers, and reflects the local concerns of the various partners. This is in sharp contrast to the approach promoted by the international epistemic community, which views ecosystems as being composed of highly interdependent entities and interconnected levels of organization. However, the main strength of the UKBAP has been to effectively coordinate a wide range of individuals and organizations, including experts, and both governmental and nongovernmental organizations. Moreover it has increased the use of the available knowledge by implementing a single reporting system able to deal with very long lists of species and habitats. This has been a major improvement over the veritable cottage industry of single-species NGOs which used to compete for public attention in the United Kingdom. In sum, UKBAP has made substantial progress in its principal knowledge-generating activities: prioritization (of species and habitats), planning (of targets and activities), and monitoring (of inputs and the achievement of targets). This in turn has helped to frame and consolidate the more local, dispersed initiatives of environmental associations and community organizations in the field of biodiversity monitoring and assessment. It has resulted in useful knowledge about the implementation of actions plans, although it has not contributed significantly to developing the knowledge base on stakes and issues.

Case Studies on Community and Citizen Involvement in the Use of Natural Resources

The third cluster shown in figure 13.1 consists of community-based processes. These are among the best performers for generating knowledge on solutions, but their performance on issues is more varied. We illustrate the four types of mechanisms in this cluster by first discussing the service-providing NGO model and community management organizations, which are characterized by explicit organization of the decision making and have the best overall performance. We then focus on the mechanisms based on spontaneous citizen involvement, which are less good at generating knowledge, especially knowledge of issues.

To a large extent, **carbon compensating agencies** can be considered as forms of organized local activism that are illustrative of service-providing NGOs. These agencies run projects to avoid carbon emissions or buy certified emission reductions under the clean development mechanism of the Kyoto Protocol of the UN climate convention. Many of them have an NGO background, or are still run as NGOs, and were constituted in an inclusive spirit in the sense of our framework.

As expected, this mode of governance performs well in developing adequate knowledge on solutions (e.g., on ways of organizing travel in a more carbon-friendly manner). These agencies aim to find new solutions to compensate for CO_2 emissions. However, their (relatively) narrow ends mean that they do not tend to contribute to the development of knowledge on issues (e.g., on the contribution of traveling to global warming). Carbon compensating agencies simply attempt to raise public awareness of the problems of carbon emissions generated by travel, and by flying in particular. Being interested in attracting "customers," they rely heavily on the Internet to spread information about the problems of CO_2 emissions, and the solutions they propose to deal with the issue. While duplication of effort among carbon compensating agencies in the generation of knowledge on solutions could be significant, due to potential competition among them, their inclusive orientation means that in practice it is quite low. The agencies cooperate among themselves, are often comparatively transparent, and implement quite similar solutions.

A more decentralized form of community and citizen involvement, which is especially relevant to GPGs such as climate change mitigation and biodiversity conservation, is the provision of ecosystems management services through collaborative management organizations. A case in point is the **Kristianstad watershed** in southern Sweden (Olsson et al. 2007). The Kristianstad watershed is one of Sweden's most productive agricultural areas, and it also contains one of the largest groundwater reserves in northern Europe. Since 1989 a collaborative approach to management has been in place in part of the watershed, which has evolved into the adaptive comanagement system of the broader Kristianstad Vattenrike Biosphere Reserve (KVRB). This system relies on a social network of concerned individuals and organizations and a multi-member organization, the Biosphere Office, which plays a key role in facilitating and coordinating the collaborative process to maintain the ecosystem services of the area. In particular the Biosphere Office has been able to facilitate information flows, identify knowledge gaps, and create nodes of expertise of significance for ecosystem management.

The inclusion of a broad range of organizations in the social network and in the Biosphere Office has led to the GPG aspects of the project being taken into account, even though its official scope is local management of the watershed. Through the networking of a set of existing organizations and actors, the learning process has been able to produce a set of cross-cutting concepts, such as landscape management, that reflect the mix of local and global issues at stake. The main strength of the decentralized collaborative mechanism resides in its capacity to enhance the revelation and accessibility of relevant knowledge. The Biosphere Office has been active in involving disparate actors (from local farmers to international nature conservation associations) in collective decision making, organized around clusters of topics of common concern. However, the other side of the coin is the high coordination costs induced by the decentralized nature of the project, and the slowness of the learning process because of the need to manage a complex set of independencies among the actors.

An illustration of the contribution of local activist networks to knowledge generation is provided by the **Danish windmill industry** (Smith 2006). Danish windmills were developed in the 1980s by a network of local activists with the help of farmers, and the industry became economically sustainable by selling electricity through local cooperatives. Lessons learned through years of user involvement in testing designs and techniques have led to major improvements. The success of this innovation is illustrated by the fact that today the knowledge produced in these local networks is used by the national government and major private corporations. As a result, the Danish windmill industry has grown from its initial grassroots and became a world leader in the sector.

In terms of our framework, the Danish windmill industry is an example of a centralized process, because of the important role of leader-activists, which centralized the available knowledge on technical issues and on social feasibility. However, because of the absence of an explicit mechanism of decision making about knowledge production, it can also be characterized as a spontaneous process.

In terms of knowledge generation, the activists' network operates very differently for issues and for solutions. First, the development of knowledge on solutions has clearly been successful. Based on the locally available and already well-tested motor technologies in the farming industry, reliable and workable solutions have been effectively elaborated. However, because of the spontaneous character of the knowledge-generation process, a big gap remains between the issues identified by the activist network and a comprehensive approach to the energy problem. In particular, in the absence of an organized mechanism, the scaling up of spontaneous grassroots innovations can be problematic and does not necessarily reflect the idiosyncratic framing of the problems as they were initially understood. An appropriate illustration of this issue is the giant 2-megawatt offshore wind-turbine sites in northwestern Europe; these sites are an outgrowth of the windmill industry, but they do not necessarily have the same environmental and energy effects as community-based windmill cooperatives.

A focus on (local) solutions rather than on (global) issues—which are taken as a given—also characterizes our last case study: **self-supplying, carbon-free communities.** Over the past decade, several local communities in Europe have adopted carbon-free supplies of energy. They generate 100 percent of their electricity from renewable sources such as wind, biomass, or solar energy. Because of the fluctuation in wind and solar energy, all such communities need either biomass or hydropower as backup technologies to ensure a continuous supply of electricity. While they remain connected to the national grid, they produce as much electricity as they consume. Several of the German 100-percent carbon-free communities, such as the energy village of Jühnde in Lower Saxony, have developed from research projects. However, the initiatives are in most cases spontaneous because they do not follow a general pattern and are not organized according to a general plan. Such initiatives correspond to neighborhood action in our theoretical framework.

Neighborhood action can take many different forms, and local and public authorities usually only facilitate coordination among local actors. Most efforts at knowledge generation are dedicated to apply existing (technical) solutions in local contexts. Within any one community, knowledge generation and sharing is generally rather efficient, but there are no guarantees of efficient translation or accumulation of knowledge across communities. Also, since the knowledge generated is mostly technical and specific, it is not easily accessible to third parties, either lay citizens or outside specialists. A network of carbon-free communities seems to be emerging, which might encourage more effective generation of knowledge and coordination of efforts in the future. Nevertheless, the high level of decentralization and low level of formalization of these local spontaneous initiatives has a structural tendency toward the duplication of effort.

Case Studies on Market Approaches and Global Activism

In this last section, we will examine case studies from the category of governance mechanisms—a category that is generally the worst at generating knowledge about issues, while also being poor (or at least only moderately good) at enhancing collective cognition on solutions. Among the market-like coordination mechanisms, we first discuss those that are worst on issues or solutions. Then we turn to examples of local self-regulation and global activism.

Bioprospecting agreements, as envisioned in the 1992 Convention on Biological Diversity, constitute a clear example of the global free-market mode of governance in respect of environmental resources. These agreements constitute an example of a "Coasean" solution to compensation for environmental externalities (Coase 1960). By granting property rights on biological resources to local communities and national organizations, these agreements assume that monetary compensation for the use of these resources by private companies will provide financial income to the owners and be an incentive for increased stewardship for biodiversity. Since the Convention many bioprospecting contracts have been signed (Rosenthal, Beck, and Bhat 1999; OMPI 2001), but many of them have failed to deliver on this promise.

From the point of view of the adequacy of the knowledge about biodiversity it generates, this mechanism is rather poor. It tends to concentrate on the most accessible and already revealed knowledge, without a structured and systematic large scale (scientific) effort to analyze the natural milieu and the knowledge available in traditional communities. With the exception of some cases (such as Costa Rica) in which there has been major government involvement in establishing an inventory of biological resources in biodiversity hotspots, the knowledge produced by bioprospecting contracts has focused on identifying compounds by the "blind" screening of large quantities of biological materials, and has not addressed the complexity of interdependencies between the different levels of organization of coupled human and ecological systems. Moreover the sharing and spillover of this knowledge tends to be poor. There is no organized coordination among the main knowledge providers, and no efforts have been made to involve scientists, government branches, or local communities (beyond the extraction stage). As a result, these actors do not systematically investigate the issues that could contribute to the overall knowledge base. For instance, no research is done into the most sustainable way to exploit a particular bio-resource, once it has been discovered. This has even led to the depletion of valuable compounds identified in the natural environment. The privatization of knowledge and the decentralization inherent in the contracting logic leads to duplication of effort, with no mutual learning from parallel experience. The only advantage of the logic of bilateral contracting seems to be speed. The spontaneous, decentralized mechanism allows quick-fix methods for working on potentially interesting molecules to emerge, although the quality of the knowledge generated by these agreements between companies and communities is often very poor.

Local legal activism is often presented as a way to alleviate some of the negative aspects of the pure market solution in the field of bioprospecting. However, except for its local character, it shares a lot of the characteristics and weaknesses of the global free market. A well-studied example is the widely acclaimed **Kani model of benefit sharing**). This was the first case in which payments were made to holders of traditional knowledge for a successfully developed pharmaceutical product. The agreement resulted from the incidental discovery of the therapeutic properties of a small herb by a group of scientists from a botanical garden who were visiting the Kani tribe in southern India. The scientists took the lead in negotiating a profit-sharing deal between their employer, the local community, and an Indian pharmaceutical company. As with the global-market mechanism, the only real advantage of this approach to generating knowledge on GPG provision is that it provides incentives for the speedy exploitation and development of the most accessible knowledge. However this case is really just an example of a windfall effect. The knowledge was only revealed by chance. Even though it resulted in benefits to the local community, the activist intervention did not seem to have much impact on knowledge generation.

Another way of improving bioprospecting agreements can be found in governance based on global self-regulation. The idea here is to have coordination on the user's side of the biomaterial in order to prevent a race to the bottom between the laboratories that are competing for new biomolecules. A recent example of such an attempt is the drafting of a standard agreement for transfers of biomaterials in the **European Culture Collections' Organization** (ECCO). The main advantage of this mechanism is the building of a common library of bio-resources, which then becomes a platform for liaison between the biological hotspots in the South, and the users, mainly industrial clients · and academic researchers located in the North. In spite of this major improvement in access to genetic resources, ECCO does not address the main negative aspects of the bioprospecting logic that lead to a focus on the extraction of single biomaterials that are no longer understood in relation to their context. By definition, an *ex-situ* collection can only contain a small fraction of the knowledge that exists in the natural environment.

The chemical industry's **Responsible Care Initiative** provides an example of local self-regulation. Nowadays, almost all large chemical manufacturers of the world are involved in this initiative, which was originally launched in Canada. It is a voluntary undertaking that requires participating firms to comply with a set of fundamental environmental, health, and safety norms, coordinated by national chemical industry associations. No state authorities or other societal groups were involved in the establishment and implementation of the rules, and compliance is voluntary (Gunningham 1995; King and Lenox 2000). Despite its global coordination, the Responsible Care Initiative leaves most decisions to local firms and their plant operators. This is why it is discussed as an example of local self-regulation. Like other self-regulation initiatives, this one implicitly aims to preempt more public and mandatory regulation, and it seems to be quite successful in that respect.

The knowledge generated within and through the Responsible Care Initiative is mostly focused on solutions to the problems of chemical factories, their employees, and their neighborhoods. The Initiative does little to address more generic problems, such as health risks due to the massive spread of chemical substances, or the environmental problems due to an accumulation of these substances in the soil, air, rivers and oceans. It concentrates on solutions for individual plants. Most of the knowledge that is revealed and shared among participants is technical. Since this knowledge is related to industrial processes, confidentiality issues are important and knowledge-sharing among firms is limited. The same is true of stakeholder dialogues. There are severe limitations on what and how much knowledge is shared, including the sharing of scientific knowledge with academic communities. Progress reports on the initiative itself are rather broad and do not go into detail. Thus knowledge diffusion occurs in a slow and filtered way that hinders spillovers and encourages the duplication of effort.

Greenpeace is well known to the broader public through its media campaigns and spectacular protest activities. Its climate-change campaigns are an example of our global-activism model of governance. Greenpeace is well equipped to raise public awareness about global environmental problems and to promote solutions. Through its centralized decision-making structure, it is able to act quickly and to diffuse new insights rapidly. It does not need to discuss and coordinate content at great length with numerous stakeholders, and it relies on the mass media to have an emotional impact on public opinion. However, Greenpeace is not a research body, and it rarely produces original knowledge on either the issues or the solutions. Moreover, it does not stimulate the production of new knowledge by stakeholders. Its target is really the public, not organizations or networks. It is worth noting that Greenpeace's national and local campaigns are better than its international campaigns at promoting solutions and raising awareness about particular environmental issues. Access to the mass media is the difference. Although local branches often cannot afford to finance large media campaigns, they can use their networks to support specific practical solutions (such as CFC-free refrigerators and tend to focus on cooperation-oriented activities aimed at dealing with issues by proposing solutions to the actors.

Global climate-change campaigns by **individual advocacy** (emotional collective action) have similar insufficiencies. For instance, between 2000 and 2008, the former U.S. vice president Al Gore organized a U.S.-focused, but globally active campaign to combat climate change. The campaign, and the activities of Al Gore and his team, emphasized providing knowledge on the dimensions, causes, and impacts of climate change. They did not generate new knowledge as such, but they packaged and disseminated existing knowledge. Whether this action aimed at raising public awareness will have a long-term impact on collective incentives to deal with climate change remains open to question. In the short run, it is clear that campaigns such as those by Greenpeace and Al Gore tend to ride the crest of the wave of established public opinion, rather than transform it. Radically new ideas usually have difficulty finding their way to a wider public.

Conclusion

This chapter has considered the global governance of global public goods. We have pushed further the idea that knowledge matters, and that institutional design also has an impact on cognitive capabilities. We have therefore sought to better understand how efficient alternative institutional solutions actually are in generating knowledge and in ensuring its distribution so that well-informed citizens can take collective decisions.

To analyze how alternative decision/governance mechanisms affect the process of knowledge generation, we have reviewed how the characteristics of the collective decision-making process impact on the various criteria for its performance with regard to knowledge generation. Since knowledge about issues is different from knowledge about solutions (the first being oriented toward the establishment of collective preferences, while the second is oriented toward the search for the most effective— and least costly—ways of addressing these issues), we analyzed the influence of the various characteristics of governance on the two types of knowledge separately.

Generally speaking, when the organizational dimensions that induce the best performances are considered, the three categories of performance require the following different governance characteristics:

• The best solutions for generating knowledge on issues associate wide scope and inclusiveness, while the best solutions for generating knowledge on solutions are characterized by inclusiveness and decentralization.

- The best solutions for producing knowledge of issues that is quickly and widely available combine narrowness and organization; for knowledge of solutions, they combine narrowness with decentralization.
- The best way of minimizing costs is to rely on processes with a narrow scope, based on exclusive interests and centralized forms of knowledge generation.

It is therefore clear that the design of efficient governance mechanisms should rely on hybridization among governance principles based either on mechanisms combining various logics of decision making or on the combination of alternative mechanisms in the same process of governance.

When assessing the best overall performances on generating knowledge on issues and solutions, our analysis shows some contrasting effects. First, scope has a strong influence on the provision of knowledge on solutions: narrow scope is always preferable to wide scope, irrespective of the other organizational characteristics. Second, the best solutions for generating knowledge on issues are characterized by organized decision making, independent of the scope. Finally, the most balanced solutions for knowledge of both issues and solutions are characterized by narrow scope, inclusive orientation, and organized decision-making.

Methodologically, this chapter has built a framework for assessing the trade-offs between quality, relevancy, and cost in the overall performance of different governance mechanisms. Two methodological principles have emerged from this framework. First, the best balanced overall performance is not the result of a linear combination of organizational characteristics on single criteria, but a complex integration of several contrasting effects and trade-offs. There is no direct extrapolation from reasoning on single criteria to a multi-criteria analysis. Second, our analysis has proven to be a good heuristic for discovering and identifying some of the gaps in governance mechanisms that have very good performance on one criterion only. An important challenge that we have identified in this context is the need to combine these mechanisms with other institutional frameworks. The particular design rules for these hybrid mechanisms cannot however be known in general, but will depend on their fit with individual situations.

14

From Rationalism to Reflexivity? Reflections on Change in the UK Biodiversity Action Plan

Anna Lawrence and Star Molteno

Human survival relies on continued ecosystem functioning, access to genetic diversity for various utilitarian benefits (e.g., crop breeding, medicines), and psychological well-being associated with a connection to nature. Some of these benefits are non-excludable, while others (such as genetic diversity) are subject to attempts to privatize them. In 1992 the Convention on Biological Diversity (CBD) simultaneously globalized and nationalized the problem of biodiversity conservation, by emphasizing the universal human interest but responding to that (somewhat controversially) through a focus on sovereign rights to benefits.

Because the definition of biodiversity includes genes, species, and ecosystem processes, it refers to a complex mixture of goods and services that are, under various circumstances, either excludable or not, and subject to rivalrous or non-rivalrous consumption. Therefore, the national biodiversity strategies and action plans that were mandated by the CBD have an ambiguous role in both protecting a national (at times private) good and demonstrating commitment to protecting (and sharing information about) a global public good. This creates the interesting situation whereby a large and diverse range of stakeholders is involved in balancing decisions about a complex concept and resource. This chapter explores the experiences of the UK approach to biodiversity since 1992 and the ways in which the concept of reflexivity helps to analyze those experiences. The focus is on how and under what conditions a more reflexive approach to knowledge generation over biodiversity conservation emerged, demonstrating a clear need to adjust the concept of biodiversity conservation to the norms and understandings of the diverse range of concerned stakeholders.

Complexity, Learning, and Reflexivity

Environmental systems have long been managed in a reductionist way based on command and control styles of intervention (Scott 1998). Increasingly, however, the "environment" or (here) biodiversity is conceptualized as "complex" (Kouplevatskaya-Yunusova and Buttoud 2006; Lansing 2003; Olsson and Folke 2001). Complex systems are characterized by many interlinked components that relate to each other in a nonlinear fashion. In other words, an effect on one part may have an unpredictable effect on another part because of feedback loops and emergent properties.

Management of such systems demand learning on at least two levels. We can relate these levels to the concepts of *single-loop learning* and *double-loop learning* developed in the field of organizational learning (Argyris and Schön 1978; Bateson 1972). Single-loop learning leads actors to modify their behavior to adjust to goals within the status quo, while double-loop learning challenges mental models and the policies based on them and involves learning from others as well as from one's own experience.

Applying these ideas to environmental governance, Voß and Kemp (2006) argue that sustainability requires a focus on processes rather than outcomes, with a key element being reflexivity—a form of learning. They distinguish between first-order reflexivity and second-order reflexivity. In the former, rationalist approaches to problem solving reduce the problem to a simplified form and end up facing new problems which were unforeseen. They see the growth of modern society as characterized by a never-ending cycle of attempts to develop solutions that in turn produce more problems.

In second-order reflexivity, however, cognition of the complexity of the system can lead to innovation in methods for tackling these issues that are typically more "open, experimental and learning oriented" (Voß and Kemp 2006, 6). They suggest that second-order reflexivity is achieved through: systems analysis to cope with complexity; a readiness to adjust goals collaboratively as both context and understanding of the context evolve; and interactive strategy implementation, recognizing that power is held by a range of actors, who need to work together deliberatively, to learn and implement change.

In this chapter we examine the evolving approach to biodiversity conservation in the United Kingdom, to explore the extent to which these paths to reflexivity are evident and effective. We take an empirical approach to survey the current highly dynamic situation, through analysis of documents and interviews with key actors from governmental and nongovernmental organizations (with relevant quotations from these interviews appearing throughout the chapter).

Governance Strategies in the UK Biodiversity Action Plan

The United Kingdom's response to the CBD is the UK Biodiversity Action Plan (UKBAP), developed between 1994 and 1996 and marked by its reliance on "target-based conservation." The original UKBAP proposed fifty-nine steps reflecting a more holistic view of the task of conserving UK biodiversity. Over time, this wider view narrowed to focus mostly on separate species and habitats. Scientific committees prepared the initial national plan in 1994, and by 1999 the plan included 391 Species Action Plans (SAPs) and 45 Habitat Action Plans (HAPs) (DEFRA 2006). In addition, by 1996 a framework was established for developing Local Biodiversity Action Plans (LBAPs), with 162 of them prepared by 2004. The UK Biodiversity Partnership—coordinated by the Joint Nature Conservation Committee (JNCC) and chaired by the Department for Environment, Food and Rural Affairs (DEFRA)—draws together experts, government agencies and nongovernmental organization (NGO) representatives. Reporting to the Partnership is the responsibility of the UK Biodiversity Partnership Standing Committee, which includes representatives of the four country Biodiversity Groups (England, Scotland, Northern Ireland, and Wales), government agencies, and conservation NGOs (JNCC 2004). So the UK approach to biodiversity policy and implementation covers a particularly diverse range of stakeholders and scales.

The UKBAP is a document, partnership, and process that relies to a large extent on three principal activities: prioritization (of species and habitats), planning (of targets and activities), and monitoring (of inputs and achievement of targets). The approach is a prime example of a modernist (reductionist and rationalist) approach to environmental management (Adams 1997).

Reporting and revision are built into the UKBAP. The standard reporting cycle is three years, and relates to the agreed framework of species, habitats, and targets. Separately, since 2005 the framework for the UKBAP has been completely revised, with two major review exercises conducted simultaneously: the Priorities Review (to reassess the species and habitats), and the Targets Review (to reassess both the targets and the approach to setting targets). Both review processes were overseen by the Biodiversity Reporting and Information Group (BRIG) chaired by JNCC and with members from the devolved countries and the NGOs. The Priorities Review was begun ten years after the initial UKBAP list of species and habitats was drawn up. It was seen as "an opportunity to take into account emerging priorities, conservation successes, and the large amount of new information that has been gathered over the past decade" (Biodiversity Reporting and Information Group 2007, 4). The Targets Review set out to reassess the published targets for existing plans, with the aims of updating targets in light of new information, resetting time-limited targets that have expired, further standardizing targets, and determining the different country contributions to each UK target (Biodiversity Reporting and Information Group 2007.

The formal aspects of this evolution in the UKBAP are well documented (UK Biodiversity Action Plan 2007b). Our interest here, however, lies in the influences and processes that brought about those changes, and in particular the extent to which the process was reflexive. We address this through stakeholders' perceptions of the key stages and influences on change, from the early days of the first UKBAP, through the accumulation of data and experience, to the committees and process of recent restructuring. Our approach is based on interviews with individuals from the Biodiversity Standing Committee, from government agencies, and from NGOs; analysis of government documents, NGO publications, and correspondence between government and NGOs; and the experience of participation in a training course for new biodiversity officers, which included components designed to bring them up to date with new structures and debates within the UKBAP.

The key characteristics of the UKBAP approach are set out in the 2007 UK Biodiversity Partnership Standing Committee document, "Conserving Biodiversity—The UK Approach":

The UKBAP *drew together existing instruments and programmes* for nature conservation throughout the UK, set out a series of activities for a 20 year period, and *recognised the need for specific biological targets and plans* for the recovery of *species and habitats* to help drive forward their conservation. This approach has achieved many conservation successes, and continues to provide a focus for action by *government and civil society*. (UK Biodiversity Partnership Standing Committee 2007, 4; emphasis added)

This process in the United Kingdom has been marked from the start by a symbiotic relationship between government and NGOs. In the same year that the UK government established the UK Biodiversity Steering Group, an alliance of conservation NGOs produced a report entitled

Biodiversity Challenge (Wynne et al. 1995), which spearheaded the move toward the UKBAP's distinctive focus on "target-based conservation" (Lindenmayer et al. 2000), and provided much of the impetus for the first round of species and habitat plans.

Stakeholders now are largely positive. Comments from government and NGO respondents in our interviews with them describe the UKBAP as "an excellent document," "very comprehensive," "a rigorous way of assessing what action we are taking and what biological outputs we are delivering."

But they also emphasize the unavoidably ad hoc nature of it:

In 1994 . . . people were going, you know, oh, back of an envelope, I think we could do that, . . . let's set down some challenging but fairly realistic targets based on gut feeling. (Interview with habitat-based NGO, conducted by the authors)

The most recent reporting round highlighted the achievements of the BAP showing that 22 percent of habitats and 11 percent of priority species are increasing, and decline is slowing for 25 percent of all habitats and 10 percent of all species. DEFRA notes an improvement not only in conservation but also in the reporting process itself. However "there remain significant gaps in monitoring information for UK priority species and . . . habitats" (DEFRA 2006, 1).

As the partners gained experience of the approach, stakeholders began to reassess the choice of species and habitats (the "priorities"), the way in which the plans were structured (the "targets" and the "actions"), and the inclusiveness of the approach. Described as "a robust document that has stood the test of time and has driven many conservation successes" (UK Biodiversity Partnership Standing Committee 2007, v), the UKBAP has nevertheless changed since its inception, both in terms of structure and process. In the next sections, we describe those changes through the eyes of respondents, and explore the extent to which change is based on first-order reflexivity (adjustment within the parameters of the BAP), second-order reflexivity (more radical change of goals and organization through the paths lists by Voß and Kemp), or a combination of other more external factors.

Planned Change: Reviews and Reporting Mechanisms

Much of the development of the UKBAP is a result of learning mechanisms built into the plan and of improvements in information and interactive Web site technology.

Some ten years after the start of the UKBAP, it was decided to reassess all the targets for the current species and habitats, in the light of progress and new information. This was also an opportunity to standardize targets, encouraging lead partners to set targets following the SMART principle, which refers to indicators that are specific, measurable, achievable, realistic, and time-bound. In the context of devolution, targets have now been set for each country. They are nearly all "quantified and allocated to standard categories, making assessment more objective and facilitating links to local biodiversity partnership targets" (UK Biodiversity Action Plan, 2007a, 1). More information is also given on how to monitor and deliver the targets.

Running concurrently with the targets review, but managed by a different subgroup, was a review of the species and habitats included in the UKBAP. To be included on the UK priority list, species and habitats had to meet the criteria listed in table 14.1.

As a result of increased data and a more inclusive and systematic process, many species met these criteria and the list grew from 577 species and 45 habitats, to 1,149 species and 65 habitats (Biodiversity Reporting and Information Group 2007).

The considerable growth in these lists has resulted in a need to adopt a more streamlined approach to developing action plans. The strategy developed for managing the longer list has been to "signpost" the actions and group the species according to the types of delivery mechanism best suited, such as further research, application of agri-environment schemes, or habitat restoration.

These reviews, which were anticipated as part of the original plan, are accompanied by moves toward more rigorous and structured reporting. The UKBAP agreed to a process of reporting on the HAPs and SAPs every three years. The first reporting round occurred in 1999 and was conducted through a paper-based questionnaire of all lead partners. In 2002 the reporting took the form of a Web-based questionnaire, this time asking for data from lead partners and LBAPs.

The most recent round in 2005 made use of a newly developed online reporting system called BARS (Biodiversity Action Reporting System) into which lead partners and LBAPs were asked to insert their own data. BARS was created to meet both the internal and external reporting needs of organizations involved in the UKBAP. The hope was that by bringing the data together in one place it would become easier to assess the achievements of plans at various (local, country, and UK) levels.

Table 14.1
Criteria for including species and habitats in the revised priorities lists

---

Criteria for including species in the revised priorities lists
1. International threat.
2. International responsibility (of the UK) + moderate decline in the UK.
A species that has declined by more than 25% in the last 25 years in the UK may qualify if the UK supports 25% or more of the global or European population.
3. Marked decline in the UK.
A species which has declined by 50% or more over the past 25 years qualifies under this criterion.
4. Other important factor(s).
Where a species does not qualify under Criteria 1, 2, or 3, there may still be a case for listing it as a candidate. However, evidence of extreme threat is required.

Criteria for including (non-marine) habitats
1. Habitats for which the UK has international obligations.
2. Natural and semi-natural habitats at risk, such as those with a high rate of decline in extent and/or quality, especially over the last 20 years, or which are rare.
3. Habitats important for assemblages of key species.
4. Habitats which are "functionally critical," i.e., those "essential for organisms inhabiting wider ecosystems," may be useful in some cases as a supporting criterion but is unlikely to be a qualifying criterion in its own right (Biodiversity Reporting and Information Group 2007, 78).

All of these changes occurred within the parameters of the original BAP. Underlying this, however, is a change in philosophy about how to approach biodiversity conservation. This constitutes a shift of thinking to an "ecosystem approach," accompanied by a reexamination of the relationship between HAPs and SAPs, and a rearrangement or development of the roles of the various stakeholders. These changes are discussed in the next section.

More Radical Change: Accumulated Experience and External Drivers

The Standing Committee attributes change in UK biodiversity policy to four primary drivers (UK Biodiversity Partnership Standing Committee 2007, iii): the need to take action to mitigate the impacts of climate change; the EU Gothenburg agreement in 2001 to halt the loss of biodiversity by 2010; the findings of the Millennium Ecosystem Assessment (highlighting the relationship between ecosystems and human well-being and the need to take action to reverse ecosystem degradation by addressing causes of degradation and valuing ecosystem services); and devolution from 1998 onwards.

Respondents from government agencies agreed that these factors had indeed supported changes not only in policy but also in BAP structure and process, particularly in moves to a more landscape-based and ecosystem approach, a greater concern with monitoring and reporting, and, concurrently, greater organizational complexity because of devolution.

Structurally, one of the most significant changes affecting UK conservation since the inception of the UKBAP is the political devolution in 1998 of the four countries that constitute the United Kingdom. With this process, political power in many fields, including the environment, has been moved from the UK government to the Scottish Executive (now Scottish Government), the Welsh Assembly. and the Northern Ireland Assembly, in addition to England, which is governed as a unitary territory by the UK central government . Each country has its own statutory agencies for biodiversity and since 2002 has written its own Biodiversity Strategy (or Environmental Strategy in Wales). Scotland has also produced its own list of priority species and habitats. Devolution has made the UKBAP more complicated. For example, the Targets Review committee developed criteria as the basis for inviting lead partners to propose new targets for SAPs and HAPs; these in turn had to be agreed in consultation with the Country Biodiversity Groups. Perhaps the most important feature of this complex decision-making structure is the historic difference in geographic coverage of the NGOs:

A country strategy focus makes it increasingly difficult for the countries to find resources to engage with the demanding UK process. NGO's, most of which are structured at a UK level, face the opposite problem and find it difficult to engage at a country level. . . . the consequence is that the NGOs and the country agencies fail to communicate effectively on some biodiversity issues. (JNCC 2004, 3)

Changes in international conservation thinking are also part of the context of change in UKBAP:

I think [climate change] is placing an absolute imperative to take an ecosystems approach because we're not working in a static world. (Interview with government department, conducted by the authors)

Those more involved with the implementation of the UKBAP, on the other hand, drew attention to the influence of cumulative experience and data. Change has been pushed by external factors, but also simply because the original plan is no longer adequate:

Why there are so many new species being put forward [for the priorities review] . . . was actually quite easy. We've got a lot more data, so we know what's happening. (Interview with species NGO, conducted by the authors)

It is important to recognize the level of personal commitment in this professional field. All our respondents demonstrated an emotional connection to nature and concern with the effectiveness of conservation:

Of course experts are not only scientifically connected with their field and their group and their taxa, but they also have a strong personal connection with that, so they want it to be conserved, they think it matters, and that's great, it's harnessed a huge amount of enthusiasm. (Interview with government department, conducted by the authors)

This commitment, combined with accumulated experience of fitting in with the BAP, can translate into frustration with procedure and structure:

It's not called the biodiversity bureaucracy for nothing; we know that it's very top heavy and very procedural. . . . There are huge communications issues between the four countries let alone with the English regional biodiversity forums, and then down to the LBAPs; I mean it's a leviathan. (Interview with habitat-based NGO, conducted by the authors)

How Change Took Place

So change processes have been a mixture of planned and unplanned, a result of both formally identified external drivers and the accumulation of experience. However respondents resisted a sense of clear separation of internal and external drivers:

It was just, I think, fortuitous. . . . All of these things were coming through at the same time, the pressure of the 2010 targets, it just came together at the right time that enabled people to look more critically about how they were doing things. (Interview with government agency, conducted by the authors)

These claims of serendipity and synchronicity complicate a simple analysis based on first-order and second-order reflexivity. However there are some clear strands in the change process: the formal, internal review (which can map on to the idea of first-order reflexivity); accumulated experience highlighting the need to "look more critically about how [we] were doing things" (which can map on to second-order reflexivity); and underlying all of this, more global shifts in consciousness of complexity and environmental change, with the responding move toward ecosystem thinking.

Although planned, by the time of the Targets Reviews, wider changes were stirring up thinking:

What we were actually trying to get people to think about was whether they could come up with new kinds of targets that could give some sense of progress towards creating more resilient landscapes. (Interview with habitat-based NGO, conducted by the authors)

Considerable resources have gone into the Priorities Review (Biodiversity Reporting and Information Group 2007), a process that all felt was necessary but somewhat traumatic. There was a strong emphasis on making the process transparent and systematic in order to avoid the criticisms of bias that arose when the original species were chosen. Respondents were well aware of the *politics* of the process—with varying levels of satisfaction:

I think this latest review has been much more systematic, much more time has been spent on it, the criteria have been carefully applied. (Interview with government department, conducted by the authors)
What they wanted to do with this review was try and make it more transparent and get people engaged. And perhaps we feel that we haven't quite been engaged enough. (Interview with species NGO, conducted by authors)
I mean the targets took two plus years, but it was *relatively* painless and straightforward, just a lot of work. But the species and habitats priorities review has been a political nightmare. (Interview with habitat-based NGO, conducted by authors)

At the same time, responses to the accumulation of experience and bureaucracy started to emerge among the partners. This gathered momentum in a process that came to be known as "refreshing the BAP" and culminated in the publication of *Conserving Biodiversity—The UK Approach*, which emphasizes the importance of climate change and ecosystem approach (UK Biodiversity Partnership Standing Committee 2007). In December 2006 the England Biodiversity Group recognized low achievements of the UKBAP targets; internal correspondence noted that "with only 18% of maintenance and 8% of expansion targets met it was clear that we would have to raise our game." In the same month, one of the national habitat groups, responsible for the lowland heathland HAP, took action that contributed directly to the "refreshing" process that is still on-going.

The Lowland Heathland HAP group invited members of the BAP partnership to an extraordinary meeting. In particular, they noted the need for clarity and synchronization in linking strategic planning at UK level, and country, regional, and local planning and delivery. They wanted particularly to define the role of HAP groups beyond simple reporting (i.e., in terms of authority and influence over the planning process), responding to communication needs at the various decision-making scales, and responsiveness to wider issues such as climate change and air pollution. These events culminated in a call from the NGOs for a meeting of this type, which fed into the ministerial meeting of March 2007 (England Biodiversity Group 2007) and the ongoing "refreshing" process that includes moves toward an ecosystem approach, with stronger linkages between local and national BAPs and between species and habitats.

Perhaps it is not surprising that a HAP had a key role in this process. Habitats are less tangible, are more obviously linked at various geographical scales, and connect various levels of biodiversity. They therefore fit more awkwardly into classifications and priority lists (Midgley 2005) and experience any poorly articulated connections more acutely.

Does This Add Up to Second-Order Reflexivity?

To what extent is this change process characterized by the types of cognitive restructuring described as second-order reflexivity by Voß and Kemp? Some of the process is obviously more reactive and simply an attempt to deal with problems arising through experience; however, many of the actors seem to be taking those actions in full awareness of the challenges of working with a complex system. In this section we assess the evidence for the presence of the characteristics of second-order reflexivity, namely systems analysis, iterative participatory goal setting, and interactive strategy implementation.

Systems Analysis

A systemic approach sees systems as organized in sequential levels, whereby each higher level "is more than the sum of the parts" (e.g., Gunderson and Holling 2002). Biodiversity management, then, is systemic when the parts are seen to be connected and organized at higher levels in ways that transcend and include lower levels (Wilber 1996). Space does not permit us to conduct a full review of the meanings of *habitat* in relation to *species*, nor the ways in which the term *ecosystem* has mutated in recent years (but see Bowker 2000 and Midgley 2005). It will suffice here to define systems analysis as occurring when linkages within and between levels of biological organization are recognized.

The very first formulations of the UKBAP took a wide approach in outlining the fifty-nine steps but the work crystallized around the more limited aims of species and habitat target setting. Much of the current effort is moving to reintegrate a systems approach into the UKBAP practice. There is plenty of support among individual members of the BAP partnership for a systemic approach, but it was usually articulated by government actors:

[In the future] there will be a lot more emphasis on the habitats, and maybe they will start to be grouped, but then you've still got the problem of the habitat thinking going on in boxes . . . and actually then you need to think about what is the appropriate mosaic of woodland and heath, and what do you do about the interface, and are there places where you want to have heathland with a few birch trees scattered and is that what we need for the various butterflies and nightjars. (Interview with government department, conducted by the authors)

Biodiversity is a multilevel thing. So by focussing on one of the levels, it doesn't matter how good it is if you are neglecting the others. We are starting to see that we can put both of them together, the species approach and the other approach. (Interview with government agency, conducted by the authors)]

Because many of the NGOs are organized around particular groups of species, such as birds, plants, or butterflies, their interests can appear to work against this approach. Nevertheless NGO representatives explicitly challenged this notion:

The question is not whether organisations with a focus on the units are unable to understand systems, but whether organisations that purport to care about systems can actually understand units. (Species-based NGO, personal communication)

Importantly, many also recognized the wider context in which biodiversity planning was taking place:

The targets that result are shared ones, belonging to the UK Biodiversity Partnership as a whole and should be considered in the context of ecosystems, climate change, the priority list review and the need to set priorities in the light of limited resources. (UK Biodiversity Action Plan 2007a)

So the BAP approach, the target driven approach, I totally think that climate change can be accommodated within it. If you are then asking me how do we do it now, that's a different question because there is so much uncertainty. (Interview with species-based NGO, conducted by authors]

It is this wider context, and the accompanying uncertainty about behavior of the biodiversity system within it, that requires the second characteristic of second-order reflexivity, which we consider next.

Iterative Participatory Goal Setting

Our study shows that iteration is built into the UKBAP process. Some respondents expressed mock horror at the prospect of any further priorities or targets review, and the hope that they had got it right this time. Most also recognized that given the current state of knowledge, and the changing context, it should be (as one civil servant put it) "dynamic and responsive" to both conservation needs and new information.

The accumulation of data plays a big role in this:

> I think people didn't have an alternative in the beginning because they didn't have the information to set smart targets. So we reckon that ten years into the BAP we ought to be putting the targets right. (Interview with government agency, conducted by the authors)

However what is being reformulated here is the detail of the overall approach, what might be termed "first-order reflexivity" in Voß and Kemp's typology. The greater change, the overall approach, and the significance of ecosystems thinking comes not from reflexive processes built into the system, but is instead influenced by both experience of the UKBAP and by international knowledge processes and the rise of the "ecosystem services" discourse (e.g., Balmford et al. 2005; Gatzweiler 2006; Hein et al. 2006; Mooney, Cropper, and Reid 2004; Rapport 1995).

Interactive Strategy Implementation

Many respondents spoke enthusiastically about the success of the UKBAP in bringing together partners:

> It's quite unusual in a way to have such a strong partnership between government and NGOs; in this sector we do actually all sit round the table and take decisions collectively. (Interview with government department, conducted by the authors)

The collectiveness of those decisions comes into question, however, when the reality of power relations is discussed.

> We do need [the Biodiversity Partnership Conference] once a year to cement the partnership. There's always a bit of unhappiness about "how did that actually influence the policy" and "what we've taken into account"; you know that's much more nebulous, but it permeates in a more fluid sort of way. (Interview with government department, conducted by the authors)

NGOs respondents often reflected an appreciation of being "at the table" but a belief that decisions do not ultimately rest with them:

The way to do policy is to respond to all the consultations, but the way you get things done is by making friends with the policy makers and the ministers. (Interview with species-based NGO, conducted by the authors)

There are, therefore, differences of power—and also differences of scale. There is an interesting and possibly essential tension between what some characterized as the species interests of the NGOs and the habitat interests of the government agencies.

The NGOs themselves are not a community of equals. In interviews, NGO respondents complained about the power or tactics of other NGOs. But the BAP has provided an incentive for NGOs to organize and collaborate. This first took the form of Biodiversity Challenge, the group that contributed so much to the original shape of the UKBAP. Other NGOs, some of whom felt that, for example, bird conservation organizations had too much influence in Biodiversity Challenge, which contributed to pressure for a more representative forum, leading to the formation in 2000 of the Biodiversity Task Force. This group sits within the coalition of the Wildlife and Countryside Link, which brings together a wide range of conservation NGOs to present a united response to the government on policy issues.

So the partnership is really a hierarchy, and one that is complicated by devolution, which makes it four separate but connected hierarchies. The government agencies need the NGOs, and the NGOs need the government agencies. None of the respondents called for either more autonomy or more power sharing; there was a strong sense that the UKBAP is real, big, complicated, inefficient but learning; and that what partners want is greater clarity of structure and leadership.

Conclusions

The UKBAP has changed profoundly in less than a decade—going from an approach based on an ad hoc, convenient but subjective list of priority species to a focus on habitats and an "ecosystem approach." The approach has been strongly path dependent, relying on government agencies affected by wider processes of political devolution, and NGOs with membership support based on particular components of biodiversity. Reductionist approaches such as the UKBAP have been criticized for failing to engage with the complex realities of ecology (Abram 1996; Green 2000). However, our study of change within the UKBAP draws attention to two ways in which this criticism can be seen as oversimplistic.

First, the actors are aware that they are engaging with a complex system, in which each is attempting to work with a part in collaboration with others in the context of incomplete knowledge of the system. Uncertainty is always associated with complexity, but in the case of biodiversity, it is particularly associated with those attributes that are most easily classified as a global public good—ecosystem services and resilience in the face of profound environmental change. The picture emerging from the experiences described here is not one of naïvely mechanistic bureaucrats seeking to control the public environment, but rather one of experts sensitive to the challenge, committed to sustainability, obliged to start somewhere, even though as one government actor put it, "I wouldn't start from here."

Consequently, the approach is also protected by learning and adaptiveness. We see here a mixture of first-order and second-order reflexivity (in the terminology of Voß and Kemp). The first BAP was simplistic, "back-of-an-envelope"; but the actors knew that. To some extent they built change into the process. Their leap in the dark helped to show just how much really was hidden in the dark, and the first ten years have channeled research and monitoring efforts to provide the new information that helps to revise the system. Many of the actors, including the bureaucrats, are ecologists, personally committed to conservation and professionally trained in systems thinking. To the extent that rational planning focuses the production of new knowledge, that the actors are predisposed to take a systems overview, and that revision is planned, this vast ambitious exercise is reflexive in the second-order sense. However, some of the most fundamental change was also influenced by more international discourses and processes including the Millennium Ecosystem Assessment.

This learning and adaptiveness is not all the harmonious experience that might seem to be implied. It is characterized by politics, struggles to match personal commitment to the rigidities of bureaucracy, and the complications of complexity. But from this mix emerges a recognition of the need for change, and a real ongoing engagement with the challenges of planning and measuring change, in the context of that (social and ecological) complexity. We cannot just conclude that rational biodiversity planning is some glorious planned experiment, however. Without stronger reflexivity, such an experiment would be lazy and dangerous.

Both first- and second-order reflexivity characterize the UK biodiversity planning system; in fact, we conclude that the UKBAP experience calls into question the rigid distinction between first- and second-order reflexivity. Perhaps it is the case that "[s]econd-order reflexivity interrupts the automatism of executing problem-solving routines. It transcends particular rationalities, and breaks the vicious circle of first-order reflexivity" (Voß and Kemp 2006, 6), but it is not always planned that way. Complexity will always break through the modernistic boundaries created by rational planning. However, it is difficult to understand the complexity until we impose those (imaginary) boundaries of habitat categories, species priorities, and time-and-quantity targets, and allow ourselves to see what happens.

Politics, concern for organizational survival, personal interests, and a large legacy of organizational history limit the development of a systems approach and transparent deliberative participation, and some of the change in the UKBAP has been driven by external shifts in thinking. There is a real ongoing effort to grasp a more profoundly systemic way of thinking and working, to make the connections between the parts that only experience can show need to be made. The question remains: How can real reflexive governance be included more consciously in this very human context?

Notes

We thank the respondents for their time and enthusiasm in responding to this study, and in particular for the interest and commitment they showed in commenting on an earlier version of this chapter. The study was conducted in time funded by a fellowship at the Environmental Change Institute, University of Oxford.

15

Reflexive Governance and the Importance of Individual Competencies: The Case of Adaptation to Climate Change in Germany

Torsten Grothmann and Bernd Siebenhüner

Most problems of modern societies on local, domestic, and global levels (e.g., environmental protection, economic development, and social welfare) cannot sufficiently be addressed by conventional forms of policy making in which state agents collect the necessary expertise, develop a regulatory solution, and implement it through legislative and executive processes. The uncertainties, complexities, interconnectedness, multiple layers, and the numerous consequences of any (regulatory) solution necessitate a governance approach that recognizes these problem characteristics (Voß and Kemp 2006). As outlined in the contributions to this book, a reflexive governance approach particularly addresses these challenges.

However, the notion of reflexive governance implies considerable challenges for individual and collective actors to become effectively involved in these governance processes. They need to be able to generate, process, disseminate, and store various forms and bodies of knowledge; they must have the ability to participate in interactive processes to acknowledge different claims and interests and to form and formulate preferences regarding potential solutions; and they require necessary resources to implement solutions and to start new governance processes.

The literature on reflexive governance has identified knowledge, cognitions, and motives as important conditions in complex and knowledge-intensive governance processes. But these characteristics on the micro-level are not dealt with systematically and sufficiently. As yet neglected are the necessary competencies of individual actors to effectively steer and participate in reflexive governance processes. The specific focus of this chapter, therefore, lies in an extensive analysis of these necessary competencies, which integrate different psychological factors—such as knowledge, cognitions, and motives—on a higher conceptual level.

The chapter includes an exploratory study on the role of competencies in the field of adaptation to climate change, which refers to "adjustments to reduce vulnerability or enhance resilience in response to observed or expected changes in climate and associated extreme weather events" (Adger et al. 2007, 720). Potential, but highly uncertain short- and long-term impacts of climate change on different interlinked sectors and regions constitute a highly complex and uncertain problem sphere that requires knowledge-intensive and cooperative adaptation processes. Early adaptation initiatives in Germany show key elements of reflexive governance, but our data also highlight the lack of necessary competencies for the functioning of these reflexive governance elements in adaptation practice.

The chapter is structured as follows. First, we present our theoretical considerations on reflexive governance and the role of individual competencies. This includes the presentation of key areas of human behavior relevant for reflexive governance, an analysis of previous research with regard to micro-level or psychological components involved in reflexive governance processes, and a detailed description of competencies that individual actors involved in such processes should possess. The second part of the chapter illustrates the importance of individual competencies by a case study on climate change adaptation in Germany. The third part of the chapter discusses practical strategies to address individual competencies in collective reflexive governance processes, such as systematic selection and training of participating actors. The conclusions identify questions for future research.

Reflexive Governance and Individual Competencies

Areas of Human Behavior Relevant for Reflexive Governance

In this chapter, we draw on various governance approaches in the effort to identify key elements of reflexive governance. We define reflexive governance as a rule-setting and rule-implementation process that includes *interaction, deliberation,* and *adaptation* as areas of individual and collective behavior. Each of the three elements highlights particular aspects of reflexive governance processes.

Interaction   Governance is a process involving a diverse set of actors including regulatory agencies, nongovernmental actors, as well as other stakeholders. All actors pursue individual interests, maintain particular rationales, and avail themselves of specific resources (Scharpf 1997).

Reflexive governance thus integrates different actors in the governance process. Different stakeholders interact in the processes of policy goal formulation and strategy development, as well as in the implementation of solutions (Voß & Kemp 2006).

Deliberation Reflexive governance acknowledges the fact that knowledge is being generated in various domains and communities. Hence, there is not one unitary knowledge and truth system but rather multiple. In addition, knowledge and truth claims are voiced by numerous different groups in society. Different claims and bodies of knowledge often clash and struggle for greater attention in governance processes. Reflexive governance addresses this challenge by applying deliberative forms of knowledge generation. These involve transdisciplinary forms of learning in which different bodies of knowledge from science and other societal groups bring together information and experience (van Asselt and Rijkens-Klomp 2002; Kasemir et al. 2003; Siebenhüner 2004; Voß and Kemp 2006).

Adaptation Processes of reflexive governance need to be dynamic over time to allow for adaptation to novel developments inside or outside the governance system. Therefore, an iterative development of flexible strategies and institutions seems most adequate to encounter dynamic external and internal processes. These strategies can be rather easily adapted or altered to new conditions such as hitherto unknown environmental threats or social dynamics (Gigerenzer 2000; Holling 1978). Reflexive governance thus has to be adaptive, and involved actors have to regularly reassess the applicability of the policies they decided (Voß and Kemp 2006).

Reflexive Governance from a Micro-Level Perspective

Addressing the three areas of behavior in reflexive governance processes—interaction, deliberation, and adaptation—from a micro-level perspective, reflexive governance can be characterized as a *psychosocial process*, in which individuals and collective actors think and learn about complex problems, communicate and cooperate, deal with conflicting interests and solve conflicts, make decisions and adapt decisions, and implement and change strategies. In this chapter we focus on the psychological factors that seem necessary for describing, explaining, and influencing reflexive governance processes from a micro-level perspective. We state that these psychological factors can be integrated in a list of competencies that actors involved in reflexive governance processes—especially actors in key positions of the reflexive governance process—should possess. We assume that without these competencies a reflexive governance process would be strongly elongated and in some cases discontinued. We therefore see these competencies as success factors for the functioning of reflexive governance processes.

As yet, scientific debates on reflexive governance have not dealt with characteristics on the micro-level systematically or sufficiently. Often *knowledge* is identified as essential and more or less undifferentiated *cognitions* are named (e.g., Loibl 2006; Rip 2006; Voß and Kemp 2006). In a psychological terminology, both constructs—knowledge and cognition—refer to what people know and how they process this knowledge. Often *motives* and interests are named as important in reflexive governance processes (e.g., Spaeth et al. 2006; Stirling 2006; Voß, Truffer, and Konrad 2006; Wolff 2006). Motives refer to what people want and pursuit. Some authors mention psychological constructs which reflect the fact that most knowledge and cognitions are motivationally biased (Smith 2006; Wolff 2006). Literature on reflexive governance so far has neglected *emotions*. Emotions refer to subjective feelings, often accompanied by physiological changes that impel one toward action (see Scherer 2005). Due to the uncertainties, complexities, interconnectedness, multiple layers, and conflict potential of most problems in modern societies, actors involved in social processes of finding solutions for these problems often experience strong negative emotions, such as excessive demand, frustration, helplessness, stress, and anger (e.g., Booth and Welch 1978). Hence, it is essential to realize the importance of emotions and their effective "management" in reflexive governance processes.

Also as yet neglected in the literature on reflexive governance are the necessary *competencies* of individual and collective actors to effectively steer and participate in reflexive governance processes, whereas the discussion of civic and democratic skills has a long tradition in educational research and practice (e.g., Dewey 1916; Marshall 1955; Chawla and Cushing 2007). In this chapter we focus on individual competencies, including such civic and democratic skills as communication and cooperation competencies, along with competencies like tolerance for uncertainty and complexity, systemic and long-term thinking, and the ability for self-reflection. Such competencies seem necessary for individual actors to effectively become involved in governance processes of long-term and highly uncertain problems like climate change.

Individual Competencies for Reflexive Governance

In identifying and defining individual competencies to effectively steer and participate in reflexive governance processes we mainly draw upon the DeSeCo project (Definition and Selection of Competencies, see OECD 2005; Rychen and Salganik 2003). This international and interdisciplinary OECD (Organization of Economic Co-operation and Development) project, which ran from 1998 to 2003, set a political standard for the discussion of competencies by bringing together a wide range of experts and stakeholders to produce a coherent and widely shared analysis of the key competencies necessary for coping with the manifold challenges of today's world.

A competency involves the ability to meet complex demands, by drawing on, mobilizing, and managing psychosocial resources (including knowledge, motivations, emotions, skills, attitudes, values, and social support) in a particular context (see OECD 2005; Rychen and Salganik 2003). Going beyond knowledge and skills, the competency concept also involves motivational and emotional components and therefore reflects the psychological factors in reflexive governance processes more fully than do concepts like knowledge or cognitions.

The main advantage of the competency concept is its power to integrate different psychological factors (e.g., knowledge, cognitions, motives) on a higher conceptual level, therefore reducing the complexity of the description and explanation of reflexive governance processes (cf. Occam's razor). In addition, the competency concept holds a high practical value. By summarizing and reformulating different psychological factors that are important for reflexive governance, competencies make these factors useful in selecting and training "personnel" for reflexive governance processes.

Our main thesis is that specific competencies of individual actors involved in reflexive governance processes—especially of actors in key positions in the process—are fundamental for the functioning and effectiveness of reflexive governance. We propose to differentiate between general competencies that seem to be relevant for all reflexive governance processes—independent from the specific governance problem they address—and competencies that are problem specific. In the second part of this chapter we address the problem-specific competencies in reflexive governance of adaptation to climate change. The general competencies—interaction, deliberation, and adaptation competency—seem to be essential for the functioning of every reflexive governance process and are defined in table 15.1. They overlap to a certain extent. A major

Table 15.1
Interaction, deliberation, and adaptation competency—definitions and subcomponents

Interaction competency	Deliberation competency	Adaptation competency
Ability to interact in heterogeneous groups of different stakeholders and to build new forms of cooperation (see "interacting in heterogeneous groups" in the DeSeCo project; OECD 2005a; Rychen and Salganik 2003).	Ability for deliberative forms of knowledge generation, involving transdisciplinary forms of learning where different bodies of knowledge from science and other societal groups bring together their knowledge (see Cohen 1989; Gadamer 1960/1990; Habermas 1981; Lecher and Hoff 1997; OECD 2005a; Offe 1997; Rychen and Salganik 2003).	ability to be highly flexible and adaptive in iterative developments of strategies and institutions in reflexive governance processes, including the abandonment of previous decisions and governance solutions (see OECD 2005a, Rychen and Salganik 2003).
Subcomponents	**Subcomponents**	**Subcomponents**
Ability to relate well to others	*Motivation to learn*	*Ability for self-reflection/ reflectiveness*
Ability "to respect and appreciate the values, beliefs, cultures and histories of others" (OECD 2005a, 12), requiring empathy, self-reflection, and effective management of emotions.	Motivation to gain new knowledge and an understanding of the beliefs, interests and values of other actors involved in this process, including the ability to take responsibility for his or her learning and harness emotions, even negative ones, and manage them to achieve learning.	Ability to regularly reassess the applicability of policies from a neutral point of view, requiring the ability to think reflectively (i.e., to question and change personal and institutional thoughts and practices to use metacognitive skills (thinking about thinking), to take a critical stance on previous thoughts, decisions and practices (see OECD 2005a), and to deal with feelings of frustration when policies fail
Ability to cooperate	*Ability to perceive, understand and tolerate others' beliefs, knowledge claims, interests and values*	*Ability to accept failures as a natural part of the management of complex tasks/"failure-friendliness"*
Ability "to balance commitment to the group and its goals with his or her own priorities" and "to share leadership and to support others" (OECD 2005a, 13), requiring communication skills or the ability to present ideas in an understandable way and listen to those of others (see Cohen 1998); an understanding of the dynamics of debate and following an agenda; ability to construct tactical or sustainable alliances; ability to negotiate; capacity to make decisions that allow for different shades of opinion (OECD 2005a); confidence in one's ability to achieve goals by working with a group (see Chawla and Cushing 2007).	Ability to detect, decipher and tolerate differences in beliefs, knowledge claims, interests and values in a governance process of manifold actors (cf. Cohen 1989).	

Table 15.1
(continued)

Ability to manage and resolve conflicts: ability to recognize conflict as "a process to be managed rather than seeking to negate it" (OECD 2005a, 13), requiring the capacity to "analyze the issues and interests at stake (e.g., power, recognition of merit, division of work, equity), the origins of the conflict and the reasoning of all sides, recognizing that there are different possible positions; identify areas of agreement and disagreement; reframe the problem; and prioritize needs and goals, deciding what they are willing to give up and under what circumstances" (OECD 2005a, 13).

Ability to deal with complexity
Ability to anticipate long-term systemic effects of action strategies (Voß and Kemp 2006), i.e., long-term thinking in decades and centuries, involving a minimum of systemic or ecologic thinking (see Lecher and Hoff 1997), the capability to evaluate and organize partly inconsistent knowledge and information, and the ability to cope with feelings of excessive demand, frustration and helplessness.
Ability to find integrated and creative solutions
Ability not to rush to a single answer, to an either-or solution, but rather handle tensions by integrating seemingly contradictory or incompatible goals as aspects of the same reality, requiring to take into account the manifold "interrelations between positions or ideas that may appear contradictory, but that may sometimes only superficially be so" (OECD 2005a, 9) and requiring a certain amount of creativity to find innovative solutions that go beyond traditional ways of problem solving.

Ability to accept failures as a natural part of reflexive governance processes without blaming a person or institution when things go wrong in order to keep stakeholders integrated in the processes
Ability to identify innovative and creative solutions
Ability to adapt policies after previous policies failed or new conditions such as hitherto unknown threats or dynamics emerged (large overlap with the "ability to find integrated and creative solutions," subcomponent of deliberation competency).

component of all three competencies is the effective management of emotions.

The Case of Climate Change Adaptation in Germany

To illustrate our micro-level perspective and the importance of competencies for the success of reflexive governance approaches, we refer to the case of adaptation to climate change. Empirically we base our analysis on data from an exploratory case study on climate change adaptation in Germany.

Adaptation to Climate Change

Adaptation to climate change refers to "adjustments to reduce vulnerability or enhance resilience in response to observed or expected changes in climate and associated extreme weather events" (Adger et al. 2007, 720). For example, building higher dykes and flood retention basins because of an increased risk of flooding due to climate change and higher precipitation qualifies as an adaptation measure. (Please note that the term *adaptation* is used differently here from its usage as a general element of reflexive governance in previous parts of the chapter.)

Adaptation to climate change cannot be substituted by mitigation of climate change; that is, the reduction of greenhouse gas emissions, which cause climate change to a large extent. "Even the most stringent mitigation efforts cannot avoid further impacts of climate change in the next few decades . . . which makes adaptation unavoidable. However, without mitigation, a magnitude of climate change is likely to be reached that makes adaptation impossible for some natural systems, while for most human systems it would involve very high social and economic costs" (Klein et al. 2007, 747).

With its high uncertainties and complexity, adaptation to climate change represents an appropriate and challenging field of application for reflexive governance. As yet, reflexive governance has not been used to describe or govern climate change adaptation processes. Much recent literature on the adaptation to climate change refers to the importance of elements incorporated in the reflexive governance approach, including the importance of micro-level factors such as cognitions (e.g., Grothmann and Reusswig 2006; Grothmann and Patt 2005; Weber 2006). Although human capital (the stock of productive skills and technical knowledge available in a society or group of people)—a concept close to that of competency—is identified as an essential condition for successful adaptation to climate change (Adger et al. 2007), there is not yet any detailed analysis of the necessary human capital or competencies for climate change adaptation processes.

Competencies for Reflexive Governance of Climate Change Adaptation

To effectively become involved in reflexive governance processes of climate change adaptation, individuals require not only general competencies for reflexive governance but also a problem-specific "uncertainty competency." This competency is essential because so far many initiatives for adaptation to climate change have been impeded by the significant uncertainty of future climate change impacts (see Adger et al. 2007). Individuals are often uncomfortable with uncertainty due to its inherent lack of predictability. Uncertainty creates a feeling of vulnerability or anxiety that can lead to actively distorting perceptions and information, which in turn can produce premature closure, false dichotomies, and rejection of relevant information (Clampitt and Williams 2000). Often people reduce uncertainty through "heuristics which sometimes yield reasonable judgments and sometimes lead to severe and systematic error" (Kahneman, Slovic, and Tversky 1982, 48). Therefore, uncertainty competency is needed. We define the uncertainty competency based on literature from social psychology and organizational research (see table 15.2).

Climate Change Adaptation in Germany—an Exploratory Case Study

To gain some empirical hint for our hypothesis of the importance of competencies for knowledge-intensive governance processes, we conducted a case study on climate change adaptation in Germany. The first and (as yet) only comprehensive study on potential climate change impacts in Germany by Zebisch et al. (2005) indicates that especially southwestern Germany, the central parts of eastern Germany, and the Alps are vulnerable to climate change. In southwestern Germany the high temperatures will cause problems in the health sector. In eastern Germany, low-water availability and the risk of summer droughts will in particular impact agriculture and forestry, as well as the transport sector (river navigation). The Alps are very vulnerable to climate change especially in nature conservation, flood protection, and winter tourism.

Different from mitigation efforts to reduce greenhouse gas emissions, adaptation activities related to the impacts of climate change are just beginning in Germany and their outcome cannot yet be evaluated. Although these adaptation initiatives do not explicitly apply reflexive governance principles, some show key elements of this governance

Table 15.2
Uncertainty competency for climate change adaptation—definition and sub-components

---

Uncertainty competency
Ability to make reasoned adaptation decisions under the uncertainty of climate change impacts.

Subcomponents
Ability to understand uncertainty
Ability to perceive and understand the uncertainty of future climate change impacts in its full dimension, including an understanding of the uncertainty differences between different climate change impacts, regions and time-scales.

Tolerance for uncertainty
Cognitive and/or emotional orientation (Furnham 1995), which allows people to tolerate the uncertainty of future climate change impacts, including the ability to accept the uncertainty in its full dimension without reducing, ignoring or eliminating it immediately through heuristics or rules of thumb. This tolerance also includes the ability to cope with feelings of vulnerability or anxiety, which often arise when individuals are confronted with uncertainty.

Ability to make reasoned decisions under uncertainty
Basic knowledge of rules (e.g., maximin, maximax, Hurwicz, Laplace, or minimax regret) and formal procedures for decision making under uncertainty (e.g., Kárný 2005), including practical guidelines for decision making with regard to climate change adaptation (see Willows and Connell 2003).

---

approach (e.g., extensive deliberation processes and stakeholder dialogues). Therefore, a study on the influence of individual competencies on these adaptation initiatives can provide some empirical indicators for the importance of competencies in reflexive governance processes. We want to emphasize that our case study is an exploratory study and that its results are just indicators (not evidence) of the importance of competencies in knowledge-intensive participatory governance processes.

We applied three data collection methods: (a) half-standardized questionnaires with ten experts from different federal government institutions in Germany, who have in-depth knowledge of adaptation activities in their federal states; (b) narrative interviews with two independent experts on one perennial climate change adaptation activity on flood hazard management in Germany; and (c) participatory observation of four workshops on adaptation to climate change in Germany. We analyzed the data gained by content-analytic methods.

In the half-standardized questionnaires, the experts were asked to recall projects and initiatives on adaptation to climate change in their federal states. On this basis, they assessed whether specific competencies are lacking for the success of these adaptation projects and initiatives (on a four-point scale from "do not agree at all" to "totally agree"). To guarantee the comprehensibility of the named competencies, they were described differently from the definition of competencies in this chapter. Eight experts "agreed" or "totally agreed" that there is a lack of uncertainty competency and complexity competence. Uncertainty competency was described as "acceptance of and adaptation despite the uncertainty of climate scenarios," complexity competence was defined as "acceptance of and adaptation despite the complexity of climate change impacts." In this chapter, this competence is included as "the ability to deal with complexity" in the deliberation competency. Seven experts "agreed" or "totally agreed" that there is a lack of sustainability competence, which was described as "long-term thinking in decades and centuries" (also included in "the ability to deal with complexity" in this chapter). Five respondents perceived a lack of communication competence, "the ability for an understandable communication of climate change impacts and adaptation options." Four experts identified a lack of cooperation competence, "the ability for interdisciplinary and transdisciplinary cooperation between different stakeholders." In this chapter, both—communication and cooperation competence—are part of the interaction competency. Hence, the respondents highly agreed on the importance and the lack of competencies for climate change adaptation, especially of the competencies to deal with uncertainty, complexity and long-term thinking.

The narrative interviews with two independent experts[1] focused on a specific climate change adaptation process in flood hazard management in Germany. This process is summarized in note form as follows: (1) initiative of water management agency to "be the first" in Germany to show proactive adaptation to climate change; (2) application of a regional model of climate change to calculate flood risk; (3) perennial political process in which the uncertainty of the climate change scenario was presented as being relatively small by the water management agency due to the perceived unwillingness of the responsible decision makers/politicians to decide under uncertainty; (4) political decision for increase of dyke height; (5) new and more reliable climate change model outputs become available, which shows smaller flood risk than previous model; (6) and water management agency does not explicitly communicate the new results to politicians because it worries that the former decision for an increase of dyke height will be annulled and a new perennial decision process will start. This adaptation process presents an example of a lack of uncertainty competency. Obviously, the water management agency and probably also the involved politicians did not have the ability to adequately deal with the uncertainty of climate change. After new and better information on climate change became available, the water management agency tended to negate this information.

Also the participatory observation of four different workshops on adaptation to climate change in Germany generated a lack of uncertainty competency as the main result. The observation of a workshop on the adaptation of biodiversity management, agriculture, and forestry in Germany also revealed the lack of another competence: The interaction competency of many participants was very low. Because of this lacking competency, the workshop came to no conclusions, and no compromise between the conflicting positions was found.

Our data highlight a lack of necessary competencies for processes of adaptation to climate change. The results indicate that a lack of uncertainty competency is a major barrier for successful adaptation processes in Germany. But also other competencies—including interaction, deliberation, and adaptation competence—seem lacking, which is mainly indicated by the results of the expert questionnaire.

Integrating Individual Competencies in Collective Reflexive Governance

To our knowledge, there are as yet no experiences from reflexive governance processes on how to address competencies. Nevertheless, we now want to elaborate on some practices that seem suited for this challenge. As has been noted before, competencies summarize and reformulate different psychological factors, which are important for reflexive governance, and make these factors addressable for selection and training of "personnel" for reflexive governance processes. To improve the practice of reflexive governance processes and advance their chances of success, necessary competencies among participating individuals should be systematically taken into account in the design of these processes. But "designing participatory exercises responding to . . . a whole array of personality related factors is still at least as much an art as a science" (Toth and Hizsnyik 1998, 205). Nevertheless, some promising practices addressing individual competencies can be named—practices that should be applied at least for the "inner circle" of participating actors and stakeholders in the reflexive governance process. In the following, we differentiate between practices that can be included in the design of specific reflexive governance processes (e.g., training modules in workshops) and practices that support the development of reflexive governance competencies and civic skills on a more general level (e.g., school education).

Practices addressing individual competencies in specific reflexive governance processes can be ordered along a temporal dimension. One of the first steps in the governance process should be the commitment of the initiator(s) of the process to pay attention to the role of competencies in the whole process. Soon after, the initiator(s) have to decide upon further persons (stakeholders and management personnel) to be included in the participatory reflexive governance process. Here, there should be efforts to systematically select persons who possess the competencies to become effectively involved in the reflexive governance processes, especially for those who will occupy key positions in the process.

However, one has to recognize that not all participating individuals will possess the necessary competencies to optimally contribute to the process. In many cases, stakeholders who lack some of the desirable competencies need to be included for political reasons, but such individuals can be trained and educated before and during the governance process. Whereas the management personnel of the reflexive governance process (e.g., members of a government institution) can be trained before the start of the process, on-the-job training during the process seems to be the most feasible way for participating stakeholders, who are unlikely to be motivated to take part in training sessions before the governance process begins. In addition, people normally do not like to be told that they lack some competencies. One promising solution is the inclusion of a neutral education professional with no stake in problems being addressed by the governance process. He or she can observe the stakeholder meetings, give feedback on observed problems in the process (e.g., difficulties in dealing with complexity), and can design training sessions to educate the group in solving these problems (e.g., education in systemic thinking). In designing training modules for the interaction, deliberation, and adaptation competency, one can refer to different sources, primarily the experiences from school education presented in the next paragraph, but also to other sources such as community psychology (e.g., Tasseit 1983). If there is no willingness among participating individuals to take part in these trainings it is useful to make the reflexive governance process resilient to people who lack the competencies to constructively take part in the process. One option is an agreement by the majority of the participating actors to follow some norms for cooperation during the reflexive governance process (e.g., to respect and appreciate the values, beliefs, cultures, and histories of others). Another option is to prepare standard answers for typical arguments that hinder reaching a solution in the governance process.

Reflexive governance competencies can also be supported outside specific governance processes, mainly in the educational system. As has been noted before, the discussion of civic and democratic skills has a long tradition in educational research and practice (e.g., Dewey 1916; Marshall 1955; Chawla and Cushing 2007). "Deliberative civic education is broadly conceived as instruction that utilizes varying forms of classroom deliberation and deliberative exercises to enhance the democratic skills of citizenship and to increase understanding of democratic practice" (Murphy 2004, 74). Hillygus (2005) has shown that the content of higher education, especially a curriculum that develops language and civic skills, is influential in shaping participation in American democracy—a result that indicates how the interaction competency, which includes participatory skills, can be supported in general education. Many other scholars studied the role of the educational system for the development of civic skills and give recommendations for improving current practice (e.g., Conover and Searing 2000; Dobozy 2007; Galston 2001; Morreale and Backlund 2002; Reinders and Youniss 2006).

Other life domains have also been studied regarding their contribution to the development of civic skills. For example, Adman (2008) could not find empirical evidence for the hypothesis that by practicing civic skills and democratic decision making at the workplace, citizens become more active in politics. Contrary to previous work, the results of Djupe and Grant (2001) indicate that church-gained civic skills and religious tradition do not directly affect political participation among those currently active in religious institutions.

Summary and Future Research

Previous publications on reflexive governance neglected the necessary competencies of individual actors to effectively steer and participate in reflexive governance processes. The specific focus of this chapter, therefore, has been an extensive analysis of these necessary competencies, integrating different psychological factors (e.g., knowledge, cognitions and motives) on a higher conceptual level. Based on competency research we differentiated between three general competencies (interaction, deliberation, and adaptation competency), which seem relevant for all reflexive governance processes, and competencies that are problem specific (e.g., uncertainty competence). The case study on adaptation to climate change in Germany illustrated that these competencies constitute important prerequisites and barriers of reflexive governance processes and should be addressed either by systematic selection and training of participating actors or the development of reflexive governance competencies and civic skills on a more general level (e.g., in school education).

This chapter represents only a first draft and illustration of necessary competencies for reflexive governance processes. Nevertheless, it seems promising to integrate micro-level factors and especially individual competencies in future models of reflexive governance. Additional research should test and differentiate these competencies—preferably with more rigid methodologies than applied in this study—to determine whether a lack of competencies qualifies as an important barrier of reflexive governance processes in other fields of application (apart from climate change adaptation). In addition to competencies, these studies should address further success factors and barriers to gain insight into the relative importance of competencies for the functioning of reflexive governance processes. For example, cooperative behavior could be a function of an individual's degree of organizational freedom rather than individual competency. Further on, the competencies need to be made operational in two ways: First, reliable and valid instruments need to be developed to measure competencies, not only for research purposes but also for the selection of people for key positions in reflexive governance processes. Second, operational tools, procedures, and conditions need to be designed for training individuals and stakeholders in necessary competencies that will allow them to become effectively involved in reflexive governance processes.

Notes

1. The two interviewees had access to information on how the adaptation process proceeded but were not involved in this activity. Therefore, they had no reason to present the adaptation process in a positively biased way. They were questioned independently from each other and their "stories" of the adaptation process were congruent.

Conclusion

Tom Dedeurwaerdere, Eric Brousseau, and Bernd Siebenhüner

Since the publication of the ground-breaking work on global public goods by Inge Kaul and her associates a decade ago (Kaul, Grunberg, and Stern 1999; Kaul et al 2003), many political initiatives have been launched, a wide number of governance experiments have been run, and much research has been carried out at the interface of economic, political, and environmental sciences. This interdisciplinary book has looked into the new challenges in the governance of global public goods in fields of environmental concern and emerging global issues such as global health, food security, and technological risks. It condensed the knowledge that has been accumulated over the years and develops novel perspectives for understanding and designing governance of global public goods.

Following Kaul's argument, this book started out with the insight that the traditional political approach of public good provision is oversimplified because it is fundamentally state-centered (both at the national and international level) and fiscally focused, and therefore fails to consider the broader politics and economics of multi-stakeholder and transnational public good provision. As a consequence, global public good approaches remain insufficiently aligned with the specific understandings and the incentives of the various actors that play a role in their provision, such as nongovernmental organizations, civic movements, social networks, and international organizations. Moreover, and this is the central argument of this volume, most traditional approaches underestimate the fact that the knowledge of the actors about issues at stake and about governance is bounded, resulting in the need to share and generate knowledge through appropriate governance solutions.

At the same time, the analysis in this book shows that the state/government continues to play a key role in any solution for improving the provision of GPG, whether through its involvement in transnational coordination to overcome global tragedies of the commons, or through the design of markets or incentives aimed at impacting on behaviors and coordination though economically grounded mechanisms.

Nevertheless, while it recognizes that any policy for GPG provision should build upon this conventional layer of policy making, the insufficiency of the traditional perspective focused either on command and control or market-based mechanisms has been increasingly clear. First, states tend to ignore the actual motivations (and their diversities) of all kinds of stakeholders and, therefore, their likelihood to contribute to the provision of public goods. Ignoring social or intrinsic nonmonetary values when designing instruments leads to unexpected consequences; crowding out being one of the worse. Second, governments also lack knowledge about the many decentralized social interactions that might open opportunities for cooperation at many levels and that are often the crucible of innovations due to the meeting of evolving needs with transforming opportunities and capabilities. Therefore states fail to correct both market and regulation insufficiencies without the involvement of the individual and collective actors affected by the collective decision making over GPG.

As explained in part I, many GPG problems are quite abstract or complex, such as global genetic diversity or technological risks, and extend far beyond the usual areas of legitimacy of the states, which are built within the boundaries of their jurisdiction and within the frame of specific constitutional pacts encompassing, before all, security and economic prosperity. As a result, many individuals have no clear collective preferences over GPG, nor do they recognize themselves necessarily as members of a global community. Moreover, as in other cases of public goods provision, they have to balance many conflicting claims, such as between economic, social, and environmental goals. Therefore, in the absence of the organization of processes of social learning over GPG, and without the involvement of the civil society organizations that play a role in this social learning (e.g. consumer movements, user organizations, or professional federations), the new policies will most likely fail to deliver and would probably face low rates of adoption.

The main insight that comes out of the analysis of these governance needs as developed in this book is that the effective governance of global public goods needs to be democratic, reflexive, and knowledge based. As seen throughout the book, this has major implications for the various disciplines that analyze GPG provision, in which many new approaches and lines of research have been developed to address broadening the conventional approach to public good provision, such as within economics, political science, and social studies of the science-policy interface. At the same time, these insights also have important practical implications. Many new experiments have been run, with a view toward organizing more participatory modes of knowledge gathering—for example, through the involvement of user groups and stakeholders, along with scientific experts, in environmental impact assessment or in deliberative policy planning. Examples discussed in this volume include citizen juries, multi-stakeholder processes, consensus conferences, and comanagement arrangements. Moreover, taking into account knowledge and values/ beliefs reinforces the interest of multilevel governance. Indeed, the provision of many public goods, while they are transnational or global, can rely on efforts undertaken at the local level; the issue of governance being then to coordinate the various levels at which governance is performed.

The results of these governance innovations, however, have been mixed so far. First of all, as shown in chapter 5, these innovations have not been without ambiguity. Indeed, the turn toward more reflexive forms of rule making has been accompanied in some countries by a restriction of state involvement in public good provision. In these cases, the new forms of governance are used as a substitute to state intervention, instead of a necessary complement to the conventional state and market based contributions to GPG governance as discussed above. Second, in other situations, some of these governance innovations have lead to sub-optimal provision of public goods, whether through a partial capture of the process by private sector actors which attempt to water down the regulatory targets, as discussed in chapter 10, or through the existence of major information asymmetries that leave the non-informed parties worse off, as shown for example in the case study of bioprospecting agreements in chapter 6.

Because of these and other difficulties, a critical assessment of the new modes of governance is essential to improve their contribution to GPG provision. Such a critical assessment, which is already established in many areas of the social sciences and humanities, can build on the new research directions in economics, political science, and science and society studies developed in this book. They call for a further reform of GPG policies from a double critical perspective. First, as clearly summarized in chapter 2, GPG policies need to move away from a technocratic and abstract approach to GPG and organize instead a discussion on GPG around the three dimensions of publicness in matter of access, use, and decision making. Second, while recognizing the key role of formal criteria such as transparency, adequacy, and equity in building the normative legitimacy of deliberation (the focus of much work on reflexive governance processes, such as that of Hajer and Wagenaar [2003]), real-world constraints on the processes of social learning, the effects of complex incentives, and the coordination costs involved in knowledge gathering on collective preferences over GPG and the design of solutions, deserve greater attention in the organization of deliberation over GPG.

The empirical research developed in this book aims to contribute to such an assessment. The results of these studies have important policy implications for further reform of GPG policy. Four cross-cutting themes with direct implications for policy making have emerged from the analysis in this book.

First, policies for global goods, such as biodiversity, sustainable farming, and food security need to address both monetary and nonmonetary values, as shown in various chapters in this volume. An example of a policy innovation reflecting this need, which is reviewed in chapter 12, is the establishment of value articulating institutions at the science and policy interface, which aim at combining quantitative assessment and social learning over values by involving concerned stakeholders in systematic multi-criteria assessment over various scenarios of GPG provision. Another example, analyzed in chapter 11, is the reform of conventional regulation of natural resources through the establishment of decentralized comanagement authorities that make decisions based on extensive deliberation on management priorities among owners, users, and managers of these resources.

A second cross-cutting policy implication is the need to create a better fit between the adopted policy measures on the one hand, and the social norms and collective preferences of citizens and social movements at various levels of governance on the other. The analysis of the role of social norms in compliance processes shows the need to shift from a sole focus on global citizenship as a basis for building legitimacy for policy making on GPG to a recognition of the contribution of initiatives undertaken at many levels, including very local ones. An illustration of this is the discussion in chapter 7 of the measures to be taken for implementing the precautionary principle. As shown, minimal standards for risk regulation developed at the global level should be complemented with a recognition of national and regional collective preferences that might call for stronger measures, such as those expressed by consumer and environmental movements in Europe. Similarly, the case study in chapter 8 of climate-friendly regulation at a subnational level in Brazil showed how a complex interaction between subnational and global social movements and policy initiatives built legitimacy for effective climate policies, when the national government failed to take appropriate action.

Third, a more interactive knowledge-generation process is needed to support planning and evidence-based policy making for GPGs, with a view that better reflects both local knowledge and preferences, and the complex interactions between ecological and social dynamics. As shown in the analysis of the United Kingdom's biodiversity policy in chapter 14, the failure of a bureaucratic process centered on the sole gathering of biological species data, led to reconsider the dynamic interactions between the social economic system and the natural environment. This made it possible to involve the many stakeholders and more effectively bring their input into a collective planning exercise. Similarly, as analyzed in chapter 9, introducing multifunctional agriculture in the European Union played a key role in reframing the deliberation process in the reform of its common agricultural policy.

Finally, the analysis of knowledge generation shows the need to address important trade-offs when building institutional arrangements for deliberation on GPG provision. Indeed, as shown in chapter 13, the latter is not only a matter of organizing the generation of knowledge, but also of finding the most appropriate way to make it available into the collective decision making, which includes the formation of individual and collective preferences. Examples of cost-effective solutions for addressing such cognitive needs for social learning and deliberation discussed in this chapter can be found in umbrella organizations such as the IUCN or the civil society partnerships proposed at the world summit in Johannesburg. Another case, analyzed in chapter 15, is the organization of a more interactive water management policy in Germany, with a view to overcoming the learning deficiencies of centralized bureaucratic administrations that fail to define appropriate risk levels to deal with the consequences of global climate change.

As can be seen from this overview of the policy implications of the theoretical and empirical analysis of GPG governance in this volume, the move toward more reflexive, knowledge-based, and democratic governance calls for a rebalancing of the role of markets, states, and civil society in the policy-making process. As a result, instead of the usual debate on more or less state involvement as compared to the markets, the policy recommendations point to the need for a qualitative broadening of the role of the state beyond its conventional function in direct regulation to new roles in accompanying processes of norm formation and decentralized collective problem solving. However, as also appears from our analysis, the proposed reforms in governance are part of an ongoing journey with many uncertainties still ahead. Nevertheless, we hope that the increased attention to reflexive governance processes advocated in this volume will contribute to a better understanding of the need for improvement of GPG provision and the possible options for doing so in an increasingly cosmopolitan world order.

References

Abbott, A. 1988. *The system of professions: An essay on the division of expert labor*. Chicago: University of Chicago Press.

ABEMA. 2008. Web site of the Brazilian Association of State Departments of Environmental Protection. http://www.abema.org.br.

Abram, D. 1996. *The spell of the sensuous*. New York: Vintage.

Ackrill, R. 2005. The common agricultural policy. In *Handbook of public administration and policy in the European Union*, ed. M. P. van der Hoek, 435–487. Boca Raton, FL: Taylor & Francis.

Adams, W. M. 1997. Rationalization and conservation: Ecology and the management of nature in the United Kingdom. *Transactions of the Institute of British Geographers* 22:277–291.

Adger, W. N., S. Agrawala, M. M. Q. Mirza, C. Conde, K. O'Brien, J. P. R. Pulhin, B. Smit, and K. Takahashi. 2007. Assessment of adaptation practices, options, constraints and capacity. In *Climate change 2007: Impacts, adaptation and vulnerability. Contribution of Working Group II to the fourth assessment report of the Intergovernmental Panel on Climate Change*, ed. M. L. Parry, O. F. Canziani, J. P. Palutikof, P. J. van der Linden, and C. E. Hanson, 717–743. Cambridge: Cambridge University Press.

Adman, P. 2008. Does workplace experience enhance political participation? A critical test of a venerable hypothesis. *Political Behavior* 30 (1): 115–138.

Akerlof, G. A. 1984. *An economic theorist's book of tales*. Cambridge: Cambridge University Press.

Albin, C. 2001. *Justice and fairness in international negotiation*. Cambridge: Cambridge University Press.

Alchian, A., and H. Demsetz. 1972. Production, information costs and economic organization. *American Economic Review* 62 (5): 777–795.

Aldred, J. 2006. Incommensurability and monetary valuation. *Land Economics* 82 (2): 141–161.

Alfsen, K., and T. Skodvin. 1998. The Intergovernmental Panel on Climate Change (IPCC) and scientific consensus. How scientists come to say what they say about climate change. [Center for International Climate and Environmental Research, Oslo.] *CICERO Policy Note* 1998:3.

Allen, P. 2001. Knowledge, ignorance and the evolution of complex systems. In *Frontiers of evolutionary economics—competition, self-organization and innovation policy*, ed. J. Foster and J. S. Metcalfe, 313–350. Cheltenham, UK: Edward Elgar.

Anand, P. B. 2004. Financing the provision of global public goods. *World Economy* 27 (2): 215–237.

Anderson, E. 1993. *Value in ethics and economics*. Cambridge, MA: Harvard University Press.

Anderson, P. W., K. J. Arrow, and D. Pines. 1988. *The economy as an evolving complex system*. Reading, MA: Addison-Wesley Pub. Co.

Anheier, H., M. Glasius, and M. Kaldor, eds. 2004. *Global civil society 2004/05*. London: SAGE Publications.

Aoki, M. 2001. *Toward a comparative institutional analysis*. Cambridge, MA: MIT Press.

Arce, D. G. 2001. Leadership and the aggregation of international collective action. *Oxford Economic Papers* 53 (1): 114–137.

Arce, D. G., and T. Sandler. 2001. Transnational public goods: Strategies and institutions. *European Journal of Political Economy* 17 (3): 493–516.

Arce, D. G., and T. Sandler. 2002. *Regional public goods: Typologies, provisions, financing, and development assistance*. Stockholm: Almqvist and Wiksell International.

Argyris, C., and D. A. Schön. 1978. *Organizational learning: A theory of action perspective*. Reading, MA: Addison-Wesley.

Argyris, C., and D. A. Schön. 1996. *Organizational learning II: Theory, method, and practice*. Reading, MA: Addison-Wesley.

Arrow, K. J. 1950. A difficulty in the concept of social welfare. *Journal of Political Economy* 58 (4): 328–346.

Arrow, K. J. 1962. Economic welfare and the allocation of resources for invention. In *The rate and direction of inventive activity: Economic and social factors*, ed. H. M. Groves, 609–626. Cambridge, MA: National Bureau Committee for Economic Research.

Ayres, I., and J. Braithwaite. 1992. *Responsive regulation: Transcending the deregulation ebate*. New York: Oxford University Press.

Bache, I., and M. Flinders, eds. 2004. *Multi-level governance*. Oxford: Oxford University Press.

Balmford, A., P. Crane, A. Dobson, R. E. Green, and G. M. Mace. 2005. The 2010 challenge: Data availability, information needs and extraterrestrial insights. *Philosophical Transactions of the Royal Society B-Biological Sciences* 360:221–228.

Baranek, E., and B. Günther. 2005. Erfolgsfaktoren von Partizipation in Naturschutzgroßprojekten—Das Beispiel: Moderationsverfahren im Gewässerrandstreifenprojekt Spreewald. In *Partizipation, Öffentlichkeitsbeteiligung, Nachhaltigkeit. Perspektiven der Politischen Ökonomie*, ed. P. H. Feindt and J. Newig. Marburg, Germany: Metropolis-Verlag: 299–319.

Bardach, E., and R. Kagan. 1982. *Going by the book: The problem of regulatory unreasonableness*. Philadelphia: Temple University Press.

Bastmeijer, K., and J. Verschuuren. 2005. NGO-business collaborations and the law: Sustainability, limitations of law and the changing relationship between companies and NGOs. In *Corporate social responsibility, accountability and governance*, ed. Istemi Demirag, 314–329. Sheffield, UK: Greenleaf.

Bateman, I. J., and J. Mawby. 2004. First impressions count: Interviewer appearance and information effects in stated preference studies. *Ecological Economics* 49 (1):47–55.

Bateson, G. 1972. *Steps to an ecology of mind: Collected essays in anthropology, psychiatry, evolution, and epistemology*. Chicago: University of Chicago Press.

Baylis, R., L. Cornnell, and A. Flynn. 1998. Sector variation and ecological modernization: towards an analysis at the level of the firm. *Business Strategy and the Environment* 7:150–161.

Beck, U. 1992. *The risk society—towards a new modernity*. Thousand Oaks, CA: Sage Publications.

Beck, U., A. Giddens, and S. Lash. 1994. *Reflexive modernization*. Cambridge, MA: Polity Press.

Beck, U., W. Bonss, and C. Lau. 2003. The theory of reflexive modernization: Problematic, hypotheses and research programme. *Theory, Culture & Society* 20 (2):1–33.

Beck, U. 2007. The cosmopolitan condition: Why methodological nationalism fails. *Theory, Culture & Society* 24 (7–8):286–290.

Becker, G. S. 1976. *The economic approach to human behavior*. Chicago: Chicago University Press.

BEESP. 2006. *Balanço energético do Estado de São Paulo 2006—ano base 2005*. São Paulo: Secretaria de Energia.

Beierle, T. C., and J. Cayford. 2002. *Democracy in practice. Public participation in environmental decisions*. Washington, DC: Resources for the Future.

Beinat, E., and P. Nijkamp. 1998. *Multicriteria analysis for land-use management*. Dordrecht, Netherlands: Kluwer Academic Publishers.

Belvèze , H. 2003. The precautionary principle and its legal implications in the area of food safety. *Revue Scientifique et Technique* [International Office of Epizootics] 22 (2):387–393.

Biermann, F., and P. Pattberg. 2008. Global environmental governance: taking stock, moving forward. *Annual Review of Environment and Resources* 33:277–294.

Biodiversity Reporting and Information Group. 2007. *Report on the species and habitats review*. UK Biodiversity Partnership.

Black, J. 2001. Decentering regulation: Understanding the role of regulation and self-regulation in a post-regulatory world. *Current Legal Problems* 54:103–146.

Black, J. 2006. Managing regulatory risks and defining the parameters of blame: A focus on the Australian Prudential Regulation Authority. *Law & Policy* 28 (1): 1–30.

Bluff, L., and N. Gunningham. 2004. Principle, process, performance or What? New approaches to OHS standard setting. In *OHS Regulation for a Changing World of Work*, ed. L. Bluff, N. Gunningham, and R. Johnstone. Sydney: Federation Press.

Bodansky, D. 1999. The legitimacy of international governance: a coming challenge for international environmental law? *American Journal of International Law* 93 (3): 596–624.

Bohman, J. 2004. Republican cosmopolitanism. *Journal of Political Philosophy* 12 (3): 336–352.

Bohnet, I., B. S. Frey, and S. Huck. 2000. More order with less law: On contract enforcement, trust and crowding. *American Political Science Review* 95:131–144.

Boltanski, L., and L. Thévenot. 2006. *On justification—economies of worth.* Princeton, NJ: Princeton University Press.

Booth, A., and S. Welch. 1978. Stress, health, and political participation. *Social Biology* 25 (2): 102–114.

Bora, Alfons. 2006. Scientific norms, legal facts, and the politics of knowledge. http://www.uni-bielefeld.de/iwt/personen/bora/pdf/Alfons%20Bora%20-%20Scientific%20norms%202006-03%2020%20KorrGA%20AB.pdf.

Bosgroep Zuiderkempen. 2006. Werkplan v.z.w. Bosgroep Zuiderkempen (January 1, 2007–December 31, 2012). Westerlo, Belgium.

Bosgroepen. 2005. Bosgroepen, missie en visie.Unpublished manuscript. Brussels, Belgium.

Bowker, G. C. 2000. Biodiversity datadiversity. *Social Studies of Science* 30:643–683.

Boyle, J. 2007. Mertonianism unbound? Imagining free, decentralized access to most cultural and scientific material. In *Understanding knowledge as a commons*, ed. C. Hess and E. Ostrom, 123–144. Cambridge, MA: MIT Press.

Braithwaite, J. 2002. *Restorative justice and responsive regulation.* New York: Oxford University Press.

Braun, D. 1993. Zur Steuerbarkeit funktionaler Teilsysteme. Akteurtheoretische Sichtweisen funktionaler Differenzierung moderner Gesellschaften. In *Policy-Analyse. Kritik und Neuorientierung, Sonderheft der Politischen Vierteljahresschrift 24*, ed. A. Héritier, 199–222. Opladen, Germany: Westdeutscher Verlag.

Brennan, G., and P. Pettit. 2004. *The economy of esteem: An essay on civil and political society.* Oxford: Oxford University Press.

Brousseau, E., and E. Raynaud. 2011 . Climbing the hierarchical ladders of rules: The dynamics of institutional frameworks. *Journal of Economic Behavior & Organization* 79: 65–79.

Brousseau, E., and J.-M. Glachant, eds. 2008. *New institutional economics: A guidebook*. Cambridge: Cambridge University Press.

Brown, H., M. De Jong, and T. Lessidrenska. 2007. Can the global reporting initiative become a global institution. Paper presented at the Amsterdam Conference on the Human Dimensions of Global Environment Change, Amsterdam. http://www.2007amsterdamconference.org.

Brown, T. C., and G. L. Peterson, and B. L. Tonn. 1995. The values jury to aid natural resource decisions. *Land Economics* 71 (2): 250–260.

Browne, W. P., J. R. Skees, L. E. Swanson, P. B. Thompson, and L. J. Unnevehr. 1992. *Sacred Cows and Hot Potatoes: Agrarian Myths in Agricultural Policy*. Boulder, CO: Westview Press.

Brunson, M. W., D. T. Yarrow, S. D. Roberts, D. C. Guynn, Jr., and M. R. Kuhns. 1996. Non-industrial private forest owners and ecosystem management: can they work together? *Journal of Forestry* 94 (6): 14–21.

Buchanan, J. M., and R. A. Musgrave. 1999. *Public finance and public choice: Two contrasting views on the state*. Cambridge, MA: MIT Press.

Bulkeley, H. 2005. Reconfiguring environmental governance: Towards a politics of scales and networks. *Political Geography* 24:875–902.

Bulkeley, H., and A. P. J. Mol. 2003. Participation and environmental governance: Consensus, ambivalence and debate. *Environmental Values* 12 (2): 143–154.

Bulkeley, H., and M. Betsill. 2003. *Cities and climate change—urban sustainability and global environmental governance*. London: Routledge.

Bullock, R. J., and M. E. Tubbs. 1987. The case meta-analysis method for OD. *Research in Organizational Change and Development* 1:171–228.

Burgess, H. 1983. Environmental mediation (the Foothills case). In *Resolving environmental regulatory disputes*, ed. L. Susskind, L. Bacow, and M. Wheeler, 156–221. Cambridge, MA: Schenkman Publishing Company.

Burgess, H., and D. Smith. 1983. The uses of mediation (the Brayton Point coal conversion case). In *Resolving environmental regulatory disputes*, ed. L. Susskind, L. Bacow, and M. Wheeler, 122–155. Cambridge, MA: Schenkman Publishing Company.

Burgess, H., D. Hoffman, and M. Lucci. 1983. Negotiation in the rulemaking process (the 301 (h) Case). In *Resolving environmental regulatory disputes*, ed. L. Susskind, L. Bacow, and M. Wheeler, 222–256. Cambridge, MA: Schenkman Publishing Company.

Burgess, J. 2000. Situating knowledges, sharing values and reaching collective decisions: The cultural turn in environmental decision-making. In *Cultural turns/geographical turns*, ed. S. Naylor, J. Ryan, I. Cook, and D. Crouch, 273–287. Harlow, UK: Prentice Hall.

Burroughs, R. 1999. When stakeholders choose: Process, knowledge, and motivation in water quality decisions. Society & Natural Resources 12 (8): 797–809.

Camacho, A. 2007. Can regulation evolve? Lessons from a study in maladaptive management. *UCLA Law Review* 55:293–358.

Cameron, J., and W. D. Pierce. 1994. Reinforcement, Reward, and Intrinsic Motivation: A Meta-Analysis. *Review of Educational Research* 64:363–423.

Carraro, C., ed. 2003. *Governing the global environment.* Cheltenham, UK: Edward Elgar.

Charnovitz, S. 2005. An analysis of Pascal Lamy's proposal on collective preferences. *Journal of International Economic Law* 8 (2): 449–472.

Chawla, L., and D.-F. Cushing. 2007. Education for strategic environmental behavior. *Environmental Education Research* 13 (4): 437–452.

Chichilnisky, G., and G. Heal, eds. 2000. *Environmental markets—equity and efficiency.* New York: Columbia University Press.

Choo, E. U., B. Schoner, and W. Wedley 1999. Interpretation of criteria weights in multicriteria decision making. *Computers & Industrial Engineering* 37:527–541.

Christoforou, Th. 2002. The origins, content and role of the precautionary principle in European Community Law. In *Le principe de précaution—Aspects de droit international et communautaire,* ed. Ch. Leben and J. Verhoeven, 205–230. Paris: Ed. Panthéon-Assas.

Clampitt, P. G., and M. L. Williams. 2000. Managing organizational uncertainty: Conceptualization and measurement. Paper presented at the ICA convention.

Clark, J., J. Burgess, N. Dando, D.Bhattachary,K.Heppel,J. Murlis, and P. Wood. 1998. Prioritising the issues in local environment agency plans through consensus building with stakeholder groups. London, Environment Agency, R&D Technical Report W114.

Clinton, W., and A. Gore. 1995. *Reinventing environmental regulation.* http:// govinfo.library.unt.edu/npr/library/rsreport/251a.html.

Coase, R. 1937. The nature of the firm. *Economica* 4:386–405.

Coase, R. 1960. The problem of social cost. *Journal of Law & Economics* 3 (1): 1–44.

Coase, R. 1988. *The firm, the market and the law.* Chicago: The University of Chicago Press.

Coglianese, C. 1997. Assessing consensus: The promise and performance of negotiated rule-making. *Duke Law Journal* 46:1255–1346.

Coglianese, C., and J. Nash, eds. 2006. *Leveraging the private sector.* Washington, DC: RFF Press.

Cohen, J. 1989. Deliberative democracy and democratic legitimacy. In *The good polity,* ed. A. Hamlin and Ph. Pettit, 17–34. Oxford: Blackwell.

Cohen, J., and C. Sabel. 2003. Sovereignty and solidarity: EU and US. In *Governing work and welfare in a new economy: European and American experiments*, ed. J. Zeitlin and D. Trubek, 345–375. Oxford: Oxford University Press.

Cohen, Joshua. 1998. The significance of critical communication skills. In *The public voice in a democracy at risk*, ed. M. Salvador and P. M. Sias, 41–56. Westport, CT: Praeger.

Cohen, M. 1997. Risk society and ecological modernisation. *Futures* 29 (2): 105–119.

Coleman, W. D. 1998. From protected development to market liberalism: Paradigm change in agriculture. *Journal of European Public Policy* 5 (4): 632–651.

Coleman, W. D., and W. Grant. 1998. Policy convergence and policy feedback: Agricultural finance policies in a globalizing era. *European Journal of Political Research* 34 (2): 225–247.

Coleman, W. D., G. D. Skogstad, and M. M. Atkinson. 1997. Paradigm shifts and policy networks: Cumulative change in agriculture. *Journal of Public Policy* 16 (3): 273–301.

Coleman, W. D., W. Grant, and T. Josling. 2004. *Agriculture in the new global economy*. Cheltenham, UK: Edward Elgar.

Collier, P. 1997. The failure of conditionality. In *Perspectives on aid and development*, ed. C. Gwin, and J. M. Nelson, 51–77. Washington, DC: Overseas Development Council.

Collier, P., L. Elliott, H. Hegre, A. Hoeffler, M. Reynal-Querol, and N. Sambanis. 2003. *Breaking the conflict trap: Civil war and development policy*. Washington, DC: World Bank and Oxford University Press.

Commission of the European Communities. 2000. *Communication on the precautionary principle*. Brussels.

Commission of the European Communities. 1985. *Perspectives for the common agricultural policy*. Brussels.

Commission on Global Governance. 1995. *Our global neighbourhood*. Oxford: Oxford University Press.

Conceição, P., and R. U. Mendoza. 2006. Identifying high-return investments: A methodology for assessing when international cooperation pays—and for whom. In *The new public finance: Responding to global challenges*, ed. I. Kaul and P. Conceição. New York: Oxford University Press.

Conover, P., and D. Searing. 2000. A political socialization perspective. In *Rediscovering the democratic purposes of education*, ed. L. McDonnell, P. Timpane, and R. Benjamin. Lawrence: University Press of Kansas.

Cooke, B. 2001. The social psychological limits of participation? In *Participation: The new tyranny?* ed. B. Cooke and U. Kothari, 102–121. London, New York: Zed Books.

Cooke, B., and U. Kothari, eds. 2001. *Participation: The new tyranny?* London, New York: Zed Books.

Cornes, R., and T. Sandler. 1984. Easy riders, joint production, and public goods. *Economic Journal* 94 (3): 580–598.

Cornes, R., and T. Sandler. 1996. *The theory of externalities, public goods, and club goods.* 2nd ed. Cambridge: Cambridge University Press.

Cullis, J., and P. Jones. 1998. *Public finance and public choice: Alternative perspectives.* New York: Oxford University Press.

Cupps, D. S. 1977. Emerging problems of citizen participation. *Public administration review* 37 (5): 478–487.

Dahl, R. A. 1994. A democratic dilemma: System effectiveness versus citizen participation. *Political Science Quarterly* 109 (1):23–34.

Dahl, R. A. 1999a. Can international organizations be democratic? A skeptic's view. In *Democracy's edges*, ed. I. Shapiro and C. Hacker-Cordon, 19–36. Cambridge: Cambridge University Press.

Dahl, R. A. 1999b. The shifting boundaries of democratic governments. *Social Research* 66 (3): 915–931.

Daugbjerg, C. 2003. Policy feedback and paradigm shift in EU agricultural policy: The effects of the MacSharry reform on future reform. *Journal of European Public Policy* 10 (3): 421–437.

Davies, G., J. Burgess, and A. Stirling 2003. *Deliberative mapping: Appraising options for addressing "the kidney gap."* London, Final Report to the Wellcome Trust.

Dawes, R. M. 1988. *Rational choice in an uncertain world.* San Diego, New York: Harcourt, Brace, Yovanovich.

Delmas, M. A., and O. Young. 2009. *Governance for the environment: New perspectives.* Cambridge: Cambridge University Press.

De Montis, A., P. De Toro, B. Droste-Franke, I. Omann, and S. Stagl. 2005. Criteria for quality assessment of MCDA methods. In *Alternatives for environmental evaluation*, ed. M. Getzner, C. Spash, and S. Stagl, 99–133. London: Routledge.

De Schutter, O., and S. Deakin, eds. 2005. *Social rights and market forces: Is open coordination of employment and social policies the future of social Europe?* Brussels: Bruylant.

Deci, E. L. 1971. Effects of externally mediated rewards on intrinsic motivation. *Journal of Personality and Social Psychology* 18 (1): 105–115.

Deci, E. L., and R. Flaste. 1995. *Why we do what we do: The dynamics of personal autonomy.* New York: Putnam.

Deci, E. L., and R. M. Ryan. 1985. *Intrinsic motivation and self-determination in human behavior.* New York: Plenum Press.

Deci, E. L., R. Koestner, and R. M. Ryan. 1999. A meta-analytic review of experiments examining the effects of extrinsic rewards on intrinsic motivation. *Psychological Bulletin* 125 (6): 627–668.

Dedeurwaerdere, T. 2005. From bioprospecting to reflexive governance. *Ecological Economics* 53 (4): 473–491.

Dedeurwaerdere, T. 2006. The institutional economics of sharing biological information. *International Social Science Journal* 188:351–368.

Dedeurwaerdere, Tom. 2009. Engaging with reflexive governance. Presentation at the IDDRI-AgroParisTech-REFGOV-IUFRO International Symposium, Nancy, France. http://www.iddri.org/Activites/Conferences-Internationales/090622 _Nancy_IUFRO_RefGov_Dedeurwaerdere.pdf.

DEFRA. 2006. The UK Biodiversity Action Plan: Highlights of the 2005 reporting round. http://jncc.defra.gov.uk/PDF/UKBAP_2005ReportHighlights.pdf.

Delli Carpini, M. X., F. L. Cook, and L. R. Jacobs. 2004. Public deliberation, discursive participation, and citizen engagement: A review of the empirical literature. *Annual Review of Political Science* 7:315–344.

Dembart, L., and R. Kwartler. 1980. The Snoqualmie River conflict: Bringing mediation into environmental disputes. In *Roundtable justice. Case studies in conflict resolution*, ed. R. B. Goldmann, 39–58. Boulder, CO: Westview Press.

Demsetz, H. 1969. Information and efficiency: Another viewpoint. *Journal of Law & Economics* 12:1–22.

Dewey, J. 1916. *Democracy and education: An introduction to the philosophy of education*. New York: Macmillan.

Diduck, A., and A. J. Sinclair. 2002. Public involvement in environmental assessment: The case of the nonparticipant. *Environmental Management* 29 (4): 578–588.

Dienel, P. C. 1989. Contributing to social decision methodology: Citizen reports on technological projects. In *Social decision methology for technological projects*, ed. C. Vlek and G. Cvetkovic, 133–150. Dordrecht, Netherlands: Kluwer Academic Publishers.

Dienel, P. C., and O. Renn. 1995. Planning cells: A gate to "fractal" mediation. In *Fairness and competence in citizen participation—evaluating new models for environmental discourse*, ed. O. Renn, T. Webler, and P. Wiedermann, 117–140. Dordrecht, Netherlands: Kluwer Academic Publishers.

Dingwerth, Klaus. 2007. *The new transnationalism: Private transnational governance and its democratic legitimacy*. Basingstoke, UK: Palgrave Macmillan.

Diringer, E. 2003. Overview. In *Beyond Kyoto: Advancing the international effort against climate change*, ed. Joseph Aldy. Washington, DC: Pew Center on Global Climate Change.

Djupe, P. A., and J. T. Grant. 2001. Religious institutions and political participation in America. *Journal for the Scientific Study of Religion* 40 (2): 303–314.

Dobozy, E. 2007. Effective learning of civic skills: Democratic schools succeed in nurturing the critical capacities of students. *Educational Studies* 33 (2): 115–128.

Dodgson, J., and M. Spackman, A. Pearman, and L. Phillips, 2000. Multi-criteria analysis: A manual. London, Department for Transport, Local Government and the Regions (DLTR). http://eprints.lse.ac.uk/12761/1/Multi-criteria _Analysis.pdf

Dolsak, N., and E. Ostrom, eds. 2003. *The commons in the new millennium*. Cambridge, MA: MIT Press.

Dorf, M., and C. Sabel. 1998. A constitution of democratic experimentalism. *Columbia Law Review* 89:267–473.

Doyle, T. 2000. *Green power: The environmental movement in Australia*. Sydney: UNSW Press.

Dressel, K. 2002. *BSE—the new dimension of uncertainty: The cultural politics of science and decision making*. Berlin: Edition Sigma.

Dryzek, J. 1997. *The politics of the Earth: Environmental discourses*. New York: Oxford University Press.

Dryzek, J., D. Downes, C. Hunold, and D. Schlosberg. 2005. Green political strategy and the state: Combining political theory and comparative history. In *The state and the global ecological crisis*, ed. J. Barry and R. Eckersley, 75–96. Cambridge, MA: MIT Press.

Dumortier M., L. De Bruyn L., M. Hens M., J. Peymen, A. Schneiders, T. Van Daele, W. Van Reeth, G. Weyembergh, and E. Kuijken. 2006. Biodiversity Indicators 2006. State of nature in Flanders (Belgium). Brussels: Research Institute for Nature and forest.

Durkheim, E. [1893] 1967. De la division du travail social. Huitième edition. Paris: Les Presses universitaire de France.

Edgar, S. L. 1990. Wisconsin groundwater legislation negotiations. In *Environmental disputes: Community involvement in conflict resolution*, ed. J. E. Crowfoot and J. M. Wondolleck, 226–253. Washington, DC: Island Press.

Eggertsson, T. 2005. *Imperfect institutions*. Ann Arbor: University of Michigan Press.

Elder, P. S. 1982. Project approval, environmental assessment and public participation. *Environmentalist* 2:55–71.

Elliott, E. 1994. Environmental TQM: Anatomy of a pollution control program that works! *Michigan Law Review* 92:1840–1849.

Elliott, M. L. P. 1984. Improving community acceptance of hazardous waste facilities through alternative systems for mitigating and managing risk. *Hazardous Waste* 1 (3): 397–410.

Elster, J. 1998. Deliberation and constitution making. In *Deliberative democracy*, ed. J. Elster, 97–122. Cambridge: Cambridge University Press.

Engel, K. H., and B. Y. Orbach. 2008. Micro-motives and state and local climate change initiatives. *Harvard Law and Policy Review* 2:119–137.

England Biodiversity Group. 2007. Refreshing the Biodiversity Partnership in England. Notes of a workshop on March 1, 2007. http://www.ukbap.org.uk/ebg/library/WorkshopNote_01_03_07.pdf.

Estevadeordal, A., B. Franz, and T. R. Nguyen, eds. 2004. *Regional public goods: From theory to practice*. Washington, DC: Inter-American Development Bank and Asian Development Bank.

Eswaran, M., and N. Gallini. 1996. Patent policy and the direction of technological change. *Rand Journal of Economics* 27:722–746.

European Commission. 2001. White paper on European Governance European Commission 2001. http://eur-lex.europa.eu/LexUriServ/site/en/com/2001/com2001_0428en01.pdf.

European Commission. 2006. Report on the distribution of direct aids to the producers (financial year 2004). Brussels. http://ec.europa.eu/agriculture/fin/directaid/2004/annex2_en.pdf.

European Community. 2006a. Council regulation (EC) No 509/2006 of 20 March 2006 on agricultural products and foodstuffs as traditional specialities guaranteed.

European Community. 2006b. Council Regulation (EC) No 510/2006 of 20 March 2006 on the protection of geographical indications and designations of origin for agricultural products and foodstuffs.

European Community. 2006c. EC 1907 regulation No 1907/2006 of the European Parliament. http://eur-lex.europa.eu/LexUriServ/LexUriServ.do?uri=CELEX:32006R1907:EN:NOT.

European Council. Resolution on the precautionary principle, Annex III of Conclusions of Presidency, European Council of Nice, 7–9 December 2000.

European Parliament and Council of the European Union. Regulation (EC) No 178/2002 of 28 January 2002 laying down the general principles and requirements of food law, establishing the European Food Safety Authority and laying down procedures in matters of food safety. *Official Journal of the European Communities*, L31: 1–24.

European Union. 2002. Guidance on public participation in relation to the Water Framework Directive: Active involvement, consultation, and public access to information. Common implementation strategy guidance document No. 8. Luxemburg.

Evenson, R., D. Gollin, and V. Santaniello, eds. 1998. *Agricultural values of genetic resources*. London: CABI.

Farnsworth, N., ed. 1988. *Screening plants for new medicines*. Washington, DC: National Academy Press.

FBMC. 2008. Web site of the Brazilian Forum on Climate Change. http://forumclima.org.br.

Feagan, R. 2007. The place of food: Mapping out the "local" in local food regimes. *Progress in Human Geography* 31 (1): 23–42.

Feindt, P. H. 2007. Harmonisierung, Problemdruck, Kommunikation. Konvergenz in der Agrarpolitik der OECD-Länder, 1986–2004. In *Transfer, Diffusion und Konvergenz von Politiken. PVS-Sonderheft 38/2007*, ed. K. Holzinger, H. Jörgens, and C. Knill, 496–521. Wiesbaden, Germany: VS Verlag.

Feindt, P. H., and A. Flynn. 2009. Policy stretching and institutional layering: British food policy between security, safety, quality, health and climate change. *British Politics* 4 (3): 386–414.

Feindt, P. H., and J. Lange, eds. 2007. *Agrarpolitik im 21. Jahrhundert. Konflikte, Optionen, Verständigungsbedarf, Loccumer Protokoll.* Loccum, Germany: Evangelische Akademie Loccum.

Feindt, P. H., M. Gottschick, T. Mölders, F. Müller, R. Sodtke, and S. Weiland. 2008. Nachhaltige Agrarpolitik als kontroverses Diskursfeld. In *Nachhaltige Agrarpolitik als reflexive Politik*, ed. P. H. Feindt, M. Gottschick, T. Mölders, F. Müller, R. Sodtke, and S. Weiland, 277–302. Berlin: Edition Sigma.

Ferroni, M., and A. Mody, eds. 2002. *International Public Good: Incentives, Measurement, and Financing.* Boston: Kluwer Academic Publishers.

Fietkau, H.-J., and H. Weidner. 1998. *Umweltverhandeln: Konzepte, Praxis und Analysen alternativer Konfliktregelungsverfahren—ein erweiterter Projektbericht.* Berlin: Edition Sigma.

Fiorino, D. 1999. Rethinking environmental regulation: Perspectives from law and governance. *Harvard Environmental Law Review* 23 (2): 441–469.

Fischer, F. 2003. *Reframing public policy: Discursive politics and deliberative practices.* Oxford: Oxford University Press.

Fischer, F. 2005. Participatory governance as deliberative empowerment: The cultural politics of discursive space. *American Review of Public Administration* 36 (1): 19–40.

Fischer, F., and J. Forester, eds. 1993. *The argumentative turn in policy analysis and planning.* Durham, NC Duke University Press.

Fisher, E., J. Jones, and R. von Schomberg, eds. 2006. *Implementing the precautionary principle—perspectives and prospects.* Cheltenham, UK: Edward Elgar.

Fitzhugh, J. H., and D. P. Dozier. 1996. *Finding the common good.* Montpelier: Sugarbush Water Withdrawal.

Folke, C., T. Hahn, P. Olsson, and J. Norberg. 2005. Adaptive governance of social-ecological systems. *Annual Review of Environment and Resources* 30:441–473.

Foray, D. 2004. *The economics of knowledge.* Cambridge, MA: MIT Press.

Forester, J. 2009. *Dealing with differences: Dramas of mediating public disputes.* Oxford: Oxford University Press.

Foulon, J., P. Lanouie, and B. Lapante. 1999. Incentives for pollution control: Regulation and information. Policy research working paper. Washington, DC: World Bank.

Frank, G., J. Latham, D. Little, J. Parviainen, A. Schuck, and K. Vandekerkhove. 2005. Analysis of protected forest areas in Europe—Provisional results of COST Action E27 PROFOR. In *Natural forests in the temperate zone of Europe: Values and utilisation*, ed. B. Commarmot, and F. D. Hamor, 377–386. Birmensdorf: Swiss Federal Research Institute.

Frank, R. H. 1988. *Passions with reason. The strategic role of the emotions.* New York: Norton.

Frey, B. S. 1984. *International political economics.* Oxford: Blackwell.

Frey, B. S. 1992. *Economics as a science of human behaviour*. Boston, Dordrecht, London: Kluwer.

Frey, B. S. 1997. *Not just for the money: An economic theory of personal motivation*. Cheltenham, UK: Edward Elgar.

Frey, B. S. 2001. *Inspiring economics. Human motivation in political economy*. Cheltenham, UK: Edward Elgar.

Frey, B. S., and R. Eichenberger. 1994. *The new democratic federalism for Europe. Functional, overlapping and competing jurisdictions*. Cheltenham, UK: Edward Elgar.

Frey, B. S., and R. Jegen. 2000. Motivation crowding theory: A survey of empirical evidence. *Journal of Economic Surveys* 5:589–611.

Frey, B. S., and M. Osterloh, eds. 2002. *Successful management by motivation. Balancing intrinsic and extrinsic rewards*. Berlin, Heidelberg, New York: Springer.

Frey, B. S., and M. Osterloh. 2005. Yes, managers should be paid like bureaucrats. *Journal of Management Inquiry* 14:96–111.

Frey, B. S., and A. Stutzer, eds. 2007. *Economics and psychology. A promising new cross-disciplinary field*. Cambridge, MA: MIT Press.

Frickel, S., and D. J. Davidson. 2004. Building environmental states: Legitimacy and rationalization in sustainability governance. *International Sociology* 19 (1): 89–100.

Frouws, J. 1998. The contested redefinition of the countryside: An analysis of rural discourses in the Netherlands. *Sociologia Ruralis* 38 (1): 54–68.

Funtowicz, S. O., and J. Ravetz. 1990. *Uncertainty and quality in science for policy*. Dordrecht, Netherlands: Kluwer.

Furnham, A. 1995. Tolerance of ambiguity: A review of the concept, its measurement and applications. *Current Psychology* 14 (3): 179–200.

Furnham, A., and A. Lewis. 1986. *The economic mind: The social psychology of economic behaviour*. Brighton, UK: Wheatsheaf Books.

Gadamer, H.-G. 1960. *Wahrheit und Methode: Grundzüge einer philosophischen Hermeneutik*. Tübingen, Germany: Mohr.

Gallini, N., and S. Scotchmer. 2002. Intellectual property: When is it the best incentive system? In *Innovation policy and the economy*, ed. A. Jaffe, et al., 51–78. Cambridge, MA: MIT Press.

Galston, W. A. 2001. Political knowledge, political engagement and civic education. *Annual Review of Political Science* 4:217–234.

Gatzweiler, F. W. 2006. Organizing a public ecosystem service economy for sustaining biodiversity. *Ecological Economics* 59:296–304.

Gehl Sampeth, P. 2005. *Regulating bioprospecting: Institutions for drug research, access and benefit-sharing*. Tokyo: United Nations University Press.

Gehring, T. 2000. Die Bedeutung spezialisierter Entscheidungsprozesse für die Problemlösungsfähigkeit der Europäischen Union. In *Wie problemlösungsfähig ist die EU? Regieren im europäischen Mehrebenensystem*, ed. E. Grande, and M. Jachtenfuchs, 77–112. Baden-Baden, Germany: Nomos.

Geis, A. 2005. *Regieren mit Mediation. Das Beteiligungsverfahren zur zukünftigen Entwicklung des Frankfurter Flughafens.* Wiesbaden, Germany: VS Verlag für Sozialwissenschaften.

Giddens, A. 1990. *The consequences of modernity.* Stanford, CA: Stanford University Press.

Gigerenzer, G. 2000. *Adaptive thinking: Rationality in the real world.* Oxford: Oxford University Press.

Girardin, L. O. L., and D. Bouille. 2003. Conditions for greater commitment of developing countries in the mitigation of climate change. International Institute for Sustainable Development (IISD).

Gneezy, U., and A. Rusticchini. 2000a. Pay enough or don't pay at all. *Quarterly Journal of Economics* 115:791–810.

Gneezy, U., and A. Rusticchini. 2000b. A fine is a price. *Journal of Legal Studies* 29:1–18.

Godard, O. 1997. *Le principe de précaution dans la conduite des affaires humaines.* Paris: Éditions de la Maison des sciences de l'Homme and Inra-Éditions.

Godard, O. 2006. The precautionary principle and catastrophism on tenterhooks: Lessons from a constitutional reform in France. In *Implementing the Precautionary Principle—Perspectives and Prospects*, ed. E. Fisher, J. Jones, and R. von Schomberg, 63–87. Cheltenham, UK: Edward Elgar.

Godard, O., C. Henry, P. Lagadec, and E. Michel-Kerjan. 2002. *Traité des nouveaux risques: Précaution, crise, assurance.* Paris: Gallimard.

Goeschl, T., and T. Swanson. 2002. The economics of R&D within the biological sector and its optimal management. World Bank Working Paper.

Government of Canada. 2007. Treasury Board. 2005. Government of Canada's Implementation Plan for Smart Regulation. http://www.tbs-sct.gc.ca/media/ps -dp/2005/0324_e.asp (accessed July 14, 2007).

Graham, D. A., and J. M. Vernon. 1971. Profitability of monopolization by vertical integration. *Journal of Political Economy* 79 (4): 924–925.

Green, J., and S. Scotchmer. 1995. On the division of profit in sequential innovation. *Rand Journal of Economics* 26:20–33.

Green, M. 2000. Human nature. *Ecos* 21:47–52.

Greer, A. 2005. *Agricultural policy in Europe.* Manchester, UK: Manchester University Press.

Gregory, R., J. Flynn, S. M. Johnson, T. A. Satterfield, P. Slovic, and R Wagner. 1997. Decision-pathways surveys: A tool for resource managers. *Land Economics* 73:240–254.

Grin, J. 2006. Reflexive modernisation as a governance issue, or: designing and shaping re-structuration. In *Reflexive Governance for Sustainable Development*, ed. J.-P. Voß, D. Bauknecht, and R. Kemp, 57–81. Cheltenham, UK: Edward Elgar.

Grothmann, T., and A. Patt. 2005. Adaptive capacity and human cognition: The process of individual adaptation to climate change. *Global Environmental Change* 15 (3): 199–213.

Grothmann, T., and F. Reusswig. 2006. People at risk of flooding: Why some residents take precautionary action while others do not. *Natural Hazards* 38 (1–2): 101–120.

Gunderson, L. H., and C. S. Holling, eds. 2002. *Panarchy: Understanding transformations in human and natural systems*. Washington, DC: Island Press.

Gunningham, N. 1995. Environment, self-regulation, and the chemical industry: Assessing responsible care. *Law & Policy* 17 (1): 57–109.

Gunningham, N., and P. Grabosky. 1998. *Smart Regulation: Designing Environmental Policy*. Oxford: Oxford University Press.

Gunningham, N., P. Grabosky, and M. Phillipson. 1999. Harnessing third parties as surrogate regulators: achieving environmental outcomes by alternative means. *Business Strategy and the Environment* 8 (4): 211–224.

Gunningham, N., R. Kagan, and D. Thornton. 2003. *Shades of Green: Business, Regulation and Environment*. Stanford, CA: Stanford University Press.

Gunningham, N., and J. Rees. 1997. Industry self-regulation. *Law & Policy* 19 (4): 563–565.

Gunningham, N., and D. Sinclair. 2002. *Leaders & laggards: Next generation environmental regulation*. Sheffield, UK: Greenleaf Publishing.

Haas, P. M. 2004. Addressing the global governance deficit. *Global Environmental Politics* 4 (4): 1–15.

Habermas, J. 1968. Technology and science as ideology. In *The Habermas reader*, ed. W. Outhwaitye, 53–65. Oxford: Polity Press.

Habermas, J. 1981. *The theory of communicative action*. Cambridge: Polity Press.

Habermas, J. 1992. *Faktizität und Geltung: Beiträge zur Diskurstheorie des Rechts und des demokratischen Rechtsstaates*. Frankfurt a.M.: Suhrkamp.

Habermas, J. 1996. *Die Einbeziehung des Anderen: Studien zur politischen Theorie*. Frankfurt a.M.: Suhrkamp.

Hajer, M. A., and H. Wagenaar. 2003. *Deliberative policy analysis: Understanding governance in the network society*. Cambridge: Cambridge University Press.

Hall, P. A. 1993. Policy paradigms, social learning and the state: The case of economic policy-making in Britain. *Comparative Politics* 25 (2): 275–296.

Hamilton, K. 2006. *Business views on international climate and energy policy*. London: Business Council for Sustainable Energy UK and The Climate Group.

Hanley, N., and C. Spash. 1993. *Cost-benefit analysis and the environment*. Aldershot, UK: Edward Elgar.

Hansen, A. J., T. A. Spies, F. J. Swanson, and J. L. Ohmann. 1991. Conserving biodiversity in managed forests: Lessons from natural forests. *Bioscience* 41 (6): 382–392.

Hardin, G. 1968. The tragedy of the commons. *Science* 162:1243–1248.

Harl, Neil. 2003. Agriculture in the twenty-first century. St. Paul, Minnesota. http://www.econ.iastate.edu/faculty/harl/AgInTwentyFirstCentury.pdf.

Hassan, R., R. Scholes, and N. Ash. 2005. *Ecosystems and human well-being: Current state and trends. Findings of the Condition and Trends Working Group.* Washington, DC: Island Press.

Hayek, F. A. 1979. *The political order of a free people.* Vol. 3, Law, Legislation and Liberty. Chicago: University of Chicago Press.

Hein, L., K. van Koppen, R. S. de Groot, and E. C. van Ierland. 2006. Spatial scales, stakeholders and the valuation of ecosystem services. *Ecological Economics* 57:209–228.

Heinelt, H. 2002. Achieving sustainable and innovative policies through participatory governance in a multi-level context: Theoretical issues. In *Participatory governance in multi-level context: Concepts and experience*, eds. H. Heinelt, P. Getimis, G. Kafkalas, R. Smith, and E. Swyngedouw, 17–32. Opladen, Germany: Leske + Budrich.

Held, D. 1995. *Democracy and the global order: From the modern state to cosmopolitan governance.* Cambridge: Polity Press.

Held, D., and A. McGrew, eds. 2002. *Governing globalization.* Cambridge: Polity Press.

Hendriks, C. M., and J. Grin. 2007. Contextualizing reflexive governance: The politics of Dutch transitions to sustainability. *Journal of Environmental Policy and Planning* 9 (3–4): 333–350.

Hess, C., and E. Ostrom, eds. 2007. *Understanding knowledge as a commons.* Cambridge, MA: MIT Press.

Higgins, V., and G. Lawrence, eds. 2005. *Agricultural governance: Globalization and the new politics of regulation.* Routledge Advances in Sociology 17. London and New York: Routledge.

Hill, S. 1983. Intergovernmental grant negotiation (the Jackson case). In *Resolving environmental regulatory disputes*, ed. L. Susskind, L. Bacow, and M. Wheeler, 86–121. Cambridge: Schenkman Publishing Company.

Hillygus, D. S. 2005. The missing link: Exploring the relationship between higher education and political engagement. *Political Behavior* 27 (1): 25–47.

Hirsch, D. 2001. Symposium introduction: Second generation environmental policy and the new economy. Symposium on Second Generation Environmental Policy and the Law. *Capital University Law Review* 29 (1).

Hirschman, A. O. 1970. *Exit, voice and loyalty.* Cambridge, MA: Harvard University Press.

Hirshleifer, J. 1983. From weakest-link to best-shot: The voluntary provision of public goods. *Public Choice* 41 (3): 371–386.

Hirshleifer, J. 1985. The expanding domain of economics. *American Economic Review* 75:53–68.

Höhne, N., C. Galleguilos, K. Blok, J. Harnish, and D. Phylipsen. 2003. Evolution of commitments under the UNFCCC: Involving newly industrialized economies and developing countries. German Federal Environmental Agency (Umweltbundesamt).

Holley, C., and N. Gunningham. 2006. Environment improvement plans: Facilitative regulation in practice. *Environmental and Planning Law Journal* 23 (6):448–464.

Holling, C. S., ed. 1978. *Adaptive environmental assessment and management.* Chichester, UK: Wiley.

Holmstrom, B. 1982. Moral hazard in teams. *Bell Journal of Economics* 13 (2): 324–340.

Hunold, C., and J. Dryzek. 2005. Green political strategy and the state: Combining political theory and comparative history. In *The state and the global ecological crisis*, ed. J. Barry and R. Eckersley, 75–96. Cambridge, MA: MIT Press.

Hunter, C. 1997. Sustainable bioprospecting: Using private contracts and international legal principles and policies to conserve raw medicinal materials. *Boston College Environmental Affairs Law Review* 25:129–174.

IBGE. 2008. Web page of Brazilian Institute of Geography and Statistics—IGBE (Instituto Brasileiro de Geografia e Estatistica). http://www.ibge.gov.br.

Intergovernmental Panel on Climate Change. 2007. *Climate change 2007* http://www.ipcc.ch/publications_and_data/publications_ipcc_fourth_assessment_report_synthesis_report.htm.

International Task Force on Global Public Goods. 2006. Meeting global challenges: International cooperation in the national interest. Final Report. Stockholm, Sweden. http://www.cic.nyu.edu/scarcity/docs/archive/2006/Global Challenges.pdf.

Itaya, J.-I., D. de Meza, and G. D. Myles. 1997. In praise of inequality: Public good provision and income distribution. *Economics Letters* 57 (3): 289–296.

Jacobi, P. 2000. Meio ambiente e redes sociais: Dimensões intersetoriais e complexidade na articulação de práticas coletivas. *Revista de Administração Publica* 34 (6): 131–158.

Jacobs, M. 1997. Environmental valuation, deliberative democracy and public decision-making institutions. In *Valuing nature: Economics, ethics and the environment*, ed. J. Foster, 232–246. London: Routledge.

Jaegerman, A. 1983. Behind-the-scenes negotiation in the NPDES permit process (the Hoslton River case). In *Resolving Environmental Regulatory Disputes*, ed. L. Susskind, L. Bacow, and M. Wheeler, 30–55. Cambridge: Schenkman Publishing Company.

Japp, K. 1997. Intersystemische Diskurse—Sozial und Systemintegration. In *Diskursive Verständigung? Mediation und Partizipation in Technikkontroversen*, ed. S. Köberle, F. Gloede and L. Hennen, 214–221. Baden-Baden Germany: Nomos.

Jessop, B. 2003. Governance and meta-governance: On reflexivity, requisite variety, and requisite irony. In *Governance as social and political communication*, ed. H. P. Bang, 101–139. Manchester, UK: Manchester University Press.

JNCC. 2004. The UK Biodiversity Action Plan and country biodiversity strategies. http://jncc.defra.gov.uk/pdf/comm04D11.pdf.

Jonas, A. E. G., and S. Pincetl. 2006. Rescaling regions in the state: The new regionalism in California. *Political Geography* 25:482–505.

Jonas, H. 1984. *The imperative of responsibility: In search of an ethics for the technological age*. Chicago: University of Chicago Press.

Josling, T. 2002. Competing paradigms in the OECD and their impacts on the WTO agricultural talks. In *Agricultural policy for the 21st century*, ed. L. Tweeten and S. R. Thompson, 245–264. Ames: Iowa State University Press.

Kagan, R. A., N. Gunningham, and D. Thornton. 2003. Explaining corporate environmental performance: How does regulation matter? *Law & Society Review* 37 (1): 51–90.

Kahneman, D., and A. Tversky. 1979. Prospect theory: An analysis of decision under risk. *Econometrica* 47 (2), 263–291.

Kahneman, D., P. Slovic, and A. Tversky, eds. 1982. *Judgment under uncertainty: Heuristics and biases*. Cambridge: Cambridge University Press.

Kallis, G., and N. Videira, P, Antunes, and R. Santos, eds. 2004. *Integrated deliberative decision processes for water resource planning and evaluation—guidance document, ADVISOR project*. Caparica, Portugal: New University of Lisbon.

Kanbur, R., T. Sandler, and K. Morrison. 1999. *The Future of development assistance: Common pools and international public goods. Policy Essay Series*. Washington, DC: Overseas Development Council.

Kanie, N., and P. M. Haas, ed. 2004. *Emerging forces in environmental governance*. Tokyo: United Nations University Press.

Karahan, G. R., L. Razzolini, and W. S. Shughart. 2002. Centralized versus decentralized decision-making in a county government setting. *Economics of Governance* 3:101–115.

Karkkainen, Bradley C. 2004. Post-sovereign environmental governance. *Global Environmental Politics* 72 (4): 72–96.

Kárný, M. 2005. *Optimized Bayesian dynamic advising. theory and algorithms*. Berlin: Springer.

Kasemir, B., J. Jager, C. C. Jaeger, and M. T. Gardner. 2003. *Public participation in sustainability science*. Cambridge: Cambridge University Press.

Kastens, B., and J. Newig. 2007. The Water Framework Directive and agricultural nitrate pollution: Will great expectations in Brussels be dashed in Lower Saxony? *European Environment* 17:231–246.

Kaul, I. 2006. Blending external and domestic policy demands; The rise of the intermediary state. In *The New Public Finance: Responding to Global Challenges*, ed. I. Kaul and P. Conceição, 73–108. New York: Oxford University Press.

Kaul, I. 2007. Providing (contested) global public goods. In *Authority in the global political economy*, ed. Volker Rittberger and Martin Nettesheim. Basingstokes, UK: Palgrave Macmillan.

Kaul, I., and P. Conceição, eds. 2006. *The new public finance: responding to global challenges*. New York: Oxford University Press.

Kaul, I., and P. Conceição. 2008. What is new about "the new public finance"? In *Public Finance, Monetary Policy and Market Issues*, ed. E. Shinnick, 9–42. Berlin: LIT.

Kaul, I., P. Conceição, K. Le Goulven, and R. U. Mendoza, eds. 2003. *Providing global public goods: Managing globalization*. New York: Oxford University Press.

Kaul, I., I. Grunberg, and M. A. Stern, eds. 1999. *Global public goods: International cooperation in the 21st century*. Oxford: Oxford University Press.

Kay, A. 2003. Path dependency and the CAP. *Journal of European Public Policy* 10 (3): 405–420.

Kenis, P., and D. Knoke. 2002. How organizational field networks shape inter-organizational tie-formation rates. *Academy of Management Review* 27 (2): 275–293.

Kenyon, W., and C. Nevin. 2001. The use of economic and participatory approaches to assess forest development: A case study in the Ettrick Valley. *Forest Policy and Economics* 3:69–80.

Keohane, R. O. 2006. Accountability of world politics. *Scandinavian Political Studies* 29 (2): 75–87.

Kindleberger, C. P. 1986. International public goods without international government. *American Economic Review* 76 (1):1–13.

King, A., and M. J. Lenox. 2000. Industry self-regulation without sanctions: the chemical industry's Responsible Care Program. *Academy of Management Journal* 43 (4): 698–716.

Kirchgaessner, G. 1991. *Homo Oeconomicus: Das ökonomische Modell individuellen Verhaltens und seine Anwendung in den Wirtschafts- und Sozialwissenschaften*. Tübingen, Germany: Mohr Siebeck.

Kiss, A., and D. Shelton. 2000. *International environmental law*. 2nd ed. Ardsley, NY: Transnational Publishers.

Kittredge, D. B. 2005. The cooperation of private forest owners on scales larger than one individual property: international examples and potential application in the United States. *Forest Policy and Economics* 7 (4): 671–688.

Klein, R. J. T., S. Huq, F. Denton, T. E. Downing, R. G. Richels, J. B. Robinson, and F. L. Toth. 2007. Inter-relationships between adaptation and mitigation. In *Climate change 2007: Impacts, adaptation and vulnerability. Contribution of Working Group II to the Fourth Assessment Report of the Intergovernmental Panel on Climate Change*, ed. M. L. Parry, O. F. Canziani, J. P. Palutikof, P. J. van der Linden, and C. E. Hanson, 745–777. Cambridge: Cambridge University Press.

Kleindorfer, P., and E. Orts. 1996. Informational regulation of informational risks. Working paper, University of Pennsylvania, Philadelphia.

Kloppenburg, J. 1991. No Hunting! Biodiversity, indigenous rights, and scientific poaching. *Cultural Survival Quarterly* 15 (3): 14–18.

Knetsch, J. L. 1995. Assumptions, behavioral findings, and policy analysis. *Journal of Policy Analysis and Management* 14 (1): 68–78.

Knill, C., and A. Lenschow, eds. 2000. *Implementing EU environmental policy: New directions and old problems.* Manchester, UK: Manchester University Press.

Kohler-Koch, B. 2005. Network governance within and beyond an enlarged European Union. In *Institutional and policy-making challenges to the European Union in the wake of eastern enlargement,* ed. A. Verdun and O. Croci, 35–53. Manchester, UK: Manchester Universtity Press.

Koontz, T. M., T. A. Steelman, J. Carmin, K. Smith Korfmacher, C. Moseley, and C. W. Thomas. 2004. *Collaborative environmental management: What roles for government?* Washington, DC: Resources for the Future.

Koontz, T. M., and C. W. Thomas. 2006. What do we know and need to know about the environmental outcomes of collaborative management? *Public Administration Review* 66:111–121.

Kouplevatskaya-Yunusova, I., and G. Buttoud. 2006. Assessment of an iterative process: The double spiral of re-designing participation. *Forest Policy and Economics* 8:529–541.

Krasner, S. D. 1999. *Sovereignty: Organized hypocrisy.* Princeton, NJ: Princeton University Press.

Kruglanski, A. W. 1978. Endogenous attribution and intrinsic motivation. In *The hidden costs of rewards: New perspectives on the psychology of human motivation,* ed. M. Lepper and D. Greene, 93–118. Hillsdale, NY: Erlbaum.

Kuhn, T. 1962. *The structure of scientific revolutions.* Chicago: University of Chicago Press.

Laffan, B. 1997. *The finances of the European Union.* The European Union series. Basingstoke, UK: Macmillan.

Lamy, P. 2004. The emergence of collective preferences in international trade: implications for regulating globalisation. Conference on Collective Preferences and Global Governance: What Future for the Multilateral Trading System? Brussels.

Lane, R. E. 1991. *The market experience.* Cambridge: Cambridge University Press.

Langton, S. 1996. An organizational assessment of the U.S. Army Corps of Engineers in regard to public involvement practices and challenges. Working paper, U.S. Army Corps of Engineers, Institute for Water Resources.

Lansing, J. S. 2003. Complex adaptive systems. *Annual Review of Anthropology* 32:183–204.

Larsson, R. 1993. Case survey methodology: Quantitative analysis of patterns across case studies. *Academy of Management Journal* 36 (6): 1515–1546.

Laws, D., and M. Rein. 2003. Reframing practice. In *Deliberative policy analysis*, ed. M. Hajer and H. Wagenaar, 172–206. Cambridge: Cambridge University Press.

Layzer, J. 2008. *Natural experiments: Ecosystem-based management and the environment*. Cambridge, MA: MIT Press.

Layzer, J. A. 2002. Citizen participation and government choice in local environmental controversies. *Policy Studies Journal: The Journal of the Policy Studies Organization* 30 (2): 193–207.

Lazear, E. 2000. Economic imperialism. *Quarterly Journal of Economics* 115:99–146.

Lea, S. E. G., R. M. Tarpy, and P. Webley. 1987. *The individual in the economy. A survey of economic psychology*. Cambridge: Cambridge University Press.

Leach, W. D., and P. A. Sabatier. 2005. Are trust and social capital the keys to Success? Watershed partnerships in California and Washington. In *Swimming upstream. Collaborative approaches to watershed management*, ed. P. A. Sabatier, W. Focht, M. Lubell, Z. Trachtenberg, A. Vedlitz, and M. Matlock, 233–258. Cambridge, MA: MIT Press.

Lecher, T., and E. H. Hoff. 1997. *Die Umweltkrise im Alltagsdenken*. Weinheim: Beltz.

Lee, M., and C. Abbot. 2003. Legislation: The usual suspects? Public participation under the Aar-hus Convention. *Modern Law Review* 66 (1):80–108.

Leibenstein, H. 1976. *Beyond economic man. A new foundation for microeconomics*. Cambridge, MA: Harvard University Press.

Lenoble, J. 1996. Law and indecidability: A new vision of the proceduralization of law. *Cardozo Law Review* 17:2901–2970.

Lenoble, J. 2005. Open method of coordination and theory of reflexive governance. In *Social rights and market forces: Is the open coordination of employment and social policies the future of social Europe?* ed. O. De Schutter and S. Deakin, 19–38. Louvain, Belgium: Collection du Centre des Droits de l'Homme de l'Université Catholique de Louvain.

Lenoble, J., and M. Maesschalck. 2010. *Democracy, law and governance*. Aldershot, UK: Ashgate.

Lepper, M. R., and D. Greene, eds. 1978. *The hidden costs of reward: New Perspectives on psychology of human motivation*. Hillsdale, NY: Erlbaum.

Levi-Faur, D., and J. Jordana. 2005. The rose of regulatory capitalism: The Global diffusion of a new order. *Annals of the American Academy of Political and Social Science* 598 (1):12–32.

Liftin, K. T. 2000. Environment, wealth and authority: Global climate change and emerging modes of legitimation. *International Studies Review* 2 (2):119–148.

Lind, E. A., and T. R. Tyler. 1988. *The social psychology of procedural justice*. New York: Plenum Press.

Lindenmayer, et al. 2000. Biodiversity indicators for ecologically sustainable forestry. *Conservation Biology* 14 (4): 941–950.

Loibl, M. C. 2006. Integrating perspectives in the practice of transdisciplinary research. In *Reflexive governance for sustainable development*, ed. J.-P. Voß, D. Bauknecht, and R. Kemp, 294–311. Cheltenham, UK: Edward Elgar.

Luhmann, N. 1977. Differentiation of society. *Canadian Journal of Sociology* 2:29–53.

Luhmann, N. 1986. *Ökologische Kommunikation: Kann die moderne Gesellschaft sich auf ökologische Gefährdungen einstellen?* Opladen, Germany: Westdeutscher Verlag.

Luhmann, N. 2000. *Die Politik der Gesellschaft.* Frankfurt, Suhrkamp.

MacMillan, D. C., L. Philip, N. Hanley, and B. Alvarez-Farizo. 2002. Valuing the non-market benefits of wild goose conservation: A comparison of interview and group based approaches. *Ecological Economics* 43 (1): 49–59.

Macnaghten, P., and M. Jacobs. 1997. Public identification with sustainable development: Investigating cultural barriers to participation. *Global Environmental Change* 7 (1): 5–24.

Maesschalck, M. 2010. *Transformations de l'éthique. De la phénoménologie radicale au pragmatisme social.* Brussels: Peter Lang.

Mangerich, M. K., and L. S. Luton. 1995. The Inland Northwest Field Burning Summit: A case study. In *Mediating environmental conflicts: Theory and practice*, ed. J. W. Blackburn and W. M. Bruce, 247–265. Westport, CT: Quorum Books.

March, J. G. 1991. Exploration and exploitation in organizational learning. *Organization Science* 2 (1): 71–87.

March, J. G., and J. P. Olsen. 1989. *Rediscovering institutions: The organizational basis of politics.* New York: Free Press.

Marsden, T. 1993. *Constructing the countryside.* London: UCL Press.

Marsden, T., R. Lee, A. Flynn, and S. Thankappan. 2009. *The new regulation and governance of food: Beyond the food crisis?* London: Routledge.

Marshall, K. E. 1955. Working with a street gang. *Autonomous Groups Bulletin* 11 (2–3): 7–10.

Martinez-Alier, J., G. Munda, and J. O'Neill. 1998. Weak comparability of values as a foundation for ecological economics. *Ecological Economics* 26 (3): 277–286.

Mascarenhas, R., and T. Sandler. 2005. Donors' mechanisms for financing international and national public goods: Loans or grants? *World Economy* 28 (8): 1095–1117.

Mauss, M. 1924. Essai sur le don: Forme et raison de l'échange dans les sociétés archaïques. *L'année Sociologique* 1923–1924.

May, K. O. 1954. Intransitivity, utility, and the aggregation of preference patterns. *Econometrica* 22:1–13.

Mayer, P. 2006. Biodiversity—the appreciation of different thought styles and values helps to clarify the term. *Restoration Ecology* 14:105–111.

Mayntz, R., and F. W. Scharpf, eds. 1995. *Gesellschaftliche Selbstregelung und politische Steuerung.* Frankfurt: Campus.

Mayntz, R., B. Rosewitz, U. Schimank, and R. Stichweh, eds. 1988. *Differenzierung und Verselbständigung. Zur Entwicklung gesellschaftlicher Teilsysteme.* Frankfurt: Campus.

Mazmanian, D. A. 1979. *Can organizations change? Environmental protection, citizen participation, and the corps of engineers.* Washington, DC: The Brookings Institution.

McDaniels, T., R. Gregory, J. Arvai, and R. Chuenpagdee. 2003. Decision structuring to alleviate embedding in environmental valuation. *Ecological Economics* 46:33–46.

McDonald, J. 2006. Tr(e)ading cautiously: precaution in WTO decision making. In *Implementing the precautionary principle—perspectives and prospects,* ed. E. Fisher, J. Jones, and R. von Schomberg, 160–181. Cheltenham, UK: Edward Elgar.

McKenzie, R. B., and G. Tullock. 1975. *The new world of economics.* 2nd ed. Homewood, IL: Irwin.

MCT. 2004. *Comunicacao Inicial do Brasil a Convencao-Quadro das Nacoes Unidas sobre Mudanca do Clima.* Ministerio de Minas e Energia.

Mech, T., and M. Young. 2001. *Voluntary environmental management arrangements.* Canberra, Australia: RIRDC.

Midgley, A. C. 2005. Governing nature and nature conservationists: Rationalization and the management of biodiversity. Paper presented at the RGS-IBG Annual Conference, London, Aug. 30–Sep. 1, 2005.

Milgrom, P., D. North, and B. Weingast. 1990. The role of institutions in the revival of trade: The medieval law merchant, private judges, and the champagne fairs. *Economics and Politics* 1:1–23.

Ministerial Conference on the Protection of Forests in Europe. 1998. Resolution L2: Pan-European Criteria, Indicators and Operational Level Guidelines for Sustainable Forest Management. Lisbon, June 2–4, 1998. http://www.foresteurope.org/filestore/foresteurope/Conferences/Lisbon/lisbon_resolution_l2.pdf.

Mitchell, R. B., W. C. Clark, D. W. Cash, and N. M. Dickson, eds. 2006. *Global environmental assessments: Information and influence.* Cambridge, MA: MIT Press.

MMA. 2008.Web site of the Brazilian Ministry of Environmental Affairs. http://www.mma.gov.br.

Mol, A. J. P. 1995. *The refinement of production.* Utrecht: Van Arkel.

Mol, A. J. P. 2007. Bringing the environmental state back: Partnerships in perspective. In *Partnerships, governance and sustainable development,* ed. P. Glasbergen, F. Biermann, and A. Mol, 173–193. Cheltenham, UK: Edward Elgar.

Mooney, H. A., A. Cropper, and W. Reid. 2004. The millennium ecosystem assessment: What is it all about? *Trends in Ecology & Evolution* 19: 221–224.

Morgan, K., T. Marsden, and J. Murdoch. 2006. *Worlds of food: Place, power, and provenance in the food chain.* New York: Oxford University Press.

Mori, S. 2004. Institutionalization of NGO involvement in policy functions for global environmental governance. In *Emerging forces in environmental governance*, ed. P. Haas, 157–175. Tokyo: United Nations University Press.

Morreale, S. P., and P. M. Backlund. 2002. Communication curricula: History, recommendations, resources. *Communication Education* 51:2–18.

Moyer, W., and T. E. Josling. 2002. *Agricultural policy reform: Politics and process in the EU and US in the 1990s.* Aldershot, UK: Ashgate.

Müller-Erwig, K.-A. 1995. Der Münchehagen-Ausschuß. Eine qualitative Betrachtung der sozia-len Prozesse in einem Mediationsverfahren. *Schriften zu Mediationsverfahren im Umwelt-schutz.* Discussion paper, Wissenschaftszentrum Berlin.

Munda, G. 1995. *Multicriteria evaluation in a fuzzy environment: Theory and applications in ecological economics.* Heidelberg: Physica-Verlag.

Munda, G. 1996. Cost-benefit analysis in integrated environmental assessment: some methodological issues. *Ecological Economics* 19 (2): 157–168.

Munda, G. 2004. Social multi-criteria evaluation: Methodological foundations and operational consequences. *European Journal of Operational Research* 158 (3): 662–677.

Murdoch, J. C., T. Sandler, and K. Sargent. 1997. A tale of two collectives: Sulphur versus nitrogen oxides emission reduction in Europe. *Economica* 64 (2): 281–301.

Murphy, T. 2004. A deliberative civic education and civil society: A consideration of ideals and actualities in democracy and communication education. *Communication Education* 53 (1): 74–91.

NAE. 2005. *Cadernos NAE: Mudança do Clima.* Vol. 1. Brasília: Núcleo de Assuntos Estratégicos da Presidência da República, Secretaria de Comunicação de Governo e Gestão Estratégica.

Nagan, W. P., and C. Hammer. 2005. The changing character of sovereignty in international law and international relations. *Columbia Journal of Transnational Law* 43 (1): 141–187.

Nelson, K. C. 1990a. Pig's eye attempted mediation. In *Environmental disputes: Community involvement in conflict resolution*, ed. J. E. Crowfoot, and J. M. Wondolleck, 209–225. Washington, DC: Island Press.

Nelson, K. C. 1990b. Sand Lakes Quiet Area issue-based negotiation. In *Environmental disputes: Community involvement in conflict resolution*, ed. J. E. Crowfoot, and J. M. Wondolleck, 183–208. Washington, DC: Island Press.

Nelson, R. R. 1959. The simple economics of basic scientific research. *Journal of Political Economy* 67:297–306.

Neuman, J. C. 1996. Run, river, run: Mediation of a water-rights dispute keeps fish and farmers happy—for a time. *University of Colorado Law Review* 67 (2): 259–340.

Newig, J. 2007. Does public participation in environmental decisions lead to improved environmental quality? Towards an analytical framework. *Communication, Cooperation, Participation/International Journal of Sustainability Communication* 1 (1): 51–71.

Newig, J., and O. Fritsch. 2009. The case survey method and applications in political science. APSA Toronto 2009 Meeting Paper. http://papers.ssrn.com/sol3/papers.cfm?abstract_id=1451643.

Nguyen, G. D., and T. Pénard. 2007. Network cooperation and incentives within online communities. In *Internet and digital economies*, ed. E. Brousseau and N. Curien, 220–236. Cambridge: Cambridge University Press.

Niemeyer, S., and C. L. Spash. 2001. Environmental valuation analysis, public deliberation, and their pragmatic syntheses: a critical appraisal. *Environment and Planning. C, Government & Policy* 19:567–585.

Noiville, C. 2000. Principe de précaution et Organisation mondiale du commerce: Le cas du commerce alimentaire. *Journal du Droit International* 127 (2): 263–297.

North, D. 1990. *Institutions, institutional change and economic performance.* Cambridge: Cambridge University Press.

North, D. 2005. *Understanding the process of economic change.* Princeton, NJ: Princeton University Press.

NRG4SD. 2008. Web site of Network of Regional Governments for Sustainable Development. http://www.nrg4sd.net.

O'Brien, E. A. 2003. Human values and their importance to the development of forestry policy in Britain: A literature review. *Forestry* 76 (1): 3–17.

O'Riordan, T., ed. 2001. *Globalism, localism and identity.* London: Earthscan Publications.

O'Rourke, D. 2000. Monitoring the monitors: A critique of Pricewaterhouse Coopers (PWC) labor monitoring. http://web.mit.edu/dorourke/www/PDF/pwc.pdf.

Oates, W. E. 1999. An essay on fiscal federalism. *Journal of Economic Literature* 37 (3): 1120–1149.

O'Connor, M. 2000. Pathways for environmental evaluation: A walk in the (Hanging) Gardens of Babylon. *Ecological Economics* 34 (2): 175–193.

OECD. 1975. *The polluter pays principle: Definition, analysis, implementation.* Paris: OECD Publ.

OECD. 1987. The 1987 OECD Ministerial Principles for agricultural policy reform. http://www.oecd.org/document/34/0,2340,en_2649_33773_31852962_1_1_1_1,00.html#_ednref5.

OECD. 2001. *Multifunctionality: Toward an analytical framework.* Paris: OECD Publ.

OECD. 2005a. The definition and selection of key competencies: Executive Summary. http://www.oecd.org/dataoecd/47/61/35070367.pdf.

OECD. 2005b. Producer and Consumer Support Estimates. OECD Database 1986–2004. http://www.oecd.org/document/54/0,2340,en_2649_33773 _35009718_1_1_1_1,00.html#NME.

OECD. 2007. *Agricultural policies in OECD countries: Monitoring and evaluation*. Paris: OECD Publ.

Offe, C. 1997. Micro-aspects of democratic theory: What makes for the deliberative competence of citizens? In *Democracy's victory and crisis*, ed. A. Hadenius, 81–104. Cambridge: Cambridge University Press.

Olsson, P., and C. Folke. 2001. Local ecological knowledge and institutional dynamics for ecosystem management: A study of Lake Racken Watershed, Sweden. *Ecosystems (New York, N.Y.)* 4:85–104.

Olsson, P., C. Folke, V. Galaz, T. Hahn, and L. Schulz. 2007. Enhancing the fit through adaptive co-management: Creating and maintaining bridging functions for matching scales in the Kristianstads Vanttenrike Biosphere Reserve Sweden. *Ecology and Society* 12 (1): art 28. http://www.ecologyandsociety.org/vol12/iss1/ art28.

OMPI. 2001. *Rapport de l'OMPI sur les missions d'enquête consacrées à la propriété intellectuelle et aux savoirs traditionnels (1998–1999)*. Geneva: Organisation Mondiale de la Propriété Intellectuelle.

O'Neill, J. 1993. *Ecology, policy and politics*. London: Routledge.

Orden, D., R. Paarlberg, and T. Roe. 1999. *Policy reform in American agriculture: Analysis and prognosis*. Chicago: University of Chicago Press.

Orsato, R., and S. Clegg. 2005. Radical reformism: Towards critical ecological modernization. *Sustainable Development* 13:253–267.

Orton, M. 2005. The Colorado River through the Grand Canyon: Applying alternative dispute resolution methods to public participation. In *Public participation in the governance of inter-national freshwater resources*, ed. C. Bruch, L. Jansky, M. Nakayama, and K. A. Salewicz, 403–432. Tokyo, New York, Paris: United Nations University Press.

Orts, W. E. 1995. Reflexive environmental law. *Northwestern University Law Review* 89 (4): 1227–1340.

Osborne, D., and T. Gaebler. 1992. *Reinventing government: How the entrepreneurial spirit is transforming the public sector*. Boston: Addison-Wesley.

Osterloh, M. 2007. Human resources management and knowledge creation. In *Handbook of knowledge creation*, ed. I. Nonaka and I. Kazuo, 158–175. Oxford: Oxford University Press.

Osterloh, M., and B. S. Frey. 2000. Motivation, knowledge transfer, and organizational forms. *Organization Science* 11: 538–550.

Osterloh, M., and B. S. Frey. 2004. Corporate governance for crooks? The case for corporate virtue. In *Corporate governance and firm organization*, ed. A. Grandori, 191–211. Oxford: Oxford University Press.

Osterloh, M., and B. S. Frey. 2006. Shareholders should welcome knowledge workers as directors. *Journal of Management & Governance* 10 (3): 325–345.

Ostrom, E. 1990. *Governing the commons: The evolution of institutions for collective action*. Cambridge: Cambridge University Press.

Ostrom, E. 2001. Decentralisation and development: The new panacea. In *Challenges to Democracy: Ideas, Involvement and Institution*, ed. K. Dowding, 237–256. New York: Palgrave Publishers.

Ostrom, E. 2008. The danger of prescribing institutional blueprints. Workshop on "Which Governance for Which Environment?" Cargèse, France, February 4–8, 2008.

Ostrom, E., R. Gardner, and J. Walker. 2003. *Rules, games, and common-pool resources*. Ann Arbor: University of Michigan Press.

Ostrom, V. 1997. *The meaning of democracy and the vulnerability of democracies*. Ann Arbor: University of Michigan Press.

Ott, K., G. Klepper, S. Lingner, A. Schäfer, J. Scheffran, and D. Spring. 2004. Reasoning goals of climate protection—specification of Article 2 UNFCCC. Berlin, Federal Environmental Agency (Umweltbundesant). http://www.umweltdaten.de/publikationen/fpdf-l/2747.pdf.

Owens, S., T. Rayner, and O. Bina. 2004. New agendas for appraisal: reflections on theory, practice, and research. *Environment & Planning A* 36:1943–1959.

Pahl-Wostl, C., and M. Hare. 2004. Processes of social learning in integrated resources management. *Journal of Community & Applied Social Psychology* 14 (3): 193–206.

Parker, C. 2000. Summary of the scholarly literature on regulatory compliance. Annex to reducing the risk of policy failure: Challenges for regulatory compliance. Working Paper 77. Paris: OECD.

Parker, C., and V. Nielsen. 2006. Do corporate compliance programs influence compliance? University of Melbourne Legal Studies Research Paper No 189. http://ssrn.com/abstract=930238 (accessed February 23, 2007).

Parsons, T. 1966. *Societies*. Englewood Cliffs, NJ: Prentice-Hall.

Pattberg, P. 2005. The institutionalization of private governance: How business and non-profits agree on transnational rules. *Governance: An International Journal of Policy, Administration and Institutions* 18 (4): 589–610.

Payne, J. W., and J. R. Bettman. 1999. Measuring constructed preferences: Towards a building code. *Journal of Risk and Uncertainty* 19:243–270.

Pearce, D. 1998. Cost-benefit analysis and environmental policy. *Oxford Review of Economic Policy* 14 (4): 84–100.

Pellizzoni, L. 2003. Uncertainty and participatory democracy. *Environmental Values* 12 (2): 195–224.

Perlman, D. L., and G. Adelson. 1997. *Biodiversity: Exploring values and priorities in conservation*. Oxford: Blackwell Scientific.

Perrings, C., and J. Touza-Montero. 2004. Spatial interactions and forest management: policy issues. Working Papers of the Finnish Forest Research Institute 1.

Peters, G. 1996. Agenda-setting in the European Union. In *European Union: Power and decision-making*, ed. J. Richardson, 61–76. London: Routledge.

Petschow, U., J. Rosenau, and E. Ulrich von Weizsäcker. 2005. *Governance and sustainability. New challenges for states, companies and civil society*. Sheffield, UK: Greeleaf.

Pickhardt, M. 2006. Fifty years after Samuelson's "the pure theory of public expenditure": What are we left with. *Journal of the History of Economic Thought* 28 (4):439–460.

Pimm, S. L. 1984. The complexity and stability of ecosystems. *Nature* 307 (5949): 321–326.

Putnam, H. 2002. *The collapse of the fact/value dichotomy and other essays*. Cambridge, MA: Harvard University Press.

Radnitzky, F. P., and P. Bernholz, eds. 1987. *Economic imperialism: The economic method applied outside the field of economics*. New York: Paragon.

Radulova, E. 2007. The OMC: An opaque method of consideration or deliberative governance in action. *European Integration* 29 (3): 363–380.

Raffensperger, C., and J. Tickner, eds. 1999. *Protecting public health and the environment. Implementing the precautionary principle*. Washington, DC: Island Press.

Raffer, K. 1999. ODA and global public goods: A trend analysis of past and present spending patterns. Office of Development Studies Background Paper, United Nations Development Program, New York. http://homepage.univie.ac.at/kunibert.raffer/UNDP.pdf.

Rapp, M., G. Wolschner, and W. Hafner. 2000. European Union Network on the Implementation and Enforcement of Environmental Law Conference on Environmental Compliance and Enforcement. Final report. Klagenfurt, Austria.

Rapport, D. J. 1995. Ecosystem services and management options as blanket indicators of ecosystem health. *Journal of Aquatic Ecosystem Health* 4: 97–105.

Rausser, G. C., and A. Small. 2000. Valuing research leads: Bioprospecting and the conservation of genetic resources. *Journal of Political Economy* 108 (1): 173–206.

Rawls, J. 1971. *A theory of justice*. Cambridge, MA: Harvard University Press.

Rees, J. 1988. *Reforming the workplace: A study of self-regulation in occupational safety*. Philadelphia: University of Pennsylvania Press.

Rei, F. C. F. 1994. Los aspectos jurídico-internacionales de los câmbios climáticos. Faculdad de Derecho, Universidad de Alicante, Alicante.

Rein, M., and D. Schön. 1993. Reframing policy discourse. In *The argumentative turn in policy analysis and planning*, ed. F. Fischer and F. Forester, 145–166. Durham, NC: Duke University Press.

Reinders, H., and J. Youniss. 2006. School-based required community service and civic development in adolescents. *Applied Developmental Science* 10 (1): 2–12.

Reinicke, W. H., and F. Deng. 2000. *Critical choices: The United Nations, networks and the future of global governance.* Ottawa: International Development Research Council.

Renn, O. 2005. Partizipation—ein schillernder Begriff. *GAIA—Ecological Perspectives for Science and Society* 14 (3): 227–228.

Renn, O., and T. Webler. 1998. Der kooperative Diskurs—Theoretische Grundlagen, Anforderungen, Möglichkeiten. In *Abfallpolitik im kooperativen Diskur: Bürgerbeteiligung bei der Standortsuche für eine Deponie im Kanton Aargau,* eds. O. Renn, H. Kastenholz, P. Schild, and U. Wilhelm, 3–103. Zürich: Hochschulverlag AG an der ETH Zürich.

Renn, O., T. Webler, H. Rakel, P. C. Dienel, and B. Johnson. 1993. Public participation in decision making: A three-stage procedure. *Policy Sciences* 26:189–214.

Rhodes, R. A. W. 1997. *Understanding governance: Policy networks, reflexivity and accountability.* Milton Keynes, UK: Open University Press.

Rip, A. 2006. A co-evolutionary approach to reflexive governance—and its ironies. In *Reflexive governance for sustainable development,* ed. J.-P. Voß, D. Bauknecht, and R. Kemp, 82–101. Cheltenham, UK: Edward Elgar.

Rogowski, R. 2006. Reflexive coordination: Thoughts on the social model of the European Union. http://www1.law.nyu.edu/nyulawglobal/fellowsscholars/documents/gffrogowskipaper.pdf

Rosenthal, J. P., D. Beck, A. Bhat, et al. 1999. Combining high-risk science with ambitious social and economic goals. *Pharmaceutical Biology* 37 (supplement): 6–21.

Rowe, G., and L. J. Frewer. 2005. A typology of public engagement mechanisms. *Science, Technology & Human Values* 30 (2): 251–290.

Rueschemeyer, D. 1974. Reflections on structural differentiation. *Zeitschrift für Soziologie* 3:279–294.

Ruhl, J., and J. Saltzman. 2003. Mozart and the red queen: The problem of regulatory accretion in the administrative state. *Georgetown Law Journal* 91 (4): 757–850.

Rychen, D. S., and L. H. Salganik. 2003. *Key competencies for a successful life and a well-functioning society.* Göttingen, Germany: Hogrefe & Huber.

Rydin, Y., and T. Matar. 2006. The New Forest, England: Cooperative planning for a commons. In *Networks and Institutions in Natural Resource Management,* ed. Y. Rydin and E. Falleth, 34–56. Cheltenham, UK: Edward Elgar.

Sabel, C., and J. Zeitlin. 2006. Learning from difference: The new architecture of experimentalist governance in the European Union. Paper prepared for ARENA Seminar, Centre for European Studies, University of Oslo, June 13, 2006.

Sabel, C. 1994. Learning by monitoring. In *The handbook of economic sociology,* ed. N. Smelser and R. Swedberg, 137–165. Princeton, NJ: Princeton UP-Russell Sage Foundation.

Sabel, C., A. Fung, and B. Karkkainen. 2000. *After backyard environmentalism.* Boston: Beacon Press.

Salati, E., A. Santos, A. A. Kablin. 2006. Temas ambientais relevantes. *Revista de Estudos Avançados* 56 (20): 107–127.

Samuelson, P. A. 1954. The pure theory of public expenditure. *Review of Economics and Statistics* 36 (4): 387–389.

Sandler, T. 1992. *Collective action: Theory and applications.* Ann Arbor: University of Michigan Press.

Sandler, T. 1997. *Global challenges.* Cambridge: Cambridge University Press.

Sandler, T. 1998. Global and regional public goods: A prognosis for collective action. *Fiscal Studies* 19 (3): 221–247.

Sandler, T. 2003. Assessing the optimal provision of public goods: In Search of the Holy Grail. In *Providing global public goods: Managing globalization,* ed. I. Kaul, et al. New York: Oxford University Press.

Sandler, T. 2004. *Global collective action.* Cambridge: Cambridge University Press.

Sandler, T., and D. G. Arce. 2002. A conceptual framework for understanding global and transnational public goods for health. *Fiscal Studies* 23 (2): 195–222.

Savage, L. J. 1954. *The foundations of statistics.* New York: Wiley.

Scharpf, F. 1999. *Governing Europe: Effective and democratic?* Oxford: Oxford University Press.

Scharpf, F. W. 1997. *Games real actors play: Actor-centered institutionalism in policy research.* Boulder, CO: Westview Press.

Scharpf, F. 2000. Institutions in comparative policy research. *Comparative Political Studies* 33 (6–7): 762–790.

Schelling, Thomas C. 1980. The intimate contest for self-command. *Public Interest* 60:64–118.

Scherer, Klaus. 2005. What are emotions and how can they be measured? *Social Sciences Information. Information sur les Sciences Sociales* 44 (4): 695–729.

Schimank, U. 2005. *Differenzierung und Integration der modernen Gesellschaft. Beiträge zur akteurzentrierten Differenzierungstheorie 1.* Wiesbaden, Germany: VS Verlag.

Schlicht, E. 1998. *On custom in the economy.* Oxford: Clarendon Press.

Schmidheiny, S. 1992. *Changing courses.* Cambridge, MA: MIT Press.

Schön, D. A. 1983. *The reflective practitioner: How professionals think in action.* London: Temple Smith.

Schön, D. A., and M. Rein. 1994. *Frame reflection: Toward the resolution of intractable policy controversies.* New York: Basic Books.

Scitovsky, T. 1976. *The joyless economy: An inquiry into human satisfaction and dissatisfaction.* Oxford: Oxford University Press.

Scotchmer, S. 1991. Standing on the shoulders of giants: Cumulative research and the patent law. *Journal of Economic Peerspectives* 5:29–41.

Scotchmer, S., and J. Green. 1990. Novelty and disclosure in patent law. *Rand Journal of Economics* 21:131–146.

Scott, C. 2004. Regulation in the age of governance: The rise of the post regulatory state. In *The politics of regulation: Institutions and regulatory reforms for the age of governance*, ed. J. Jordana and D. Levi-Faur. Cheltenham, UK: Edward Elgar.

Scott, J. C. 1998. *Seeing like a state*. New Haven,CT: Yale University Press.

Secretariat of the International Task Force on Global Public Goods. 2006. Meeting Global Challenges: International Cooperation in the National Interest. Final Report. Stockholm, Sweden.

Selten, R. 1990. Bounded rationality. *Journal of Institutional and Theoretical Economics* 146:649–658.

Sen, A. K. 1977. Rational fools: A critique of the behavioral foundations of economic theory. *Philosophy & Public Affairs* 6:317–344.

Serbruyns, I., and S. Luyssaert. 2006. Acceptance of sticks, carrots and sermons as policy instruments for directing private forest management. *Forest Policy and Economics* 9 (3): 285–296.

Sidikou-Sow. Balkissa. 2005. Has globalization as yet changed standard theory? A survey of textbooks in public finance and public economics. UNDP/ODS Background Paper. United Nations Development Programme, Office of Development Studies, New York. http://www.thenewpublicfinance.org.

Siebenhüner, B. 2002. How do scientific assessments learn? Part 1. Conceptual framework and case study of the IPCC. *Environmental Science & Policy* 5:411–420.

Siebenhüner, B. 2004. Social learning and sustainability science: Which role can stakeholder participation play? *International Journal of Sustainable Development* 7 (2): 146–163.

Siebenhüner, B., and J. Suplie. 2005. Implementing the access and benefit-sharing provisions of the CBD: A case for institutional learning. *Ecological Economics* 53:507–522.

Sigurdson, S. G. 1998. The Sandspit Harbour mediation process. In *Alternative dispute resolution in environmental conflicts: Experiences in 12 countries*, ed. H. Weidner, 133–162. Berlin: Edition Sigma.

Simon, H. A. 1957. *Models of man: Social and rational*. New York: John Wiley & Sons.

Simon, H. A. 1978. Rationality as process and as product of thought. *American Economic Review* 68 (2): 1–16.

Simon, H. A. 1983. *Reason in human affairs*. Oxford: Blackwell.

Simon, H. A. 1986. Rationality in psychology and economics. *Journal of Business* 59 (4): 209–224.

Skogstad, G. 1998. Ideas, paradigms and institutions: Agricultural exceptionalism in the European Union and the United States. *Governance: An International Journal of Policy and Administration* 11 (4): 463–490.

SMA. 2002. *Agenda 21 in São Paulo 1992–2002*. São Paulo: São Paulo State Department of Environmental Protection.

SMA. 2005. No reason to wait: The benefits of greenhouse gas reduction in São Paulo and California. Hewlett Foundation. http://www.climatechange.ca.gov/publications/others/GOLDEMBERG_LLOYD_2005-12-02.PDF.

Smart, B. 1992. *Beyond compliance: A new industry view of the environment*. Washington, DC: World Resources Institute.

Smith, A. 2006. Niche-based approaches to sustainable development: radical activist versus strategic managers. In *Reflexive governance for sustainable development*, ed. J. P. Voß and D. Bauknecht, 313–336. Cheltenham, UK: Edward Elgar.

Smith, G. 2003. *Deliberative democracy and the environment*. London: Routledge.

Sondergard B., O. E. Hansen, and J. Holm. 2004. *Journal of Cleaner Production* 12 (4): 337–352.

Sonnino, R., and T. Marsden. 2006. Beyond the divide: Rethinking relationships between alternative and conventional food networks in Europe. *Journal of Economic Geography* 6 (2): 181–199.

Sørensen, E., and J. Torfing. 2009. Making governance networks effective and democratic through metagovernance. *Public Administration* 87 (2): 234–258.

Sørensen, E. 2006. Metagovernance: The changing role of politicians in processes of democratic governance. *American Review of Public Administration* 36 (3): 98–114.

Spaeth, Philipp, H. Rohracher, K. M. Weber, and I. Oehme. 2006. The transition towards sustainable production systems in Austria: A reflexive exercise?" In *Reflexive governance for sustainable development*, ed. J.-P. Voß, D. Bauknecht, and R. Kemp, 355–382. Cheltenham, UK: Edward Elgar.

Steele, J. 2001. Participation and deliberation in environmental law: Exploring a problem-solving approach. *Oxford Journal of Legal Studies* 21 (3): 415–442.

Stern, N. 2006. *The economics of climate change: The Stern review*. London: HM Treasury, UK Cabinet Office.

Stewart, R. 2001. A new generation of environmental regulation? *Capital University Law Review* 29:21–168.

Stigler, G. J. 1984. Economics—the Imperial Science? *Scandinavian Journal of Economics* 86:301–313.

Stiglitz, J. 2002. New perspectives on public finance: Recent achievements and future challenges. *Journal of Public Economics* 86:341–360.

Stirling, A. 1997. Multi-criteria mapping: Mitigating the problems of environmental valuation? In *Valuing nature? Ethics, economics and the environment*, ed. J. Foster. London: Routledge.

Stirling, A. 2006. Precaution, foresight and sustainability: Reflection and reflexivity in the governance of science and technology. In *Reflexive governance for sustainable development*, ed. J.-P. Voß, D. Bauknecht, and R. Kemp, 225–272. Cheltenham, UK: Edward Elgar.

Stirling, A., O. Renn, and P. van Zwanenberg. 2006. A framework for the precautionary governance of food safety: integrating science and participation in the social appraisal of risk. In *Implementing the precautionary principle—perspectives and prospects*, ed. E. Fisher, J. Jones, and R. von Schomberg, 284–315. Cheltenham, UK: Edward Elgar.

Strange, S. 1996. *The retreat of the state: The diffusion of power in the world economy*. Cambridge: Cambridge University Press.

Sullivan, T. J. 1983. The difficulties of mandatory negotiation (the Colstrip power plant case). In *Resolving environmental regulatory disputes*, ed. L. Susskind, L. Bacow, and M. Wheeler, 56–85. Cambridge: Schenkman Publishing Company.

Sunstein, C. 2005. *Laws of fear—beyond the precautionary principle*. Cambridge: Cambridge University Press.

Sunstein, C. R. 1997. *Free markets and social justice*. Oxford: Oxford University Press.

Susskind, L., L. Bacow, and M. Wheeler, eds. 1983. *Resolving environmental regulatory disputes*. Cambridge: Schenkman Publishing Company.

Swanson, T. 1995. *Intellectual property rights and biodiversity conservation*. Cambridge: Cambridge University Press.

Tableman, M. A. 1990. San Juan National Forest mediation. In *Environmental disputes: Community involvement in conflict resolution*, ed. J. E. Crowfoot and J. M. Wondolleck, 32–65. Washington, DC: Island Press.

Talbot, A. R. 1984. *Settling things. Six case studies in environmental mediation*. Washington, DC: The Conservation Foundation.

Tansey, G., and T. Rajotte, eds. 2008. *The future control of food: A guide to international negotiations and rules on intellectual property, biodiversity, and food security*. Sterling, VA: Earthscan.

Tasseit, S. 1983. Partizipieren lernen. Ein gemeindepsychologischer Versuch. [Learning to participate. A community psychological attempt.] In Gemeindepsychologische Perspektiven. Band 2: Interventionsprinzipien, ed. S. Fliegel, W. Stark, and B. Roehrle, 116–123. Tuebingen, Germany: Deutsche Gesellschaft fuer Verhaltenstherapie.

te Velde, D. W., O. Morrissey, and A. Hewitt. 2002. Allocating aid to international public goods. In International public goods: Incentives, measurement and financing, ed. M. Ferroni, and A. Mody, 119–156. Boston: Kluwer Academic Publishers.

Teubner, G. 1983. Substantive and reflexive elements in modern law. *Law & Society Review* 17 (2): 239–286.

Teubner, G. 1989. *Recht als autopoietisches System*. Frankfurt am Main: Suhrkamp.

Teubner, G., L. Farmer, and D. Murphy, eds. 1994. *Environmental law and ecological responsibility: The concept and practice of ecological self-organization*. Chichester, UK: Wiley.

Thaler, R. H. 1992. *The winner's curse: Paradoxes and anomalies of economic life*. New York: Free Press.

Thomas, J. C. 1995. *Public participation in public decisions: New skills and strategies for public managers*. San Francisco: Jossey-Bass Publishers.

Todd, S. 2002. Building consensus on divisive issues: A case study of the Yukon wolf management team. *Environmental Impact Assessment Review* 22:655–684.

Toth, F. L., and E. Hizsnyik. 1998. Integrated environmental assessment methods: Evolution and applications. *Environmental Modeling and Assessment* 3:193–207.

Touffut, J.-P., ed. 2009. *Changing climate, changing economy*. Cheltenham, UK: Edgar Elgar.

Tracy, M. 1989. *Government and agriculture in Western Europe 1880–1988*. New York: Harvester Wheatsheaf.

Trubek, D., and L. Trubek. 2007. New governance & legal regulation. *Columbia Journal of European Law* 13:540.

Turner, M. A., and Q. Weninger. 2005. Meetings with costly participation: An empirical analysis. *Review of Economic Studies* 72 (1): 247–268.

Tweeten, L. 1989. *Farm policy analysis*. Boulder, CO: Westview Press.

Tyler, T. R. 1998. Trust and democratic governance. In *Trust and governance*, ed. V. Braithwaite and M. Levi, 264–294. New York: Russell Sage Foundation.

UK Biodiversity Action Plan. 2007a. Targets Review information note. http://www.ukbap.org.uk/library/brig/TargetsReview06/Final/TargetsReview_EndnoteFINAL.pdf.

UK Biodiversity Action Plan. 2007b. UK Biodiversity Action Plan Timeline. http://www.ukbap.org.uk/GenPageText.aspx?id=53.

UK Biodiversity Partnership Standing Committee. 2007. Conserving Biodiversity—the UK Approach. http://jncc.defra.gov.uk/_ukbap/UKBAP_ConBio-UKApproach-2007.pdf

UNCTAD. (United Nations Conference on Trade and Development). 2007. World Investment Report. Geneva: UNCTAD.

UNEP. 1997. *Global environment outlook 1*. Nairobi: UNEP.

UNEP. 2000. *Global environment outlook 2000*. Nairobi: UNEP.

UNEP. 2002. *Global environment outlook 3. Past, present and future perspectives*. London: Earthscan.

UNEP 2007. *Global environment outlook 4: Environment for development.* Valetta, Malta: Progress Press.

UNFCCC. 2006a. *Key GHG data 2006—highlights from greenhouse gas (GHG) emissions data for 1990–2004 for Annex I parties.* Bonn: UNFCCC.

UNFCCC. 2006b. Working paper 7: Submission from government of Brazil, April 18, 2006.

United Nations. 2001. Report of the high-level panel on financing development [Zedillo Report]. A/55/1000. http://www.un.org/reports/financing/full_report .pdf.

United Nations. 2005. *The millennium development goal report 2005.* New York: United Nations.

Van Asselt, M. B. A., and N. Rijkens-Klomp. 2002. A look in the mirror: Reflection on participation in integrated assessment from a methodological perspective. *Global Environmental Change* 12 (3): 167–184.

Vatn, A. 2004. *Institutions and the environment.* Cheltenham, UK: Edward Elgar.

Vatn, A., and D. W. Bromley. 1994. Choices without prices without apologies. *Journal of Environmental Economics and Management* 26:126–148.

Verheyen, K., N. Lust, M. Carnol, L. Hens, and J. J. Bouma. 2006. *Feasibility of forests conversion: Ecological, social and economic aspects, Final Report of SPSD II MA/04.* Brussels: Belgian Science Policy.

Vicary, S. 1990. Transfers and the weakest-link: An extension of Hirshleifer's analysis. *Journal of Public Economics* 43 (3):375–394.

Vicary, S., and T. Sandler. 2002. Weakest-link public goods: Giving in-kind or transferring money. *European Economic Review* 46 (8): 1501–1520.

Vieillefosse, A. 2003. MSc. Dissertation in Environmental and Resource Economics. London, University College London.

Vincent, M. 2007. Extending protection at the WTO to products other than wines and spirits: Who will benefit? *Estey Centre Journal of International Law and Trade Policy* 8 (1): 57–68.

Vogel, D. 1995. *Trading up: Consumer and environmental regulation in the global economy.* Cambridge, MA: Harvard University Press.

von Winterfeldt, D. 1987. Value tree analysis, an introduction and an application to offshore oil drilling. In *Insuring and mananging hazardous risks: From Seveso to Bhopal and beyond,* ed. P. R. Kleindorfer and H. C. Kunreuther, 139–477. Berlin: Springer.

von Winterfeldt, D., and W. Edwards. 1986. *Decision analysis and behavioural research.* Cambridge: Cambridge University Press.

Voß, J.-P., D. Bauknecht, and R. Kemp, eds. 2006. *Reflexive governance for sustainable development.* Cheltenham, UK: Edward Elgar.

Voß, J.-P., and R. Kemp. 2006. Sustainability and reflexive governance: Introduction. In *Reflexive governance for sustainable development,* ed. J.-P. Voß, D. Bauknecht, and R. Kemp, 3–28. Cheltenham UK: Edward Elgar.

Voß, J.-P., B. Truffer, and K. Konrad. 2006. Sustainability foresight: reflexive governance in the transformation of utility systems. In *Reflexive governance for sustainable development*, ed. J.-P. Voß, D. Bauknecht, and R. Kemp, 162–188. Cheltenham: Edward Elgar.

Voß, J.-P., J. Newig, B. Kastens, J. Monstadt, and B. Nölting. 2008. Steering for Sustainable Development: a Typology of Problems and Strategies with respect to Ambivalence, Uncertainty and Distributed Power. In *Governance for Sustainable Development. Coping with ambivalence, uncertainty and distributed power*, ed. J. Newig, J.-P. Voß, and J. Monstadt, 1–20. London: Routledge.

Ward, H. 1999. Citizens' juries and valuing the environment: A proposal. *Environmental Politics* 8 (2): 75–96.

Weber, E. U. 2006. Experienced-based and description-based perceptions of long-term risk: Why global warming does not scare us (yet). *Climatic Change* 77 (1–2): 103–120.

Weber, M. 1922. *Grundriß der Sozialökonomik*. Vol. 3. Wirtschaft und Gesellschaft. Tübingen, Germany: Mohr.

Webler, T. 1995. "Right" discourse in citizen participation: An evaluative yardstick. In *Fairness and competence in citizen participation: Evaluating models for environmental discourse*, ed. O. Renn, T. Webler, and P. Wiedemann, 35–86. Dodrecht, Netherlands: Kluwer Academic Publisher.

Whelan, J., and K. Lyons. 2005. Community engagement or community action: Choosing not to play the game. *Environmental Politics* 14 (5): 596.

Wiedemann, P. M., F. Claus, and D. Gremler. 1995. *Ergebnisse des Forums "Abfallwirtschaft Lü-beck": Arbeiten zur Risiko-Kommunikation*. vol. 15. Ed. U. Programmgruppe Mensch. Umwelt, Technik.

Wilber, K. 1996. *A brief history of everything*. Dublin: Gill and Macmillan.

Wilkinson, K., P. Lowe, and A. Donaldson. 2010. Beyond Policy Networks: Policy Framing and the Politics of Expertise in the 2001 Foot and Mouth Disease Crisis. *Public Administration* 88 (2): 331–345.

Williamson, O. 1985. *The economic institutions of capitalism: Firms, markets, relational contracting*. New York: Free Press.

Williamson, O. 1996. *The mechanisms of governance*. Oxford: Oxford University Press.

Willke, Helmut. 1997. *Supervision des Staates*. Frankfurt: Suhrkamp.

Willows, R., and R. Connell, eds. 2003. *Climate adaptation: Risk, uncertainty and decision-making. UKCIP Technical Report*. Oxford: UKCIP.

Wolff, F. 2006. The transformation of agriculture: reflexive governance for agrobiodiversity. In *Reflexive governance for sustainable development*, ed. J.-P. Voß, D. Bauknecht, and R. Kemp, 3–28. Cheltenham, UK: Edward Elgar.

World Bank. 2001. *Global development finance: Building coalitions for effective development finance*. Washington, DC: World Bank.

World Trade Organization. 2004. WTO agriculture negotiations: The issues, and where we are now. http://www.wto.org/english/tratop_e/agric_e/agnegs_bkgrnd_e.pdf.

Wynne, B. 1993. Public uptake of science: A case for institutional reflexivity. *Public Understanding of Science (Bristol, England)* 2 (4): 321–337.

Wynne, G., M. Avery, L. Campbell, S. Gubbay, S. Hawkswell, T. Juniper, M. King, P. Newberry, J. Smart, C. Steel, T. Stones, A. Stubbs, J. Taylor, C. Tydeman, and R. Wynde. 1995. *Biodiversity challenge,* 2nd ed. Sandy: Royal Society for the Protection of Birds.

Yeung, K., and B. Morgan. 2007. *An Introduction to law and regulation: Text and materials.* Cambridge: Cambridge University Press.

Young, O. R. 1994. *International environmental governance: Protecting the environment in a stateless society.* Ithaca, NY: Cornell University Press.

Young, O. R., ed. 1997. *Global governance: Drawing insights from the environmental experience.* Cambridge, MA: MIT Press.

Young, O. R., H. Schroeder, and L. A. King, eds. 2008. *Institutions and environmental change: Principal findings, applications, and research frontiers.* Cambridge, MA: MIT Press.

Zander, J. 2010. *The application of the precautionary principle in practice: Comparative dimensions.* Cambridge, UK: Cambridge University Press.

Zebisch, M., T. Grothmann, D. Schröter, C. Hasse, U. Fritsch, and W. Cramer. 2005. Climate change in Germany—vulnerability and adaption of climate sensitive sectors. Umweltbundesamt, Dessau, Germany. http://www.umweltbundesamt.de/uba-info-medien/mysql_medien.php?anfrage=Kennummer&Suchwort=2974.

Zierhofer, W. 2007. Representative cosmopolitan: Representing the world within political collectives. *Environment & Planning A* 39 (7): 1618–1631.

Zürn, M. 2000. Democratic governance beyond the nation-state: The EU and other international institutions. *European Journal of International Relations* 6 (2): 183–221.

Index

Politics, Science, and the Environment
Peter M. Haas and Sheila Jasanoff, editors